Developments in Russian and Post-Soviet Politics

Developments in Russian and Post-Soviet Politics

Edited by

Stephen White

Alex Pravda

Zvi Gitelman

Duke University Press
Durham, NC

First published 1990 as DEVELOPMENTS IN SOVIET POLITICS
Reprinted 1990, 1991
Second edition (DEVELOPMENTS IN SOVIET AND POST-SOVIET
POLITICS) 1992
Reprinted 1993
Third edition (DEVELOPMENTS IN RUSSIAN AND POST-SOVIET
POLITICS) 1994

Published in the USA by
DUKE UNIVERSITY PRESS
Durham, North Carolina
and in Great Britain by
THE MACMILLAN PRESS LTD
Basingstoke and London

Printed in Great Britain

Library of Congress Cataloging-in-Publication Data
Developments in Russian and post-Soviet politics / edited by Stephen
White, Alex Pravda, and Zvi Gitelman. —3rd ed.
p. cm.
Rev. ed. of Developments in Soviet and post-Soviet politics.
1992.
Includes bibliographical references and index.
ISBN 0–8223–1507–6. — ISBN 0–8223–1518–1 (pbk.)
1. Soviet Union—Politics and government—1985–1991.   2. Soviet
Union—Economic policy—1986–1991.   3. Soviet Union—Social
conditions—1970–1991.   4. Perestroika.   5. Former Soviet republics—
Politics and government.   I. White, Stephen, 1945–   .
II. Pravda, Alex, 1947–   .   III. Gitelman, Zvi Y.   IV. Developments
in Soviet and Post-Soviet politics.
DK286. 5.D47   1994
947. 085' 4—dc20
                                                    94–10629
                                                        CIP

Contents

List of Illustrations and Maps

Illustrations

List of Tables and Exhibits

Tables

Exhibits

Preface

In our preface to the first edition of this book we explained that this was above all a guide for students, but hoped it might be considered more than 'just' a textbook. As befitted a volume on developments, we made no attempt to cover every aspect of what could still be described as the Soviet political system; our aim, then and now, was to allow ourselves a little more room in which to concentrate upon the more important changes in a rapidly evolving system, and to deal with the (often controversial) issues of interpretation to which they give rise. We also thought it proper, dealing with issues of this kind, to allow for a diversity of approach within a common framework.

As we wrote in 1990, our assumptions about Soviet politics were 'changing almost daily'. But not even we could claim to have foretold the changes with which we deal in this third edition, with the end of Communist Party rule and of the former USSR, and with privatisation, an emerging party system and (from December 1993) a strongly presidential Russian republic. This is accordingly a very different book: all of the chapters have been rewritten, most of them are entirely different, and several of the contributors as well as the subjects with which they deal are new to this edition. Our aim, however, remains the same: to offer an interpretative framework for what is now a group of political systems whose evolution – in an age of nuclear weapons and tele-communications – matters almost as much to the outside world as to their own citizens.

Once again, for this third edition, we would like to thank our chapter authors for their contributions and for their willingness to provide us with revisions almost to the point of publication so that this book can be as up-to-date as possible. We would like particularly to thank our publisher, Steven Kennedy, whose commitment to this series and to this book in particular has been a great inspiration. We hope that not just our students, but a wider circle of scholars and members of the general public, will find that the outcome justifies the effort that has been invested in it.

Stephen White
Alex Pravda
Zvi Gitelman

Notes on the Contributors

Mary Buckley is Reader in Politics at the University of Edinburgh. Her books include *Soviet Social Scientists Talking* (1986), *Women and Ideology in the Soviet Union* (1989), *Perestroika and Soviet Women* (edited, 1992) and most recently *Redefining Russian Society and Polity* (1993).

Simon Clarke is Reader in Sociology at the University of Warwick and the author of *What about the Workers?* (with others, 1993). With Peter Fairbrother he has been researching the restructuring of management, industrial relations and labour organisation in Russia since 1990, in collaboration with teams of Russian researchers in four contrasting Russian regions.

Zvi Gitelman is Professor of Political Science and Judaic Studies at the University of Michigan, Ann Arbor. A specialist in Soviet and Russian political sociology and ethnic issues, his books include *Jewish Nationality and Soviet Politics* (1972), *Public Opinion in European Socialist Systems* (coedited, 1977), *Becoming Israelis* (1982), *A Century of Ambivalence: The Jews of Russia and the Soviet Union* (1988), and *The Politics of Nationality and the Erosion of the USSR* (edited, 1992).

Ronald J. Hill is Professor of Comparative Government at Trinity College, Dublin. His books include *The Soviet Communist Party* (with Peter Frank, 3rd ed., 1987), *The USSR: Politics, Economics and Society* (1989), *Communism under the Knife: Autopsy or Surgery?* (1991); he is also the author of numerous contributions to professional journals and symposia, with particular reference to local goverjnment and the CPSU, and a member of the board of the *Journal of Communist Studies and Transition Politics*.

Leslie Holmes has been Professor of Political Science at the University of Melbourne since 1988, and is currently acting Director of the Centre for Russian and Euro–Asian Studies. Among his many publications are *Politics in the Communist World*

(1986), *The End of Communist Power* (1993), and a forthcoming study of *Post-Communism*.

Alex Pravda is a Fellow of St Antony's College and Lecturer in Politics at Oxford University, and was previously Director of the Soviet foreign policy programme at the Royal Institute of International Affairs (Chatham House). His books include *Trade Unions in Communist States* (with Blair Ruble, 1986), *British–Soviet Relations since the 1970s* (coedited, 1990), *Perestroika: Soviet Domestic and Foreign Policies* (coedited, 1990), and *The End of the Outer Empire: Soviet–East European Relations in Transition* (edited, 1992).

Thomas F. Remington is Professor of Political Science at Emory University, Atlanta. His books include *Politics in the USSR* (with Frederick Barghoorn, 1986), *The Truth of Authority: Ideology and Communication in the Soviet Union* (1988), *Politics and the Soviet System* (edited, 1989) and *Parliaments in Transition: New Legislative Politics in the Former USSR and Eastern Europe* (edited, 1994); he is also a member of the board of *Russian Review*.

Peter Rutland is Associate Professor in the Department of Government at Wesleyan University, Middletown, Connecticut. A specialist on Soviet and Russian political economy, his books include *The Myth of the Plan* (1985), *The Politics of Economic Stagnation in the Soviet Union* (1993) and a forthcoming study entitled *Russia, Eurasia and the Global Economy*.

Richard Sakwa is Senior Lecturer in the Faculty of Social Sciences at the University of Kent, Canterbury. His many publications include *Soviet Politics* (1989), *Gorbachev and his Reforms 1985–1990* (1990) and *Russian Politics and Society* (1993), as well as contributions to journals and symposia. He is a member of the board of the *Journal of Communist Studies and Transition Politics*.

Robert Sharlet is Professor of Political Science at Union College in Schenectady, New York, and an Associate of the Harriman Institute of Columbia University. A specialist on Soviet and Russian law and politics, he has published six books of which the most recent is *Soviet Constitutional Crisis: From De-Stalinization to Disintegration* (1992).

Darrell Slider is Associate Professor of International Studies at the University of South Florida, Tampa. He is the author of a number of articles on Soviet and post-Soviet politics and is the coauthor, with Stephen White and Graeme Gill, of *The Politics of Transition: Shaping a Post-Soviet Future* (1993).

Stephen White is Professor and Head of the Department of Politics at the University of Glasgow. His recent books include *After Gorbachev* (4th ed., 1993), *The Soviet Transition: From Gorbachev to Yeltsin* (coedited, 1993), *Developments in East European Politics* (coedited, 1993), and *The Politics of Transition: Shaping a Post-Soviet Future* (with Graeme Gill and Darrell Slider, 1993); he is also chief editor of *Coexistence* and of the *Journal of Communist Studies and Transition Politics*.

John P. Willerton is Associate Professor of Political Science at the University of Tucson, Arizona. A specialist on Russian and post-Soviet elite politics and the policy proces, he is the author of *Patronage and Politics in the USSR* (1992); his other publications have appeared in *Slavic Review*, *Soviet Studies*, *Studies in Comparative Communism* and other journals and professional symposia.

List of Abbreviations and Terms

Apparat	Party administrative apparatus
Apparatchik	Full-time party official
Arbitrazh	Tribunal system for disputes between state enterprises
birzhy	commodity exchanges
Bolshevik	Radical ('majority') faction of Russian Social Democratic Labour (later Communist) Party
CC	Central Committee
CIA	Central Intelligence Agency (USA)
CIS	Commonwealth of Independent States
CPD	Congress of People's Deputies
CPE	Centrally planned economy
CPSU	Communist Party of the Soviet Union
CSCE	Conference on Security and Cooperation in Europe
Glasnost	Openness, publicity
GNP	Gross national product
Gorkom	City party committee
Gosagroprom	State Agroindustrial Committee
goskazy	state orders
Gospriemka	State quality control
Gossnab	State Committee on Supplies
gosudarstvennost	statehood
Goszakaz	State order
INF	Intermediate-range nuclear force
gosudarstvenniki	national democrats
Ispolkom	Executive committee of a soviet
Kadry	Cadres, staff
KGB	Committee of State Security
Khozraschet	Cost accounting
Kolkhoz	Collective farm

xvi

Komsomol	Young Communist League
Krai	Territory
Menshevik	Moderate (minority) faction of the Russian Social Democratic Labour (later Communist) Party
mir	peasant land commune
NEP	New Economic Policy (1921–8)
Nomenklatura	List of party-controlled posts
Oblast	Region, province
Obshchestvennik	Activist
obshchina	community
Okrug	Area, district
Perestroika	Restructuring
Plenum	Full (plenary) meeting
Podmena	Substitution, supplantation
PPO	Primary party organisation
pravovoe gosudarstvo	law-based state
privatizatsiya	privatisation
prikhvatizatsiya	asset grabbing
Raikom	District party committee
RSFSR	Russian Soviet Federal Socialist Republic (now Russian Federation)
samizdat	underground literature
Sblizhenie	Drawing together (of nationalities)
Sliyanie	Fusion (of nationalities)
sobornost	communality
sovnarkhozy	economic regions
soyuz	union
zemstvo	local government unit
USSR	Union of Soviet Socialist Republics
Val	Gross output
WTO	Warsaw Treaty Organisation
Zastoi	Stagnation

The Former

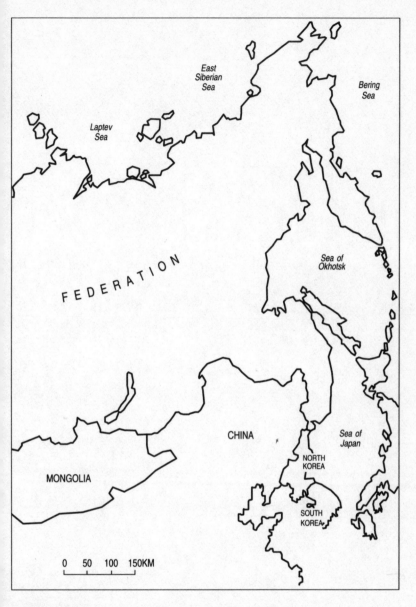

Soviet Union

1

Introduction: From Communism to Democracy?

STEPHEN WHITE

In 1990, when the first edition of this book appeared, the Soviet political system was still one that older generations of students would have recognised. The 1977 Constitution, adopted during the years of stagnation under Brezhnev, was still in force. Article 6, which gave legal effect to the Communist Party's political monopoly, had just been reformulated to allow other parties and movements the right to take part in the administration of public life. Yet none of them, in members or influence, could hope to compete with the CPSU; and the party, under the leadership of Mikhail Gorbachev, was still insisting that it should pay a dominant role in the multiparty politics of the future, though now it would have to win its majorities through the ballot box rather than imposing them on the basis of its 'scientific understanding' of the laws of social development. There was a working Soviet parliament, elected for the first time on a largely competitive basis; yet a higher proportion of deputies were party members than ever before, and party members still virtually monopolised positions of influence within government and outside it. The economy was based on a modified form of planning and state ownership, and political controls were still strong in the armed forces, the courts, and the mass media.

By 1992, and the appearance of the second edition of this book, almost all of these features of the traditional Soviet system had

1

been altered beyond recognition. Gone, for a start, was the Communist Party of the Soviet Union, fairly described in the first
edition of this book as 'not simply a feature of Soviet political life
but its central and defining characteristic'. Gone, too, was
Mikhail Gorbachev, the architect of *perestroika*, both as party
leader and as the first and last Soviet President. Gone, indeed,
was the state itself: the union treaty, originally concluded in 1922,
was repealed in December 1991, leaving 11 (later 12) of the 15
republics to seek their future in a loose and ill-defined 'Commonwealth of Independent States' (CIS). There was no Soviet government any more, and no national parliament, although the
members of the outgoing Congress of People's Deputies voted to
pay themselves their deputies' salaries until their term expired in
1994. A determined start had meanwhile been made on privatising
a substantial part of the Soviet economy, and the right to buy
and sell land – for the first time since 1917 – had been conceded.
In a fitting change of symbols, out went the hammer and sickle
and in – or back, perhaps – came the Russian Republic's new
version of the imperial double-headed eagle. Leningrad, by
popular agreement, reverted to its original name, St Petersburg;
the Lenin Museum in Moscow was handed back to the city government; the Marx and Engels Museum became the Noblemen's
Club; and surplus copies of Gorbachev's speeches began to be
reprocessed as wrapping paper.

This, then, was 'Russian and post-Soviet politics'; and yet our
volume is also concerned with the period of Soviet and communist rule, not just because of its historical importance but because
it continued to shape much of the political system that had succeeded it. Indeed in one important sense it was still a 'Soviet'
political system, at least until 1993, in that power continued to be
exercised by the elected councils or (as they were still called)
soviets that had first been established in 1905, long before the
Bolsheviks had taken power. Within those councils, indeed, power
was often exercised by the same people, although they no longer
called themselves communists. Boris Yeltsin himself had been a
member of the party's Politburo and Secretariat, and left its ranks
as late as 1990. His prime minister, Viktor Chernomyrdin, had
been a member of the Central Committee. The Ukrainian president, Leonid Kravchuk, left the party in 1991; and the influential Kazakh president, Nursultan Nazarbaev, was a member of

the Politburo until just after the coup attempt against Gorbachev in August 1991. The Communist Party, after a ruling by the Russian Constitutional Court, was allowed to reconstitute itself and become one of the largest parties in the new Russian parliament; in some other republics, especially in Central Asia, it changed its name but remained a dominant force in local politics. The bulk of economic activity was still concentrated in the hands of the state, and although the old union had disappeared Russia remained the dominant actor within the territory it had formerly occupied. As compared with Eastern Europe in 1989, this was much less clearly the overthrow of a system and its replacement by multiparty capitalism: not surprisingly, perhaps, because the Soviet system had not originally been an external imposition.

The Gorbachev Agenda

A very different atmosphere had prevailed when in March 1985 a vigorous, stocky Politburo member from the south of Russia became general secretary of what was still a united and ruling party. Gorbachev, according to his wife at least, had not expected the nomination and spent some time deciding whether to accept it; all that was clear was that (in a phrase that later became famous) 'We just can't go on like this'. The advent of a new general secretary had certainly made a significant difference in the past to the direction of Soviet public policy, although any change took some time to establish itself as the new leader marginalised his opponents and coopted his supporters on to the Politburo and Secretariat. Gorbachev, however, told the Politburo meeting that agreed to nominate him that there was 'no need to change our policies' (*Istochnik*, 1993, no. 0, p. 74) and there was little public evidence of his objectives, or even of his personal background. He had not addressed a party congress, and had no published collection of writings to his name; and he had made only a couple of important visits abroad, to Canada and the UK, on both occasions as the head of delegation of Soviet parliamentarians. Only a few important speeches – in particular an address to an ideology conference in December 1984 and an electoral address in February 1985, which mentioned *glasnost*, social justice and participation – gave some indication of his personal priorities.

The new general secretary's policy agenda, in fact, took some time to develop. In his acceptance speech Gorbachev paid tribute to his immediate predecessors, Yuri Andropov and Konstantin Chernenko, and pledged himself to continue their policy of 'acceleration of socio-economic development and the perfection of all aspects of social life'. At the first Central Committee he addressed as leader, in April 1985, he spoke in a fairly orthodox manner about the need for a 'qualitatively new state of society', including modernisation of the economy and the extension of socialist democracy. The key issue, in these early months, was the acceleration of economic growth. This, Gorbachev thought, was quite feasible if the 'human factor' was called more fully into play, and if the reserves that existed throughout the economy were properly utilised. This in turn required a greater degree of decentralisation, including cost accounting at enterprise level and a closer connection between the work that people did and the payment that they received; but there was still no talk of 'radical reform', let alone a 'market'. The months that followed saw the gradual assembly of a leadership team that could direct these changes and the further extension of what was still a very limited mandate for change.

Of all the policies that were promoted by the Gorbachev leadership, *glasnost* was perhaps the most distinctive and the one that had been pressed furthest by the end of communist rule. *Glasnost*, usually translated as 'openness' or 'publicity', was not the same as freedom of the press or the right to information; nor was it original to Gorbachev (it figured, for instance, in the 1977 Brezhnev Constitution). It did, however, reflect the new general secretary's belief that without a greater awareness of the real state of affairs and of the considerations that had led to particularly decisions there would be no willingness on the part of the Soviet people to commit themselves to his programme of *perestroika*. Existing policies were in any case ineffectual, counterproductive and resented. The newspaper *Sovetskaya Rossiya* reported the case of Mr Polyakov of Kaluga, a well-read man who followed the central and local press and never missed the evening news. He knew a lot about what was happening in various African countries, Polyakov complained, but had 'only a very rough idea what was happening in his own city'. In late 1985, another reader complained, there had been a major earthquake in Tajikistan in Soviet Central Asia, but no details were made known other than that 'lives had been lost'. At about the same time there had been an earthquake in Mexico and a volcanic eruption in Colombia, both covered extensively with on-the-spot reports and full details of the casualties. Was Tajikistan really further from Moscow than Latin America?

Influenced by considerations such as these, the Gorbachev leadership made steady and sometimes dramatic progress in removing taboos from the discussion of public affairs and exposing both the Soviet past and Soviet present to critical scrutiny. The Brezhnev era was one of the earliest targets. It had been a time, Gorbachev told the 27th Party Congress in 1986, when a 'curious psychology – how to change things without really changing anything' – had been dominant. A number of its leader representatives had been openly corrupt, and some (such as Brezhnev's son-in-law, Yuri Churbanov) were brought to trial and imprisoned for serious state crimes. More generally, it had been a period of 'stagnation', of wasted opportunities, when party and government leaders had lagged behind the needs of the times. The Stalin question was a still more fundamental one, as for all Soviet reformers. Gorbachev, to begin with, was reluctant even to concede there was a question. Stalinism, he told the French press in 1986, was a 'notion made up by enemies of communism'; the 20th Party Congress in 1956 had condemned Stalin's 'cult of personality' and drawn the necessary conclusions. By early 1987, however, Gorbachev was insisting that there must be 'no forgotten names, no blank spots' in Soviet literature and history, and by November of that year, when he came to give his address on the 70th anniversary of the revolution, he was ready to condemn the 'wanton repressive measures' of the 1930s, 'real crimes' in which 'many thousands of people inside and outside the party' had suffered.

In the course of his speech Gorbachev announced that a Politburo commission had been set up to investigate the political repression of the Stalinist years, and this led to the rehabilitation of many prominent figures from the party's past (and thousands of others) from 1988 onwards. The most important figure to be restored to full respectability in this way was the former *Pravda* editor Nikolai Bukharin, whose sentence was posthumously quashed in February 1988 (later in the year his expulsions from the party and the Academy of Sciences were both reversed). Two other old Bolsheviks, Grigorii Zinoviev and Lev Kamenev, were rehabilitated later in the year. Trotsky had not been sentenced by a Soviet court and there was therefore no judgement to be reversed; but his personal qualities began to receive some recognition in the Soviet press, and from 1989 onwards his writings began to appear in mass-circulation as well as scholarly journals. An extended discussion took place about the numbers that Stalin had condemned to death: for some it was about a million by the end of the 1930s, but for others (such as the historian and commentator Roy Medvedev) it was at least 12 million, with a further 38 million repressed in other ways (the numbers were almost certainly a 'world record' of their kind, according to Alec Nove (Getty and Manning, 1993, p. 274)). Perhaps more significant, a number of mass graves of the Stalin period began to be uncovered, the most extensive of which were in the Kuropaty forest near Minsk. The victims, as many as 40,000, had been shot between 1937 and 1941; this, and the other graves that were still being discovered in the early 1990s, was an indictment of Stalinism more powerful than anything the historians and writers could hope to muster.

Glasnost led to further changes in the quality of Soviet public life, from literature and the arts to statistics and a wide ranging discussion on the future of Soviet socialism. Public information began to improve, with the publication of statistics on crime, abortions, suicides and infant mortality. Subjects that had been taboo during the Brezhnev years, such as violent crime, drugs and prostitution, began to receive extensive treatment. Many events of the past, such as the devastating earthquake in Ashkhabad in 1948 and the nuclear accident in the Urals in 1957, were belatedly acknowledged. Figures for defence spending and foreign debt were revealed to the Congress of People's Deputies for the first time in 1989; figures for capital punishment followed in 1991. The Congress itself was televised in full and followed avidly throughout the USSR; so too were Central Committee plenums, Supreme Soviet committee hearings and other public occasions. Still more remarkably, the Soviet media were opened up to foreign journalists and politicians, and even (in a few cases) to emigres and open opponents of Soviet socialism; and the first 'spacebridges' were instituted, linking together studio audiences in the USSR and many Western nations. Opinion polls suggested that *glasnost*, for all its limitations, was the change in Soviet life that was most apparent to ordinary people and the one that they most valued.

The 'democratisation' of Soviet political life was an associated change, and was similarly intended to release the human energies that, for Gorbachev, had been choked off by the bureaucratic centralism of the Stalin and Brezhnev years. The Soviet Union, he told the 19th Party Conference in the summer of 1988, had pioneered the idea of a workers' state and of workers' control, the right to work and equality of rights for women and all national groups. The political system established by the October revolution, however, had undergone 'serious deformations', leading to the development of a 'command–administrative system' which had extinguished the democratic potential of the elected soviets. The role of party and state officialdom had increased out of all proportion, and this 'bloated administrative apparatus' had begun to dictate its will in political and economic matters. Nearly a third of the adult population were regularly elected to the soviets, but most of them had little influence over the conduct of government. Social life as a whole had become unduly politicised, and ordinary working people had become 'alienated' from the system that was supposed to represent their interests. It was this 'ossified system of government', with its command-and-pressure mechanism', that was now the main obstacle to *perestroika*.

The Conference duly approved the notion of a 'radical reform' of the political system, and this led to a series of constitutional and other changes from 1988 onwards that are discussed – together with the changes that followed in the post-Soviet period – in several chapters of this book. An entirely new electoral law, for instance, approved in December 1988, broke new ground in providing for (though not specifically requiring) a choice of candidate at elections to local and national-level authorities. A new state structure was established, incorporating a relatively small working parliament for the first time in modern Soviet political history and (from 1990) a powerful executive Presidency. A constitutional review committee, similar to a constitutional court, was set up as part of a move to what Gorbachev called a 'socialist system of checks and balances'. Judges were to be elected for longer periods of time, and given greater guarantees of independence in their work. And the CPSU itself was to be 'democratised', although in practice the changes were less far-reaching than in other parts of the political system and in the end were not sufficient to preserve the party's authority. Leading officials, it was agreed, should be elected by competitive ballot for a maximum of two consecutive terms; members of the Central Committee should be involved much more directly in the work of the leadership; and there should be much more information about all aspects of the party's work, from its finances to the operation of its decision-making bodies.

Together with these changes, for Gorbachev, there must be a 'radical reform' of the Soviet economy (these and other changes are considered further in Chapters 6 and 7). Levels of growth had been declining since at least the 1950s. In the late 1970s they reached the lowest levels in Soviet peacetime history, and may altogether have ceased per head of population. Indeed, as Gorbachev explained in early 1988, if the sale of alcoholic drink and of Soviet oil on foreign markets were excluded, there had been no increase in national wealth for at least the previous 15 years. Growth, at least for many reforming economists, could not be an end in itself; what was important was the satisfaction of real social needs. But it was equally apparent that without some improvement in living standards there would be no popular commitment to *perestroika*, and no prospect that socialism would recover its appeal to other nations as a means by which ordinary working people could live their lives in dignity and sufficiency. There was indeed a real danger, in the view of economists like Nikolai Shmelev, that without radical reform the USSR would enter the 21st century a 'backward, stagnating state and an example to the rest of the world how not to conduct its economic affairs' (*Znamya*, 1988, no. 7, p. 179).

Radical reform, as Gorbachev explained to the 27th Party Congress and to an important Central Committee meeting in the summer of 1987, involved a set of related measures. One of the most important was a greater degree of decentralisation of economic decision-making, leaving broad guidance of the economy in the hands of the State Planning Committee (Gosplan) but allowing factories and farms throughout the USSR more freedom to determine their own priorities. They should be guided in making such decisions by a wide range of 'market' indicators, including the orders they received from other enterprises and the profits they made on their production. Retail and wholesale prices would have to reflect costs of production much more closely so that enterprises could be guided by 'economic' rather than 'administrative' regulators, and so that the massive subsidies that held down the cost of basic foodstuffs could be reduced. Under the Law on the State Enterprise, adopted in 1987, enterprises that persistently failed to pay their way under these conditions could be liquidated; some economists were willing to argue that a modest degree of unemployment was not simply a logical but even a desirable feature of changes of this kind. The state sector, more generally, should be gradually reduced in size, and coopera- tive or even private economic activity should be expanded in its place. Gorbachev described these changes, which were gradually brought into effect from 1987 onwards, as the most radical to have taken place in Soviet economic life since the adoption of the New Economic Policy (NEP) in the early 1920s.

There was a still larger objective, discussed by academics and commentators as well as the political leadership: the elaboration of a 'humane and democratic socialism' that would build on Soviet achievements but combine them with the experience of other nations and schools of thought. Khrushchev had promised that the USSR would construct a communist society 'in the main' by 1980 in the Party Programme that was adopted under his lea- dership in 1961. His successors swiftly dropped that commitment and began to describe the USSR, from the early 1970s, as a 'developed socialist society', whose evolution into a full commu- nist society was a matter for the distant future. Brezhnev's succes- sors in turn made it clear that the USSR was at the very beginning of developed socialism, whose proper development would require a 'whole historical epoch'. Gorbachev, for his part, avoided the term 'developed socialism' and opted instead for 'developing socialism', in effect a postponement into the still more distant future of the attainment of a fully communist society. Later still, in 1990, the objective became 'humane, democratic socialism'; in 1991 the revised version of the Party Programme was entitled 'Socialism, Democracy, Progress', with communism mentioned only in passing.

It remained unclear, these generalities apart, how a socialist society of this kind was to be constructed and how its further development was to be assured. Gorbachev resisted calls to set out the way ahead in any detail: did they really want a new

Stalinist *Short Course*, he asked the Party Congress in 1990, referring to the discredited Marxist primer produced in 1938? And what was the point of programmes like railway timetables, with objectives to be achieved by particular dates; wasn't an authentic socialism the achievement of the people themselves, not something they were directed towards by others? Gorbachev's objectives emerged as a set of fairly general propositions: a humane and democratic socialism would assume a variety of forms of property and would not necessarily exclude small-scale capitalism; it would be ruled by a broad coalition of 'progressive' forces, not just by Communists; it would guarantee freedom of conscience and other liberties; and it would cooperate with other states in an 'interconnected, in many ways interdependent' world. However adequate as an expression of general principle, this could scarcely offer practical guidance to party members and the broader public in their daily life; nor did it necessarily carry conviction at a time of economic difficulty, nationalist discontent and the acknowledgement of mistakes in public policy for which a party that had monopolised political power could hardly avoid responsibility.

In the end, the search for a 'third way' that would combine democracy with social justice turned out to be a delusion. More open elections led, not to the return of committed reformers, but to the success of nationalist movements in several of the non-Russian republics and to the election of anti-communist mayors in Moscow, Leningrad and several other large cities. The opportunity to organise outside the framework of the CPSU led to 'informal' movements and popular fronts, and then to political parties that were openly hostile to the CPSU and socialism. There were demonstrations on an enormous scale, not in support of a humane and democratic socialism, but (in early 1990) for the removal of the party's political monopoly from the constitution. Writers and academics, protected by *glasnost*, moved steadily towards an explicit critique of Marxism and of Lenin as the founder of what they described as a 'totalitarian' system, and then to a more general attack upon revolutions as progenitors of violence and repression. The economy hovered between plan and market, combining many of the worst features of both. Abroad, the Warsaw Treaty Organisation and the Council for Mutual Economic Assistance disappeared leaving no obvious basis for the conduct of relations with the former Soviet and communist states, still less the outside world.

It was far from clear, in fact, why the Soviet system had collapsed so ignominiously at the end of 1991. Was it, for instance, the result of falling rates of economic growth, and of the strain this placed upon the 'social contract' that was sometimes held to exist between regime and public? Perhaps; but national income fell much more sharply, anything from 15 to 20 per cent, in the early postcommunist years without the same kind of consequences. Was it a repudiation of the CPSU and of its political legacy? To some extent; but there was no popularly supported wave of opposition of the kind that had swept across Eastern Europe, even the Baltic, and the party, when it was allowed to revive in postcommunist Russia, was the largest of all in terms of membership and one of the largest in the new parliament. Had people rejected Marxism–Leninism? But the party itself, in its draft Programme of July 1991, had moved to a position that could more properly be described as social democratic, and there was still a strong commitment, if polls were any guide, to public ownership and comprehensive social welfare. Even the USSR had hardly been repudiated: 76 per cent had supported the idea of a 'reformed federation' in a referendum in March 1991, and almost as many, asked by interviewers, were prepared to support it long after it had disappeared. What had been rejected, and what had been retained, was still unclear years after the apparent demise of the world's first socialist society.

A Presidential Republic?

The new Russian constitution, when it was published in November 1993, seemed to provide more evidence of a change of regime: and a change, following a great deal of public and private discussion, towards a strongly presidential as well as democratic and postcommunist republic. The constitution's opening words – 'We, the multinational people of the Russian Federation' – appeared to borrow the famous opening of its American counterpart. The Russian state was described, in Chapter 1, as a 'democratic federal legally-based state with a republican form of government'. The laws of the state as a whole were to have pre-

EXHIBIT 1.1   *Russia's republics and regions (according to the 1993 Constitution)*

Republics (21)	Leningrad Oblast
Republic of Adygeya	Lipetsk Oblast
Altai Republic	Magadan Oblast
Republic of Bashkortostan	Moscow Oblast
Republic of Buryatia	Murmansk Oblast
Chechen Republic	Nizhnii Novgorod Oblast
Republic of Dagestan	Omsk Oblast
Chuvash Republic	Orel Oblast
Ingush Republic	Orenburg Oblast
Kabardino-Balkar Republic	Penza Oblast
Republic of Kalmykia-Khalmg-Tangch	Perm Oblast
Karachai-Cherkess Republic	Pskov Oblast
Republic of Karelia	Rostov Oblast
Khakass Republic	Ryazan Oblast
Republic of Komi	Sakhalin Oblast
Republic of Marii El	Samara Oblast
Republic of Mordovia	Saratov Oblast
Republic of North Ossetia	Smolensk Oblast
Republic of Sakha (Yakutia)	Sverdlovsk Oblast
Republic of Tatarstan	Tambov Oblast
Republic of Tuva	Tomsk Oblast
Udmurt Republic	Tula Oblast
	Tver Oblast
Krais (6)	Tyumen Oblast
Altai Krai	Ulyanovsk Oblast
Khabarovsk Krai	Vladimir Oblast
Krasnodar Krai	Volgograd Oblast
Krasnoyarsk Krai	Vologda Oblast
Primorskii Karai	Voronezh Oblast
Stavropol Krai	Yaroslavl Oblast
Oblasts (49)	*Federal Cities Enjoying Status*
Amur Oblast	*Equivalent to an Oblast (2)*
Arkhangelsk Oblast	Moscow
Astrakhan Oblast	St Petersburg
Belgorod Oblast	
Bryansk Oblast	*Autonomous Oblast (1)*
Chelyabinsk Oblast	Jewish Autonomous Oblast
Chita Oblast	
Irkutsk Oblast	*Autonomous Okrugs (10)*
Ivanovo Oblast	Agin Buryat
Kaliningrad Oblast	Chukchi
Kaluga Oblast	Evenk
Kamchatka Oblast	Khanty-Mansi
Kemerovo Oblast	Komi-Permyak
Kirov Oblast	Koryak
Kostroma Oblast	Nenets
Kurgan Oblast	Taimyr
Kursk Oblast	Ust-Orda Buryat
	Yamal Nenets

cedence over those of the 89 units that composed it, a provision
that was meant to end the 'law of wars' that had previously
undermined the USSR (for a listing of the 'subjects of the Federation' under the new Constitution see Exhibit 1.1). The Constitution itself was to have 'supreme legal force' throughout the
territory of the Federation, although it was less than clear that
Bashkortostan, Tartarstan and some of the other 'autonomies'
would accept these claims and (not least) pay their taxes, still less
the tiny republic of Chechnya which, in its view, had become fully
independent in late 1991.

The old Soviet parliament, in September 1991, had adopted a
'Declaration of the rights and freedoms of the individual', and a
statement on these matters had been incorporated into the
Russian constitution in April 1992. The 1993 constitution devoted
a whole chapter to the subject, one that could not be modified by
subsequent legislation. There was to be 'ideological' and 'political
diversity', together with 'multipartyism'. There could be no state
or official ideology. The Russian state was to be a secular one,
based in the separation of church and state, with religious organisations independent of political control and equal before the law.
Freedom of movement, within or across the boundaries of the
federation, was guaranteed. Citizens must be allowed to have
access to any information that was held about them by public
bodies (in effect, a freedom of information act); and censorship
was specifically prohibited. There was freedom of assembly and
association, and freedom to engage in any entrepreneurial activity
not forbidden by law. The constitution also provided for a system
of social security, and a right to housing (where necessarily, free
of charge). All had the right to free medical care, and to a free
education: provisions that were in some ways reminiscent of the
constitutions of the Soviet period, with their emphasis upon social
rights and welfare. In the courts, similarly, all had the right to a
qualified defence lawyer, and were presumed innocent until
proved guilty.

The state itself was based upon a separation of legislative,
executive and judicial powers, and upon an elaborate system of
federal government (the background to these changes is considered further in Chapters 2, 3 and 5). The most important
matters of state were reserved for the federal government, including socio-economic policy, the budget, currency emission and

on, energy, foreign affairs and defence. Other matters, ...ding the use of land and water, education and culture, health and social security, were to be under the 'joint' management of the federal and local governments, which also had the right to legislate within their sphere of competence. There was to be a single unit of currency, the ruble; a single capital, Moscow; and a single state language, Russian, although the constituent republic could endow their own languages with the same rights if they chose to do so.

A central role was accorded to the president, who defined the 'basic directions of domestic and foreign policy' and represented the state internationally. The President was directly elected for a period of 4 years, and for not more than two consecutive terms. He or she must be at least 35 years old, a Russian citizen, and a resident of Russia for at least the previous 10 years (there was no formal retirement age, which presumably reflected a wish to allow Yeltsin – already 63 – the possibility of a second term). The president had the right to appoint the prime minister, and (on his nomination) to appoint and dismiss deputy premiers and other ministers. If he thought it necessary he could dismiss the government as a whole. The President, equally, nominated the chairman of the State Bank, and judges to higher courts (including the Constitutional Court); he headed the Security Council, and appointed his 'plenipotentiary representatives' throughout the federation. Additionally, the President could call elections or a referendum; he could declare a state of emergency; he issued his own decrees, which had the force of law; he could dissolve parliament in appropriate circumstances; he could initiate legislation; and he gave an annual 'state of the union' address to the Federal Assembly. He could, finally, be impeached, but only for serious anti-state crimes and after a complicated procedure had been initiated.

The new parliament was called a Federal Assembly (the term 'soviet' appeared nowhere in the document and there was a determined attempt to eliminate it at all levels of government). The 'representative and legislative organ of the Russian Federation', the Assembly consisted of two chambers: a Council of the Federation and a State Duma. The Council of the Federation, or upper house, consisted of 178 deputies, two from each of the 89 subjects of the Federation. The State Duma, or lower house, con-

sisted of 450 deputies chosen for a four-year term. The first a
in effect transitional Federal Assembly, elected in December 1993,
would however be dissolved after two years. Any citizen aged
over 21 could be elected to the State Duma, but could not at the
same time be a member of the upper house or of other representative bodies, and all deputies were to work on a 'permanent
professional basis'. Both houses elected a chairman, committee
and commissions.

The Council of the Federation, under the new constitution,
considered all matters that applied to the federation as a whole,
including state boundaries, the declaration of martial law, and the
use of Russian forces beyond state borders. The Duma approved
nominations to the premiership and adopted federal laws (they
were also considered by the Council of the Federation, but any
objection could be overridden by a two-thirds majority; objections
on the part of the President could be overridden by both houses
on the same basis). The Duma could for its part reject nominations to the premiership, but after the third such rejection it
would be automatically dissolved. The Duma might equally be
dissolved if it twice voted a lack of confidence in the government
as a whole, or if it refused to express confidence in the government when the matter was raised by the prime minister. The
whole document was put to the country in a referendum on 12
December 1993; 54.8 per cent of the registered electorate were
reported to have taken part, of whom 58.4 per cent voted in
favour (*Rossiiskie vesti*, 25 December 1993).

This was less than a resounding endorsement (indeed there was
some doubt if the constitution had been adopted at all, as the legislation on referendums insisted on a majority of the electorate
and not just of voters declaring in favour), and there was continuing criticism of the new constitution, after as well as before it
had been put to the electorate. The extraordinary powers attributed to the president aroused particular concern (Gorbachev, for
instance, complained that the Russian president had more powers
than the tsar had done before the revolution), and there were calls
for the discussion to continue so that a process of amendment
could take place. Yet even a document of this fundamental kind
was not enough, it appeared, to resolve the tension that had
developed between president and parliament, or to establish the
authority of the central government over local areas. Nearly half

of the republics had voted against the new constitution and some might not accept it; and the results of the December 1993 elections, in which Communists, Agrarians and the far-right Liberal Democrats secured a large share of the vote, left Yeltsin facing a parliament at least as hostile as the one he had dissolved in September 1993 but one that had a new and convincing democratic mandate. Yeltsin himself had promised to stand in a further presidential election in June 1994, but the promise was withdrawn and it appeared he would stand down no later than the end of his 5 year term in 1996. This left him something of a 'lame duck' president, confronting a parliament and government that enjoyed much closer relations. The prime minister, Viktor Chernomyrdin, in turn had a decisive influence in the shaping of the moderately reforming government that was formed in January 1994, and he made it clear that there would be no more 'market romanticism'.

Citizens or Subjects?

Was government, under this postcommunist constitution, moving any closer to the people from whom it claimed to derive authority? The early years of *perestroika* had seen almost a rebirth of politics as informal movements blossomed into political parties, and demonstrations took place with half a million or more participants. A million Armenians had demonstrated in Yerevan in 1988 in support of the incorporation of Nagorno-Karabakh into their republic; the turnout was such a high proportion of the local population that it entered the *Guinness Book of Records*. In the Baltic, in August 1989, two million joined hands to protest against the Nazi–Soviet pact of 50 years earlier which had led to the in corporation of the three republics into the USSR. A mass of popular and street literature developed, bolstered by the law on the mass media that had been adopted in October 1990; there was an ecological press, a gay press, a business press, even a monarchical press. In August 1991, when the attempted coup was resisted by thousands of Muscovites in defiance of a curfew and at the risk of their lives, it did appear that Russians had at least become active participants in the shaping of their own lives, rather than the passive spectators they had been throughout the Soviet years. For Boris Yeltsin, speaking just after the coup had collapsed, the Russian people had finally 'thrown off the fetters of seventy years of slavery'; for others it was nothing less than the birth of a 'liberal democratic state' (*Literaturnaya gazeta*, 28 August 1991).

But did Russians, by the mid-1990s, feel involved in the politics that was being conducted, sometimes violently, all around them? Fewer and fewer, in fact, were prepared to take an interest in politics and to play a part in public life (see Table 1.1), with an increasing proportion disillusioned or alienated. There was general agreement, in Russia-wide polls in 1993, that the country was in a 'tense' or 'explosive' situation, and general agreement that neither president, nor government, and still more so the Supreme Soviet, were in a position to take the country out of its crisis. Who, in fact, was in control? As a series of polls made clearly, it was hardly the president or government. In their own

TABLE 1.1 *Political interest and participation, 1988–92*

	1988	1989	1990	1991	1992
Can you say of yourself that you . . . always took and still take part in socio-political life?	10	13	7	4	3
have found new opportunities for political participation?	11	4	1	1	0.5
have no more opportunity to participate in socio-political life than before?	33	22	21	17	10
have recently become disillusioned with politics?	n.d.	12	14	16	16
for you, the main thing is the fate of your own people?	34	32	26	28	26
that politics doesn't interest you and you don't understand it?	11	12	11	1	25

Source: Adapted from *Ekonomicheskie i sotsial'nye peremeny*, 1993, no. 3, p. 5 (Public Opinion Research Centre data, $N = 1045$, 1498, 2081, 2110, 1771 respectively; don't knows excluded).

town or district, for instance, 28 per cent in July 1993 thought there was 'no real locus of authority', 25 per cent thought it was 'speculators or the mafia', and 21 per cent found difficulty in responding. For 19 per cent the local soviet was still in charge, but 12 per cent thought the old party apparatus was still the dominant force (*Ekonomicheskie i sotsial'nye peremeny*, 1993, no. 5, p. 38). And in Russia as a whole, 16 per cent thought Yeltsin was in charge but 23 per cent thought it was the mafia, 13 per cent no-one at all, and 6 per cent thought it was still the Communist Party and its officials (*Moskovskie novosti*, 1993, no. 12, p. 9A).

Political leaders as well as institutions were held in low regard. Mikhail Gorbachev, for instance, enjoyed the support of 51 per cent of those who were asked to nominate the 'man of the year' in 1988, but just 1 per cent in 1992. Boris Yeltsin was better regarded in 1992, with a 17 per cent rating, but his support was also in decline and it had never been as high as that of Gorbachev in the heady days of *perestroika*. Measured in terms of 'trust', Yeltsin enjoyed a better level of support than almost all other branches of government; but two or three times as many had little or no confidence in the Russian president (see Figure 1.1). As for parties, fewer than a quarter of those who were asked in late 1993 could name a single one, and the party that was most widely identified – the Liberal Democrats – was also the party that was most generally disliked (*Argumenty i fakty*, 1993, no. 38, p. 1). The overwhelming majority, in surveys, thought there were no parties that represented their interests, and very few (just 3 per cent, in other surveys) connected their hopes for the future with parties and politicians. There was, in fact, a strong antipathy towards the concept of party, associated as it was with 70 years in which the CPSU had monopolised power and abused its dominant position.

What, in these circumstances, could ordinary Russians do to express their views and defend their interests? Not a lot, if surveys (again) were any guide. What, for instance, were the forms of protest or political action that ordinary Russians thought acceptable or appropriate? About a third (33.6 per cent) thought there were none; other suggestions included 'discussions at the workplace' (21.7 per cent), 'protest letters' (12.6 per cent), 'strikes' (12.3 per cent) and 'pickets, meetings and demonstrations' (11.8

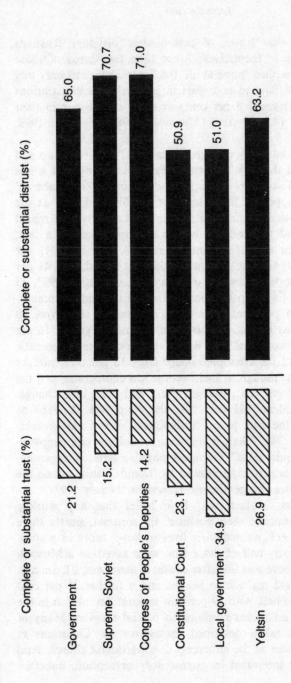

Complete or substantial distrust (%)

Government — 65.0
Supreme Soviet — 70.7
Congress of People's Deputies — 71.0
Constitutional Court — 50.9
Local government — 51.0
Yeltsin — 63.2

Complete or substantial trust (%)

Government — 21.2
Supreme Soviet — 15.2
Congress of People's Deputies — 14.2
Constitutional Court — 23.1
Local government — 34.9
Yeltsin — 26.9

FIGURE 1.1   *Trust in government, 1993*

Source: Adapted from *Mir mnenii i mneniya o mire*, 1993, no. 72 (based on a Russia-wide survey of August–September 1993, *N* =1740; don't knows excluded).

...t). But what forms of action were ordinary Russians ...to engage in themselves? More than two-thirds of those who were asked replied 'none at all' (68.7 per cent), and only tiny minorities were willing to take part in pickets or demonstrations (7.8 per cent), strikes (6.8 per cent) or even 'discussions in their labour collective' (4.9 per cent) (*Mir mnenii mneniya o mire*, 1993, no. 58).

Indeed, what had really changed since 1991? Had the coup and its defeat opened the way to democracy, or to changes of a less welcome kind? Two years later, fewer Muscovites 'remembered' that they had supported the defence of the White House at the time, and fewer were inclined to support if it there was a repeat performance. Had the collapse of the attempted coup, in fact, brought about the end of communist rule? A year later, 41 per cent of the Russians who were asked thought it had, and 41 per cent took the opposite view. Two years later, in August 1993, 43 per cent thought the coup had brought about the end of communist rule, but 45 per cent were more pessimistic (*Izvestiya*, 20 August 1993). Was Russia, by this time, a democracy? Just 16 per cent thought it was. And had Russia become more democratic since the defeat of the attempted coup? Only 18 per cent thought it had; 28 per cent thought it had become less democratic; and the largest group, 44 per cent, thought there had been little change. For most respondents (43 per cent) the coup was likely to be remembered, in the end, as an 'insignificant' event (*Moskovskie novosti*, 1993, no. 34). What, in any case, could you call people in these postcommunist days? The most popular term, it appeared, was still 'comrades', closely followed by 'friends'; only among the young was it 'ladies and gentlemen' (*Izvestiya*, 24 July 1993).

Many Russians, in fact, had little belief that any worldly changes would improve their position. By contrast, nearly three out of four, in 1993, wanted their lives to have 'more of a spiritual content'. Nearly half of those who were asked, in a Moscow survey, thought there was life after death; if there was, 21 per cent thought they would make it to heaven and a further 20 per cent expecting to go to hell, with 59 per cent unsure. An interest in the spiritual was by no means confined to official religion. Many of those who were asked described themselves as 'Christians in general', rather than as the adherents of a particular church. And many more were interested in extrasensory perception, unorthodox medicine, and various forms of oriental wisdom. The national television service, and many of the popular papers, offered a nightly astrological forecast as well as more conventional news; 71 per cent, according to the surveys, thought forecasts of this kind had a 'certain scientific basis' (*Moskovskie novosti*, 1993, no. 39). Bookstalls reflected the same emphases: there was L. Ron Hubbard and the Bhagavad-Gita, Sigmund Freud and the Tibetan Book of the Dead, Nostradamus and Madame Blavatskaya, as well as Emmanuelle and Western management manuals. The first experience of democratic politics had clearly been a disenchanting one; it remained to be seen if the informed and participatory citizenry of Western textbooks on government would emerge at a later stage.

PART ONE

The Russian Political System

2

Yeltsin and the Russian Presidency

JOHN P. WILLERTON

The most critical political struggles occurring in the late Soviet and post-Soviet periods have revolved around new divisions of power and authority, the forging of new institutional arrangements, and the delination of new political rules governing the actions of policy-makers. This has been true both in Moscow and in the regions. Russia and other states of the former Soviet Union have been in the midst of fundamental socioeconomic change as new political systems emerge. Most elements of the political elite and broader society are agreed in rejecting the Soviet past, but there continues to be considerable uncertainty and much disagreement about transitional policies and longer-term goals.

In this setting, the most fundamental principles underlying policymaking and governance are subject to debate. In Russia, politicians have been struggling to forge a new constitution and then to sort out the divisions of power and responsibility both among and within government branches, while concomitantly structuring a dynamic new relationship between the political centre – Moscow – and the regions. Post-Soviet executive and legislative branches emerged out of collapsed Soviet structures, with officials in both branches covering their own institutional and sectoral interests at the same time as they promoted their own career ends.

Arguably the most influential politician in the dynamic struggles underway since the failed August 1991 coup has been

Russian Federation President Boris Yeltsin. Yeltsin's political authority – grounded in unrivalled popular support and a forceful leadership style – has lent considerable weight to efforts at constructing a strong post-Soviet political executive. Certainly the legacy of the Tsarist and Soviet past pointed to a forceful executive. The political and institutional disarray of the later 1980s and the 1990s reinforced the efforts of many to create a strong political executive, and given apprehensions about a return to the excessively powerful executive of the Soviet period. However, the general ineffectiveness of the Yeltsin regime's economic reform programme bolstered the position of political rivals who championed different policy and institutional interests.

The locus of such opposition, up to October 1993, was the national legislature: the popularly-elected Congress of People's Deputies and its smaller working body, the Supreme Soviet. Parliamentary Chairman Ruslan Khasbulatov – a one-time ally of Yeltsin who quickly emerged as a leading spokesperson for those opposing the President and his initiatives – proved quite savvy in directing the legislature and safeguarding the prerogatives it secured during the late Soviet period. The struggles between Yeltsin and Khasbulatov were already quite pointed by late 1992, contributing to a political gridlock that reflected not only the politics of personality, but the politics of fundamental system and institution building, and they led to a crisis in late 1993 that ended with the dissolution of parliament itself.

The post-Soviet governing elite now encompasses a wide range of actors and interests, including not simply government officials, Presidential appointees, and elected legislators, but also industrialists and entrepreneurs whose activities are crucial to the revival of the economy. No politicians has proven able to forge a working consensus across these varied interests. Protracted debates and political inaction have left most citizens dissatisfied with post-Soviet Russia's initial democratisation experience. President Yeltsin finally moved to break the gridlock by dissolving the legislature in September 1993. The bloody outcome of this dramatic showdown in early October left the executive intact and more powerful than at any point since the collapse of the USSR, but Yeltsin and his government were tarnished by having unilaterally violated the constitution and used military force to crush their opposition.

Federal-level institutions and officials have been engulfed at the same time in complex manoeuvrings with regional and local actors who are energetically striving for greater policy-making autonomy. Russian Federal republics such as Bashkortostan, Sakha (formerly Yakutia) and Tatarstan continue to challenge Moscow's preeminence with the adoption of new constitutions and proclamations of the supremacy of their laws. Republic and lower-level officials are using efforts to strengthen their bailiwicks' decision-making prerogatives to enhance their own political standing with constituencies. Considerable political and economic power has shifted to subnational actors in the past few years. It is hardly surprising that on more than one occasion President Yeltsin has turned to regional executives for support in his struggles with federal-level rivals. Moreover, from the earliest days of his presidency, Yeltsin has sought to develop institutional means to enhance his influence over republic and provincial executive and legislative bodies.

A focal point for all of these horizontal and vertical power struggles within the Russian Federation has been the construction of a new post-Soviet constitution. Under the 1977 Brezhnev Constitution and subsequent constitutional amendments, the legislative branch was granted supreme governing powers. Ironically, Yeltsin, as chairman of the national legislature, had played a critical role in enhancing the legitimacy of legislative prerogatives during the last year of Soviet rule. Legal amendments guaranteed that the powers of the executive were derived from the legislature, with political accountability extending from the former to the latter. New post-Soviet realities quickly altered the view of Yeltsin, members of the executive branch, and many reformers, as they struggled for new constitutional arrangements, modelled somewhat on the French system, and designed to bolster the executive. Divisions within the parliament and its leadership constrained legislative dominance during 1992–3, but Yeltsin failed to find the legal means – either by directive or national referendum – to secure a preeminent decision-making position for the executive branch. Only a Presidential crackdown in late 1993 enabled the executive to secure a preeminent position, which was entrenched in the constitution adopted in December. But the power vacuum left with the dissolution of legislative bodies was temporary, and battles over the 'rules of the game' continued as politicians struggled to forge a new set of working relationships. As has been true through the period since the collapse of the USSR, pressing policy problems were exacerbated by fundamental institutional cleavages, leaving the political arena dynamic and unstable.

The Political Executive in the Russian and Soviet Past

Traditional Norms and Institutions

Both the pre-Soviet and Soviet political systems assumed a strong executive, with considerable authority resting with the top decision-maker – whether tsar or Communist Party General Secretary. The centralised autocracy of the tsars, grounded in the influence of Byzantium and Mongol domination, was predicated on a steep power hierarchy, with the chief executive's position religiously legitimated, and the political system conferring decisive decision-making prerogatives. The Tatars initiated the long-term development of an administrative bureaucracy supporting the political executive. Peter the Great rationalised and professionalised that bureaucracy in the 18th century, simultaneously enhancing the power of central executive agencies – especially those closely tied to the tsar. By the 19th century, an extensive system of ministries and advisory councils assisted the tsar, assuming critical information gathering, consultation, and policy coordinating roles. This administrative apparatus assumed the key role in enabling the executive to react forcefully against any challenges to its authority. There were pressures to develop representative bodies, ranging from the prepetrine *Zemskii Sobor* (assembly of nobility, clergy, and bourgeoisie) to elected councils (*dumas*) and assemblies (*zemstvos*), and culminating in the *Duma* created by Tsar Nicolas II in 1905. But throughout the pre-Soviet period the chief executive was never constrained by such institutions, and the executive could ignore and even dissolve such bodies when necessary.

Soviet power built on this legacy, albeit with its founder, Vladimir Lenin, rejecting the personal trappings of power and assuming an unpretentious if dominant role within the regime. The Soviet system relied upon strong political executives – wellensconced within the Communist Party apparatus – to direct the

massive state bureaucracy. Essential characterist
tional Soviet political system were its centralise
nature, with a massive set of interconnected bureau
all institutions and interests into an apparatus rule
and relatively homogeneous Slavic and Russian e
Forceful chief executives such as Stalin, Khrush   , and
Brezhnev devoted much attention to consolidating power within
the party–state apparatus, with programmatic success contingent
upon their organisational prowess.

The 'First' or 'General' Secretary within the CPSU apparatus
was the country's top executive, wielding far-reaching supervisory
power over all other Secretaries and all subordinate organs of the
party and state. He assumed the critical role in the mobility of
political elites and the formation of governing coalitions. With the
General Secretary at the helm, broad policy-making and supervisory powers rested with the CPSU Politburo and Secretariat,
whose approximately 25 members constituted the top decision-
making elite of the country. The CPSU Central Committee, with
roughly 400 members drawn from all major federal and lower-
level institutions, legitimated the policy line set by these top
executives. Meanwhile, the CC apparatus, with roughly 20
departments and thousands of professional Communist Party
workers, coordinated the activities of those and other party and
soviet bodies, transmitting themselves up and down the institutional hierarchies. Power was hierarchically organised and quite
concentrated in the Soviet system, and the political executive
enjoyed a hegemonic position in the wider society.

Matters of policy implementation and administration fell to
state organisations, led by the Council of Ministers (with approximately 100 ministries and state committees), its governing council
(or Presidium), and the prime minister. The 'popularly elected'
federal legislature – the Supreme Soviet – with deputies selected
through single-candidate elections, provided *post hoc* legitimation
for the CPSU leadership's initiatives. Taken together, these executive, administrative, and legislative bodies unified the policy-
making, implementing, and legitimating functions into a single
interconnected hierarchy controlled by the CPSU elite. This
pattern of power organisation was replicated at the republic and
lower levels, providing the party executive with a dominant
position throughout the Soviet system.

While Lenin and Stalin played the key roles in forging Soviet executive norms, Leonid Brezhnev proved to be the quintessential Soviet leader, effectively developing a large patronage network and building a governing coalition across major elite cohorts which survived for nearly two decades (1964–82). In 1977, Brezhnev combined the considerable decision-making powers of the CPSU General Secretaryship with the largely honorific Chairmanship of the Supreme Soviet Presidium to bolster his standing as the country's chief executive. On paper at least, the merging of these two posts – a precedent followed by Brezhnev's successors – widened the chief executive's already extensive power base. Mikhail Gorbachev subsequently used such executive prerogatives to his advantage as he attempted to initiate his radical political and economic reform programme.

Gorbachevian Initiatives

Institutional and policy reforms of the Gorbachev period (1985–91) laid the groundwork for the political norms and policy struggles of post-Soviet Russia and the other successor states. Gorbachev, operating under traditional Soviet political norms, found reform of the executive and of the overall political process necessary for the realisation of his programmatic goals. Gorbachev had inherited from Brezhnev and the interregnum regimes a complex agenda of unresolved and deepening domestic and foreign policy problems. Several years of intricate political manoeuvring by Gorbachev and other reformers resulted in both the ouster of numerous long-dominant conservative politicians and the fashioning of the coalition necessary to effect more fundamental policy change. But Gorbachev and his allies quickly learned that any prospect of success for the *perestroika* programme was tied to fundamental institutional reforms: reforms designed to diminish the resistance of the entrenched party–state apparatus.

Policy reform required a strong chief executive not constrained by resistant subordinate institutions. Similar to earlier general secretaries, Gorbachev demonstrated the considerable discretionary power of the top executive as he set about reorganising the apparatus and restructuring power relations among its constituent institutions. Major steps were taken to streamline party

and government agencies so as to lessen sources of resista
while enhancing the viability of reform-oriented executive dire
tives. Decision-making responsibilities were redistributed: the
Politburo and Secretariat, as well as the subordinate CC and its
apparatus, were downgraded, their powers being transferred to
newly-created bodies such as Central Committee commissions and
later a series of bodies tied to the newly-created USSR presidency.
New rules were introduced, such as multiple candidate elections
for top executive posts and term limits for most executives, to
alter the composition of the political elite and make that elite
more accountable to pressures from below that were sympathetic
to the Gorbachev regime and its reformist policy line.

By 1990, the decision-making initiative had been shifted away
from the party–state apparatus and to a rejuvenated governmental executive branch and a reworked system of popularly-
elected soviets. Gorbachev replaced Andrei Gromyko as Supreme
Soviet Chairman in October 1988, enabling him to oversee the
upgrading of the parliament and its previously honorific membership. Over the next two years considerable powers were transferred to the Supreme Soviet chairmanship as Gorbachev
consolidated his position while accelerating the reform process.
There were strong institutional needs to build a broad consensus
through – among other means – a viable legislative branch. That
legislature would be legitimated by popular election and would be
more inclined to cooperate with a reform-oriented executive.
Accordingly, the largely ceremonial USSR Supreme Soviet, which
traditionally was convened only twice a year for 2–3 day sessions,
was replaced by a two-tiered legislature. A popularly-elected and
large Congress of People's Deputies (2250 members) represented
the range of political and socio-economic interests, while a smaller
deliberative body, named the Supreme Soviet (542 members) and
drawn from the ranks of the Congress, operated over lengthier
sessions lasting 3–4 months each. With many members selected
through multi-candidate, secret ballot elections, these bodies
rapidly became independent entities willing to challenge the
executive and the party–state apparatus. The legislature now
included full-time parliamentarians, with considerable authority to
address all policy issues. Especially noteworthy was the emergence
of a system of committees and standing commissions which put
considerable pressure on the executive. Legislators now took

seriously the confirmation of leading government officials, such as the Prime Minister and members of the Council of Ministers, and they proved willing to oppose and even reject nominees backed by Gorbachev or his Prime Minister. They likewise subjected government policies to considerable public scrutiny. With the emergence of an influential and contentious federal-level parliament, the precedent was set for comparable republic and lower-level legislative bodies. Boris Yeltsin and other politicians would use such sub-federal institutions to champion their own interests as they challenged the hegemonic position of Soviet federal authorities.

For a brief period Gorbachev assumed a commanding position of authority as the head of a reinvigorated legislature and as the chief executive within the traditionally powerful apparatus. Further institutional changes – in particular, the creation in March 1990 of a USSR Presidency – were intended to make Gorbachev independent of party–state apparatus pressures from below while simultaneously giving him an independent base of power and enhanced authority in dealing with the more powerful and increasingly independent legislature. As President, Gorbachev had considerable power in directing the work of the Prime Minister and government through the Council of Ministers. The chief executive appeared to be in a very formidable position, structuring the activities of all major political institutions.

But in fact, the struggles and institutional changes of the 1985–91 period resulted in the forging of a new political system, with a new balance of power among executive, legislative, and other institutions. New formal and informal 'rules of the game' – in particular, contested secret-ballot elections – gave non-traditional and reformist interests mounting influence in the political process. Late Gorbachev period institutional adjustments – including the granting of extraordinary decision-making powers to the President, the downgrading of the Council (renamed Cabinet) of Ministers, and the creation of a Council of the Federation (drawing in republic leaders to a top Presidential advisory body) and a Presidential Council – were intended to help the political executive cope with these mounting political challenges. Yet the growing momentum of power decentralisation and democratisation hampered the efforts of any individual or group to channel dynamic reform processes. Gorbachev did not enjoy the legitimacy of a popular mandate as chief executive since he chose to be elected President by the Congress and not by direct popular election. In some cases his Presidential decrees were ignored or even rejected by the legislature. Meanwhile, the heightened authority of regional and local officials enhanced their ability to challenge the preferences of the long-dominant central authorities – whether executive or legislative. These officials' career interests were increasingly driven by regional and local constituencies rather than by the interests of Moscow. As a result, republic and provincial executives and volatile subfederal elected assemblies confronted federal authorities on all basic resource and policy issues. Both horizontal and vertical political cleavages undermined the federal executive's ability to govern and to channel the reform process. Further federal-level institutional and personnel changes, combined with a final effort to draft a viable new Union Treaty among the republics and federal government, failed to preserve both the federal executive's position and the besieged Soviet system.

Developments of the Gorbachev period underscored the need for strong executive leadership, but a leadership attuned to increasingly democratic realities and skilled in rather different political qualities. Politicians needed to understand and address complex economic problems as post-Soviet society underwent a fundamental transition to a regulated market system. In this setting it was incumbent on officials to build coalitions and attempt to forge consensus among openly competing institutions and interests. This meant adjusting to parliamentary manoeuvring and negotiations among governmental institutions as well as nascent political parties and newly-emergent business and entre-preneurial interests. Officials were now accountable both before subordinate institutions and the public. Gorbachev, a master player in Soviet apparatus politics, ultimately failed to adjust to new political realities. It fell to Yeltsin and other post-Soviet politicians to cope with these new political conditions.

Yeltsin and the Russian Political Elite

Boris Yeltsin played a leading role in challenging and eventually helping to bring down the centralised Soviet regime, but as Russian Federation President he inherited the political and socio-economic conditions requiring a strong executive. After the failed August 1991 coup Yeltsin became the central official responsible for holding together the Russian Federation in the face of powerful centrifugal forces that he had helped to launch. He also became the key figure responsible for forging a reform pro- gramme capable of extricating Russia from its deepening economic crisis.

Yeltsin brought a commanding presence and considerable poli- tical authority to his position as the *de facto* successor to Gorba- chev. His political authority stemmed in large measure from his open challenge of the CPSU and his resistance to the August 1991 coup. His past commitment to rooting out corruption and cham- pioning the interests of common workers had earned him strong support from diverse elements within Russian society. Meanwhile, his institutional position as Russian President had been legiti- mated by popular election; during the late Soviet period he sub- mitted himself on several occasions to election, whether directly by voters or indirectly by voters' representatives within the legis- lature. His actions and past career revealed him as a forceful per- sonality who had a vision to move Russia from its authoritarian communist past towards a democratic free market future.

Yeltsin had made a career in the CPSU and had risen to a top provincial party post (in Sverdlovsk) before coming to Moscow in December 1985 to help clean out a corrupt city party leadership. After splitting with Gorbachev and the CPSU leadership a few years later, Yeltsin had fallen from power but in the process earned considerable regard in the eyes of reformers and those dis- gruntled by apparently half-hearted *perestroika* reform policies. Yeltsin returned to the national limelight with his election to the new Congress of People's Deputies in March 1989. A year later, in May 1990, with the revival of the Russian Federation legis- lature, Yeltsin was picked as its Chairman. During his tenure in the legislature Yeltsin championed Russia's sovereignty, leading the parliament in claiming the supremacy of Russia over Soviet law. His highly-publicised resignation from the Communist Party at the 28th CPSU Congress (July 1990) bolstered his standing with the reform element. His political legitimacy was further strengthened by his June 1991 popular election to the newly- created Russian presidency: in a multi-candidate race in which several rivals were given resource and media advantages of the

TABLE 2.1 *Political spectrum of leading Russian Federation politicians and officials*

I	II	III	IV	V
Radical reformers	(Centre-rightists)	Centrists	(Centre-leftists)	Conservatives and nationalists
Gaidar	Chernomyrdin	Lobov	Skokov	Khasbulatov
Shumeiko	Petrov	Volsky	Travkin	Rutskoi
Yeltsin	Shakhrai	Yarov	Zorkin	Zyuganov
Fedorov	Yavlinsky	Khizha	Rybkin	Zhirinovsky

TABLE 2.2 *Leading Russian Federation politicians and officials*

	Year born	Current (or most recent) position	Political orientation*
Burbulis, Gennadii	1945	President, *Strategiya* (Jan. 1993–); adviser to Yeltsin	I
Chernomyrdin, Viktor	1938	Prime Minister (Dec. 1992–)	II
Chubais, Anatolii	1955	Deputy Prime Minister (June 1992–)	I
Filatov, Sergei	1936	Chief, Presidential Administration (Jan. 1993–)	I
Fedorov, Boris	1958	Deputy Prime Minister (Dec. 1992–Jan. 1994)	I
Gaidar, Yegor	1956	1st Deputy Prime Minister (Sept. 1993–Jan. 1994)	I
Grachev, Pavel	1948	Defence Minister (May 1992–)	–
Khasbulatov, Ruslan	1942	Chairman, Russian Federation Supreme Soviet (Oct. 1991–Oct. 1993)	V
Khizha, Georgii	1938	Deputy Prime Minister (May 1992–Sept. 1993)	III
Kozyrev, Andrei	1951	Foreign Minister (Oct. 1990–)	I
Lobov, Oleg	1935	Secretary, Security Council (Sept. 1993–)	III
Luzhkov, Yuri	1936	Mayor, Moscow (June 1992–)	I
Petrov, Yuri	1939	Chairman, State Investment Corporation (Feb. 1993–)	II
Poltoranin, Mikhail	1939	Chief, Russian Federal Information Centre (Dec. 1992–)	I
Popov, Gavriil	1936	Cofounder and Leader, Russian Movement for Democratic Reforms (Feb. 1992–)	I

Rutskoi, Alexander	1947	Vice President (June 1991–October 1993)	V
Rybkin, Ivan	1947	Chairman, State Duma (Jan. 1994–)	IV
Shakhrai, Sergei	1956	Deputy Prime Minister (Nov. 1992–)	II
Shumeiko, Vladimir	1945	1st Deputy Prime Minister (June 1992–)	I
Skokov, Yuri	1938	Secretary, Security Council (June 1992–May 1993)	IV
Sobchak, Anatolii	1937	Mayor, St. Petersburg (June 1991–)	I
Travkin, Nikolai	1946	Cofounder and Leader, Democratic Party of Russia (1990–)	IV
Volsky, Arkadii	1932	Chairman, Russian Union of Industrialists and Entrepreneurs (Jan 1992–)	III
Yarov, Yuri	1942	Deputy Prime Minister (Dec. 1992–)	III
Yavlinsky, Grigorii	1952	Chairman, Economic and Political Research Centre (1991–)	II
Yeltsin, Boris	1931	President (June 1991–)	I
Zhirinovsky, Vladimir	1946	Founder and Leader, Liberal Democratic Party (March 1990–)	V
Zorkin, Valerii	1943	Chairman, Constitutional Court (Dec. 1991–Oct. 1993)	IV
Zyuganov, Gennadii	1944	Chairman, Communist Party of the Russian Federation (Feb. 1993–)	V

*See Table 2.1 for description of categories. Defence Minister Grachev has not articulated a particular political orientation, but rather has stressed military professionalism and the government's non-involvement in the political process. When called upon, he has been supportive of the Yeltsin government.

Soviet federal authorities, he earned 57 per cent of the vote to win on the first ballot. This mandate strengthened Yeltsin in his growing public rivalry with Soviet President Gorbachev, who had avoided placing his candidacy before the public a year earlier.

Yeltsin's policy goals were straightforward: he championed Russian Federation independence, promoted the country's democratisation, and supported the introduction of radical market-oriented economic reforms. Between mid-1991 and early 1994 his regime's policy programme and strategies evolved, reflecting a changing balance of elite elements within his government and a dynamic domestic political and economic situation. Central to the Yeltsin policy approach was the 'shock therapy' reform package which began to emerge as early as late October 1991, more than a month before the final collapse of the USSR. This strategy entailed rapid and widespread privatisation, the freeing of prices (including those on energy), and a tightening of monetary policies. As the programme emerged, it encompassed the use of joint-stock arrangements in the dispersion of mid-sized enterprises and the introduction of a system of vouchers freely distributed to the popular so that citizens could acquire former state enterprises and property. This programme assumed a foreign policy of cooperation with Western countries and international organisations such as the International Monetary Fund to secure external investment and assistance. It was also predicated on the assumption of a diminishing – though not insubstantial – role for government in the management of the economy and the fostering of investment.

Yeltsin's policy preferences placed him squarely in the midst of those elements pressing for fundamental root and branch political and economic reform. The post-Soviet Russian political elite was quite diverse in policy orientations, ranging from extremist reformers drawn to Western democratic and capitalist experience to chauvinist slavophile nationalists inspired by the pre-Soviet Russian past. Among the varying ideological positions staked out in the early post-Communist period we can identify three major groupings which influenced the Russian political scene: (a) radical reformers, (b) conservatives and nationalists, and (c) centrists adopting selected positions held by reformers and conservatives. In addition, some politicians expressed policy preferences placing them between the centrists and either the reformist (centre-right) or the conservative-nationalist (centre-left) groupings. Table 2.1 provides an attitudinal spectrum setting out the relative positions of these groups. Table 2.2 lists leading Russian Federation politicians during the post-Soviet period, indicating their broad policy orientations along that spectrum.

Radical Reformers

Radical reformers supported a rapid shift to a market economy, favouring a shock therapy approach which would quickly privatise trade and services, free prices, and harness government involvement, while opening up the economy to domestic and foreign entrepreneurs. Radical reformers looked to the Western experience and Western assistance in bolstering reform efforts. They were especially supportive of the foreign policy line promoted by Andrei Kozyrev, Russia's Foreign Minister since 1990. Kozyrev's policy line favoured close political and economic relations with the West, full-scale disarmament, and rapid integration in to the global economy. Radical reformers also put great stock in an unrestricted press which would illuminate both Russia's systemic problems and relevant foreign and domestic policy responses. Mikhail Poltoranin – a reformist journalist whose association with Yeltsin went back to the mid-1980s when Yeltsin was Moscow city boss – played a critical role in helping the government harness the media to advance its reform agenda.

Many leading radical reformers emerged from academia, with some of the most prominent, like Yegor Gaidar and Grigorii Yavlinsky, trained as economists. A number of political movements and nascent parties fell into this group, with Democratic Russia arguably the most influential. Democratic Russia had arisen in spring 1990 to aid reformers seeking regional and local offices, and it had played an important role in Yeltsin's successful drive for the presidency a year later. Another nascent radical reformist party of some influence was the Russian Movement for Democratic Reforms, founded in 1991 by two high-profile reformers, Moscow Mayor Gavriil Popov and St Petersburg Mayor Anatolii Sobchak. Yeltsin loyalists such as Gennadii Burbulis attempted to form some kind of political movement to support the government's radical reform programme, but these nascent parties failed to coalesce as effective political organisations, falling victim to considerable factionalisation and division.

Conservatives and Nationalists

At the other end of the ideological spectrum were conservatives and nationalists who quickly came to oppose Yeltsin's reform efforts. Emphasising a unified and indivisible Russia, many conservatives and nationalists wanted to see a return to the pre-revolutionary borders of 1914. They were sceptical of Western motives and hesitant about asking Western assistance, preferring that Russia rely on its own resources as it addressed its economic woes. Their economic reform proposals favoured the traditional military–industrial sector. There was a commitment to restoring Russian national culture and a concomitant hostility to the Westernisation of the country's culture. Many turned to Russian Orthodoxy as a spiritual–philosophical base. While advocating economic reform, conservatives and nationalists stressed the revival of the Russian peasantry on the basis of individual economy in the traditional *obshchina* (community).

The more extreme conservatives and nationalists favoured a return to the command political–economic system, rejecting all market-oriented reforms. Extremists adopted strongly anti-semitic positions, pointing to a global Zionist conspiracy said to be undermining Russia's socioeconomic and political transformation. Several conservative and nationalist anti-reform blocs, for example the Russian People's Assembly and the National Salvation Front, emerged to help form an anti-Yeltsin coalition. Such groups strove to take executive powers away from the radical reformers and reverse the Yeltsin policies. They sought to restore order and stop corruption. In the economic realm, they attempted to stop privatisation, stabilise prices, and minimise international economic (and political) connections. All such extremists gave attention to strengthening Russia's military capabilities.

Among the most influential conservatives were parliamentary chairman Ruslan Khasbulatov and Vice President Alexander Rutskoi. Both men had assumed more moderate – centrist – positions when the Russian Federation was struggling against Soviet authorities, but they rapidly moved toward the conservatives as Yeltsin's radical reform programme emerged and as Yeltsin increased the power of the presidency. By the time of the 1993 Presidential–legislative showdown, both men were firmly aligned with conservative elements and adopting decidedly more extreme policy positions. After the 'October events' of that year, both were under arrest.

Vladimir Zhirinovsky, the leader of the Liberal-Democratic Party, was arguably the most influential of the conservative–nationalist extremists. Zhirinovsky had championed a quasi-fascist policy stance in the June 1991 Russian Federation presidency election, drawing 6 million votes. He and other extremists, however, had difficulty working with other conservatives and nationalists. Likewise, communists – who were divided among nearly a half-dozen different party groups in the post-Soviet period – proved weak and unable to assume much influence either within the conservative ranks or within the political process overall. Some Russian sociologists estimated that the number of committed communists did not exceed 5 per cent of the country's population, with the communist platform appealing only to the elderly, pensioners and others especially hurt by the Yeltsin programme. Communists and Liberal Democrats were nonetheless among the most successful contenders in the December 1993 elections, and they were well represented in the new Russian parliament.

Centrists

Situated between these radical reform and conservative–nationalist groups were a variety of centrists who attempted to synthesise and balance selected aspects of reformers' and conservatives' policy preferences and strategies. It is difficult to generalise across all centrists, but suffice it to note that most of them sought national compromises with more modest political and economic reform programmes. In general, centrists were committed to political democratisation and economic privatisation, but without the excesses and trauma of the shock therapy strategy. Likewise, centrists were committed to a unified Russia and to avoiding any measures that would contribute to the country's disintegration, but they did not champion a return to 1914 borders – with its threatening implications for the now independent former Soviet states. Finally, centrists stressed Russian domestic resources, preferring a less prominent Western role in providing investment and assistance.

A number of important political movements (such as Nikolai Travkin's Democratic Party of Russia and Alexander Rutskoi's People's Party of Free Russia) emerged in the late Gorbachev period in support of these centrist policy perspectives. But especially important to the ranks of the centrists were the highly influential industrial directors and technocrats, whose enterprises accounted for nearly 85 per cent of the industrial potential of the state sector. These directors and technocrats were a complex mix of interests, spanning (a) directors of enterprises successfully adapted to the privatised and market setting, (b) directors of military–industrial complex and heavy industry enterprises with much potential but still dependent on the government, and (c) directors of unprofitable enterprises which were unlikely to survive without major government subsidies. Arkadii Volsky – a former high-ranking CPSU official with strong ties to the country's military-industrial complex – formed the Scientific–Industrial Union in May 1990 to bridge these disparate elements. Its policy positions fell between the more reformist preferences of the first group and the very conservative stances of the third group, with an overriding interest in slowing down the privatisation of industries. Two years later Volsky – together with Rutskoi and Travkin – helped to form Civic Union, a coalition that has intended to solidity the centre's political position *vis-à-vis* the Yeltsin government, and within a few months it presented an economic programme meant to serve as a feasible alternative to the shock therapy strategy. The programme stressed the impossibility of moving to a market economy in one leap, stressing a 'realistic' strategy of conversion, with appropriate government safeguards to minimise social dislocations and economic disruptions (for example, through government maintenance of energy prices). Civic Union committed itself to the development of a societal safety net during the lengthy transition period, while also promising to shore up Russia's statehood after the collapse of the USSR.

Centre-right and Centre-left Elements

As Tables 2.1 and 2.2 indicate, a number of politicians had policy preferences which bridged either centrist-reform or centrist-conservative policy orientations. Among the former were Prime Minister Viktor Chernomyrdin, long-time Yeltsin protege and one-time Presidential chief-of-staff Yuri Petrov, and Deputy Prime Minister Sergei Shakhrai. These officials assumed critical roles in the Yeltsin government, but they favoured more cautious reform measures than those promoted by radical reformers such as Gaidar. Their general preference was to proceed with privatisation more slowly while preserving a larger role for government agencies in the conduct of the country's economic life. Many of these officials' career were tied to the state industrial sector. Centre-left elements were fundamentally opposed to the shock therapy strategy, though they were not opposed to the long-term emergence of a regulated market economy. They favoured stronger state control over the economy and considerable subsidies for the state industrial sector. Among those bridging the centrists and conservatives were one-time Security Council Secretary Yuri Skokov, Democratic Party of Russia leader Nikolai Travkin, and former Constitutional Court Chairman Valerii Zorkin. These politicians ultimately became harsh critics of the Yeltsin programme. Skokov, for instance, had been a top associate of Yeltsin's, serving as a key adviser on security issues before becoming Security Council Secretary. However, he broke with Yeltsin in spring 1993 and aligned himself with centrist and conservative opponents. Centre-left politicians, rather than joining the ranks of extremist opponents, engaged in consensus-building efforts with industrialists and centrists such as Arkadii Volsky. They were, however, part of a broad spectrum of opposition to the reformist regime.

The Executive: Institutions and Personalities

Because real executive powers had been created in the CPSU apparatus during the Soviet period, governmental executive bodies had been of secondary importance, significantly primarily in the implementing of CPSU decisions. Russian Federation institutional and procedural changes of the late Gorbachev period (1990–1) laid the groundwork for the institutional and policy cleavages which emerged in the wake of the USSR's collapse. Following the precedent set by the 1989 USSR Congress of People's Deputies election and first sessions, republic-level elections were held in 1990 in Russia and elsewhere to select new parliaments. Competitive secret-ballot elections yielded much more assertive republic-level legislatures which were willing to challenge central authorities. As initially constituted, the Russian parliament selected its own executive, a chairman, but within a year it separated the executive from the legislative, permitting the direct popular election of a Russian Federation President. Yeltsin helped bolster the parliament's authority during his tenure as its chair, and as a consequence he maintained a good working relationship with the parliament during its late Soviet-period struggles with the federal authorities. Indeed, Yeltsin's successor as parliamentary chair, Ruslan Khasbulatov, was a political ally whom Yeltsin helped recruit into the parliamentary leadership when he himself became President. It was only with the final collapse of the Soviet system – and assumption of decision-making power by Russian Federation officials – that the policy preferences of the Russian President and parliament began to diverge, rapidly leading to a fundamental executive–legislative conflict which overwhelmed the first two years of the post-Soviet regime.

Institutions

The Russian Federation President emerged as the primary policy initiator and coordinator, as well as the chief arbiter among openly competing interests within the post-Soviet system. During the post-August 1991 transition Yeltsin immediately assumed the top decision-making position, effectively pushing aside the politically compromised Soviet President as he assumed Gorbachev's executive powers. An economic management committee, headed by the Russian Prime Minister Ivan Silaev, was created to oversee economic reform, but Silaev's powers were quickly assumed by Yeltsin. There was a need for a strong executive in the midst of considerable organisational disarray, with Yeltsin initially attempting to govern Russia by decree. He was assisted by a team of young, well-educated, reform-oriented advisers, with a ra economic reform package already emerging within months.

A fundamental Presidential–parliamentary institutional rivalry was bound to arise in the earliest days of Russian Federation sovereignty. According to late Soviet-period constitutional arrangements, the executive was subordinate to the legislative branch: the Congress of People's Deputies was the supreme political body. Thus, while the President nominated the Prime Minister and other leading members of the Council of Ministers, the Prime Minister and other top Ministers were subject to confirmation by the parliament. The President's ability to structure the federal-level policy agenda was significantly enhanced when, in November 1991, the Congress gave Yeltsin extraordinary powers to promote his radical economic reform programme. Yeltsin's decrees were made equal to law, while he was also empowered to appoint heads of local administrations and Presidential representatives to regions to supervise their performance. Implicit in the parliament's action, however, was its prerogative to take such powers away: something the parliament would do in the spring of 1993. Ultimately, the parliament had the ability to impeach the President, should two-thirds of all members vote accordingly. The President did not have comparable constitutional authority to disband the parliament, though this did not stop Yeltsin from threatening to do so on a number of occasions (and doing so, unconstitutionally, in September 1993).

In fact, the Russian Federation executive operated on a system where competing actors, with independent bases of power, could resist his policy preferences. Democratic Russia had helped put Yeltsin into office, but he operated without a political party base. Yeltsin needed to use his considerable public standing and Presidential prerogatives to build bridges to important political and societal elements. He exhibited considerable policy flexibility as he constantly adjusted his team and his policy line to accommodate dynamic domestic interests. During his first years in the presidency, Yeltsin's image shifted from being a President primarily representing Democratic Russia to being a balancer of diverse reformist and centrist interests. Yeltsin's actions during 1992–3 revealed an unpredictable application of his institutional and personal powers: at times he was assertive and quite willing to directly take on his opponents; at other times, he appeared distant and less decisive. The new constitution adopted in December 1993 endowed the President with new and still more formidable powers (see Exhibit 2.1), but it remained unclear in the confused post-election situation how these powers would be exercised and how far in political terms they extended.

The post of Vice President was created along with that of the President in spring 1991. Beyond being the immediate successor should the President die or be impeached, his role and responsibilities were unclear. There was no past precedent for this post. Indeed, a major dilemma of the Soviet political system had been the uncertainty surrounding the succession arrangements should the chief executive depart his office. As was true of other political systems with positions of this kind, the President proved central in determining the functions of the Vice President. Alexander Rutskoi, an air force general and hero of the Afghan war who had shared Yeltsin's policy positions during the late Gorbachev period, had run with Yeltsin as a vice-presidential candidate in June 1991. While supportive of Yeltsin during the first months of their administration – Rutskoi had organised the defence of Russia's 'White House' during the August 1991 coup attempt – Rutskoi was already criticising the Yeltsin economic reform programme by November 1991. He had close ties to the military-industrial complex, and was opposed to the shock therapy strategy. Moreover, Rutskoi was critical of the pro-Western foreign policy of Andrei Kozyrev, which he viewed as undermining Russian security needs. Yeltsin gave Rutskoi responsibility for overseeing agrarian reforms (February 1992–April 1993). But Rutskoi allied himself with farm managers and local officials who were holdovers from the Soviet period, undercutting fundamental system reform in favour of more traditional policy approaches to improve agricultural productivity.

Increasingly different policy preferences emerged during 1992–3 that further distanced the two men and left Rutskoi and his aides isolated from the mainstream executive. In spring 1993 Rutskoi announced he would run for the presidency, and by late 1993 he was presenting himself as Yeltsin's successor when the parliament attempted to strip Yeltsin of the presidency during the September 1993 Presidential–parliamentary showdown. Rutskoi's actions suggested the potential for the Vice President to function as a counterweight and rival to the President. It was not surprising

EXHIBIT 2.1 *The Russian Presidency, 1993*

Under the December 1993 Constitution, the President of the Russian Federation is:

head of state (Art. 80:1);
the guarantor of the Constitution (Art. 80:2), to which he swears an oath (Art. 82:1);
he 'defines the basic directions of the domestic and foreign policy of the state' (Art. 80:3), and represents the Russian Federation domestically and internationally (Art. 80:4);
he is elected for four years by direct and secret vote (Art. 81:1); he must be at least 35 years old, and have lived in the Russian Federation for at least 10 years (Art. 81:2), and may not be elected for more than two consecutive terms (Art. 81:3);
he 'appoints with the agreement of the State Duma the Chairman of the Government of the Russian Federation'; 'takes decisions on the resignation of the Government of the Russian Federation'; nominates candidates for the Chairmanship of the State Bank; on the recommendation of the prime minister, he appoints and dismisses deputy premiers and federal ministers; nominates candidates for the Constitutional Court and Supreme Court; forms and heads the Security Council; appoints and dismisses his plenipotentiary representatives in the regions; appoints the high command of the armed forces (Art. 83); additionally, he calls elections for the State Duma; he dissolves the Duma in appropriate circumstances; calls referenda; initiates legislation; reports annually to the Federal Assembly on 'the situation in the country' and the 'main directions of the domestic and foreign policy of the state' (Art. 84);
he is Commander in Chief (Art. 87), and can introduce a state of emergency (Art. 88);
he issues decrees that have the force of law throughout the territory of the Federation (Art. 89).

---

that the constitutional reforms proposed by Yeltsin abolished the vice presidency, making the chairman of the parliament the successor should the President leave his position. Rutskoi, in the event, sided with the parliament against Yeltsin and was arrested and ousted in October 1993.

At the top of the state administrative structure was the Council of Ministers, led by a Prime Minister nominated by the President and subsequently approved by the parliament. The Council of Ministers assisted the President and his advisers in the formulation of policies while implementing and administering policies. In

theory, the Prime Minister was the top adviser and leading architect for the executive's programme. In fact, the Prime Minister
played an important role in linking the executive and legislative
branches and in marshalling support for Presidential initiatives in
parliamentary bodies. The Prime Minister helped in selecting ministers who themselves regularly accounted to legislative standing
committees.

The importance of the position of prime minister was reflected
by Yeltsin himself assuming the post in November 1991 as he was
setting out his reform agenda. Yeltsin wanted to signal his involvement in forging a new economic reform programme while
directly dealing with the parliamentarians who would need to
approve it. First Deputy Prime Minister Gennadii Burbulis essentially fulfilled the prime minister's routine tasks, while Yegor
Gaidar, a monetarist inspired by the work of the American economist Milton Friedman and appointed Deputy Prime Minister for
economic policy, developed the actual reform programme. By
spring 1992 it was clear Yeltsin needed someone to assume the
prime ministership to rally support for government policies
among parliament members. Gaidar, as the Yeltsin reform programme's key architect and most forceful proponent, was the
natural choice, though the lack of majority support for him in the
parliament compelled him to serve as acting Prime Minister.
Although besieged, Gaidar maintained this 'point man' position
for 8 months before parliamentary pressures finally led to his
ouster and replacement by a more centrist politicians, Viktor
Chernomyrdin. Chernomyrdin, a lacklustre bureaucrat drawn
from the energy sector, bridged more centrist elements as he
advocated a more moderate reform strategy. In fact, the shock
therapy approach continued under Chernomyrdin. Radical reformers held the upper hand in the governing coalition even while
centre-right or centrist elements were coopted into the government. Chernomyrdin, meanwhile, helped to hold together Yeltsin's fragile coalition throughout 1993; it was no accident that
Yeltsin appointed him acting Vice President in the wake of the
late 1993 crisis and he was influential in the formation of a
centrist administration in early 1994 following the December elections.

Yeltsin, Gaidar, Chernomyrdin and their associates operated in
the midst of considerable institutional disarray as the struggle

over policy reforms continued. Russian Federation governmental bodies had coopted the positions of USSR ministries after the failed August 1991 coup. During this period many governmental institutions sought autonomy; this was especially likely where government bodies had powerful domestic constituencies or significant resources. Some institutional experimentation was attempted by the top-level executive. For instance, a Russian State Council, with roots in the 19th century tsarist experience, was created to help top executives harness the state bureaucracy. Gennadii Burbulis assisted in the creation and supervision of a system of state counsellors, though it never got off the ground and was disbanded by summer 1992. An influential presidential administration, however, did arise, filling the void left by the collapsed Soviet party–state apparatus. First headed by Yuri Petrov, and since January 1993 by Yeltsin's top lieutenant in the parliament, Sergei Filatov, the presidential administration included a wide array of advisory councils, committees, and groups, with a growing number of advisers, experts, and staff members.

A significant bureaucratic dilemma for the executive involved policy coordination in the face of overlapping and competing institutions. There was considerable jockeying for administrative position and for governmental and private resources. For instance three different bodies emerged in the Yeltsin government to address the all-important need for foreign investment: besides the Ministry of Foreign Economic Relations, a holdover from the late Soviet period that was headed initially by a Gaidar associate, a Russian Agency for International Cooperation and Development was set up with Alexander Shokhin at its head, and a new State Investment Corporation was established and chaired by Yeltsin's former chief of staff, Yuri Petrov. There was especially noteworthy institutional confusion in the area of foreign policy, with the Foreign Ministry constantly struggling to safeguard its prerogatives against various institutions. A series of inconsistent governmental decrees and statements throughout 1992 left doubt as to the Foreign Ministry's real authority in pursuing its controversial pro-Western foreign policy line. The June 1992 establishment of a Russian Federation Security Council – whose voting membership included the President, Vice President, Prime Minister, parliamentary First Deputy Chairman, and a secretary, but with the Foreign Minister only a non-voting member – raised questions regarding where policy originated. The Security Council was said to set broad policy goals and engage in long-term strategic planning, and many viewed it as operating along the lines of the communist-period Politburo. Over times its focus came to encompass a widening set of foreign and domestic policy matters related to Russia's sovereignty, stability, and security. But with Security Council Secretary Skokov holding more conservative policy positions than Foreign Minister Kozyrev, questions arose about the Yeltsin government's foreign policy. Eventually, Skokov's break with Yeltsin resulted in his ouster, though institutional uncertainty regarding the foreign policy process continued.

While struggling to forge a coherent reform programme, the Yeltsin government was also beset with the dilemma of cultivating a reliable and professional cohort of political appointees and civil servants. Reformers since the earliest days of the Gorbachev regime had wrestled with the lack of professional civil servants. In March 1992 the Yeltsin government established the Main Administration for Training Civil Service Cadres, designed to help develop a reserve pool of civil servants who were reform-oriented and who understand the norms of a regulated market system. Proposals were forthcoming from Burbulis and Petrov, among others, for a civil service law. One suggested approach was to use the old tsarist Table of Ranks system to develop approximately 12 civil service levels, separated into four groups. Such efforts were intended to help alleviate mounting problems of corruption. The results to date have been unclear. What has been clear is that the executive still copes with a large and cumbersome state bureaucracy. By late 1992, the post-Soviet state apparatus was already larger than the combined central Communist Party and state apparatus of the USSR and former Russian Republic.

The Yeltsin Leadership

Yeltsin drew from a variety of settings in forming his government. A number of top advisers and allies had past associations from Sverdlovsk (now Yekaterinburg), such as Yuri Petrov. Yeltsin also turned to politicians with whom he had forged allegiances during the struggles of the late Soviet period, like Sergei Filatov. Many academics from outside of the traditional political establishment assumed key decision-making roles (for instance, Gaidar).

Members of two basic ideological groups comprised the Yeltsin team: radical reformers, and centrists and technocrats. Developments of the first 2 years of the regime revealed that radical reformers generally assumed the decisive positions within the Yeltsin coalition. Most top policy-making posts in the executive were held by such reformers. Centrists and technocrats were recruited to build bridges to their institutional constituencies, thus broadening the Yeltsin coalition's base. Mounting domestic political pressures required changes in tactics and an occasional rotation of personnel. For instance, Sergei Shakhrai – a leading Yeltsin adviser and reformer dealing with legal and nationalities issues – moved in and out of several top government posts during the regime's first year. In spring 1992 he resigned as the Deputy Prime Minister supervising the important Ministries of Internal Affairs, Justice, and Security, only to return to the same high-level post less than 6 months later.

The Yeltsin team evolved over the period commencing in late 1991. The force of events immediately following the collapse of the Soviet system contributed to at least a short-term strengthening of the Russian Federation executive branch, with President Yeltsin in the helm as acting Prime Minister. As we have noted, the broad contours of the Yeltsin radical reform programme emerged during this period, with Burbulis and Gaidar overseeing the development of the policy programme and Petrov overseeing the presidential administration. By spring 1992, mounting pressure from the parliament forced personnel changes, with Burbulis ousted and Gaidar elevated as acting Prime Minister. Representatives from the industrial sector (such as Vladimir Shumeiko and Georgii Khizha) were brought into top governmental positions, suggesting some balancing of centrist interests with the dominant reformist ones. However, these industrialists and centrist-reformers were integrated into the Gaidar team, while Burbulis was working behind the scenes to strengthen the presidential apparatus.

Outside pressures led to another Yeltsin accommodation with the centrists at the end of 1992, as the centre-right Chernomyrdin replaced Gaidar as Prime Minister. Chernomyrdin was drawn from the industrial energy field and was known to favour greater state controls and a slower pace of reform. But most of the Gaidar team was retained. Indeed, a radical reformer, Sergei Filatov, replaced the more centrist Petrov as head of the presidential administration. Filatov was a Yeltsin ally who worked with Yeltsin in the Russian parliament in the early 1990s. As the parliament's First Deputy Chairman, Filatov had been a counterweight to Khasbulatov's increasingly conservative stances. Filatov brought a number of leading reformers into Yeltsin's policy-making group (much as Petr Filippov and Vyacheslav Volkov, cofounders of the Democratic Russia Movement, and Sergei Yushenkov, coleader of the parliamentary group, Democratic Choice). He pushed for the creation of an executive branch Federal Information Centre, for be headed by another reformer and Yeltsin loyalist, Mikhail Poltoranin. Meanwhile, in late 1992 Boris Fedorov was appointed Deputy Prime Minister for financial and economic policy, thus assuming the same post Gaidar had held a year earlier when Gaidar had been crafting the shock therapy programme. Committed to fiscal responsibility and fundamental economic reform, Fedorov would assume a decisive role in overruling an early Chernomyrdin decision to reintroduce price controls in early 1992. Such appointments proved critical as reformers maintained the policy initiative *vis-à-vis* centrists.

This balancing of reformers and centrists continued in 1993. Yeltsin made a number of gestures toward the increasingly influential Civic Union: two deputy prime ministers (Oleg Lobov and Oleg Soskovets), for instance, were recruited from the industrial lobby to oversee that sector. Lobov brought strong centrist industrial credentials to his post, but he rapidly became a trusted member of the Yeltsin team, ultimately filling the role of Security Council Secretary.

The results of the April 1993 referendum – in which nearly 59 per cent of voters expressed confidence in Yeltsin and 53 per cent expressed approval of his socioeconomic reform policies – bolstered the confidence of reformers as they moved ahead with privatisation and reform efforts. The parliament, however, in spite of the referendum results, attacked government policies at every turn. It challenged the government's foreign policy line, revised the budget and increased spending (and the projected budget deficit), and attacked top reformers through parliamentary investigations into alleged corruption. By the second half of 1993 events were moving toward a high stakes executive–legislative showdown. Yeltsin, undaunted by the continuing parliamentary opposition, returned Gaidar to the First Deputy Prime Minister position in September 1993. The dissolution of the parliament and ousting of Vice President Rutskoi a few weeks signalled at least a temporary victory of the radical reformist executive branch; the adoption of a new and strongly presidential constitution in December 1993 appeared to hold out the prospect of a more enduring dominance.

System-building Amidst Political Uncertainty

The entire post-Soviet period has been characterised by profound institutional cleavages and policy debates. The division of political responsibilities among Russian federal, regional, and local actors is still being determined more than two years after the demise of the USSR. All organisations and political elites are angling to enhance their positions. During the past five years there has been a discernible deconcentration of power, at least until President Yeltsin's offensive in late 1993. The new Russian Constitution – approved through a popular referendum in December 1993 – formally bolstered the position of federal authorities and the President *vis-à-vis* regional and local interests. But the powers of sub-federal actors are still not entirely clear, with republic and regional leaders struggling to maintain, if not further enhance, the political prerogatives that they had secured over the past five years.

Considerable uncertainty abounds in Moscow as federal institutions continue to struggle over their own powerbases. The new Constitution sets out a powerful presidency with minimal legislative and judicial checks. Constitutional arrangements, generally reflecting presidential preferences articulated in drafts issued earlier in 1993, provide the executive with important unilateral prerogatives as well as the ability to dissolve the government and – under certain conditions – the parliament itself. The President may declare a state of emergency or declare war without legislative approval; he need only inform the legislature of such actions. But the executive–legislative rivalry and policy stalemate are far from over, especially given the December 1993 electoral results and victory of anti-reform conservative and centrist forces. New constitutional arrangements provide for legislative review of the government's programme and performance and they do permit legislative policy initiative. The conservative and centrist coalition which dominated legislative proceedings before the dissolution of the parliament has been replaced with another conservative-centrist coalition which will continue to challenge Yeltsin reformism.

The balance of power among the Russian political elite also remains confused and unclear after the December 1993 elections. After the dissolution of the late Soviet-period parliament in October, radical reformers had been left in a dominant position to dictate the federal government's reform programme; their consolidation of power was followed by additional measures to free prices and to expand the privatisation of property. But the impressive electoral showing of conservative and nationalist elements in December – winning the largest share of party-list seats in the Duma – served as a powerful brake on reformers' efforts at accelerating the reform process. In the wake of reformers' poor showing, Yeltsin backed off from his radical reform programme. He pledged to balance his government's efforts at controlling inflation with greater attention to helping the poor and those hurt by shock therapy initiatives. Centrist elite elements, relatively low-key during the tumult of late 1993, emerged as an important factor in further elite coalition-building efforts. With centrist party members and sympathisers constituting at least 20 per cent of the new parliament's membership, they assume a critical position in future legislative battles. There is still considerable public support for state involvement in the economy and state provision of a social safety net: core centrist policy ends. The Yeltsin regime will have to accommodate these policy preferences if it is to fashion an effective governing coalition.

Overall, the post-Soviet political elite remains fragmented. The absence of viable political parties undermines the ability of politicians to operate in more coherent and organised ways. Political parties have not dominated the president, did not play a role in the formation of the government, and have not provided discipline to parliamentary proceedings. As we have seen, the Yeltsin-led coalition is not grounded in an organised party but only in the vaguest bloc of reform-oriented elements. That bloc's organisational weaknesses were clearly revealed in the reformers' poor electoral showing in late 1993. Meanwhile, past experience suggests it will be difficult for Vladimir Zhirinovsky and other conservative and nationalist party leaders to secure policy agreement and voting constraint among their parliamentary supporters.

Although institutional and elite cleavages at the federal level are of continuing importance to the evolution of a nascent democratic system, we must now look to the increasingly regional character of Russian politics. Autonomous republics and provinces continue to seek economic sovereignty and greater political autonomy from federal authorities. In the recent past they have taken advantage of presidential–parliamentary struggles to bargain for new rights. It was no accident that an important Yeltsin initiative after the October 1993 crushing of the old parliament was to crack down on regional leadership, especially those which had resisted his directives. He disbanded lower-level soviets, ordered new elections to such soviets, and gave more power to heads of administration who were selected by and responsible to him; the new Constitution, equally, was supposedly binding throughout the Federation. Only time will tell whether such unilateral moves by the federal executive will effectively shore up the political centre's influence over the vast periphery.

Meanwhile, significant resource differences among the Russian provinces are dividing the political agendas of regional leaders. Many Siberian regions seek control over their massive natural and energy resources, while traditional urban and industrial centres (especially in the Central Economic Region) press for political arrangements (often requiring a strong central government) to maintain their access to such resources. Yeltsin and the federal government must balance these divergent regional needs while attempting to maintain the integrity of the Federation.

Other post-Soviet states have experienced institutional rivalries and complex policy struggles comparable to those in Russia. Powerful political executives, such as Ukraine's President Leonid Kravchuk and Kazakhstan's Nursultan Nazarbaev, dominated their countries' political scenes in the months following the collapse of the USSR, initiating policy changes while often coopting the positions of opponents. Kyrgyzstan's popularly elected President Askar Akaev, for instance, initiated political and economic reforms and attracted considerable international attention to his country's economic dilemmas. But Akayev and these other executives quickly confronted serious challenges from rival elite and institutional interests which brought political gridlock. As in the Russian Federation, sources of opposition have emerged within increasingly powerful and independent-minded legislatures. Chief executives continue to struggle to assert their institutional prerogatives while attempting to forge governing coalitions and find consensus policy programmes.

Past tradition and more recent developments suggest a continuing need for a strong executive leadership branch and presidency. But with only two or three years of post-Soviet experience and a new Constitution which is yet to be tested, it is difficult to be definitive about the role and institutional prerogatives of the federal executive. Everyone, including President Yeltsin, seems committed to a formal division of executive, legislative, and judicial powers, but the route by which such a separation will be realised is long and uncertain. The executive branch's unilateral dissolution of the legislative branch – and undermining of the judicial branch – set a precedent that is subject to future manipulation. Events of the post-Soviet period more generally make clear that the development of a balanced set of governmental branches – with shared political power – is critical to the long-term prospects for democratisation in Russia. Yet as actors compete to carve out large niches within the political system, it is unclear how an institutional separation of powers will be accomplished – either in Moscow, or in the 89 varied units that together constitute the Federation.

3

Representative Power and the Russian State

THOMAS F. REMINGTON

Russia traces its lineage as an organised polity to the princedom called 'Rus' which arose over one thousand years ago in Kiev, today the capital of Ukraine. For most of its history, Russia has been ruled autocratically. Since 1991, when the USSR dissolved and communist rule ended, Russia has been rebuilding its political institutions. Its future as a democratic state remains shrouded in uncertainty, however. President Boris Yeltsin's decrees of September and October 1993, abolishing the parliament, demanding new elections, and then (in November) issuing the draft of a new and strongly presidential constitution, illustrate yet again the dilemma for an autocratic reformer: the use of authoritarian means, even to achieve democratic ends, reinforces the autocratic principle.

Russia's vast geographic size and distinctive pattern of historical development have often been cited as factors helping to explain the difficulty that modern Russia has had in escaping the authoritarian trap. As the historian Richard Pipes points out, through its territorial aggrandizement, Russia had become the largest state in the world in physical terms by the middle of the 17th century (Pipes, 1974, p. 83). Today, even after the breakup of the USSR, it remains the world's largest state. The inescapable fact of its great expanse has always set before its rulers the challenging of controlling their domain, comprising numerous indigenous peoples, covering some of the world's most unfavourable

57

terrain, and surrounded by dozens of actual and potential enemies. As a result, Russia's rulers historically have placed great emphasis on their capacity to penetrate and regiment society, especially in order to mobilise the realm's human and natural resources for war. Robert C. Tucker calls attention to the importance of military power in the development of the Russian state by quoting the great 19th century Russian historian Vasilii Klychevsky as follows: 'The expansion of the state territory, straining beyond measure and exhausting the resources of the people, only bolstered the power of the state without elevating the self-confidence of the people . . . The state swelled up, the people grew lean' (Tucker, 1987b, p. 111).

Conquest and assimilation of new territories – a process that Russians call 'the gathering of Russian lands' – brought many non-Russian-speaking peoples under Russian rule. Like other European and Asian states, Russia considered its monarch an emperor and the state a multi-national empire. Russia's history therefore differs from the model of an emerging nation-state such as was the outgrowth of political development in Western Europe (Szporluk, 1990, 1992). Some principles of Western liberal philosophy did influence Russian thought and practice in the 19th and early 20th centuries, but by and large currents of revolutionary socialism were more powerful than was liberal democracy. These movements put forward radical ideologies of class struggle. One of them, represented by Lenin's wing of the Russian Marxist party, demanded the overthrow of the old regime in order to create a new state based on the power of the industrial working class and endless strata of the peasantry. Thanks in large measure to Russia's exhaustion in World War I, Lenin's Bolshevik party succeeded in taking state power in the October Revolution of 1917.

The Bolshevik revolution was a class revolution only in part, however. The breakdown of imperial rule left a vacuum in many of the national territories which nationalist movements, some liberal but most populist or socialist, filled by seizing power. Lenin's strategy for taking power explicitly called for allying the Bolsheviks with radical nationalism in the periphery, on the grounds that tsarist imperialism was the common enemy of socialists and nationalists. Following the October Revolution, however, the Bolsheviks were forced to reconstruct state power both to defend their revolution against internal and external enemies and to transform social relations. In some outlying regions of the old empire Lenin's party allied itself temporary with local nationalists; in others it suppressed them militarily. Eventually the Bolsheviks drove out all groups with autonomous political bases and imposed Moscow's rule. Nationalism, including Russian nationalism, was outlawed and prevented from forming the basis of an independent, rival political force that might challenge Moscow's socialist programme.

Rather than giving the new Bolshevik state a specifically Russian identity – or indeed, any ethnic–national identity at all – Lenin's comrades named their state according to its ideological tenets. The name finally adopted in the 1924 Constitution, the 'Union of Soviet Socialist Republics', incorporated two major substantive points of Bolshevik ideology, socialist economy and soviet rule, and two formal elements, represented by the notion of a union of republics. *Socialist* referred to the programme by which the government seized productive assets from their private owners, declaring them state property and placing them under the control of an immense bureaucratic mountain for planning and administration; and the *soviet* element referred to the democratic, participatory element in the new government, through which the state comprised a pyramid of popularly-elected councils which fused law-making and executive power. Each of the constituent members of the union was to take the form of a nominally sovereign, self-governing *republic*, but together they formed a *union* that was both federal and unitary. Thus Bolshevik ideology rather than Russian nationality defined the identity of the new state.

Names aside, the problem of imposing a centralised, socialist, soviet system throughout the ethnically diverse territory that the Bolsheviks' Red Army conquered was tremendously difficult. Many peoples in the periphery resented the restoration of centralised Russian rule. While never reluctant to resort to force to suppress any armed resistance to Soviet power, Lenin sought as much as possible to pacify nationalist sentiments through symbolic concessions. Among these were a federal structure for the state: the state's principle constituent elements would be legally equal in status and would each represent a numerous indigenous nationality on its territory. Russia, in Lenin's plan, would simply be one of the constituent members of this new soviet and socialist union.

Another concession, also mainly symbolic, was the grant of linguistic and cultural sovereignty to those ethnically designated territories, except for those issues where the Bolshevik rulers found cultural independence threatening to the state's unity. Such matters were numerous, especially in the harshest periods of communist rule, when virtually any utterance might be taken as the expression of dangerous anti-Soviet nationalism. Finally, Lenin and his successors encouraged the formation of cadres (organisers and managers who assumed responsibility for politics and administration) from among the indigenous nationalities. The formation of an industrial working class, the creation of technical and managerial staff for the economy, and the swelling up of agencies of state military, ministerial, scientific and police power, all created millions of new positions for the ambitious of every nationality so long as they accepted Moscow's rule and faithfully carried out its orders.

At the heart of Lenin's model of the new Soviet state, though, was the bifurcation of authority between party and government. The Communist Party intertwined itself with state and society so thoroughly that ordinary citizens considered the authorities to comprise one great seamless chain of power stretching all the way to Moscow. In actuality the Communist Party always preserved its own identity and structure in order to be the ultimate seat of power in the state. It was the final arbiter of disputes among the competing agencies of government, the source of leadership and pressure in society, the judge of individuals' political reliability. Admission to the party became the ticket for career mobility. Especially in the post-war decades, the regime systematically recruited members of the non-Russian nationalities into the party and gave some opportunities for advancement up the career ladder. Some gained symbolic positions of influence in the structures of Soviet-wide power – such as in the departments of the Communist Party at the all-union level – but for the most part, the non-Russian party cadres tended to rise and remain within their own national territories, while positions of power in the all-union structures of party and state went to ethnic Russians.

Russia occupied a contradictory position in the Soviet state. On the one hand it was advantaged since Russians had rebuilt the state almost entirely on the territory of the prerevolutionary tsarist empire: of the lands encompassed by the empire at the height of its power, only Finland, Poland, and the Baltic States became independent of Moscow. In language and culture, the Soviet regime was Russian. Physically, Russia dominated the Soviet state: at the point that the Soviet Union itself dissolved, the territory of the Russian republic occupied three-quarters of Soviet territory, and comprised half its population.

Yet Russia itself, as a territorial state representing the national aspirations of the Russians, was peculiarly disadvantaged as well. It lacked certain instruments of rule that the other republics possessed: Soviet leaders readily understood that if the Russian republic had its own republic-level branch of the Communist Party or KGB, for instance, these would be too powerful for their all-union counterparts to control. Instead, Russia's regions were ruled directly by the structures of the union-wide bureaucracy. This gave Russia's regions direct access to the highest levels of power, but tended to weaken the organisational potential that Russia itself might have had as a national republic within the union. In the words of Ramazan Abdulatipov, formerly Chairman of the Council of Nationalities of the Supreme Soviet, Russia was strongly 'woven into' the fabric of the nation. As a result, the collapse of the union has had greater disintegrating effects on Russia than it has had on the other successor states (*Pravda*, 19 February 1992).

Generally, however, the threat of Russia's breakup is easily exaggerated. To be sure, in some respects, Russia's political development in the last several years has closely paralleled that of the USSR, with events in the Russian case lagging behind those at the USSR level by about one year. The same political and constitutional impasse that led to the emerging 'war of laws' between the central union government and the governments of the constituent republics form mid-1990 to mid-1991 and the confrontation between Presidents Gorbachev and Yeltsin in the winter of 1990–1 was repeated in Russia in 1992–3 with the constitutional confrontation between President Yeltsin and the leadership of the Supreme Soviet. The new post-communist Russian government has had the same difficulty in enforcing laws in breakaway territories claiming independence that Gorbachev's regime had with separatist union republics. Yeltsin has faced a similar task of building a consensus on a new federal treaty, one with some teeth in it, that can define the constitutional authority of the federal government *vis-à-vis* its constituents. Russia's own rights and duties in relation to its new neighbours (what it calls the ('near abroad') and, more delicately, in relation to the 25 million Russians who have suddenly found themselves living in foreign countries after the union split up, have also been a major pre-occupation of the law makers.

Faced with a nearly identical set of crises and starting with a nearly identical constitutional structure, the Russian governmental system has undergone an organisational evolution parallel to that of the union government, but every step has been about one year later.

The paths also differ, of course. Yeltsin sought and won popular election as president in 1991, whereas in 1990 Gorbachev evidently calculated that the risk of defeat in a direct election was too great. Accordingly, he sought to legitimate his assumption of the new presidency by putting his candidacy before the Congress of People's Deputies instead. In the intensifying rivalry between Gorbachev and Yeltsin, where the former embodied state power in the union and the other was rising as preeminent leader of the union's major component republic, Yeltsin's solid popular backing proved a crucial political advantage. Unlike Gorbachev, and indeed unlike any other politician in Russia, Yeltsin had won three direct, contested, and democratic popular elections in as many years, as candidate for USSR deputy from Moscow in 1989, for Russian Republic deputy from Sverdlovsk in 1990 (he was subsequently elected parliamentary chairman), and as president of Russia in 1991.

Moreover, the balance of forces between centre and constituents differed between the union and Russia. One important difference is in population: while the Soviet population was only half Russia, Russia's is more than 80 per cent Russian. Another is the relationship between the ethnic–national territories and the federal government. Constitutionally, Soviet Russia preceded the formation of its internal ethnic–national subdivisions, whereas the Soviet Union was formed through a merger of already existing republics. Although both the USSR and Russia were nominally federations, there was no purely 'USSR' territory or nationality separate from its constituent republics. As the republics attained independence in late 1991, therefore, the union-level ministries and other Soviet-wide structures of power became a government without a country. But in Russia, on the other hand, the territories created to give ethnic–national groups special recognition constitute only about half of the territory of the country.

Constitutional Crisis

The Russian state is threatened by a different crisis from that which the union state faced. This is the lack of consensus on a constitutional framework that might be capable of reconciling parliamentary power with presidentialism. The collision between President Yeltsin and his opponents in the Russian parliament reached a climax in the spring and summer of 1993 when the parliament attempted to remove Yeltsin from power. Yeltsin's decree of 21 September then disbanded parliament, stripped all deputies of their legal mandates, and demanded new parliamentary elections in December 1993. Some deputies obeyed Yeltsin's orders, but others resisted and barricaded themselves inside the White House, as the official residence of the parliament was called. Parliamentary chairman Ruslan Khasbulatov convened a rump Congress of People's Deputies, which passed motions declaring Vice-President Alexander Rutskoi acting president of Russia, and naming a new government, but the deputies were impotent to enforce their actions. For 10 days demonstrators opposed to Yeltsin's decrees confronted the riot troops who surrounded the White House. These protestors included both militant communist and Russian nationalist groups. Appeals by moderates for compromise were unavailing, and Church-mediated negotiations between Yeltsin and the White House forces broke down.

Then, on the weekend of 3–4 October, the loosely organised paramilitary units opposing Yeltsin broke through police lines and joined forces with some of the group holed up in the White House. Together, they stormed the building just next to the White House where the Moscow mayor's offices were located, and then pushed on to try to take over Ostankino, the television tower where Russia's main national television broadcast facilities are housed. Both at the mayor's offices and the television tower, the attackers drove trucks through the entrance, smashed offices, and exchanged gunfire with police. Dozens of people were killed.

Rutskoi and Khasbulatov seem to have expected this action to spark a national revolt against Yeltsin, or, at the very least, a large-scale defection of military units to their side; in the heat of the moment they called on their followers to 'seize the Kremlin'. In the end, after several tense hours of indecision, the army moved decisively to back Yeltsin and crush the uprising. Khasbulatov, Rutskoi, and the other leaders of the rebellion were arrested. In the assault on the White House that followed, heavy shelling caused yet more loss of life, and gravely damaged the building. The White House, which had been the site of heroic Russian and democratic resistance to the August 1991 coup, was quickly dubbed the 'Black House' by Muscovites.

Confrontation between the President and the parliament had been growing since early in 1992, when Yeltsin's government launched a programme of radical economic liberalisation and macro-economic stabilization ('shock therapy'). In March 1993 the deputies, meeting in the 8th Congress of People's Deputies, voted on a motion to remove Yeltsin from power: the proposal failed by only 72 votes to clear the two-thirds hurdle required for impeachment of the president. As the impasse deepened, each branch attempted to block the other's enactments. Yeltsin attempted to find ways to bypass parliament, for example by convening a broadly representative Constitutional Assembly in the summer of 1993, and, later in the year, by forming a 'Federal Council' consisting of two representatives from each of Russia's constituent regions and republics. This Council was to serve as a surrogate upper chamber of the prospective new parliament, with elections to fill the lower chamber until a new and final constitution was adopted and a regular parliament could take office. The parliamentary leadership meantime extended its control over local and regional soviets, preparing for another attempt to remove President Yeltsin.

Looking at the crisis more closely, it is clear that Russia inherited the results of Gorbachev's strategy of piecemeal reform. Unable to contain the political and economic pressures that were awakened by his democratising measures, the old Soviet system gave way to a struggle in its successor states between opposing political forces. Yet the reforms of the Gorbachev era did not bring about the full-scale transition to democratic government that occurred in Central Europe. As a result, Russia has undergone a protracted constitutional battle. Since his election as president in June 1991, Boris Yeltsin committed the power and authority of his office to a programme of radical social and economic liberalisation which if successful would end the economic protectionism and state control that preserved the old communist order. His embattled opponents include those groups intend upon restoring a centralised, socialist state as well as various ultra-nationalists, all of whom polled strongly in the December 1993 elections.

Behind the struggle for constitutional supremacy between president and parliament over 1990–3 thus stands a larger and continuing contest between the forces aspiring to a liberal, Western-oriented political and economic order, and those trying to return to some version of the Soviet or Russian past. Neither group was strong enough to impose its will on the other and each defended a different model of rule. Yeltsin demanded a presidential republic with strong executive power; his preferred system, now enacted in a new constitution, resembles the French Fifth Republic. The forces opposing him generally sought a system of parliamentary supremacy, with a weak presidency. Some of the communists even proposed a constitution that almost perfectly replicated the old Soviet system. As the president and parliament fought for supremacy, the state's actual power decayed: the central government grew divided internally and unable to enforce its will over the regional governments as the wealth and resources of the country are divided up through a process that some have called 'spontaneous privatisation'.

From Soviet to Representative Democracy

Behind the turbulent events of the last few years one can discern four distinct but overlapping phases:

- First, over 1989–90, a wave of expanding democratic participation through elections to the soviets;
- Second, through 1990–1, an opposing trend to strengthen executive authority by creating powerful executive positions such as presidencies and mayoralties;
- Third, from 1991 until 21 September 1993, when Yeltsin

decreed the dissolution of parliament, a deepening confrontation between executive and legislative branches.
• Finally, following the elections of December 1993 and the constitutional referendum, a new presidential republic and a new
parliament dominated by opponents of the Yeltsin programme.

The first of these stages was the heyday of Gorbachev's democratisation programme in 1989–90, when the prospect of competitive elections to the soviets stimulated groups of democratic
activists to mobilise their followers to elect known reformers and
to defeat candidates representing the old communist establishments. In this phase, the reformers saw free elections to the
soviets as a way to overcome the power of the Communist Party
and the class of elite office-holders (the *nomenklatura*) that it supported. Consequently, leaders of the democratic movement such
as the distinguished former dissident, the physicist and member of
the Soviet Academy of Sciences, Andrei Sakharov, advanced the
old Leninist slogan of 'all power to the soviets'. For the reformers
this meant using the newly democratised soviets to wrest political
power from the Communist Party and the state bureaucracy. The
democrats' strategy suited Gorbachev as well, for whom the
democratisation of the soviets was a way to reinforce his own
power to enact reform and weaken his opponents.

Even as Gorbachev was attempting to strengthen his own hand,
however, his democratisation programme multiplied the arenas of
power outside the central level of government. Gorbachev's plan
for elections to a new system of legislative power at the level of
the Soviet Union in 1989 and to the Supreme Soviets in the
republics in 1990 was faithfully implemented. At the union level,
Gorbachev's proposal for a two-tiered legislature came into being
following elections in March 1989. The voters throughout the
Soviet Union elected USSR deputies, who convened in a vast,
2250-seat body called the Congress of People's Deputies. The
Congress had power to amend the constitution and adopt laws,
and would in turn elect from among its membership 542 deputies
to a bicameral parliament called the Supreme Soviet. In a novel
departure from the traditionally brief and ceremonial proceedings
of the Supreme Soviet of the past, the new Supreme Soviet, Gorbachev declared, would exercise real parliamentary power. It
would stay in session for most of the year, deliberating on legisla-

tion and exercising oversight over government (see Urban, 1990a; Kiernan, 1993; Chiesa, 1993).

Pressed between the conservative old guard who demanded that Gorbachev kept democratic reform from getting out of hand, and a democratic intelligentsia that was spearheading popular movements in industrial regions and national republics, Gorbachev devised numerous safeguards against excessive independence by the new legislative branch. For one thing, a third of the seats in the Congress would be filled directly by officially recognised public organisations, such as the Communist Party, the trade union federation, and the Komsomol (the other two-thirds were to be filled by elections from ordinary constituencies and national–territorial areas). Second, the complicated procedures for nominating and registering candidates would be overseen by the same electoral commissions that had been supervising elections to the soviets for decades and which were thoroughly controlled by local Communist Party officials. Third, many aspects of the old structure of the Supreme Soviet were preserved, including a powerful inner parliament, the presidium, to guide agenda formation and control the proceedings, considerable discretion in the hands of the chairman of the Supreme Soviet to govern floor proceedings, and precedence of unicameral structures such as committees and presidium over the nominal division of responsibilities between the two chambers.

The democratic forces won a number of important and impressive victories. Once elected, they created, for the first time in Soviet history, an independent legislative caucus. Yet the results of the elections of 1989 to the Congress and Supreme Soviet did not satisfy the aspirations of either the democratic reformers or of Gorbachev. The democratic movement's attainment of a visible public forum did, however, threaten the interests of the powerful ruling bureaucracies, such as the Communist Party apparatus, the ministries and agencies of the state, and elements of the military and security forces. Moreover, Gorbachev had lost his ability as party leader to control the pace of change in the outlying republics. In some, local communist leaderships found themselves forced to align themselves with powerful movements for national independence, while in others, the leaders increased repression of opposition in order to tighten their hold over their republics. In Russia, the democratic forces appealed to widespread antagonism toward the stultifying power of the central bureaucracy, linking the call for radical democratic and economic reform with the demand for a powerful and sovereign Russia.

Flanked by increasingly active opponents, from the hard-line conservatives based in the central state bureaucracies on his right and on his left from democratic forces allied with the movements for national sovereignty in the union republics, Gorbachev moved in early 1990 to strengthen his own political position further. Railroading constitutional amendments on the creation of a state presidency through the Congress of People's Deputies, Gorbachev won the deputies' approval for a presidency. Moreover, in place of direct popular elections, he urged that – for this one time – the Congress elect the president. Dominating the proceedings with an almost cynical display of power, Gorbachev had himself elected president of the USSR, becoming the first, and last, person to hold that position.

In keeping with his dual strategy of consolidating his personal power while expanding mass participation in the political system, the presidential office Gorbachev created was (at least on paper) an extremely powerful one. The president could name and dissolve the government, suspend legislative enactments, declare emergencies, and impose presidential rule. Moreover, in a pattern that was to become familiar under Yeltsin, he sought further to expand his own political base by multiplying the official bodies directly answerable to him. For example, he created an advisory council called the 'Presidential Council', as well as a 'Federation Council' which would give him direct access to the chiefs of state of the union republics. Later in 1990, when the Supreme Soviet failed to agree on an economic programme, parliament granted him still more powers which would allow him to enact laws through presidential decree. And, in December 1990, as his real power was slipping still further, he compensated by demanding even greater formal power and reorganised the executive branch yet again.

Gorbachev's attempt to create a powerful executive presidency at the union level did not, however, inhibit the gathering momentum of popular movements for republican sovereignty and democratic reform. These movements were given a new impetus by the round of elections to the legislative organs of all the union republics which were held in 1990. In most republics, elections of deputies to all lower-level soviets were held simultaneously. Throughout the USSR, therefore, around 2 million deputies' seats were filled in 1990. As in 1989, the democratic forces fought to nominate and elect candidates defending the cause of radical reform and to defeat prominent representatives of the ruling establishment.

For its new legislative system the Russian Republic, alone among the union republics, adopted the two-tiered structure that Gorbachev had introduced at the all-union level. It rejected, however, the principle of reserved seats for public organisations. The lower tier, the Congress of People's Deputies, was assigned 1068 seats; the number was arrived at by creating 900 territorial seats plus 168 seats for national–territorial districts. The Congress of People's Deputies in turn would elect a 252-member bicameral Supreme Soviet. As at the union level, the two chambers of the Supreme Soviet (the Council of Nationalities and Council of the Republic) were of equal size and equal powers.

At the time of the 1990 election the RSFSR had 28,758 local soviets, including those of autonomous territories. For these races, 726,000 election districts were formed, of which 10,000 were multi-seat districts. In 1861 village and settlement soviets all voters were given a common list of candidates and seats: that is, the territorial district represented by the local soviet was not sub-divided into electoral districts. Altogether around 1.2 million people ran for nearly three quarters of a million seats at various levels. The degree of contestation was much higher at the republican and city levels. Indeed, in many localities it was difficult to persuade enough candidates to run to fill the available seats.

More than the 1989 elections of USSR deputies, the 1990 republic and local elections in Russia were conducted along partisan lines. Although competing parties as such were absent, in stark contrast to the 'founding elections' that ushered in post-communist governments in Eastern Europe, many of the Russian candidates often affiliated themselves with a political movement. Most prominent was the coalition of reform-minded candidates who campaigned under the banner of 'Democratic Russia'. Democratic Russia – also known as DemRossiya or DR – was a broad, loosely organised coalition of candidates for soviets at all levels who pressed for radical political and economic change: the end of the power and privilege of the Communist Party, a turn toward a free market economy, and democratic rights and freedoms for citizens. On the eve of the elections, over 5000 candidates identified themselves as members of the Democratic Russia movement (Brudny, 1993). Opposing them was a far smaller alliance called the 'Bloc of Public and Patriotic Movements of Russia' which had an aggressively nationalist and authoritarian stance.

The democratic forces won a number of notable victories. Around 40 per cent of the newly elected RSFSR deputies identified themselves with the democratic cause (Sobyanin, 1994). In the city soviets of Moscow, Leningrad and Sverdlovsk, democratically oriented deputies won majorities. At the same time, candidates openly identified with the ultra-conservative, nationalist cause were overwhelmingly defeated. In Moscow the 200 candidates running on the platform of the 'Bloc of Public and Patriotic Movements of Russia' received around 2–3 per cent of the vote. Of the 498 deputies elected to the Moscow soviet, the conservative-patriotic faction had only 10. In Leningrad, where the conservative bloc ran 150 candidates, only two reached the runoff round. The bloc's defeat owed both to the unpopularity of its positions and to its near total inactivity during the campaign. As one Soviet analyst put it, the patriots, unlike the democrats, simply were unwilling to stand outdoors campaigning in the cold for days on end, handing out literature at metro stations and factory gates.

The democrats quickly acted on their electoral victories in the republic-wide and local races. In Moscow, Leningrad and Sverdlovsk, the democrats used their majorities to elect prominent democratic politicians – Gavriil Popov, Anatolii Sobchak and Yuri Samarin, respectively – as chairmen of the city soviets. In the Russian congress, the democrats succeeded, after three ballots, in winning the election of Boris Yeltsin as Chairman of the Supreme Soviet. In turn, by assuming control of the powers of the chairmanship, Yeltsin helped ensure that the committees of the Supreme Soviet were headed by democratically-oriented deputies.

Soon, however, the democratic forces at all levels began to splinter into rival factions. Inexperienced, with few incentives to maintain any sort of partisan discipline, and lacking independent political bases, the newly elected legislators soon expressed frustration over their inability to seize hold of the levers of power and force the state to become more responsive to the will of the country. Many, indeed, found themselves forced to go cap in hand and seek favours from individual officials and ministers on behalf of various constituents. Professional government officials in turn treated the newly elected deputies with a mixture of disdain and resentment, complaining of their incompetence and meddlesomeness. In many local soviets, the new chairmen created 'off-budget' streams of revenue and expenditures which were out of the reach of the soviet itself. In the Oktyabrsky ward of Moscow, for instance, the new chairman of the soviet was a young, partially crippled democrat named Ilya Zaslavsky. Zaslavsky was intend upon turning Oktyabrsky District into a showcase for market-oriented economic reform, and moved rapidly to encourage privatisation and leasing of state assets. The enormous profits realised from selling off and leasing out building space went into an off-budget account under the control of a quasi-independent agency that was linked to the executive committee of the soviet but was outside the control of the soviet itself. Sessions of the local soviet, as this writer witnessed, often disintegrated into bitter shouting matches as the opposition demanded a proper accounting of the transactions taking place in the soviet's name. Many of Zaslavsky's original supporters turned against him. Eventually the soviet found himself unable to take any action at all because one side or another would invariably walk out in order to deny the session a quorum before a major vote.

At the level of the Russian-wide Congress of People's Deputies, the democratic forces and the opposition were rather evenly matched. For the first four congresses, from May 1990 to May 1991, around 40 per cent of the deputies voted consistently with the democratic wing and about the same proportion voted consistently with the anti-reform wing over a wide spectrum of issues. Taking the most divisive motions on which rollcall votes were held at each congress, i.e. those votes which most clearly separated the democratic from the conservative deputies, and using them to construct a voting score for each deputy, we find that only a very small number of deputies fail to vote consistently with one side or the other (Sobyanin, 1994).

Although the democratic and conservative sides were roughly equal in strength, Yeltsin and his supporters had several advantages that enabled them to win a number of significant legislative victories on the first year of the Congress's existence. One was the strength of popular hostility to communist power and privilege, which was strongest in large cities and industrial centres and weakest in rural areas, where conservatives and high-ranking officials faced little significant opposition. This made many deputies reluctant to fight the tide of democratic reform. Second, the democrats allied themselves with the popular cause of Russian resistance to the central government. It was difficult for any but the most committed communists to oppose the call for a 'strong, sovereign Russian state'. Yeltsin's own position was strengthened, rather than weakened, by Gorbachev's clumsy attempts to undermine him, as when Gorbachev appealed to the heads of the autonomous republics within Russia with an offer to sign a new union treaty on an equal footing with the Russian republic. Likewise, when Gorbachev deployed tanks and armoured personnel carriers around the Kremlin on the opening day of the 3rd Congress in March 1991, Yeltsin appealed for solidarity among Russian politicians against the bullying tactics of the union leadership. The 3rd Congress, in fact, had been convened at the initiative of the communists, who tried to use it to remove Yeltsin from power. Yeltsin rallied a majority of deputies, however, and won their endorsement of his proposal for a powerful, directly elected Russian president.

The third factor that strengthened Yeltsin during the year he served as Chairman of the Supreme Soviet was the strategic opportunity that the chairmanship gave him to cultivate alliances within the Supreme Soviet. One way he did this, for example, was by distributing key positions in the leadership to deputies from both his camp and the opposition. Although all of the individuals he chose to fill the positions of first deputy and deputy chairmen later turned against him, he made good use of the opportunity to influence the choice of committee chairs and thus the makeup of the presidium.

Presidential Power

Ironically, Yeltsin's departure from the Supreme Soviet upon being elected Russian president led to the surge in strength of the conservative wing of the deputies, because he lost much of his ability to build the tactical agreements needed to win a majority of the deputies. Establishment of the presidency brought about the problem of 'competing mandates' between legislative and executive branches which many scholars of comparative politics believe to be a source of instability in presidential systems (see for instance Linz, 1990; Lijphart, 1992; Mainwaring, 1993; and Shugart and Carey, 1992). At the very minimum, the institution of the presidency, although supported by the required two-thirds of the deputies needed to pass constitutional amendments, was treated as an incremental alteration of a constitutional order that was already a contradictory mixture of soviet and parliamentary elements. Deep conflict over the proper division of powers between president and legislature eventually resulted. The democrats' frustration over what could be accomplished through the vehicle of 'soviet power' was matched by a wave of popular disillusion both with the soviets and with the democrats. As 1990 wore on, public pressure built for a stronger executive branch. This phase saw a widespread trend for the creation of new chief executive posts: presidencies of the union and autonomous republics, and mayoralties of cities. As the pendulum swung back to executive power, presidents of republics began to claim the power to appoint their own regional representatives and administrators rather than to allow such positions to be filled by popular elections.

The model of soviet power that developed under communism had treated state power as a single, undivided whole: the soviets combined rule-making power with the right to allocate resources and directly oversee the executive branch (Anweiler, 1974). Although the theoretical unit of state power in the soviets was never an accurate description of how power in the Soviet state was exercised (since, after all, the Communist Party made all the major decisions), it did serve to facilitate the party's power over state and society. The demise of the old regime left the question of the division of responsibilities between soviets and state administrators undecided. The new deputies elected on the democratic wave of 1989 and 1990 frequently found themselves unable to take charge of the generally conservative, hostile bureaucracy, and demanded stronger executive authority that could monitor and control the powerful agencies of the state. Nationalists in the republics demanded powerful presidents who could stand up to the central government in Moscow. As the Communist Party began to weaken and disintegrate, many groups, both conservative and reformist, came to regard strong presidencies as the only solution to the decay of order and authority in the state. The chairmen of soviets began acting autonomously of the soviets and demanding the creation of independently elected executive positions – mayoralties, governorships, and presidencies. The public, frequently dismayed at the inability of the soviets to transform social conditions, generally supported the call for stricter power and accountability.

Consequently, over 1990–1 there was a counter-movement back towards greater centralisation of executive power within the state. In January 1991, responding to Gorbachev's call for a union-wide referendum on the concept of a 'renewed' federal union, Yeltsin won the agreement of the Russian parliament's leadership to the idea of placing another question on the referendum ballot in Russia. This would test the Russian electorate's support for creating a Russian presidency. Yeltsin's conception of a presidency went one better than Gorbachev, however – Russia's president would be directly elected by the people, and would thus have an enormous moral and political advantage over the union president.

About 70 per cent of the voters in the March 1991 referendum in Russia endorsed the proposal for a Russian presidency. Soon afterward, in a dramatic confrontation with Gorbachev, who had allied himself with the most reactionary elements of the union bureaucratic interests, and with his own communist-led opposition, Yeltsin won another major victory at the 3rd Congress of the Russian Republic People's Deputies in March 1991, which approved his plans for a powerful executive presidency. The election was held in June; Yeltsin won with over 57 per cent of the vote in a field of six candidates. At the same time, the cities of Moscow and Leningrad (which later took back its old prerevolutionary name of St Petersburg) elected the chairmen of their city soviets, Popov and Sobchak, as mayors.

The establishment of a presidency, however, as we have seen in Chapter 2, set off a chain of events leading to the sharp confrontation between president and parliament which defined the third phase. In fact the polarisation of political forces might have occurred somewhat sooner but for the August coup, since it tended to unite most groups against the hard-line elements at the centre who seized power, briefly and unsuccessfully, in the name of restoring centralised Soviet rule. The surge of popular resistance to the coup in Moscow, Leningrad and other cities, and Yeltsin's role as its focal point, gave the Russian leader a substantial political bonus. Many of his communist opponents in the congress lost their political bases through a series of decrees which suspended, and later outlawed, the activity of the CPSU and confiscated its considerable property. In October 1991, at the 5th Congress, Yeltsin won several significant victories, the last time he was to do so at one of the congresses. He sought and received special powers to enact economic reform measures by decree; he won the Congress's consent to put off elections of local heads of government until 1 December 1992; he won approval of constitutional amendments giving him the right to suspend the acts of lower authorities in Russia if he found that they violated the constitution and to suspend legal acts of the union if they violated Russian sovereignty; and the Congress approved his programme for radical economic transformation. Shortly after the Congress concluded, Yeltsin issued new decrees banning the activity of the Communist Party and nationalising its property. A few days later Yeltsin assumed the position of prime minister himself, named a new cabinet dominated by young economists committed to rapid economic liberalisation, and issued a package of decrees launching the programme of radical 'shock therapy' from the start of the following year.

Making full use of his expanded powers, Yeltsin pursued his programme of reform throughout 1992. Although the harsh edges of the 'shock therapy' effort were considerably softened as the year proceeded, the government accelerated privatisation of small state-owned enterprises, kept state industry on a limited ration of government credit, and allowed prices to float freely on most goods. Inflation rose to 25–30 per cent a month by the end of the year. Yeltsin had lost his majority by the time of the 7th Congress in December. The Congress was called upon to approve a candidate for prime minister since Yeltsin's head of government, Yegor Gaidar, held only the status of acting Prime Minister, and the legal limit of his powers had expired. Either Gaidar or another individual had to be approved by the Congress for prime minister. One major fight at the Congress therefore concerned

Gaidar and the programme of reform associated with him. Another was the law on the government, which specified its powers and the extent to which the parliament could approve its composition and structure. Yeltsin and the deputies had been at loggerheads over the bill all year. At a still more fundamental level, Yeltsin had been unable to win congressional approval of a draft of a new constitution that would formalise his powers *vis-à-vis* the government and the legislative branch. Under the constitution, however, only the congress had the power to amend or replace the old constitution and so far the congress had been unwilling to adopt a new one.

At the 7th Congress Gaidar strongly defended his policies and refused to make significant concessions to the conservatives or the industrial lobby. His opponents responded by intensifying their efforts to remove him while Yeltsin declared his intension to nominate him anyway as prime minister. To win at least some deputy support for Gaidar, Yeltsin offered concessions on the law on government, inviting the Congress to accept a constitutional amendment providing that the ministers for security, foreign affairs, internal affairs, and defence would be confirmed by the Supreme Soviet. This sweetener proved to be too little, however, and Gaidar was narrowly defeated (the vote was 467 in favour, 486 against). The Congress, however, passed Yeltsin's proposed amendment on the four ministries.

Yeltsin responded furiously, denouncing the Congress and chairman Khasbulatov, and demanding a national referendum that would dissolve the Congress and adopt a new constitution. At that point the chairman of the Constitutional Court, Valerii Zorkin, intervened and negotiated a compromise between the Congress and the president. Under its terms, both sides agreed that a referendum would be held in April that would decide the principles of a new constitution; it also provided a means for voting on a new prime minister that was acceptable to both Congress and president. This provided that a series of advisory votes would be held on candidates proposed by Yeltsin. Yeltsin would then choose one who appeared to enjoy a majority of support and nominate him for formal approval. This procedure was carried out and on the final day of the Congress, 14 December, Victor Chernomyrdin was proposed and confirmed as Prime Minister.

Confrontation and Collapse

If, throughout 1992, the parliament had concentrated most of its fire on the government, in 1993 it began increasingly to turn directly on Yeltsin. Over January and February the confrontation between Yeltsin and the parliamentary leadership intensified. Yeltsin and Khasbulatov could not agree on the wording of the issues to be put before the people for a vote in April. Khasbulatov demanded cancellation of the referendum and called for another Congress to decide basic constitutional issues and to cancel the referendum. Yeltsin threatened to hold a referendum without congressional approval. The congress met on 10 March and voted overwhelmingly to cancel the referendum, rejecting a plan Yeltsin offered for resolving the constitutional crisis and annulling Yeltsin's powers to adopt economic and political legislative acts by decree. Yeltsin responded with his televised 20 March address to the nation in which he said he was declaring a 'special form of administration' and assuming extraordinary powers. When his decree appeared in print on 24 March, however, the declaration of an extraordinary situation had been dropped, after it had become clear that neither the army nor the government would oppose Yeltsin, and that he had a considerable amount of public sympathy for his confrontation with the Congress. The deputies quickly met again, on 26 March, and the 9th Congress debated whether to remove Yeltsin from power. The vote to remove him failed, because of the constitutional provision that the president could be removed only by a two-thirds vote of the Congress – the vote was 617 to remove, 268 against; the close margin of 72 votes indicates how severely Yeltsin's support in the Congress had eroded. The Congress also voted on replacing Khasbulatov as chairman. Although in this instance a majority (517) would have sufficed, only 339 votes were cast against him.

Having failed to remove Yeltsin, the Congress then reversed itself and voted to hold a referendum after all. This was to be held on 25 April and was to include four items. These were carefully balanced between 'pro-Yeltsin' and 'anti-Yeltsin' questions:

1. Do you have confidence in the President of the Russian Federation?
2. Do you approve of the social-economic policy carried out by

the President and government of the Russian Federation since 1992?
3. Do you consider it necessary to hold early presidential elections?
4. Do you consider it necessary to hold early elections of people's deputies?

For a year, Khasbulatov's position had been that if early elections were to be held, they should be held both for president and parliament. This referendum was intended to tie the country's expected support for Yeltsin to its anticipated dissatisfaction with the Gaidar economic programme, and to link the popular notion of early parliamentary elections with the idea of an early presidential election.

Yeltsin proved unexpectedly successful, however. Responding to the Yeltsin camp's appeals to vote 'da, da, nyet, da', the citizens came to the polls in large numbers (there was a 62.9 per cent turnout) and supported the Yeltsin positions by 58.7, 53, 49.5 and 67.2 per cent respectively. In the case of the latter two questions, since the Constitutional Court had ruled that a majority of registered electors (and not just voters) would have to approve the measures for them to have constitutional force, the referendum failed to force new elections.

Again, however, Yeltsin was unable to capitalise on his political victory in the referendum and break the impasse in the power struggle between legislative and executive branches. Attempting to forge a broad consensus on a new draft constitution, he convened an assembly of prominent political leaders from all major sections of the political system which in due course approved a new draft constitution calling for a presidential republic and a bicameral legislature. But there still was no apparent way to win the ratification of the constitution in view of the parliament's adamant opposition. Meantime, the chairman of the Supreme Soviet, Ruslan Khasbulatov, consolidated his own grip on the legislature, rewarding his supporters with apartments, trips abroad, and other perquisites, while squeezing out any who opposed him. He also gradually extended his control over the hierarchy of local soviets, most of them dominated, like the national Supreme Soviet, by intransigent opponents of Yeltsin's power and policies. Khasbulatov maintained regular contact with the local soviets by means of conferences and a closed-circuit telephone conference call network. Corruption charges and counter-charges flew back and forth between parliament and leading government ministers. Vice-President Rutskoi made serious accusations of corruption against Yeltsin's ministers, and was in turn accused of corruption himself. In August, Yeltsin suspended his Vice-President from his duties and stripped him of all privileges. Russian central politics descri-bed into a discouraging mixture of powerlessness and diatribe.

Finally, on 21 September, Yeltsin cut the Gordian knot with a series of decrees that lacked constitutional foundation but offered a political solution to the impasse. He shut down parliament, declared the deputies' powers null and void, and called elections for a new parliament to be held on 11 and 12 December. Decrees soon afterward dissolved city, district, and village soviets and called for elections to new, far smaller, bodies of representative power; Yeltsin also called upon regional soviets to disband and hold elections to new representative organs that were to conform with guidelines that he also issued by decree. In effect, Yeltsin was attempting to end the system of *soviet* power, which he had denounced as intrinsically undemocratic the preceding June. In their place were to be small, purely deliberately and representative bodies at the local level, and a national parliament (called a Federal Assembly) with two chambers (see Exhibit 3.1). The upper chamber, the Council of the Federation, was to resemble a typical European upper house in that it was much weaker than the lower house, and gave equal representation to each of Russia' 89 regions and republics (called 'subjects of the federation'). The lower house, the State Duma, was to introduce a fundamentally new principle into Russian legislative institutions: proportional representation. Half of the Duma's 450 seats were to be filled by the candidates listed on parties' electoral lists according to the share of votes that party received in the election in a single federal-wide district. The other half of the seats were to be filled in traditional single-member-district contests. Each voter thus had, in effect, four votes for the Parliament: two for the two deputies from his or her region to the upper house, and two for the lower house, one to fill the local district seat, and the other for a party list.

On 21 September Yeltsin had also declared that new presidential elections would be held the following June, two years ahead of

EXHIBIT 3.1   *The Russian Federal Assembly, 1993*

Under the terms of the December 1993 Constitution, the *Federal Assembly* or parliament of the Russian Federation is the 'representative and legislative organ of the Russian Federation' (Art. 94).

The Federal Assembly consists of two chambers: the Council of the Federation and the State Duma (Art. 95).

The State Duma is elected for a four-year term (Art. 96); deputies must be citizens, aged at least 21 years, who enjoy electoral rights (Art. 97); deputies cannot simultaneously hold seats in the Council of the Federation and the State Duma, or in the State Duma and other representative bodies (Art. 98).

The *Council of the Federation* is responsible for changes in borders between subjects of the Federation; it confirms the declaration of martial law; it approves the deployment of Russian troops beyond Russian borders; it calls presidential elections, and (under appropriate circumstances) can impeach the President (Art. 102).

The *State Duma* approves candidates for the chairmanship of the Government; expresses its confidence or otherwise in the Government (Art. 103); and considers legislation (Art. 104) and federal laws (Art. 105). Laws on taxation, budgetary and related matters, the approval or denunciation of international treaties, and declarations of war or peace, additionally require the approval of the Council of the Federation (Art. 106). Laws may be suspended by the President, but are adopted if a two-thirds majority in the Council of the Federation and State Duma vote accordingly (Art. 107).

---

schedule, but later changed his mind and announced that he intended to serve out his term until 1996. To provide a constitutional foundation for the state, Yeltsin reconvened the constitutional assembly to produce a draft constitution to be approved in a popular referendum held the same day as parliamentary elections. When the text was published on 10 November there were few surprises. Yeltsin's draft provided for a very strong presidency: the president had to win the consent of the lower house (State Duma) of the new parliament for his appointed prime minister but if, after three attempts, the president still could not get a majority to approve his choice, he could dissolve parliament and hold new elections. It was clear that the president's advisors were strongly attracted to the strong executive presidency model of France, Mexico or the United States. Clearly they were unimpressed by the arguments of those Western political scientists who argued that presidentialism entailed a very high risk of further

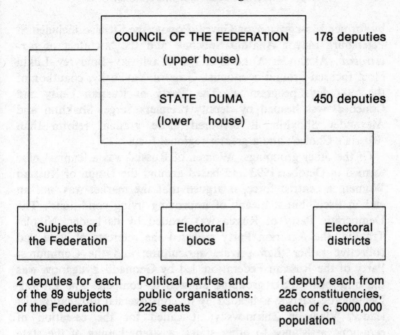

FIGURE 3.1 The Russian Federal Assembly, 1993

political instability because of the rivalry that would develop between president and legislature for control of government.

Elections took place on this basis to the Federal Assembly on 12 December 1993 (see Figure 3.1). In all there were 3797 candidates, of whom 494 were seeking places in the Council of the Federation and 1586 in the constituency section of the State Duma; the other half of the seats in the State Duma were contested on a party list basis, with 1717 candidates in all (*Rossiiskaya gazeta*, 11 December 1993). There had originally been 21 parties or electoral blocs but several failed to secure sufficient signatures from electors to qualify, and in the end 13 blocs were registered. The president's administration was represented by 'Russia's Choice', headed by Yegor Gaidar, although Yeltsin refused directly to endorse it; its candidates included most members of the government, including foreign minister Kozyrev, privatisation minister Chubais and finance minister Fedorov. The Democratic Reform Movement, another contender, was headed by former Moscow mayor Gavriil Popov; the list also included St Petersburg mayor Anatolii Sobchak and the 'architect of *perestroika*', Alexander Yakovlev. The 'Yavlinsky–Boldyrev–Lukin bloc' focused around economist Grigorii Yavlinsky, coauthor of the '500 days programme'. The 'Party of Russian Unity and Concord' was headed by deputy premiers Sergei Shakhrai and Alexander Shokhin; it favoured more gradual reform than 'Russia's Choice', and a greater regional focus.

Of the other groupings, 'Women of Russia' was a feminist bloc formed in October 1993 and based around the Union of Russian Women; a centrist force, it argued that the market was 'not an end in itself, but a means of improving living conditions'. The Democratic Party of Russia was headed by its leader, Nikolai Travkin; the Agrarian Party reflected the interests of state and collective rather than private agriculture; and the Communist Party of the Russian Federation, led by Gennadii Zyuganov, was the only post-CPSU grouping allowed to compete. The Liberal-Democratic party was headed by its controversial ultranationalist leader, Vladimir Zhirinovsky; it called for the cessation of economic assistance to other states, a strengthening of the state sector, a crackdown on crime, a strongly pro-Slavic and anti-Western foreign policy in former Yugoslavia and elsewhere, and the restoration of a Russian state 'within the framework of the former USSR'. Other contenders was 'The Future of Russia–New Names' (a youth grouping), 'Civic Union' (headed by Arkadii Volsky of the Russian Union of Industrialists and Entrepreneurs and reflecting the interests of what had formerly been state industry), 'Dignity and Charity' (representing veterans, Chernobyl victims and invalids) and 'Kedr' (a broadly environmentalist grouping).

The results in the constituency section were difficult to interpret as the majority of the candidates ran as independents. In the party list section, however, Zhirinovsky's Liberal Democrats came an unexpected first with about 24 per cent of the vote, followed by 'Russia's Choice' with 15 per cent, the reformed Communists with 14 per cent, the Agrarians on 9 per cent, and 'Women of Russia' with just under 9 per cent (not all the parties cleared the minimum 5 per cent threshold. The outcome, in terms of seats, is shown in Table 3.1. All voters, it appeared, were worried about inflation, the increase in crime and economic decline. Zhirinovsky

TABLE 3.1 *Groups and factions in the Federal Assembly, 1994*

State Duma (lower house)

Faction	Number of seats
Russia's Choice (radical reformist)	76
New Regional Policy (centrist)	65
Liberal Democratic Party (extreme right)	63
Agrarian Party of Russia (procommunist)	55
Communist Party of the Russian Federation	45
Party of Russian Unity and Concord (moderate reformist with strong regional policy)	30
Russian Way (Russian nationalist)	25
Yavlinsky–Boldyrev–Lukin bloc (moderate reformist)	25
Women of Russia (centrist)	23
Democratic Party of Russia (centrist)	15
Union of 12 December (radical reformist)	12

Council of the Federation (upper house)

Political affiliation	Number of seats
Proreform democrats	48
Russia's Choice	40
Yavlinsky–Bodyrev–Lukin block	3
Party of Russian Unity and Concord	4
Russian Movement for Democratic Reforms	1
Moderate reformers	23
Centrist opposition to the government	36
The communist and socialist opposition	20
Communist Party of the Russian Federation	15
Agrarian Party	3
Socialist Workers' Party	1
Labour Party	1
Extreme nationalists	2
Cossacks' movement in Kuban	1
Russian National Council	1

Source: Adapted from *RFE/RL Research Report*, 4 February 1994 (these totals are necessary approximations, especially in the Council of the Federation where most candidates did not reveal a party affiliation at the time of their election).

supporters, however, were more likely than others to be concerned about the weakness of the state itself, and about bribery and corruption (*Izvestiya*, 30 December 1993). The outcome was a new parliament that was likely to take a strongly confrontational position towards the President, but whose democratic mandate could not be questioned; while the Russian public, for its part, had given a thumbs down to existing policies but without indicating a coherent alternative.

The new parliament, when it began its work in January 1994, added some further complications. It was unclear where it would meet, for a start, and if it would meet at any time in joint session. The Council of the Federation, it emerged, was composed of regional notables who took little direct interest in parliamentary work; they did however elect Vladimir Shumeiko, a pro-reform politician who had served in the Yeltsin government, as their first chairman. The State Duma, it appeared, would be less easy for the Yeltsin administration to work with; its chairman, elected by a single vote, was Ivan Rybkin, formerly the coordinator of the communist fraction in the old Supreme Soviet, and communists and nationalists were relatively more numerous. Political coordination of the Duma is in the hands of a new structure called the 'Council of the Duma', made up of the leaders of the registered party fractions, which takes the place of the Presidium that had existed in the Soviet era. The relationship between both houses and the president was an uncertain one, though they did, for instance, assemble in February 1994 to hear Boris Yeltsin deliver the first of his 'state of the union' addresses; the relationship between the two houses – which had different but in practice overlapping responsibilities – was also a potential source of tension.

Prospects, Constraints and Opportunities

How will the future development of Russia's political system be influenced by the experience of the 1990–3 phase, when Russia's representative institutions moved across the stages from the wave of democratic mass mobilisation against the old communist order to their paralysing collision with the presidency? Are there lessons that we, as observers, and Russia's citizens and leaders, as participants, may learn about the prospects for democracy in Russia: have the odds of a democratic evolution improved with the adoption of a new and strongly presidential constitution, or has the violent, abrupt breakdown of the 1990–3 system instead so tainted the new institutional framework that it will never win widespread popular support? One might offer three rather general observations on these questions.

1. Political scientists generally agree that democracy requires a body of politicians who possess the habits and skills needed for a system built on choice, bargaining, compromise, tolerance and accountability. Where were such individuals to be found in the communist and early postcommunist regimes? Parliaments through the former communist world have proven to be a valuable recruiting and training ground for new politicians. Indeed, a very large number of Russia's present political class, both liberals and conservatives, served in either the USSR legislature of 1989–91 or the Russian legislature of 1990–3 – including Yeltsin himself. These politicians themselves frequently acknowledge the learning and maturation they have undergone as a result of having served in these new deliberative bodies, however imperfect they may have been. Contrary to the expectations of many Russians, many of the Russian deputies of the 1990–3 vintage chose to run again for the new parliament. Whatever else they brought with them, they did at least provide a leavening of useful parliamentary experience.

2. The second observation is that revolutions rarely make as abrupt a break with the past as they purport to do: behind the appearance of radical discontinuity lies, very often, the restoration of older arrangements and forms. Observers of parliaments in the postcommunist environment, for instance, are often struck at how many of the institutional features of the old communist-era legislatures survive or are recreated in the new ones. Many commentators have called attention to the parallels between the organisation of Yeltsin's presidential administration and the old communist system. In part, *de facto* continuity across deep historical disjunctures is caused by the fact that many of the same people who ran the old system resurface in leading positions in the new one. But it is also a product of the fact that certain institutional arrangements are, at least temporarily, efficient and familiar ways of getting things done. Therefore, deeper and more

lasting change in a political system often requires a longer period in which new people are brought into the political elite, new interests rise and organise, and new structures arise to meet new needs.

3. The third point relates to the second. Often social change, like biological change, occurs in an evolutionary fashion. Imposing a new constitution on a political system in which the actual distribution of power and political resources are unchanged is likely to result in either of two outcomes: the constitution is tacitly ignored, and life goes on in much the same way as before; or the constitution is explicitly rejected, and a new one more suited to the system's realities is adopted. Many observers wondered why Russia's parliament over 1990–3 failed to develop a working system of political parties. The answer may be that other structures – the centralised presidium, the functional committee, the weak fractions – met the political needs of the deputies better. Once Yeltsin resolved the impasse in presidential–parliamentary relations by dissolving parliament and calling new elections, he created a set of powerful incentives for parties to develop electoral organisations that could win seats in the new parliament. Immediately, in fact, a diverse array of party coalitions quickly scrambled to assemble lists of candidates and obtain the required number of voter signatures to register them, and to campaign for electoral support. In like manner, we may expect that to the extent that Russia's society develops along the lines of a Western-style capitalist welfare state, its politics will evolve along similar lines as well.

Consequently it is fair to say that democracy in Russia will require good constitutional engineering as well as the peaceful, organic development of liberal institutions in society. Constitutional engineers must design appropriate incentives into the relationship between legislative and executive power to reward the leaders on each side for seeking moderation, tolerance and compromise; if Russia is committed for the foreseeable future to a presidential system with a dual executive, these might be found in the sort of mixed presidential–parliamentary system that the French Fifth republic has developed, where the cabinet requires parliamentary confidence to govern and the president has wide powers to oversee the executive branch only when he is of the same party as the parliamentary majority. It also is clear that there will be a need for vigorous and competitive political parties and interest groups linking political leaders to the voters. To the extent that a competitive party system can assume some of the tasks of organising and channelling the political pressures associated with Russia's passage from communism (a subject addressed in the following chapter), the fragile institutions of the post-communist democracy may begin to overcome the heavy burden of Russia's autocratic past.

4

Parties and the Party System

RONALD J. HILL

The collapse of the Soviet Union at the end of 1991 and the stated intension of establishing a democratic political order in post-Soviet Russia has confronted the people of that country with new challenges in circumstances of economic and social collapse that can hardly be judged the most propitious for the establishment of stable, effective and responsive institutions and procedures. After more than seven decades of political monopoly exercised by the Communist Party of the Soviet Union, from 1917 until the spring of 1990, no citizens alive today have direct experience of a functioning party system such as forms the basis of modern representative democracy. The lack of appropriate experience, the continuation into the post-Soviet era of institutions, attitudes and values that were instilled into citizens by generations of authoritarian rule, and, finally, a fairly rudimentary appreciation of how democracy actually works in a complex society, all combine to form a legacy of communist party rule that makes the emergence and establishment of a recognisable *party system* somewhat problematic.

The Legacy of Communist Party Rule

Throughout most of the 20th century the country has been dominated by the Communist Party of the Soviet Union, or CPSU. According to the 1977 Constitution, it was 'the leading and guiding force of Soviet society and the nucleus of its political system, of all state organs and public organisations'. It supposedly 'determined the general perspectives of the development of society and the course of the home and foreign policy of the USSR, directed the great constructive work of the Soviet people', and imparted 'a planned, systematic and theoretically substantiated character to their struggle for the victory of communism'. It claimed to recruit the 'best' representatives of all social categories – workers, peasants, members of the intelligentsia, and almost all national and ethnic groups. By 1989, with a peak membership of almost 20 million, it embraced almost a tenth of the adult population; 45.4 per cent of these were classified as workers, 11.4 per cent as collective farm peasants, and the remaining 43.2 per cent as white-collar employees, including the intelligentsia, drawn from a wide range of professions and occupations (a breakdown for 1990, using slightly different criteria, is given in Table 4.1). It had representatives of 'over 100' nationalities, with members in practically all workplaces. Clearly, for a wide segment of today's Russian society – including those who counted communists within their family or circle of acquaintances – the experience of political parties was with the peculiar model offered by the CPSU.

The party, as an institution, possessed a complex set of offices and committees, which overlapped with those of the state, economic management and the trade unions and offered a career structure for the politically ambitious. Party membership was, indeed, a necessary qualification for a successful career in administration, and millions of Soviet citizens depended on the party in their working life – some for their very livelihood. It was an enormous organisation that functioned through thousands of local offices; an important employer in its own right, it offered jobs to politicians at all levels and to thousands of auxiliary staff, ranging from secretaries and office staff, janitors, and chauffeurs, to computer operators, office managers, and even social scientists.

As a major national organisation, the party owned or used large amounts of office space and other property; it possessed fleets of vehicles, and could call on those of other organisations; it ran publishing houses, hotels and vacation homes; and in performing its political functions it consumed office furniture and equipment, paper, ink, typewriter ribbons, floppy disks and other

TABLE 4.1 *The CPSU in 1990*

		(%)
Membership	19,228,217	
of which candidates	372,104	
of which women	5,813,610	(30.2)
Social composition		
workers	5,313,524	(27.6)
collective farmers	1,466,361	(7.6)
white collar staff	7,793,048	(40.5)
students	101,415	(0.5)
pensioners and housewives	3,344,981	(17.4)
Others	1,208,888	(6.3)
Educational level:		
higher	6,808,715	(35.4)
incomplete higher	358,350	(1.9)
secondary	8,605,207	(44.7)
primary	1,154,880	(6.0)
less than primary	54,570	(0.3)
Age groups:		
up to 20	38,553	(0.2)
21–25	645,091	(3.4)
26–30	2,001,936	(10.4)
31–40	5,002,311	(26.0)
41–50	3,682,076	(19.1)
51–60	3,844,212	(20.0)
over 60	4,014,038	(20.9)

Source: Adapted from *Izvestiya TsK KPSS*, 1990, no. 4, pp. 113–15.

office stationery. In short, the CPSU was a substantial economic force, and through its policies it charted the course of the country's economic development. Its members' entrance fees and earnings-related monthly subscriptions, plus the profits of its eleven publishing houses and other subsidiary enterprises, enabled the party to dispose of colossal funds to cover the salaries of party officers and employees and the upkeep of various party facilities. In 1988, running the Central Committee apparatus alone cost 50.4 million rubles (3 per cent of the party's budget).

The party made enormous demands on its members. Individuals were not free to join and leave: identified at their place of work as potential recruits, they were invited to submit an application, and then subjected to a complex admissions procedure, including a year's probation, to screen out 'undesirables'. Regular study of the classic Marxist texts and a willingness to accept binding discipline in carrying out formal assignments were part of the life of the ordinary member, in addition to paying subscriptions and attending monthly branch meetings. And, while in the 1970s the party elite – the so-called *nomenklatura* officials, appointed through the party-based nomination system – exploited the system for their own private benefit (and appear to be retaining their common ties to take advantage of the new opportunities for entrepreneurship), ordinary members were subject to disciplinary procedures, up to and including expulsion, for a variety of misdemeanours. Without such an apprenticeship, however, a career of responsibility, authority or power anywhere in the system was unthinkable.

The party claimed its authority on the basis of its supposed understanding of the 'scientific' ideology of Marxism–Leninism. However, even before the Bolshevik revolution the ideology had become a means of political struggle and control; in later years it was manipulated by leaders at all levels in the hierarchy and imposed upon their subordinates as a test of loyalty. This ideology proved almost infinitely malleable, and could be involved to support surprisingly unsocialist principles of inequality and privilege, not to mention the horrors of the purges, the show trials, and the 1939 pact with nazism. In its official interpretation at a given time it was binding on all party members; this rendered it a powerful weapon in the political struggle and led to what Mikhail Gorbachev called the party's 'infallibility complex' and the arrogance of power.

The CPSU was, for all intents and purposes, a permanently ruling organisation, which deployed its members in strategic positions in the institutions of rule: legislatures, the courts, economic management, state administration. It was in a dominant position, able to have its policies adopted and applied, subject only to inefficiencies in the system and resistance among those responsible for their implementation. The Soviet state was never independent; it was politically subordinate to the Communist Party, whose policy it dutifully implemented. The relationship was often seen as one of party dictatorship, and from the earliest years *podmena*, or party interference in the work of state and other bodies, was a problem that prevented effective administration.

The CPSU ruled through a complex network of structures, from the 5-yearly congress down through conferences and committees at the levels of the republic, province, city and district, and ultimately to the branches or primary party organisations (PPOs) in almost every place of employment in the country. Every party member belonged to such an organisation (of which there were approaching 450,000 in the late 1980s), and they were allocated 'party assignments' for fulfilment. Monthly meetings discussed various concerns, including the allocation of these assignments and the admission of new members. District or city conferences formally elected the party committee and delegates to the provincial or republican conference, rising up on the hierarchy to the all-Union party congress. Although acquiring something of the quality of a rally, this forum discussed broader policy matters and formally elected the Central Committee, which in turn elected the Politburo and the General Secretary, the highest party office. Such indirect party elections, guided by the superior organs, deprived rank-and-file members of any say in the selection of the party leadership, and democratic centralism (the principle of hierarchical subordination) ensured that power resided in the hands of the officials at whatever level.

The first secretary was the most powerful politician in a given locality, and a substantial apparatus conducted the work of the party, with various administrative departments covering both internal party matters and the administrative areas that were nominally the state's responsibility. The occupants of such positions, who also controlled recruitment, extended their privileges and perquisites in the 1970s, and they later resisted Gorbachev's attempts to simply the structure and define the party's role more precisely, delineating it from the state.

In short, the CPSU created the system and directed it, using its own officers and members to ensure the compliance of other institutions, including the political security agencies, through which the population was kept under control. The party administrators, or *apparatchiki*, dominated the whole system, and were responsible to their superiors through patronage links; through *nomenk-*

latura they in turn could dispense patronage by arranging appointments for associates. Corruption, nepotism, cronyism and other anti-democratic practices invaded the apparatus and became endemic, but were hidden from the public by official party and state secrecy.

Such was the legacy of power deployment which Boris Yeltsin, former party chief in Sverdlovsk (now Yekaterinburg) and later Moscow, having resigned from the CPSU in July 1990 and subsequently as an independent won election to the presidency of Russia, moved to destroy. He did so by prohibiting its operation in state economic and administrative enterprises in Russia, nationalising the party's assets in the republic and forcing Gorbachev to resign as General Secretary; Yeltsin formally banned the party in Russia in November 1991 (although later this was partially rescinded by the Constitutional Court, and various successor organisations established themselves during 1993).

The experience of Communist Party rule shows a similar evolutionary development. In the 1920s, a machine for winning power in a revolutionary situation was converted into the central element of power for rapidly modernising a backward, politically inexperienced society; in the 1930s, an elite of committed radicals became a mechanism for imposing discipline on the new managerial class; and from the 1960s onwards that class used the party as a means of establishing its own control over a society whose increasing complexity and sophistication led it to make demands for which the CPSU was unprepared. Although various successor parties claimed the mantle – undoubtedly with a view to obtaining access to the CPSU's substantial wealth – and although a 'Restoration Congress' was held outside Moscow in February 1993, re-establishing a Communist Party of the Russian Federation, the chances of a return to power are remote. The CPSU, in attempting in the conditions of the 1930s to build communism – a model society characterised by wealth, freedom, harmony and social homogeneity, according to the official rhetoric of decades past – but having signally failed to satisfy the most basic wants and needs of a complex and demanding society, has undermined not only its own position but the very idea of socialism and communism based on Marxist ideas. That original aspiration has also been undermined by developments that have taken place as a result of the party's own policies of modernisation.

The Emergence of Pluralism of Interests

As indicated above, the CPSU's principal goal from the late 1920s was to create an industrial society as the basis for 'communism', a society envisaged as a logical advance on 19th century industrialism. The conditions of Russia in the early years of this century could hardly have been less propitious for implementing the goal – as the Mensheviks and other Marxist opponents of Lenin and the Bolsheviks argued. In effect, from the viewpoint of committed Marxists, the initial task had to be to bring Russian society to a level of development that in other countries had been achieved under capitalism. It can be plausibly argued that the priorities entailed by Stalin's slogan of 'socialism in one country' were not inappropriate for a nation that aspired to great power status, with or without the overtones of socialism and communism. It can be added that, in the circumstances of technical primitiveness, social rigidity and political inexperience that characterised Russian society, authoritarian methods may have been the ones most likely to succeed in the time-frame that was envisaged. Moreover, such an approach to modernisation was compatible with Russian historical experience: Peter the Great had used similar methods to achieve a comparable 'revolution from above' in the early 18th century.

In the 20th century, however, the scope of modernisation was far broader, entailing, in effect, the complete restructuring of society. Industrialisation – the core goal – entailed not only the building of more industry but also a range of other processes that totally altered the nature of the society. Urbanisation included both the expansion of existing cities as industrial and administrative centres and the creation of new urban communities. The new workers and managers in industry were drawn from the rural peasantry, who were induced to migrate, often over great distances, to form new urban centres, and whose steady decline in numbers is one of the marked features of Soviet social history. The workers and managers were trained for their new roles in an expanded education system, geared to the needs of the state. Furthermore, the range of new roles and occupations as industry expanded and cities developed greatly extended the opportunities for career choice and for social, leisure and entertainment activities, while the migration process undermined the traditional family structure and established new patterns of social bonding and intercourse. The cycle of the seasons, which had been the prime factor in ordering the population's life, was replaced by the clock and the needs of the industrial process: time out of the place of work allowed urban workers an opportunity for exploring new interests and engaging in fresh pursuits. The peasantry, too, collectivised for purposes of economic efficiency and political control, were required to learn new techniques and master equipment produced by industry, so as to feed an increasing urban population. They were also brought libraries, cinema, radio, the telephone and other products and services associated with town life, and in this and other ways, urban values extended into the countryside. In short, within half a century, a relatively simple, traditional rural society with modest industrial development concentrated in a few large centres was changed into a modern, complex, urban and industrial social organism in which well-educated individuals and groups had opportunities for self-expression such as their grandparents, or even parents, could never have dreamed of.

Such a society, as Western social science has argued, makes demands on the political system that a less developed society does not. The potential for conflict of interests increases with the growing complexity of society, and fresh mechanisms were required for their articulation, aggregation and incorporation into the process whereby resources are allocated. In other words, the political system must be capable of containing the potential for conflict. Procedures are needed for tapping public opinion and responding to it in a timely fashion, if the principal goal of a political system – the maintenance of the system through the resolution of conflict, preventing the collapse of order into civil war or revolution – is to be successfully carried out.

It was recognised as early as the 1960s that Soviet society already generated a broad range of interests that needed to be accommodated in the political process if the population were to grant continuing legitimacy to the party and the system. Ideological conviction and the sense of achievement in building a new society or defending the Motherland in war were less acceptable to a society growing increasingly sophisticated in its tastes, more aware of the world beyond the border and more demanding in its expectations. The goal of 'communism' served less and less to

inspire a population after two generations of 'socialist construction', and the promises of 1961 to build the material basis for
communism within two decades were so unrealistic as to be
incapable of generating the necessary support. Increasingly, as has
been observed, the emphasis shifted from getting to the utopia of
communism to managing society and its problems now.

The need for a more responsive set of institutions and procedures was argued by scholars and even by some political leaders
with increasing urgency as time passed. By the mid-1980s, analysis
of Soviet politics in terms of interests was commonplace.
Moreover, a society that had acquired the education and training
associated with modernisation, and had also gained experience of
living in a complex, modern society (and, since the 1950s, had
learnt much about the world beyond their own country), was
manifestly capable of playing a far more positive and active role
in political life than the isolated, uneducated peasantry of half a
century earlier was able to do. That partly explains the rapid
expansion of the Communist Party from the 1950s onwards, as
'the best representatives' of all social groups were recruited into
the ranks: increasingly, the 'best' were deemed to be those with
the advanced education and training in whatever field. Hence, the
changes wrought by the party's own policy of rapid modernisation made change in the way the society was governed and administered both necessary and possible.

However, a party with the ideological baggage of the CPSU
and a positive achievement to look back on felt little pressure to
reform itself, and it was becoming steadily more apparent that
entrenched groups in the party and state administration were
stifling the expression of those interests. The effect of this was to
contribute to the social malaise that involved widespread dissatisfaction, cynicism and apathy and led to economic slowdown
that threatened the country's position as a world power.

Glasnost and the Articulation of Interests

Upon coming to power as Communist Party General Secretary in
March 1985, Gorbachev sought to tackle a number of problems.
His prime goal was to invigorate a moribund economy, but it
quickly became apparent that his strategy would entail broad-

ranging efforts to release the energies of the population, both in the quest for economic expansion and in the political struggle against corruption and complacency that had become endemic in the 1970s under the indulgent leadership of Leonid Brezhnev. The policies of social and economic acceleration, *glasnost* and *perestroika* offered the population new opportunities to raise issues that had hitherto been taboo, and resulted in an explosion of challenging ideas in literature and the arts, the press, the mass media, and generally throughout society. The phrase 'pluralism of interests', which had been applied disparagingly to Western scholars' analyses of liberal democracy, was now admitted into Soviet political discourse, although qualified by the word 'socialist'. The new orthodoxy rapidly found reflection in political discussion groups and clubs, of which there were some 60,000 by the end of 1988, and two years later some 11,000 informal independent organisations were in existence. *Glasnost*, a slogan that implied giving voice to concerns that had hitherto been politically out of bounds, had long been part of the political lexicon; now, however, it was given a new content. As a weapon in the political struggle, it was officially encouraged by Gorbachev, and came to be accepted as a step on the road to greater freedom of expression – a necessary precondition for the emergence of a process of genuine political debate.

Further reforms offered opportunities for the exploiting the new freedom to challenge. A new set of representative institutions – the Congress of People's Deputies and a revamped Supreme Soviet, to which representatives were elected in conditions of political competition for the first time nationally in the spring of 1989 – permitted genuine grievances and concerns to be aired at national level. Within months of the opening of the new institutions, groupings of deputies began to form which appeared to have the potential of coalescing into political parties: the reformist Inter-Regional Group of Deputies and the traditionalist Soyuz (Union) group were coalitions of opinion that might have emerged as electoral blocs had the country's political evolution followed a different course. Further constitutional and legislative changes combined with the emergence of new aspirations, particularly in certain of the non-Russian areas, to push the development of pluralism *tout court*, leading to the emergence of political parties alongside, and in competition with, the Communist Party, which showed growing signs of internal conflict and external decline.

The Emergence of Parties

In 1989–90, the CPSU's leadership came under increasing pressure to permit still greater political self-expression by refor- mulating Article 6 of the 1977 Constitution, which identified the party as 'the leading and guiding force of Soviet society, of all state organs and public organisations'. Movements for national renewal in the Baltic republics and Ukraine, in particular, were already beginning to act as political parties, in preparing to contest republic-level elections in the spring of 1990. In February, a CPSU Central Committee plenum agreed to the amending of the Constitution, and in the following month, Articles 6 and 7 were changed to refer to 'political parties', with no particular privileges for the CPSU (changes to the Russian Republic's constitution were made in the following year). A new Law on Public Organisations, adopted in October, established rules for forming, registering and winding up political parties, as one of a number of kinds of organisations sanctioned in society.

Proto-parties were already in existence, and they registered themselves and began the arduous task of organising, recruiting members, adopting constitutions, devising membership rules, seeking funds – and awaiting a chance to test their strength at elections. There was, indeed, a proliferation of organisations calling themselves political parties over the following two years (including – as in Poland, Czechloslovakia and elsewhere – frivolous and 'divan' parties, so tiny that their entire membership could sit together on a sofa), and the CPSU itself took a considerable interest in them, if only because it needed to identify potential political allies. Shortly after its 28th Congress (July 1990) the CPSU's monthly *News of the CPSU Central committee* published a brief run-down of 15 parties with claims to national status, and it became clear that the CPSU was contemplating coalition government with one or more of these rivals, and debating which ones it might be prepared to collaborate with.

Meanwhile, *glasnost* was having an impact on the CPSU itself. As the only political party for decades, it had perforce been the only effective source of legitimate political expression. For those who wished to play an active part in Soviet society rather than cross the political line into dissident activity, with all the risks entailed in such a step, membership of the party was a *sine qua non*. It therefore served to channel and control the political activities of an exceptionally broad spectrum of individuals and groups in the society. Since 1961 it had, indeed, referred to itself as a party of the whole people, with the implied assumption – sometimes explicitly stated – that a single organisation could reflect the interests of all groups within society. So long as ideological conformity was exacted through the organisational principle of democratic centralism, a fiction of monolithic unity could be plausibly maintained. Once the winds of *glasnost* begin to blow in society at large, however, the breezes drifted into the party itself (it was, after all, closely in touch, through its own membership, with virtually all walks of life), and a variety of opinions began to be expressed. The 19th Party Conference, in June–July 1988, was the first party forum for many decades at which a facade of unity was not maintained. Delegates were clearly divided into reformers and traditionalists, as epitomised by the clash between Boris Yeltsin and Yegor Ligachev on the penultimate day of the conference. Subsequent developments enhanced the rift, and in advance of the 28th Congress in the summer of 1990, three 'platforms' published programmes that were barely compatible, if at all. The Congress itself saw the dramatic resignation of Yeltsin, accompanied by other leading reformers, and shortly thereafter the CPSU split. Parties in the republics had already declared their independence, while rump organisations 'on the programme of the CPSU' kept Moscow's flag flying – but precisely what that meant became steadily less clear as ideological and organisational fragmentation affected the unit of the party.

Towards a Party System

By the time of the prohibition of the CPSU following the attempted coup of August 1991 scores of parties and party-type institutions were in existence, representing the broad spectrum of interests and opinions in what had long been a complex and relatively sophisticated modern society which the CPSU had struggled but failed to accommodate. One analysis published after the coup (Slavin and Davydov, 1991) identified three broad blocs of parties: the 'conservative–dogmatic' political forces, including the neo-Stalinist 'Unity' organisation associated with Nina Andreeva, the supporters of the 1990 founding congress of the Russian Communist Party, and other 'defenders of socialist principles'. They based their approach on a 'vulgarised class approach', sought a renewed form of socialism – in reality a monolithic, totalitarian type of party monopoly – and denounced reformers from Khrushchev to Gorbachev as traitors to the cause whose aim was a 'bourgeois restoration' and whose policies betrayed generations of workers who strove to build socialism against the odds. Given the economic decline that contrasted so markedly with the feverish construction of the 1930s, such a position found resonance in society at large. Some of these organisations renewed their existence in early 1993, following the rescinding of the ban on Communist Party organisations by the Constitutional Court, and were involved in the constitutional crisis of September–October 1993, supporting the Congress of People's Deputies against the authority of President Yeltsin.

A second bloc comprised democratic socialists, including progressive forces from the CPSU, left social-democrats, anarcho-syndicalists and those of similar views. They pitched their appeal towards the masses of workers, recognising that the working class of today is very different from the ex-peasants who were the mainstay of the Bolshevik party under Stalin. This group of parties, itself quite heterogeneous, favoured pluralist democracy, but was concerned for the interests of the workers in the difficult period of transition from a command to a market economy, and as such they appeared to enjoy widespread support.

A third bloc, which drew most of its support from the intelligentsia, looked westwards for its inspiration, believing broadly that the salvation of what was the Soviet Union lay in the thorough-going assimilation into the mainstream of Western civilisation. Broadly liberal in orientation, they favoured the market, parliamentary democracy, ideological pluralism, and minimal state intervention in the affairs of society. A further tendency was neo-Slavophilism, which had absorbed some of the ideas of Alexander Solzhenitsyn, but also included monarchists, and was the Russian equivalent of the nationalistically-oriented movements of the Baltic republics, Georgia, Ukraine and elsewhere in the former Soviet Union. The broad aims were a resurgence of Russia on the basis of a return to traditional values such as Orthodoxy, Russian state power and a rekindled sense of pride in one's national identity.

More recent surveys classify the broad range of parties somewhat differently in the light of changing circumstances and evolving perceptions of political reality (see Table 4.2). New parties reflecting a broad range of ideological perspectives have sprung up to fill the ideological vacuum left by the discrediting of Marxism–Leninism as an official ideology, which has forced the whole nation to reassess its identity. Resurgent nationalism, patriotism, Slavophilism and Westernism have surfaced alongside more conventional ideological currents, including anarchism, monarchism, liberalism, republicanism, neo-Stalinism, Trotskyism and a host of other tendencies reflected in a shifting kaleidoscope of political groups, parties and coalitions. Individual politicians have formed 'parties' and 'movements', held 'congresses' to establish broad coalitions, split over issues of ideology, policy or personality, and attempted to project images of themselves as statesmen and women of the future. Among the best known are the historian and former dissident Roy Medvedev, whose Socialist Workers' Party retains a Marxist orientation; the former Vice President Alexander Rutskoi, who formed 'Communists for Democracy' under Gorbachev and later led the People's Party of Free Russia, which he took into the centrist bloc known as Civic Union; Nikolai Travkin, leader of the centre-right Democratic Party of Russia; Arkadii Volsky, whose organisation, the All-Russian Union for Renewal, appeals to managers and intellectuals; the writer Valentin Raputin, a member of Gorbachev's Presidential Council in 1990–1, a Russian nationalist and leading figure in the National Salvation Front and later the Russian National Union; and Father Gleb Yakunin, another former dissident, of the Russian Christian Democratic Movement and of the pro-Yeltsin Democratic Russia Movement. The personalisation of politics has led to the depiction of the political process in terms of little more than a struggle among rivals, with their changing parties and organisations relegated to a secondary role, as individuals and groups weighed their electoral chances and shifted their allegiances and alliances.

Table 4.2 *The Russian political spectrum, 1993*

'Oppositional' parties and movements			'Democratic' (pro-Yeltsin) parties and movements	
'Patriots'	*'Communists'*	*'Centrists'*	*'Democratic Movements'*	*'Democratic Parties'*
National-Republican Party of Russia (less than 1000)	United Opposition (bloc)	Civic Union (bloc)	Democratic Russia (bloc: 200–300,000 'supporters')	Social Democratic Party (5600)
Russian National *Sobor* (bloc)	All-Union Communist Party of Bolsheviks	People's Party 'Free Russia' (120,000)	Democratic Reform Movement (bloc)	Republican Party (7000)
Russian All-National Union (bloc)	Labour Russia (bloc: up to 100,000 'supporters')	All-Russian Union 'Renewal' (2000)		Free Democratic Party (2000)
National Salvation Front (bloc; 40,000 'supporters')	Russian Party of Communists (10,000)	Democratic Party of Russia (40,000)		Constitutional Democratic Party (2000 'supporters')
Liberal-Democratic Party (100,000, independent est. 1500)	Russian Communist Workers' Party (60,000)	Constitutional Democratic Party – Party of Popular Freedom (300)		Party of Economic Freedom (600)
	Union of Communists (10,000)	Agrarian Party		People's Patriotic Party (103,000)
	Socialist Workers' Party (50–80,000)			Peasant Party (14,000)
	Party of Labour			People's (Gdlyan) Party (10,000)
	Communist Party of the Russian Federation (500,000)			Christian-Democratic Union (5000)
				Russian Christian Democratic Movement (7000)

Source: Based upon *Spravochnik* (1993). Membership estimates in brackets are generally self-declared; some minor blocs or parliamentary factions have been excluded; the Liberal-Democratic Party has been reclassified as 'patriotic'.

In the circumstances of 1991–3 this was to be expected, since there were few opportunities in view for parties to play any significant role. The institutions of the communist era – the Congress of People's Deputies, the Supreme Soviet and the Presidency – seemed well entrenched and could constitutionally remain in office until the middle of the decade, and beyond in the case of the president. In such political circumstances, accompanied by dire economic conditions for the bulk of the population, it was an uphill struggle trying to set up an organisation, to recruit members, to attract subscriptions and institutional funds, to devise programmes, to identify leaders and project an appropriate image that would attract the votes of the popular masses in elections some time away – so remote, indeed, that the economic and political institutional setting was likely to look quite different and the precise problems faced by the nation when elections eventually came were unpredictable.

The Party System and the Political System

There was a further important dimension related to the last: it was far from clear what role political parties would have in the future Russian state structure. From December 1991 until October 1993 an institutional power struggle took place between the entrenched parliamentary institutions (the Congress of People's Deputies and the Supreme Soviet) and the presidency, occupied since June 1991 by Boris Yeltsin. Disagreements over policy developed into an institutional battle over where power lay and where it should like in the future system. Should Russia have presidential or a parliamentary form of democracy? This was a crucial question over which there was little rational debate: rather, various institutional interests presented different drafts of a new constitution, in which different dispositions of institutional power were defined. Until that issue was resolved, it was unclear what role political parties would play, and hence what kind of party system would evolve. To give one illustration of the issues, in a parliamentary system, such as those of Western Europe, a political party typically presents a programme of government to the electorate in the form of a manifesto, endorsement for which, through votes for the party's candidates, constitutes a mandate to implement the provisions of the programme in the next parliamentary term. It is the function of the governing party or coalition of parties to frame legislation to enact the elements of the programme and persuade parliament to give legal endorsement to those provisions. Party ideology, values and programmes are therefore important attributes of the party system. Likewise, in a parliamentary democracy, the members of the government administration – the prime minister, the ministers, the secretaries of state and other high state officers – are drawn from among those elected to parliament, so it is vital that parties should have in their leadership individuals of suitable calibre to perform such functions, and the parties need to present themselves to the electorate as possessing such capabilities.

In a strong presidential system, by contrast, the political initiative lies with the presidency, and the occupants of the principal offices of state are chosen for appointment by the president and are responsible to him, rather than to parliament. In those circumstances, a well-articulated party political programme becomes something of an irrelevance, since the parties in parliament have few opportunities to put their policy goals into action, and the president may look to any parties, or to none, when seeking individuals to appoint to the governing 'team'. The role of parties in such a system is clearly different from the one they perform in a parliamentary democracy: that is particularly true when, as in the Russian case, the president has set a precedent of being a member of no political party and eschewing such membership.

Nevertheless, the commitment to political parties seems strong among the politically active of Russia, and the election to a new State Duma precipitated by the political crisis of September–October 1993 gave the scores of new organisations an opportunity to test their campaigning skills and their popularity for the first time since the collapse of communist power. The campaign witnessed attempts to establish credible coalitions of various tendencies, whose role, once elected, would be in the initial period to test the relative powers of the presidency and the parliament to establish working political conventions to govern relations among institutions.

It is impossible – and would be pointless in view of the rapidly changing circumstances – to attempt to enumerate all the bodies that might conceivably have offered candidates, if only because some had a distinctly regional organisational base and appeal (the Greens typically organise on a city or district basis, rather than as a unified national body), others were suspended before the campaign began, and others were barred during the campaign itself, including leftist and nationalist organisations – even though individuals associated with them continued to seek electoral endorsement without the support of the party organisation. The number of parties nation-wide was substantial, and it was extremely unlikely that many of them would survive this 'founding election' as serious contenders for a long-term role. Electoral defeat would force coalitions and mergers, while other parties would convert themselves into special interest groups to pursue the concerns of those whom they claimed to represent, and still others would disappear from the scene entirely. The experience of other former communist countries looked likely to be followed: scores of parties contested the first one or two elections, and in the course of these elections and through subsequent political and governmental activity a party system gradually emerged.

In advance of the founding election of 1993, Russian sources identified 40 or so parties that appeared to have genuine claims to be taken seriously as national organisations, broadly characterised as 'oppositionist' and 'democratic' (see *Spravochnik*, 1993). The oppositionist parties included the centrist bloc, embracing Civic Union, the Democratic Party of Russia, and the Agrarian Party of Russia. The 'patriotic' bloc included the National-Republican Party of Russia and the National Salvation Front (an inter-party grouping). And the communist bloc – formed by 'refugees' from the Communist Party, and bearing the marks in terms of organisational structures and internal practices – included up to a dozen parties that claimed the mantle of the CPSU at various stages in its history, including an All-Union Communist Party of Bolsheviks, reviving the title by which the CPSU was known until 1952. 'Democratic' or pro-Yeltsin movements and parties included Democratic Russia, Democratic Choice and the Russian Movement for Democratic Reforms, while parties also identified as 'democratic' also included the Social Democratic Party, the Republican Party, the Party of Economic Freedom and the Peasant Party of Russia.

Party Orientations and Party Politics

While the names of these and other parties have a suitably cosmopolitan ring, implying at least a familiarity with world-wide ideological and philosophical trends, they are not necessarily characterised by distinct programmes and reforms. The Constitutional Democrats, for example (who revived the name of one of the pre-1917 parties in Russia, popularly known as the Cadets, from their initials in Russian – KD, pronounced Kah-Deh), are affiliated with West European Liberal parties, but their alliance with the Party of Economic Freedom, headed by Konstantin Borovoi, implies a particular approach to economic affairs rather than politics. Borovoi's party was instrumental in its turn in setting up a Council of Constructive Forces in June 1992, embracing half a dozen parties plus other groupings including trade unions; this body's influence has been marginal, however. The approach of elections naturally forced party leaderships to define their positions with greater precision so as to present a distinct identity, or to forge formal electoral alliances that could subsequently lead to mergers. This took place both before and during the election campaign of December 1993.

Most parties in Russia command a very small membership base. In very few cases has anything approaching a mass membership been attained, perhaps in reaction to the party that dominated the lives of the nation for so long, perhaps in bewilderment at the array of choice now available, and perhaps also in recognition that the future role and powers of these organisations remained unclear. Moreover, despite claims to a national role, few parties, if any, have so far established a nation-wide organisation. The Democratic Party, for example (one of the largest), headed by Nikolai Travkin, claimed a membership of only 40,000 at the beginning of 1993, with sections in a third of Russia's regions. The Peasant Party had about 14,000 members, with branches in 45 provinces, while its 'oppositionist' counterpart, the Agrarian Party, with an undisclosed membership, had sections in only 10 regions in early 1993. The various communist parties, which resurfaced following the ruling of the Constitutional Court in November 1992 concerning the legality of Boris Yeltsin's banning of the CPSU (and which were restricted in their participation in the 1993 election campaign), claimed a combined membership of

1.4 million, and their officers certainly possessed the greatest experience in organisation and campaigning (see *Spravochnik*, 1993).

The picture towards the end of 1993 therefore appeared uncertain. To be sure, parties and party leaders existed in abundance, but there was no *party system*. Nor, even after the adoption of a new constitution, was it certain what kind of party system would emerge or would be appropriate. New institutions take time to become established, and the party system is likely to take several years to evolve so as to identify its niche in the new institutional structures of post-communist Russia.

In seizing the political initiative during the constitutional crisis of September–October 1993, calling elections to a new set of state representative institutions with limited powers, and placing restrictions on a number of organisations that failed to demonstrate sufficient broad appeal (that is, those that failed to muster at least 100,000 signatures of supporters spread across several provinces), Boris Yeltsin may have encouraged the consolidation of a limited number of structures and obviated the very real risks of 'extreme pluralism': fragmentation and consequent political instability. Moreover, by devising a constitution embodying a relatively weak representative institution, he attempted to avoid placing the continuity and stability of government in the hands of a small number of political rivals whose track record as secure leaders of stable parties was at best unproven and in many cases non-existent. These were emergency measures, intended to counteract the very real pressures of social and economic instability on fledgling parties and state institutions, and it was clear that they would undergo further evolution and modification.

Assuming that the institutions established in December 1993 gain acceptance, the newly elected representatives and their parties will have ample opportunity to acquire the demeanour appropriate to a democracy and learn to present their experience in such a way as to win the confidence and support of the electorate at subsequent elections. They will therefore play a vitally important role in the further political development of Russia. Well before the end of the century, there is likely to be a tendency towards the formation of united organisations that will define a broadly conventional democratic political system, with extreme parties that command little electoral support pushed to the margins of political life. Over the medium term much depends on the type of electoral system that is introduced, the laws covering campaigning, the access to the public through the mass media, and many other factors that have been excluded from political life for practically the whole of this century – indeed, that have never been part of the population's living experience. The way ahead therefore remains fraught with obstacles of various kinds: but it does seem that the peoples of the Soviet Union have matured politically by their experience since the mid-1980s and are unlikely to tolerate a reversion to dogmatic orthodoxy, or (despite Zhirinovsky's success in the elections) a move to right-wing nationalism. The past few years have shown the Soviet people to be able to identify their interests and act upon them; the next few years will see whether they are now capable of channelling them through a new party system in Russia and the other post-Soviet republics.

5

Citizen and State under Gorbachev and Yeltsin

ROBERT SHARLET

In the political and legal landscape of Imperial Russia and its successor, the Soviet Union, the individual was traditionally relegated to a marginal status. Under the tsars, an individual was considered a 'subject' of the crown; after 1917, the Bolsheviks declared Russia a republic and the individual became a 'citizen'. Qualitatively, however, little had changed – in terms of civil and political rights, crown subject and Soviet citizen alike were both dependent creatures of a powerful state. Granted, as the USSR modernised, the citizen enjoyed a better material existence than his or her prerevolutionary predecessor. This was consistent with Soviet emphasis on social and economic rights. Nevertheless, so far as classic Western-style civil and political freedoms were concerned – such as the rights of speech, press, assembly and petition which translate into popular sovereignty, elections, accountability and limited government – Soviet Man remained politically and legally impoverished.

This divide or conceptual gulf between state and individual in Russian history has been aptly expressed in Robert C. Tucker's concept of 'dual Russia' (1971). In its 19th-century context, dual Russia was 'official Russia' and 'popular Russia', or the Russia of the imperial court, aristocracy and bureaucracy which dominated the Russia of the common people, the great mass of peasants for the most part. Dual Russia proved to be a useful analytical device

for examining the elite–mass relationship in the 20th-century
Soviet Union as well. The state of the autocracy passed into
history, replaced by the Communist party-state of the Soviet
period. Tsar and retainers were gone, succeeded by a dynasty of
party leaders and their lieutenants. The bureaucracy, however,
especially its elitist administrative culture, made safe passage from
autocracy to communism, growing enormously in power, scope
and capacity for cruelty in the process. Now, at the end of the
20th century in the wake of the collapse of the Soviet Union, has
the idea of a dual Russia finally exhausted itself or does it still
have utility for the student of post-Soviet Russia, and of its legal
culture in particular?

Soviet Rule of Law Policy and Practice Under Gorbachev

The 'Rule of Law' is a Western concept. It resonates certain
themes: (1) a government of laws not men, or the idea of limited
government; (2) an independent judiciary along with a well-
embedded due process of law – to buffer the citizen from the
superior power of the state in civil as well as criminal justice; and
(3) a viable political and legal culture, or set of supportive attitudes, beliefs and sentiments held by governed and governors
alike, to wit, that law is the preferred means for peacefully mediating and resolving political, economic and social disputes and
conflicts.

This is the worldview Mikhail Gorbachev sought to borrow
from in the late 1980s as he attempted to reform the Soviet system.
When Gorbachev became General Secretary of the Communist
Party of the Soviet Union in 1985, the USSR Constitution of 1977,
promulgated under Leonid Brezhnev, was the prevailing *formal* law
of the land. The *actual* supreme law, however, was the party's
policies, resolutions, directives and myriad secret instructions
(dubbed by a former Soviet prosecutor as 'instructive law'; see
Neznansky, 1985, pp. 32–7), by which the state (*read*: the bureaucracy) and citizen were controlled and regulated. The Constitution
itself was the product of a drafting process dominated by the party
elite. As such, it represented a 'metapolicy' or a policy on policy-
making and implementation, and bore the imprint of the Brezhnev
leadership's vision of the party–state–society relationship.

Almost at the outset, the 1977 Constitution posited the hegemony of the Communist Party over the Soviet system. In Article 6, the party was declared 'the leading and guiding force of Soviet society, the nucleus of its political system and of all state and social organisations' (Sharlet, 1978, p. 78). The party hegemony clause implied the unity of legislative, executive and judicial powers in a single, unaccountable organisation, the CPSU, and made unmistakably clear its dominance over the process of making and carrying out public policy in the USSR.

Aside from a series of fictions on popular sovereignty (Art. 1), parliamentary supremacy (Art. 2), and the federal structure of the USSR (Chap. 8), in other clauses the Constitution did provide a reasonably accurate 'map' of the state–society relationship. These clauses concerned the hierarchical structure of the state (Art. 3), its monopoly position in the economy (Art. 11), and its 'unitary' character (Art. 70).

Finally, on the subject of individual rights, the Constitution combined democratic ideals and authoritarian reality. Yes, citizens were guaranteed freedom of speech, press and assembly, *but* only for the 'purpose of strengthening and developing' the state (Art. 50). The determination of what constituted the constructive exercise of these civil rights was of course subject to party criteria enforceable through broadly written 'political' laws administered by dependent courts (see for instance Art. 190.3 on sedition and Art. 70 on subversion of the Russia Republic Criminal Code in Berman, 1972, pp. 153, 180–1). Additionally, the right to petition government for redress of individual grievances was also granted, but subject to enabling legislation which up to 1985 had not been enacted.

Nearly all Soviet citizens implicitly understood the nominal status of these rights and few ever tested them. These few, perhaps a couple of thousand brave citizens branded by the authorities as 'dissident', beginning in the late 1960s, attempted to practise their constitutional rights of unlicensed speech and petition (critical letters to the leadership), uncensored press (*samizdat* or self-published underground periodicals), and free assembly (peaceful vigils and silent demonstrations). Invariably, their initiatives were met by various forms of repression, including bureaucratic deprivation, psychiatric confinement, forced expatriation, or, for the more persistent human rights activists, one or another type of political trial followed inevitably by conviction and incarceration. The message embedded in the rights clauses of the 1977 Constitution and in the regime's repression policy was therefore clear – the party was master, the state its obedient servant, and the citizen, while free to enjoy his or her array of socio-economic rights (job, housing, health care, education *et al.*), need not apply to the political arena, a closed space.

This then was the closed political universe inherited by Gorbachev as part leader in the mid-1980s. Soon after his elevation to power, he set for himself the task of reforming the Soviet system or, in functional language, opening up the universe of discourse and the arena for political action. To accomplish and institutionalise his task, Gorbachev, a lawyer, set out on the path of constitutional reform. More than any other Soviet leader before him, Gorbachev relied on law to effect systemic change. Beginning in 1988, Brezhnev's Constitution, which had only been amended once, in a minor way in 1981, underwent a dramatic transformation.

Because the party was still the dominant actor in the Soviet political system, the impetus for constitutional reform emerged from the specially convened 19th Party Conference in June–July 1988. The conference gave life to the phrase *pravovoe gosudarstvo*, a concept which in Soviet Marxist jurisprudence of the 1920s had a pejorative 'bourgeois' meaning, but now took on positive connotations as Gorbachev began to explicitly borrow from Western constitutional norms. Literally, the phrase means 'legal state', but in the context of *perestroika*, the popular name for Gorbachev's restructuring programme, the intended meaning was 'law-based state'. In his report to the 19th Conference, Gorbachev described as the main defining characteristic of this new conception of the Soviet state 'the supremacy of law' (Sharlet, 1992b, p. 146, n. 62).

By late 1988, the compliant Soviet legislature had converted this revolutionary idea (for the USSR) of a state limited by law into a series of constitutional amendments which significantly revised one-third of the 1977 charter. The changes created a new, competitive electoral process, a two-tier legislative system including a working parliament, and a novel (again for the USSR) Committee for Constitutional Oversight. Subsequent amendments stripped the party of its monopoly on power and added an executive presidency inspired by the French and American models.

Gradually from 1988–90 onwards, an embryonic separation of powers arrangement, the first in the history of the Soviet Union, was beginning to emerge. Its corollary, an effective system of checks and balances, was, however, not yet in sight – the Constitutional Oversight Committee reported to the new parliament, which in turn delegated enormous powers to the president. Nonetheless, Gorbachev had begun the process of prying open the closed Soviet system by changing the rules of the political game from law as a party instrument to the constitution as an agent for social change.

In addition to restructuring the system, Gorbachev strove to awaken a dormant society and energise and mobilise a more activist citizenry on behalf of his reform programme. To this end he relied on policy statements and the legislative process as well as his frequent empowering speeches. Very early in his incumbency, Gorbachev defined his *perestroika* programme in terms of the policies of *glasnost* or openness, democratisation, economic reform and 'new thinking'. Distilled into constitutional language, his first two concepts, *glasnost* and democratisation, suggested the rights of speech, press and petition, and the right of assembly and participation respectively.

Under the banner of *glasnost*, a nascent freedom of the press began to develop in the Soviet Union. As a new emphasis in information policy Gorbachev had introduced *glasnost* in 1985, and formally proposed it to the 27th Party Congress in 1986 which gave the concept the CPSU's full imprimatur. As he subsequently, in speeches and other communications, reiterated his call for more openness in public information, it became clear that *glasnost*, along with democratisation, were tactical approaches to Gorbachev's more ambitious strategy of bringing about deep economic reform in a system saddled with a vast and ossified bureaucracy. Gorbachev therefore used *glasnost* to enlist the intelligentsia and unleash the press on behalf of his *perestroika* campaign. Both intellectuals and journalists became advance men in his effort to catalyse, mobilise and involve the normally passive mass public in the effort to decentralise the command economic structures and stimulate initiative and growth.

Glasnost had its first effects on Soviet journalism, which was traditionally tightly controlled by the party apparatus and state censors. As Stephen White points out, 'Secrecy is a very well-established Russian tradition' (1993, p. 74). Even the existence of censorship was classified and could not be reported. The censors who worked in the media and the arts, in turn, ensured that the party line on politics and culture was adhered to by preventing the appearance of unflattering information, negative images and anything else deemed unduly critical or 'anti-Soviet' in the legal phrase of the day. Thus, the public largely received only positive news and uplifting books, plays and films. The party's projected image of the USSR was of a placid society, well-governed and generally trouble-free.

Under Gorbachev, journalistic *glasnost* soon revealed the approved image to be a chimera in a country wracked by serious problems and overgrown with proverbial weeds and thistles. Progressively, Soviet newspaper and magazine readers 'discovered' prostitution, drug abuse and organised crime, phenomena heretofore consigned to capitalist societies in the decadent West. The revelations became ever more astonishing as enterprising editors sought to outdo each other in the quest for ever higher circulations. Many of the most dramatic disclosures concerned the hidebound, stagnant economy. Social and legal issues were discussed next in frequency, while political, military and historical matters, at least initially, were taken up more tentatively, the informal rule among editors being the closer something was to the circles of power, the greater the caution and the practice of self-censorship. By the late 1980s, the readership of *Trud*, one of the most popular newspapers, had soared to 18 million or more, *Argumenty i Fakty*, a weekly, had the highest circulation of its kind in the world.

Adding its voice to the journalism of revelation, the Soviet public sent million of letters-to-the-editor to its favourite publications. In a single year, *Pravda*, the party's main paper, received nearly half a million letters, well in excess of the volume received by comparable Western papers. The mail volume at *Ogonek*, a muckracking magazine, surged from barely 20 letters a day in 1986 to nearly 200,000 annually a few years later. Most often, the letter writers wrote of hardship, privation and unpleasant encounters with pervasive bureaucracy. Sometimes, shocked to read stridently negative news stories, correspondents reacted by criticising the 'messenger', the media for maligning Soviet reality. One bitter reader scorned a newspaper with the comment that not even an enemy of the Soviet state could have done worse. However, as Vitalii Korotich, a crusading editor of the *perestroika* period, wrote: 'Most of our letters are about pain . . .' – abandoned children, contaminated meat, mismanagement and various rights violated (Cerf and Albee, 1990, p. 14).

In a short space of time, Gorbachev's promotion of *glasnost* accomplished a lot. Soviet citizens took up his invitation to speak out in the new genre called 'readers' mail', while investigative journalists and broadcasters turned the media into a lively, critical medium for public information. *De facto* freedom of speech and press were in the making, but the party and state bureaucracies remained in place and criticism from below still met resistance from various quarters. As censorship was relaxed, telephone editing took up some of the slack with party officials calling journalists to guide or prevent stories altogether. Gorbachev himself, the author of the policy of openness, annoyed by criticism, sometimes attempted to discipline errant editors (most of whom were party members), including Korotich on one occasion. In the streets and squares of the cities, on invisible cues from powerful local elites, the police would selectively and, more often arbitrarily, crack down on some forms of public speech, as well as harass publishers and distributors of the emerging independent press.

Examples of the political pendulum swinging between tolerance and intolerance of *glasnost* abounded during the *perestroika* period. In 1989, a Soviet Estonian journalist found himself suddenly drafted after publishing an article exposing training brutality in the army, while the following year in Moscow a petitioner bearing a 'speech on a stick' with the slogan 'Let the Nitrates Eat Bureaucrats' was detained. Police harassment under Gorbachev, however, concentrated heavily on the new independent publications, most of them small in scale, over which the party-state had little leverage – neither the power of appointment nor the possibility of withholding large rolls of newsprint. In the spirit of Gorbachev's axiom 'Anything that is not prohibited is permitted', hundreds of independent newspapers, magazines and journals addressing a diverse range of issues in another single-issue focus (e.g. *Eroticheskaya gazeta* or 'Erotica' which was quite tame by Western standards) or broadside journalism, sprang up throughout the Soviet Union. These publications were usually more critical than even the boldest of the official press and often incurred the wrath of local authorities who tended to be less committed to Gorbachev's reform programme. For instance, in a 2-month period of 1989, the distributors of *Express-Khronika* 'were detained on 20 occasions . . . subjected to administrative arrest twice . . . beaten up twice . . . fined seven times, and in all a total of 1,212 copies of the newspaper were confiscated'. Later, in 1991, an employee of the paper received nearly three weeks' administrative detention for his efforts to practise freedom of the press (Sharlet, 1992a, p. 209).

In spite of vacillations, Gorbachev well understood that if *glasnost* was to be ultimately effective as a mediatory of change in irreversibly opening up Soviet society and stimulating systemic reform, the policy would have to be translated into law. In effect, *glasnost* would need to be codified, one of the legislative tasks that Gorbachev invited the newly seated parliament to take up following the 1989 all-union elections. For drafting purposes, the legislative package on information policy was divided into three parts: a statute on *glasnost* itself, another on archival information, and a third law on the press. After going through at least six draft versions, the law on *glasnost* was never realised; and because of the potentially explosive information on past repressions in the Soviet archives, the statute governing access was also marooned in the drafting process and never came to fruition in the Soviet period. The law on the media, designed to codify freedom of the press, was finally enacted in 1990, but its passage through the political process was hardly free of conflict.

The idea of a law on the media first surfaced in a 1986 legislative agenda for the old (pre-1988 constitutional revision) Supreme Soviet inherited by Gorbachev from his predecessor Chernenko in 1985. At that time the Soviet legislature was a pro-forma extension of the party policy-making process which met briefly only twice a year. Hence, legislative drafting was done within the state bureaucracy subject to approval of the party apparatus. In 1986–7, Gorbachev was outlining the contours of the general process of systemic reform already discussed, but conservatives, reluctant to relinquish central powers, remained entrenched in the administrative system and often were able to slow his policy initiatives.

Such was the case with his 1986 proposal for a media law. Since a law on the press would touch on 'core ideological and organisational matters', it was therefore not surprising that significant differences soon developed between reformers and conservatives over the content of the draft law (Remington, 1991, p. 197). With the adversarial groups, the conservatives from positions of strength in the state legal establishment and the reformers in the think tanks, law schools and among the 'democratic' factions of the parliament, unable to reach consensus, the drafting project was becalmed in the absence of either side's ability to propel it forward for the next three years.

The constitutional reforms of 1988 provided an opening for the reformers drafting the press and other laws. With the election of the new working parliament the following year, the initiative on the press law 'passed from the bureaucracy to the legislature' (Remington, 1991, p. 190). Another year went by before the law on the press finally appeared. In the interim, the party ideological secretary meddled, the Central Committee Secretariat tried to sabotage the reform version, and the censorship agency and state publishing houses, both prospective losers in a liberal law, doggedly fought a rearguard action. A crucial break occurred in early 1990 when Gorbachev supported revision of Article 6 of the 1977 Constitution, depriving the party of its leading role in the Soviet system. By June, the reformers had prevailed and the first Soviet law codifying a free press, albeit hedged somewhat, had been adopted.

The new law proclaimed the right to 'freedom of the press' and banned censorship (Art. 1). The text then proceeded to create a system of checks and balances between state and press, and between the press and the citizen. For instance, anyone who had reached the legal majority was free to establish a publication (Art. 7), but the state reserved the right to register the publication and thus give it legal status (Art. 8). The registration application looked innocent enough (Art. 9), but the review committee was stacked with conservative bureaucrats. A publication could be shut down for disclosing an official secret (then still ill-defined), advocating the violent overthrow of the constitution, as well as other grounds (Art. 5), but the law also accorded the alleged offender the right of judicial appeal (Art. 14). Finally, a journalist's right to carry out investigate resource was secured, but absent a shield law and the concept of a 'public figure' in Soviet jurisprudence, he or she could be required to verify his or her reportage (Art. 32) and could be sued for defaming the 'honour and dignity' of an organisation (Art. 35) or public official (Art. 39). From this brief analysis, it might be said that while reformers managed to introduce into the law certain libertarian principles, the conservatives still managed to box in the press between state oversight and potentially litigious individuals, especially public officials using the courts as a deterrent to media criticism.

Beginning with the new parliament in 1989, Gorbachev had hoped to have a new *perestroika*-era constitution in place within a few years, but in the end the task eluded him. Still powerful conservative forces within the national leadership were manoeuvring behind the scenes against his reforms. As the economy crumbled, a restless and deeply discontented public was in backlash as well. Ironically, Gorbachev's success in pushing *glasnost* as well as his achievement in encouraging democratisation contributed to his downfall and the ultimate collapse of the USSR. By unbridling speech and offering journalistic license to a long-fettered press, Gorbachev had inadvertently opened the door to unintended public pressure on his presidency along with runaway ethnic nationalism in the outer republics of the union. His inability to deliver on the fruits of economic reform cost him public affection while the centrifugal forces in the provinces undercut his elite support. Increasingly desperate to salvage his programme and save his presidency, Gorbachev's efforts reached their nadir in January 1991 when he secretly authorised a violent KGB assault in breakaway Lithuania, and then, denying knowledge of the operation, ducked responsibility. Finally, after the press contradicted the Kremlin's cover story, Gorbachev, in a fit of pique, briefly proposed suspending the new press law.

In retrospect, Gorbachev had unleashed freedoms which took on a life of their own and grew irresistibly beyond his control. After the abortive coup against him, power flowed to Yeltsin and other republic leaders, and all was finally lost in the last days of 1991. Nonetheless, Gorbachev left his successors a positive legacy to build on – the enhanced status of the individual *vis-à-vis* the state, as well as the significantly greater reliance on law and constitutional process as the new 'rules of the game' (Sharlet, 1993, p. 1).

Russian Constitutionalism under Yeltsin

Russia's quest for a constitutional future began in the Soviet period. Following the federal example, appropriate amendments on electoral law and legislative structure were made to the Russian Republic Constitution of 1978. Then, after the all-union parliamentary elections in 1989, similar elections were held in the union republics in 1990. A new two-tier parliament, similar to the federal structure, was in place in the RSFSR by summer. One of the early decisions of the 1st Russian Congress of People's Deputies was to establish a Russian Constitutional Commission, and task it to draft a new union republic constitution consistent with the changes then underway in the Soviet system. Thus, from the summer of 1990 through 1991, parallel all-union and RSFSR constitutional commissions, among others, were at work on constitutional reform. By the end of the USSR and the creation of the Commonwealth of Independent States in late 1991, Soviet constitutional reform efforts had foundered over the Union Treaty issue. The Russian constitutional drafting process, however, continued on into the post-Soviet period without interruption.

The Russian Constitutional Commission was chaired by Boris Yeltsin, initially in his capacity as Speaker of the Parliament and then, after his election in June 1991, as President of Russia. His deputy on the Presidium of the Parliament, Ruslan Khasbulatov, who subsequently succeeded Yeltsin as Speaker, became Vice-Chairman of the Constitutional Commission, with People's Deputy Oleg Rumyantsev as its Executive Secretary. Rumyantsev led the drafting process from the outset.

The Commission produced its first draft in November 1990 and a second version in October 1991, but neither garnered the broad support necessary among the Russian political elite. Opposition came from various directions – conservatives uneasy over the adverse implications for the command–administrative system, ambitious politicians with their own constitutional agendas, and from provincial leaders seeking more autonomy (and in some cases, even independence) for republics and regions within the Russian Federation. Finally, a third draft Russian Constitution was taken up for discussion at the Sixth Congress in April 1992. The Congress approved the draft in principle, but referred it back to the Constitutional Commission for additional work. The draft did undergo further revisions in the course of the next year.

What did the Rumyantsev draft, as it came to be called, say about power, and, in particular, about the citizen–state relationship in the post-Soviet Russia? The Russian draftsmen were committed to creating a constitution for a democratic society. Gorbachev's inspiration to develop a law-based state had evolved into full-blown interest in Rule of Law models. The Constitutional Commission showed special interest in the American and French constitutions, and in certain aspects of the West German system. Thus, the Rumyantsev draft proposed a system of separation of powers. It involved a mixed parliamentary–presidential system with a constitutional court. In this arrangement, however, parliament was the stronger branch, a feature which did not sit well with President Yeltsin. Some of his concerns for more executive power were taken into accounting subsequent revisions, but with the result that the parliamentary and presidential models coexisted increasingly uneasily within the hybrid draft Constitution.

The drafter's attempts to accommodate the progressively conflictual ambitions of the President and his conservative parliamentary opposition were inadvertently subverting the thrust of a checks and balances system. The consequence, if the Rumyantsev draft had been adopted, might have been a continuation of the then prevailing legislative–executive mutual obstruction and resulting policy paralysis.

The division of powers question between centre and periphery was even more nettlesome. Several of the ethnic republics of the Russian Federation were showing interest in separatist and even secessionist paths to the future, and a number of regions (*oblasti*) were restless for more autonomy, resenting Moscow's heavy hand in nearly all matters. To avert an open break by the more aggressive subjects of the federation, the President hurriedly negotiated a set of power-defining treaties with the federation subjects just before the Sixth Congress opened. These three treaties with the different types of administrative units among the 89 federation subjects were collectively called the Federation Treaty. The document made considerable concessions to the spirit of federalism in the direction of decentralisation of central power over the provinces. All but two republics signed the agreement and the Sixth Congress instructed the Constitutional Commission to append the Treaty to the draft Constitution. Since the Treaty, to become fully operative, required dozens of enabling statutes, the result was a politically correct but very cumbersome, asymmetrical constitutional draft.

Within this doubly conflicted political universe, the constitutional clauses on citizen and state were more promising, but not without problems. To the Western legal eye, the draft gave both the executive and the legislature too many opportunities to amend or restrict fundamental rights and freedoms. For instance, many of the rights clauses included the caveat that exceptions could be 'established by federal law', which was potentially at odds with the birthright clause which held these rights to be natural and inalienable (Art. 13). Nonetheless, given the bleak human rights landscape of the Soviet past, the tone and direction of the draft was positive. Opening with a declaration of state sovereignty (Art. 1), the Rumyantsev draft next gave priority to 'The individual and his rights and freedoms as the supreme value', endorsed international humanitarian standards, and assigned to the state as its main obligation the protection of these rights (Art. 2). Freedom of speech, assembly and petition were found in the chapter on civil and political rights, each amply defined (Arts. 25, 31 and 33).

Freedom of the press, however, was located elsewhere in the draft, in a special section on 'Civil Society'. In this section, media rights were placed in the context of property, associational, educational, cultural, and family rights, each spelled out in some detail. One might wonder if this was appropriate material for a constitution which after all was meant to be fundamental law, or whether such concerns should not have been left to private initiative as in a Rule of Law society. However, it must be borne in mind that Russia in recent years has been emerging from decades, even centuries of legal and civil darkness; hence their compelling need to write everything down in a country in the absence of a democratic political and legal culture within which language would normally resonate.

Thus, the media clause, laid out in four parts, was also quite specific, guaranteeing freedom of the press, declaring censorship impermissible (Art. 73.1), and providing for a wide variety of ownership of mass media (Art. 73.2). Normally, the latter two provisions would seem out of place in a democratic constitution, but Russia has had a long history of state censorship and only brief experience with private ownership. The troubling part was the last which permitted the state to suspend or terminate media on the basis of federal law, subject to a court decision (Art. 73.4). This echoed the authoritarian past of the Soviet period with its distrust of private initiative and intolerance of autonomous activity. On its face, the termination section negated the preceding parts of the freedom of press clause. Beyond, it directly contradicted the freedom of speech clause which included 'the unobstructed expression of opinions and convictions' (Art. 25.1).

By spring of 1993, the legislative–executive conflict had intensified and Yeltsin, still dissatisfied with the Rumyantsev draft Constitution which he considered too pro-parliament, set up a rival constitutional commission which produced a pro-presidential draft more to his liking. In June, after he had successfully won public endorsement in the April referendum, President Yeltsin convened a Constitutional Convention to bring to a conclusion the long drafting process. The Convention, which was dominated by pro-presidential delegates, considered the Yeltsin and Rumyantsev drafts, and predictably reported in favour of a composite version heavily weighted toward the President's preferences. The position of the presidency in the separation of powers was strengthened and more executive checks on the parliament were introduced. On the division of powers issue, however, Yeltsin's Convention had little choice but to endorse the arrangements negotiated in the Rumyantsev draft. By summer of 1993, the republics and regions were in too rebellious a mood toward the centre to risk further incurring their wrath.

Of special interest here, however, were the changes introduced by the Convention's draft Constitution in the area of individual rights. These can be summarised as follows: (1) Whereas the Rumyantsev draft devoted nine chapters across two sections to the subject, the successor version streamlined rights into a single chapter; (2) the Convention's version greatly circumscribed, consolidated and defined the caveat on potential legal exceptions to rights; and (3) freedom of the press lost its erstwhile position of prominence and was subsumed in the free speech clause.

In the draft Constitution which issued from the Constitutional Convention in the summer of 1993, the many distinctions and considerable detail on individual rights of the Rumyantsev draft fell away. The rights clauses were now consolidated into a single chapter (Chap. 2). Political, civil, economic and social rights; duties and obligations; and constitutional guarantees were all combined and simplified. In the process the constitutional focus on 'civil society' was dropped.

Legal caveats to individual rights were for the most part eliminated from specific constitutional clauses, although the freedom of association clause, now reduced from a chapter and five articles to a single article, still retained language allowing for abridgement under certain circumstances (Art. 29). Toward the end of the rights chapter, the allowable grounds for state infringement were enumerated. They were defence of the constitutional system, considerations of internal security and national defence, and concerns of health, morals and the legitimate competing rights of other citizens (Art. 55). The first two criteria were potentially broad and ambiguous, and in a country with Russia's past and a weak judicial culture, liable to abuse by elites pursuing private agendas behind the facade of state power.

Most interesting, however, was the subsumption of freedom of the press under the freedom of speech clause (Art. 28). Indeed, the two rights are invisibly bound together in democratic rights theory, but press freedom has usually merited a separate conceptual identity. In the Russian treatment, freedom of the press was annexed to the speech clause at the end almost as an afterthought: 'Freedom of the mass media is guaranteed. Censorship is prohibited.' Lost in the change was the right of access and pluralism of ownership as well as the worrisome termination provision. Nonetheless in the summer version of the draft Constitution, media freedom along with all other individual and group rights were still subject to limitation by the state should their exercise prove threatening to the constitutional government, the integrity of the state or the usual concerns of public safety and the equitable balancing of citizens' rights.

Apropos the tension between media rights and state sensitivity, the Russian law on the press was issued in December 1991 after extensive debate between reformers and conservatives. Initial drafts of the law had actually been regressive compared with the Soviet law of 1990, but pro-reform parliamentary deputies ultimately prevailed and a more progressive law resulted. Still while censorship was generally prohibited, a number of conditions for its re-application were listed, including advocating the violent overthrow of the government or inciting hatred against various kinds of groups (Lawyers' Committee for Human Rights, 1993, p. 86). Russian elites, in the turbulent conditions of the transition from authoritarianism, were apparently unwilling to place their faith in the Western notion of the so-called free marketplace of ideas as a check and cultural restraint on extremism in the media; hence the enumeration of journalistic behaviour which would not be countenanced by the authorities.

While press freedom was still somewhat tentative and qualified in constitutional theory and legislative language, the position of the media was even more tenuous in the everyday political and economic realities of Russia in transition. This was due to at least two reasons. First, the press got drawn into the no-holds-barred struggle for power between President Yeltsin and the Parliament headed by his rival, Speaker Khasbulatov. Secondly, beginning in 1992, the media became another casualty of the rush to the market led by Yeltsin's Young Turk economic advisors.

In Russia the press began to reflect the split in society between the rival political camps as they fought over the constitutional distribution of power (the 'war' of the drafts), and over economic policy (to go fast or proceed slowly). Thus the press became dichotomised into reformist and conservative groups with only a few publications attempting to occupy a neutral or independent middle ground. This was perhaps understandable in a country where journalism had always been a highly politicised adjunct of party-state policy rather than an autonomous actor in the public arena. In this atmosphere and given journalists' long political socialisation in the Soviet system, partisanship came quite naturally to most newsroom personnel who still practised Soviet-style essay journalism rather than Western-style news reportage.

Thus newspapers took sides – for Yeltsin, *Kommersant*, *Moskovskii komsomolets*, *Rossiiskie vesti* and *Izvestiya* among others; while the conservative opposition in parliament could rely on *Pravda*, *Sovetskaya Rossiya*, the parliament's own paper *Rossiiskaya gazeta*, and the extremist publication *Den* to cite the best known publications. With the exception of a maverick programme or two, such as '600 Seconds', however, President Yeltsin had firm control over state television along with the former Soviet news service, now ITAR TASS which was television's main feed.

Since most citizens in Russia, as in other contemporary indus-trialised societies, get their news from TV, this gave the President a decided advantage in the power struggle.

Trying to maintain a centrist or independent position in the political arena were the two independent news agencies, Interfax and Postfaktum, and the newspapers *Nezavisimaya gazeta* (which translates as 'The Independent Newspaper'), its offshoot *Segodnya*, and to a lesser extent, the older *Moscow News* or *Moskovskie novosti* which publishes English and Russian editions.

As the political struggle heated up in 1992, each side tried to silence its opponent's press. For instance, Yeltsin's press and justice ministries periodically invoked provisions of the 1991 Russian press law to harass *Den* which was indeed frequently out-rageous. In the same spirit, Khasbulatov attempted to establish parliamentary control over *Izvestiya* which regularly criticised him. Yeltsin's ministers rose to the defence of *Izvestiya*'s recent independent status. Legal issues were joined and the *Izvestiya* case eventually reached the Russian Constitutional Court, which found in favour of the paper and against the parliament.

Nonetheless, the 'war' over control of the media raged on into 1993, as the media simultaneously came under financial pressure from the invisible laws of supply and demand of the emerging market. With *glasnost* no longer a novelty and the dramatic days of the unwinding of the Soviet system past, readership had declined precipitously while the price of newsprint spiralled upward in step with skyrocketing inflation. The real battle for survival was shifting from the editorial offices and newsrooms to the business offices and circulation departments. The shakeout had begun and would go beyond the power crisis of 1993 as the print media in particular fought each other on two fronts – over policy and public personalities on the one hand, and for readership and market share on the other. Eventually, media winners and losers will be determined by market forces rather than the politicians as Russia's still aborning press freedom meets the bottom line.

Constitution and Press in the Final Crisis of the First Republic

The first post-Soviet Russian Republic came to a fiery end in late 1993. Both constitutionalism and the press, caught in the crossfire, became casualties. By late summer of 1993 the draft Constitution of the Constitutional Convention, Yeltsin's preferred version, was in trouble in the regional and republic legislatures over the division of powers between centre and periphery, as well as a related dispute between mainly Russian regions and ethnic republics over the latter's superior political and economic rights *vis-à-vis* Moscow.

Meanwhile, the President and parliament continued to exchange political body blows. During the summer, parliament proposed a package of amendments to the extant 1978 Constitution, already a patchwork from over 300 amendments, which, if adopted, would have reduced the President to a figurehead. On 21 September, Yeltsin counterattacked with his now famous Decree No. 1400 by which he suspended parts of the Constitution, dissolved parliament and took control of its newspaper *Rossiiskaya gazeta*.

For the next 12 days the two sides exchanged constitutional salvoes and press broadsides, each claiming legitimacy while decrying the illegality of its opponent's actions. Then on 3 October former Vice President Alexander Rutskoi, from his base in the besieged parliament building, called on his armed supporters to attack the main TV station. The choice of target was not accidental; the opposition had long complained of unfair treatment by state television, which was seen as a pro-Yeltsin bastion. The assault failed and the following day troops loyal to the President successfully attacked and overran the seat of parliament, the Russian White House, which Khasbulatov and Rutskoi had turned into an armed camp. Just as the idea of constitutionalism was in shreds, the press itself was bloodied in the withering crossfire. A number of journalists were killed and wounded, mostly by snipers from inside the White House, while others were beaten by Yeltsin's forces after the surrender. The battle for Moscow was over, the executive branch had won and the First Russian Republic had come to a violent end.

The State and the Press During the Interregnum

Just as his adversary Rutskoi had initiated the violence with an attack on the pro-Yeltsin television centre, the President, in the days after his military victory, launched an administrative assault against the opposition press. By executive decree, which was for the time being the only law in the land, a number of papers were banned including *Den*, several were suspended including *Pravda* and *Sovetskaya Rossiya*, and censorship was temporarily reimposed at other papers including *Nezavisimaya gazeta* and *Segodnya*, which ran blank spaces where stories had been censored. Who were the censors? They were the same experienced hands from the Soviet period called back into service. When Vladimir Solodin, the former Soviet chief censor who ran the operation was asked about this, he replied indignantly 'You wouldn't expect me to use pastry chefs, would you?' (Gambrell, 1993, p. 70).

Good news came on the heels of the banning and the censors' arrival. During the interregnum, Russia's first independent television network was established, breaking the state's long monopoly of this vital medium. Even more important, the independent and moderate papers and even the pro-Yeltsin press came together to denounce the bans, suspensions and censors. The Yeltsin administration's immediate reaction was to withdraw the censors. A deal was struck which allowed *Pravda*, after it had changed its editor, to resume publishing (although several weeks later financial conditions forced its temporary closure – another new feature of the postcommunist information marketplace).

Two months later in early December, a similar manifestation of press freedom occurred. It was during the election campaign for a new parliament decreed by President Yeltsin. A parallel campaign for a new draft Russian Constitution, an exceptionally one-sided document which Yeltsin had ordered prepared during October, was also underway for a constitutional referendum to be held on Election Day, 12 December 1993. Left-wing candidates, among others, were criticising the draft Constitution, provoking the President to threaten to pull the TV plug on their campaigns if they did not desist. Yeltsin's threat to punitively withhold media time evoked a storm of criticism from nearly every corner, even the pro-Yeltsin parties. A day or two later, the presidential press spokesman was sent before the television cameras to conciliate for the second time in the interregnum. Clarifying Yeltsin's position, he declared the President in favour of 'constructive criticism' of the constitutional draft, but against 'brazen rejection'. Nothing further was said about reducing candidates' TV time. Somehow in the carnage of October and amidst the arbitrariness of the inter-regnum, a free press culture, which had taken root in Gorba-chev's time, had not only survived Yeltsin's cavalier approach, but was beginning to flower.

The Yeltsin Constitution passed, on 12 December, ushering in the Second Russian republic. As a victor's Constitution pre-sidential supremacy has replaced the separation of powers, and the spirit of unitarism has superseded the emerging federalism. However, as most observers in Russia and abroad agree, the chapter on 'The rights and freedoms of the individual and citizen', while not unflawed in conception, constitutes a major step forward in Russia's quest for a democratic future. Will these rights, including freedom of the press, be steadfastly implemented and safeguarded, or will they turn out to be merely declarative rights which wither at the first collision with political reality? The larger question which framing this inquiry concerns the concep-tion of 'dual Russia' introduced at the beginning of this chapter. Can the dualism be consigned to the past; will the new parties and blocs help knit together and mediate between state and society? Or might Russia slip backward into a hypertrophic state looming over a stunted society and complacent citizenry? One hopes not, but Russia's journey to the future will most surely be a difficult one during which hope and despair will meet again and again.

PART TWO

Patterns of Public Policy

6

The Economy: The Rocky Road from Plan to Market

PETER RUTLAND

Six years after Gorbachev took office, his programme of economic reform was overtaken by political and economic disintegration. The attempted coup of August 1991 was a reaction to this political and economic collapse, and to the failure of Gorbachev's policies. The new leadership which took over in the wake of the coup decided that there was no alternative but to break with the old model and move the Russian economy in the direction of market economics. In October 1991 President Yeltsin appointed Yegor Gaidar as First Deputy Prime Minister in charge of economic reform. The political vacuum created by the collapse of the USSR and the dismantling of the Central Committee apparatus, which had previously steered the planned economy, gave Yeltsin and Gaidar a window of opportunity to introduce radical economic reform.

Gaidar was a 35-year-old former academic who had been an editor at several Communist Party publications, but who had not been directly involved with the reform programmes proposed under Gorbachev. He decided to take as his model the shock therapy launched in Poland in January 1990, and moved swiftly to introduce similar measures in Russia. The price liberalisation introduced in January 1992, in the event, failed to stabilise the Russian economy. Instead, the economy slid into hyperinflation while simultaneously experiencing a sharp fall in output and a

131

slump in living standards. Ensuing anger with the impact of the economic reform deepened the political confrontation between Yeltsin and the Russian parliament. Thus the events of 1991–2 set in train a downward spiral of political and economic interactions from which Russia has still not recovered.

It is important to view the economic policies of the Gaidar government in the context of the disastrous economic situation that they inherited. The system of central planning which Stalin imposed in the 1930s at tremendous human cost ground on for five decades and transformed the economy of the USSR in all its aspects: geography, institutions, social structure and psychology. After 1985, the old system started to break down. The power of central planners steadily eroded, with enterprises and republics behaving in an increasingly independent manner. From 1988 on, the previous macroeconomic and foreign trade balance of the Soviet economy also collapsed. These processes have left the post-Soviet economy in something of an institutional vacuum: it is neither a market nor a planned economy, but a curious hybrid whose laws of motion are as yet unclear.

Most articles and books written on economic policy in the post-Soviet states adopt a prescriptive rather than descriptive mode: they say what policy *should* be, rather than what it actually *is*. This chapter seeks to redress the balance by analysing the actual processes under way in the Russian economy. The reform government which took power in 1991 did not take over a *tabula rasa*: they inherited an economic system in the throes of tortuous and painful disintegration.

The Origins of the Soviet Economic System

How was it possible that the world's second superpower, capable of conquering space and building a formidable arsenal of nuclear weapons, was unable to feed its own people and provide them with the basic necessities of modern urban life? In order to grasp the paradoxes of the Soviet economy, it is necessary to view it in its historical context.

Since the 1930s the USSR operated under a centrally planned economy, or CPE. This was a highly distinctive form of economic organisation, in which the conventional laws of supply and demand, taken for granted in the West, did not apply. After all, the CPE was the result of a political struggle in which property rights were taken away from social classes and vested int he state. Stalin tried to establish a state monopoly over all forms of economic activity. Private ownership of productive assets (stores, workshops, farms, tools, factories) was abolished, to the maximum feasible extent. All such assets became the property of the state, managed by directors who were answerable to the industrial ministries based in Moscow, and to the network of political monitoring agencies (the party and the secret police) which spread down into every factory.

The CPE had its roots in Marx's vision of a unified economy which would run itself like a giant factory, free from the anarchy of the capitalist market. The New Economic Policy (NEP) which Lenin persuaded the Communist Party to accept in 1921 was a retreat from the utopian Marxist vision. NEP replaced state food requisitioning with a market in grain, and thus recognised the need for the state and private sectors to coexist (at least in the short run). In 1928 Stalin abandoned NEP, and set out to construct an economic system which would guarantee the CPSU's monopoly of political power, and enable him to impose his development goals on the economy. Independent peasants were forced to join collective farms (*kolkhozy*), whose produce was requisitioned by the state. The farmers scratched out a living from the small private plots that they were allowed to retain.

During the first 5 year plan (1928–32) Stalin launched the USSR on the path of 'extensive' growth, pumping capital and labour out of agriculture and consumption and pouring it into heavy industry. The coal mines, steel mills and power stations were seen as the key to economic growth and military preparedness. 'Intensive' growth (the expansion of production thanks to the more efficient use of resources) made only a marginal contribution at this stage.

Thanks to the vast natural and human resources of the USSR, Stalin's industrialisation strategy turned the USSR into the world's second largest economy. But Soviet citizens saw precious few of the benefits. Real living standards halved during the 1930s, and only regained the 1928 level by the late 1950s. By 1960 it was clear to the Soviet leadership that the scope for further extensive growth was exhausted. Capital accumulation was at maximum levels, and the labour reserves of the country were fully mobilised.

The running down of the rural economy meant that the USSR became a net importer of food in 1963, while popular pressure for improved living conditions was mounting. Attention turned to reforms designed to shift the Soviet economy onto a path of intensive growth.

Through the 1960s and 1970s, however, things continued pretty much as before. During the Brezhnev era (1964–82) the annual growth rate slowly declined, from 6.5 per cent to 2 per cent a year – but was still positive. Thus consumers saw their living standards roughly double. Most families acquired a television and refrigerator, although only 1 in 20 owned a car. An informal 'social contract' meant that everyone was guaranteed a job, a minimal subsistence income and rudimentary housing. The deficit of consumer durables meant that by 1990 consumers had accumulated 280 billion rubles (R280 bn) in savings accounts, a sum equivalent to 7 months' retail spending. This monetary overhang exacerbated the persistent goods 'famine'. Purchasing power comparisons show the average Soviet citizen's living standard was roughly 25 per cent of that prevailing in the developed capitalist economies. One has to go to a country such as Turkey or Mexico to find a comparison favourable to the USSR in these terms.

The economic stability of the USSR during the Brezhnev years was misleading: Soviet economic achievements were a house built on sand. Resources were poured into maintaining high output levels in heavy industry and defence plants, while investment in the social and economic infrastructure was neglected. The crunch came in the late 1970s, with crises in agriculture, transport and energy. The exhaustion of easily accessible natural resources led Brezhnev to launch hugely expensive projects in oil, gas and atomic power. At the same time, the big-spending ministries and regional party organisations forged ahead with costly prestige projects such as the Baikal–Amur railway and the 1982 'Food Programme'. Squeezed by these massive and unproductive investments, the economy stalled. There was probably zero overall growth between 1980 and 1985 (although this was disguised in the official statistics: see Table 6.1). After 1978 rationing of key food items was introduced in many outlying regions.

By 1985, when Gorbachev came to power, it was clear that the sorry condition of the economy threatened the status of the USSR as a superpower. By 1980 the USSR had lost its claims to

TABLE 6.1   *Soviet economic performance, 1971–88**

	1971–5	1976–80	1981–5	1986	1987	1988
GNP	3.2	2.2	1.9	4.0	1.3	1.5
Industry	5.6	2.4	2.0	2.7	2.9	2.4
Agriculture	−0.1	1.6	2.1	8.3	−3.1	−3.1
Consumption	3.0	2.0	0.8	−1.5	1.0	1.5
Investment	7.8	3.4	3.5	8.3	4.7	n.a.
Labour productivity	1.4	1.0	1.4	2.3	3.2	3.1

*Average annual rates of growth, per cent. The consumption figure is *per capita*.
Sources: These data are the CIA estimates, taken from *The Soviet Economy in 1988: Gorbachev Changes Course*, a paper presented by the CIA and DIA to the National Security Economic Subcommittee of the Joint Economic Committee, US Congress (14 April 1989). Figures for agriculture 1971–80 are taken from *Narodnoe khozyaistvo SSSR v 1987g* (Moscow: Finansy i statistika, 1988).

be the world's second largest economy, having been overtaken by Japan (with half the population and none of the USSR's vast natural resources). By 1986 the USSR occupied first place in the world league table only in the production of oil, steel, iron ore, potatoes and sugar – hardly the sinews of a 21st century superpower. They occupied sixth place in the production of radios (just behind Singapore), and of passenger cars (behind Italy and France). Given what is known about poor product quality and false statistics, the real situation was even worse.

Gorbachev's poor economic management added a new problem to the list of economic woes: a growing fiscal crisis. In 1988 the government ran a R36 bn deficit on a R500 bn budget, a sum equal to 7.3 per cent of Soviet GNP. Previously, one of the few advantages of the CPE had been tight control over the government budget. Budget discipline eroded after 1985, due to increasingly erratic behaviour by the political leadership, who subjected the bureaucracies to a series of bewildering reorganisations. Also, production costs were steadily rising, while prices were held constant. The gap was filled with government subsidies (food subsidies, for instance, rose from R2 bn in 1965 to R73 bn in 1990 bn). These structural imbalances were compounded by a series of exogenous shocks. Falling world oil prices meant a loss of $40 bn export revenues, while cleaning up after Chernobyl and the Armenian earthquake cost another R20 bn.

It was clear, however, that the Soviet economy was not merely suffering from poor political leadership. Nor was it facing a cyclical crisis that would clear up on its own accord after a few years. The economy experienced a steady, long-run decline in productive efficiency, which was in turn the product of deep-seated contradictions within the central planning system itself. The problem was that despite these chronic economic problems, all the key political and economic elites had a strong vested interest in the preservation of the status quo. This meant that the political leadership found it impossible to build a coalition in favour of market reform.

The Centrally Planned Economy

How, then, did centrally planning work? At the centre stood the State Planning Committee, Gosplan, which drew up a grid chart matching the flow of available inputs (labour, capital, and raw materials) with the set of desired outputs. Beneath Gosplan were some 60 economic ministries, supervising 120,000 factories, farms and other units in industry, construction, commerce and agriculture.

The ministries allocated output targets to enterprises in the form of an annual plan. Plans were altered so frequently that the 5 year plan was little more than a forecasting exercise: the annual plan was the operational document. The inputs which factories needed to fulfil their output targets were provided by the State Committee on Supplies (Gossnab). In addition to the economic ministries, there were 20 State Committees supervising functional aspects of the economy (prices, labour, etc.). Beneath the ministries, regional soviets had control of a limited amount of local industry.

This system of central planning was incredibly complicated and difficult to manage. The national leadership steered the economy through a network of political agencies which paralleled the economic bureaucracies. There was the Communist Party, which ran a network of branches in every farm and factory. Powerful regional party officials used their political muscle to play a trouble-shooting role in the local economy: forcing through a local construction project, helping a factory acquire scarce supplies, persuading factory directors to help with the harvest and so forth. The personal networks between local political and economic managers were very important to the smooth functioning of the system. The party tried to use its monopoly of political authority to lay down priorities – such as saving energy, or building a pipeline. Unfortunately, there were so many 'priorities' in force that the centre lost the ability to make much of an impact.

The huge quantity of information flowing up and down the pyramid of planning institutions had to be simplified and made manageable. The planners relied on crude, physical measures of output (thousands of cars or tons of coal). Managers knew that output targets had to be met, even if it came at the expense of other goals set by their ministry (such as introducing new products or conserving energy). The central plan targets paid little attention to product quality – only 15 per cent of their manufactured goods met current world standards for quality and reliability. Soviet consumers had little choice but to accept what ever products were made available to them. Crude physical targets may have suited the Soviet economy of the 1930s, when it revolved around a few simple products (coal, oil, steel), but they are grossly inappropriate for a modern economy.

The biggest headache facing Soviet managers on a daily basis was the unreliability of supplies. The Soviet economy seemed to operate under conditions of permanent shortage. Plans were so 'taut' that even the smallest interruption in deliveries could threaten plan fulfilment, and in response managers hoarded stocks or traded on informal networks to procure the supplies they needed.

A striking feature of the CPE was the passive role played by money and prices. Planning took place in physical terms, and money flows were only calculated after the basic plan was constructed. Prices bore scant relation to production costs – retail prices covered only about one-third of the cost of producing food, for example. Managers worried about meeting output targets, and did not care whether or nor they made a profit. They knew that at the end of the year their ministry would always cover their losses. Firms faced what Hungarian economist Janos Kornai termed a 'soft budget constraint'. Capital investment was treated as a gift from above, and there were no incentives to using it efficiency.

The planners tried to make their job easier by concentrating production in a handful of very large enterprises, such as the Kama truck plant, which had 120,000 employees in a single location. In most product categories two or three monopolists dominated the Soviet market. Supplies and equipment would be hauled over hundreds or even thousands of miles – at subsidised transport rates. These oversized firms created massive company towns, building their housing and even running their own farms to provide for their own workers.

An important behavioural feature of the Soviet planning system was the 'ratchet effect'. Productivity gains would earn firms handsome bonuses for the initial year, but would mean higher targets in subsequent years. Thus there were few incentives for managers and workers to show initiative and innovate, which meant that the CPE strongly inhibited technological progress. While the USSR enjoyed some spectacular successes such as Sputnik, it lagged 6–10 years behind the USA in leading-edge electronic and computer technology despite the vast amount of resources poured into scientific institutions.

The CPE suited some economic sectors better than others. The system had been designed to maximise the growth of the military–industrial sector, which accounted for at least 25 per cent of Soviet industry. Mining and heavy industry also did fairly well, but agriculture, construction, and consumer goods and services were all severely deformed. Agriculture was the Achilles heel of the Soviet economy. While labour productivity in Soviet industry was about 30–50 per cent of the US level, in agriculture it was 5–10 per cent. Despite having 20 per cent of the labour force in agriculture, the USSR still had to import about 10 per cent of its food needs.

Gorbachev's Economic Reforms

Economic reform did not appear on the national agenda for the first time when Gorbachev took office in 1985. On the contrary, the structural failings of the CPE had been analysed in Soviet economics journals and in the popular press since the early 1960s.

Khrushchev experimented with a broad range of reforms, the most ambitious being an attempt to devolve power from the central ministries to 102 regional economic councils. Khrushchev's reforms were hasty and poorly designed, and were reversed after his fall from power in 1964. In 1965 prime minister Kosygin tried to increase enterprise independence by replacing output targets with a number of financial indicators, such as profits. The measure was squashed by bureaucrats and party officials hostile to the changes.

What Gorbachev brought was not, therefore, a new diagnosis of the USSR's economic ill,s nor a new set of prescriptions about how to cure them. Rather, Gorbachev's assertive style convinced people that he had the energy and political will to make sure that this time around the reforms would actually be implemented.

The Learning Phase, 1985–6

Gorbachev's six-year struggle to reform the Soviet political and economic system was to end in disaster. His reforms led not to the revival of the Soviet system, but to its disintegration. Among the reasons for this failure was his unwillingness to embark upon serious economic reform.

Gorbachev chose to begin with political rather than economic reform – in contrast to the strategy followed by the Chinese leadership since 1978. While Gorbachev's political liberalisation spiralled beyond his control, his economic reforms never really materialised. As time wore on, Gorbachev became more willing to talk about radical economic reform. Unfortunately, Gorbachev proved unable or unwilling to persuade the all-union Supreme Soviet and the leaders of the Soviet republics to implement his economic plans. Historians will argue over whether *perestroika* was doomed to fail because the obstacles to success were too great, or whether Gorbachev himself can be blamed for failing to grasp the nettle of market reform.

Gorbachev's early speeches indicate that he did not think that a radical overhaul of the system of central planning was required. His initial strategy was to promote the 'acceleration' of economic growth, by shifting investment from costly irrigation projects into the machine tool sector. His initial approach to reform was traditional relying on centrally-managed political campaigns. Shortly after taking office in 1985 he launched Brezhnev-style discipline campaigns against alcoholism and corruption. These campaigns succeeded in arresting thousands of officials and slashing official alcohol sales, but had no discernible impact on economic efficiency. Another innovation typical of Gorbachev's top-down approach was the introduction of a new system of quality control, called *gospriemka*, in 1987. Teams of outside inspectors were placed in factories and told to rigorously apply state quality control standards. Vociferous opposition from managers and workers angry at the imposition of outside monitors forced the abandonment of the programme.

By mid-1986, in the wake of Chernobyl, Gorbachev started to acknowledge that some sort of radical restructuring (*perestroika*) of the economic mechanism was in order. The main thrust of the reform programme which emerged in an *ad hoc* fashion lay in three directions: decentralising decision making; promoting new forms of ownership; and opening the economy to international trade. Rather than abandon the CPE model entirely, the idea was to make it work more effectively by casting aside ideological dogmas and introducing greater flexibility. Market-type forces were to be allowed a place within the CPE, but it was not until 1988 that Gorbachev started talking openly about a 'market' economy. (And even then he usually talked of a 'planned' or 'regulated' market economy.)

Decentralisation of the Planning System

The centrepiece of Gorbachev's economic reform was the new Law on the State Enterprise, introduced in June 1987. This was a complex and contradictory measure, whose aim was to reduce ministerial interference and increase managerial freedom.

In theory, planners were to abandon mandatory targets in favour of indirect guidelines. Government purchases, through a new system of 'state orders' (*goszakazy*) would be steadily reduced and the centralised supply system would be sharply curtailed. The new system would need fewer bureaucrats, so the staff of the central ministries was cut by one-third. The industrial sections in the CPSU Central Committee apparatus were also abolished.

Enterprises were to be self-financing, and would produce according to customer contracts with freely negotiated prices.

However, political opposition to the price increases that would result (since current prices did not cover costs) meant that price liberalisation was not implemented. The new law expanded the role of 'Work Collective Councils', giving them the right to elect the factory director, in line with Gorbachev's democratisation programme. A 1990 amendment to the law revoked the right to elect directors, but by then it was too late: the ministries had effectively lost control of their enterprises.

These reforms were effectively dead on arrival. First, it was unrealistic for the Soviet leadership to insist that firms meet their targets for the twelfth 5 year plan (1986–90). This undermined the increased autonomy for firms which was supposed to be the keystone of the reform. Second, the new system suffered from some serious design flaws. Several crucial issues were fudged or ignored, such as bankruptcy, unemployment and price reform. It made no sense to give managers more freedom (for example, to increase wages) without a radical liberalisation of prices. This merely sowed the seeds of future hyperinflation.

Promoting New Forms of Ownership

In 1987 new laws encouraged the formation of cooperatives and 'individual labour activity'. Private and cooperative cafes, shops and taxis flourished, and by December 1988 they employed 787,000 (out of a workforce of 135 million), rising to 11 million by late 1991 (9 per cent of the labour force).

This was a novel development for the USSR, but a far cry from the restoration of capitalism. While the coops made life a little easier for the Soviet consumer, they were reined in by price controls, licensing requirements and limitations on hiring labour. These were mostly confined to the service sector: few got involved in manufacturing. Leasing of industrial units to teams of workers began in 1988, in emulation of Hungarian experience, and a legal framework was provided in 1989. Leaseholders took advantage of lower tax rates and slacker wage norms to boost average wages, and the number of workers in leased firms rose to 4 million by 1991.

There was considerable opposition to the new entrepreneurs, both from state managers who did not appreciate the competition, and from citizens who saw the coops as profiteering from shortages. The coops only really took root in the Baltic republics, Moscow and Leningrad. In most provinces, local officials were able to strangle the nascent cooperative movement in its cradle. This nascent private sector, moreover, did not represent the kernel of an invading market economy. The successful coops were those that found a niche within the interstices of the CPE, providing services to state enterprises (which often sponsored them), and taking advantage of the looser profit regulations.

An important flaw was that, unlike in China, *perestroika* left agricultural management virtually unchanged. In late 1988 Gorbachev started to push the idea of leasing land to individual farmers, but there were many ways in which farm managers could make life difficult for leaseholders, by denying them access to equipment and supplies. By 1991 there were only 47,000 leasehold farms, with less than 1 per cent of arable land.

Increased International Integration

The problems of economic reform seemed so daunting that leading Soviet economists persuaded Gorbachev that the task could only be tackled with outside help. International factors could assist reform in a variety of ways.

First, Western imports (of food, consumer goods and machine tools) would help keep the Soviet economy going through the dislocations which would accompany reform, and would provide incentives for managers and workers to embrace the new methods.

Second, the monopolistic structure of Soviet industry made it difficult for planners to come up with fair and realistic prices. Making the ruble partially convertible and taking world prices as a benchmark would help shorten the adjustment period.

Third, expanding cooperation with Western businesses would promote an influx of technology and know-how. In 1987 new rules were issued encouraging joint ventures, and the number of joint ventures rose from 23 in 1987 to 3,400 in April 1991, with 117,000 employees and total capital of R7 bn. In 1988 the former monopoly of the Ministry of Foreign Trade was broken, and by 1989 roughly one-third of all foreign trade was being conducted directly by Soviet enterprises.

These developments, encouraging though they were, ran into severe problems. Internationalisation was not a magic wand which could amazingly rescue the Soviet economy from its plight. The Soviet economy was highly autarchic: only 10 per cent of GNP was traded, and two-thirds of that was with the former socialist bloc (the members of the Council of Mutual Economic Assistance, or CMEA). The major constraint was the limited capacity of the Soviet economy to boost exports. The USSR ran a trade deficit in three of the four years 1987–90, and accumulated debts of $68 bn by 1991, up from $25 bn in 1985. Oil, gas, minerals and weapons accounted for 70 per cent of exports, as Soviet manufactured goods were not competitive in the West because of their low quality.

Unfortunately, the liberalisation of foreign trade only worsened the situation. Joint ventures imported twice as much as they exported, while a series of scandals revealed that firms were exporting scarce materials (such as metals and fertiliser) at bargain prices, and importing consumer goods, computers and so forth in return.

Military Conversion

In December 1988 Gorbachev announced cuts of 500,000 in the 3.2 mn armed forces. This was followed up in December 1990 with a vague plan for the conversion of defence plants to civilian production. The plan was extremely conservative, calling for vast additional investments to retool the factories according to centrally-managed programmes (R30 bn over five years). Despite promises to cut 15 per cent from defence spending, even in 1991 there were few signs of serious cuts in the funding for defence plants, and civilian production at these plants merely crept up from 43 per cent in 1988 to 54 per cent in 1991.

The Struggle for Market Reform

As *perestroika* unfolded, clear contradictions emerged between the political elements of the programme – *glasnost* and democratisation – and the economic reforms. It was not a good idea to try to democratise a political system while simultaneously launching a reform programme, in the middle of an economic crisis.

Glasnost increased the opportunities for people to express their discontent with the economic situation. Investigative journalists filled the papers with articles showing people just how badly off they really were. The elections of March 1989 and March 1990 saw humiliating defeats for Communist Party candidates, especially officials, with 'anti-establishment' candidates capitalising on popular discontent with food rationing, poor housing, pollution and corruption.

By 1989 it was clear that *perestroika* was not producing the hoped-for burst in economic growth. On the contrary, shortages of such basic items as sugar, meat, soap and cigarettes were spreading, as one after another they fell prey to panic buying and disappeared from the shops. In the summer of 1989, the deteriorating economic situation triggered a wave of strikes by some 500,000 coal miners. The government, acutely aware of its lack of popular authority, immediately capitulated to the miners' demands for improved pay and benefits. Strike threats from oil and steel workers won similar concessions in 1990. The main beneficiary of this wave of popular unrest was Boris Yeltsin, who managed to get himself elected as President of the Russian Republic in May 1990 despite intense opposition from Gorbachev.

Thus, by pursuing *glasnost* and democratisation Gorbachev sowed a field of dragon's teeth for his *perestroika* programme. His political manoeuvrings were perhaps necessary for the consolidation of his own personal power, but they sharply reduced the leadership's room for manoeuvre in economic policy. Political liberalisation made it far more difficult to take touch decisions that would hurt the interests of certain industrial sectors or social groups. Gorbachev's vision of *perestroika* was of a carefully managed process, with himself playing a pivotal role, balancing the conflicting demands of the democratic Left and the conservative Right. As time wore on, Gorbachev found it increasingly difficult to maintain this balance, and his policy lurched violently from one side to the other.

1989–90 saw a bewildering parade of economic reform proposals. Some were considered too radical, some not radical enough, but none found a consensus for action among the old and new political elites. Gorbachev became more vocal in his advocacy of reform, but repeatedly backed down in the face of conservative opposition.

The first team of reform economists, led by Leonid Abalkin, reported in November 1989. Prime Minister Nikolai Ryzhkov rejected their plan as too radical – but his own programme was in turn rejected by the USSR Supreme Soviet as being too conservative. In March 1990 Gorbachev renewed his commitment to radical economic reform, and the Abalkin team published a new, more ambitious plan. Ryzhkov again rejected Abalkin's proposals, and presented an alternative plan which proposed 100–200 per cent increases in food prices in order to balance the budget. The USSR Supreme Soviet rejected the Ryzhkov plan on the grounds that it was Polish-style 'shock therapy' without any real structural reform to sweeten the pill.

Over the summer, Soviet and Western economists set to work on a programme capable of meeting the various conflicting demands being made on Gorbachev. At one point six different teams of economists were closeted in various dachas working on draft programmes, under the auspices of different government agencies. Gorbachev's rhetoric shifted in favour of radical reform. In a speech on 17 August he used the word 'privatisation' for the first time.

Stanislav Shatalin, a former Gorbachev adviser now working for Boris Yeltsin, came up with a '500 days' plan for the transformation of the CPE into a market economy (on the basis of an earlier draft by radical economist Grigorii Yavlinsky). The plan proposed the rapid abolition of central ministries, subsidies and plan targets, but with price liberalisation postponed to the second phase of the programme. Shatalin's plan was politically appealing – although it was hard to see how subsidies could be abolished before prices were freed.

In October Gorbachev rejected the Shatalin plan, offering instead a conservative stabilisation programme. The RSFSR parliament, loyal to Yeltsin, decided to press ahead on its own with the Shatalin plan. Meanwhile, most of the other republics were unhappy with both the Gorbachev and Shatalin plans, since they seemed to leave too much central control in Moscow. (For example, Shatalin proposed a single currency issued by a federal reserve bank in Moscow. Throughout the latter part of the year Yeltsin played a game of bluff and counter-bluff with Gorbachev.

TABLE 6.2   *Economic performance of the Commonwealth of Independent States, 1989–92 (per cent change over previous year)*

	1989	1990	1991	1992
GDP	+3	−4	−8	−20
produced national income	+2.3	−3.4	−10.1	−18.5
industrial output	+1.9	−1.1	−7.8	−18.2
consumer goods output	+7.7	+6.5	−4.5	−15
agricultural output	+1.5	−2.6	−6.9	−10
capital investment	+5	+1	−12	−45
retail turnover	+8.4	+10.5	−9.6	−36.7
volume of services	+7.4	+5.2	−18.5	−35.9

Source: 'Ekonomika Sodruzhestva v 1992 godu', *Delovoi mir*, 10 March 1993, p. 10.

Many of Yeltsin's economic advisers resigned, unsure whether Yeltsin was really prepared to break with Gorbachev.

Amid a growing sense of panic and open talk of a 'Jaruzelski variant', Gorbachev won additional powers from the USSR Supreme Soviet to rule by decree. Yeltsinites were convinced that Gorbachev had abandoned reform and turned to the Right. Polls showed Gorbachev's popularity rating falling from 52 per cent in December 1989 to 21 per cent in October 1990.

In November 1990 Gorbachev used his presidential powers to raise the price of luxury goods, to enact a 40 per cent tax on the dollar earnings of exporters, and to impose output targets for 1991. In December Ryzhkov suffered a heart attack and was replaced as USSR Prime Minister by Valentin Pavlov, up to this point the finance minister. In March 1991 Pavlov raised retail prices by 60 per cent (with compensation payments for consumers). Apart from a brief general strike in Minsk, the Belorussian capital, social response to the price increases was surprisingly muted.

1991: The Collapse of the Planned Economy

The Breakdown of Central Planning

The political deadlock in Moscow and the growing 'war of laws' between Moscow and the republics caused a breakdown in the system of central planning and mounting economic chaos. In the first 9 months of 1991 GNP fell 12 per cent, consumption fell 17 per cent, and investment 20 per cent. Food output fell 8 per cent and industrial output fell 6.4 per cent. Many firms nevertheless increased profits in 1991, as they took advantage of greater laxity in price setting. By mid-1991 45 per cent of industrial products, and 60 per cent of consumer goods manufactures, were sold at 'free' prices (set by the producer) or 'contract' prices (agreed between producer and customer enterprises). In the first 9 months of 1991 retail prices rose 103 per cent, and although retail spending rose 66 per cent in money terms in real terms it fell 24 per cent. By mid-1991 the monetary overhang – unspent rubles in the hands of the population and in savings accounts – amounted to R570 bn.

The 1990 inflation was primarily a product of years of suppressed inflation. The old price structure became increasingly unrealistic, with black market prices rising 100 per cent in 1991, and standing at 3 to 5 times the official prices for the same goods – which had disappeared from the shelves.

While industrial prices rose 164 per cent, agricultural procurement prices only rose 56 per cent. Farmers were caught in a price scissors, and responded by refusing to sell grain to the state and cutting back on sowing for the next harvest. Given the imbalances in the Soviet economic system, liberalisation produced perverse outcomes. In 1990 fruit and vegetables were taken off the state procurement system – with the result that output fell while prices rose 40 per cent.

Industrial firms struck out for independence from the central planning system. A June 1990 law allowed state enterprises to convert themselves into joint stock companies (JSCs), with most shares bought by other state firms (usually their customers and suppliers). By January 1991 1200 JSCs, many of them grouped together into holding companies (variously described as 'concerns', 'associations' and so forth). This process has been described as '*nomenklatura* privatisation' or 'spontaneous privatisation', since these JSCs were effectively controlled by their old managers, now freed from ministerial tutelage.

The state firms also moved quickly to set up banking and trading networks to take over the coordination functions abandoned by the centre. In 1990 the old sectoral state banks were abolished, and more than 2000 aggressive new 'commercial' banks sprang up, mostly controlled by industrial enterprises and specialising in inter-firm lending. As a result credit issues rose 36 per cent, to R496 bn, in 1991. Before long 'bank wars' broke out as the USSR State Bank and the RSFSR Central Bank struggled to reign in the commercial banks.

1991 also saw the emergence of over 100 commodity exchanges (*birzhy*), where everything from oil to passenger cars to dollars was traded at free prices. Large state enterprises dominated the exchanges, although a new breed of aggressive entrepreneurs emerged as middlemen. The exchanges only handled less than 5 per cent of total trade turnover, but they were important in setting prices for the emerging market economy. (Although their prices were typically highly inflated.)

Tax revenues collapsed in the course of the year, to 40 per cent of the planned level. Spending contracted to 70 per cent of the planned level, leaving a R200 bn budget deficit (20 per cent of GDP) which was covered by the printing of rubles. By the end of 1991 while the 'official' commercial rate was R1.6 to the dollar the rate on dollar auctions was reaching R90 per dollar.

The International Debt Crisis

By the end of 1991 the USSR was close to defaulting on its $58 bn hard currency debt (not to mention its $17 bn debt with former CMEA members and other soft currency partners). Some $22 bn was due in repayments by the end of 1992, and there was little chance that the USSR could find such a sum. It even turned out that Gorbachev had sold off 80 per cent of Soviet gold reserves (worth some $15 bn) since 1988 in a desperate attempt to keep the economy afloat.

The collapse of CMEA and the shift to hard currency payments from January 1991 (at Moscow's insistence) caused a catastrophic 590 per cent drop in trade with East Europe. Trade with capitalist countries also fell 33 per cent, because of the disruptive reorganisation of foreign trade. The government was forced to cut imports ruthlessly in 1991 to keep the current account in balance.

The crisis stimulated urgent calls for emergency assistance from the West, such as the 'Window of Opportunity' programme authored by Graham Allison and Grigorii Yavlinsky, which proposed a $14 bn Marshall Plan to finance the transition to capitalism in the USSR. However, the London G7 meeting in July 1991 turned down such proposals, on the grounds that the political chaos in the Soviet Union meant it was unrealistic to expect any transition plan to be implemented. Germany, which was carrying half the Soviet debt, was understandably reluctant to pour in more money.

The Breakup of the Union

In 1991 the political cohesion of the USSR collapsed, and with it what was left of the old structures of central planning. The catalyst for this process was the independence movements in the Baltics, subsequently emulated by other republics. Beginning with Estonia in September 1987 a series of republics proclaimed their economic self-management, challenging the legal status of union enterprises and moving to take control over their own taxation and foreign trade. The Baltic republics were granted formal 'economic independence' in a USSR law in November 1989, but their demands escalated as the centre weakened.

One republic after another declared political sovereignty, beginning with Lithuania in March 1990, and Gorbachev found five republics refused to accept the new draft Union Treaty he proposed in December 1990. Instead of Gorbachev's formula of 'a strong centre and strong republics', they wanted a horizontal union of equals. In 1991 a 'war of laws' broke out between republican and all-union authorities, which encouraged firms to ignore output plans and refuse to pay taxes to the federal government.

Gorbachev struggled to find a consensus among public leaders for a new union. A new draft union treaty was due for signature on 20 August. The coup brought this process to an end, and triggered the break-up of the USSR. Protracted negotiations between the republics through the autumn of 1991 failed to produce agreement on how to preserve a common 'economic space' on the territory of the USSR. The republics – particularly Ukraine – insisted on sovereign control over their own economic and natural resources, and were reluctant to accept Moscow control over the common currency. On the other hand, all sides recognised how tightly their economies were intertwined after 70 years of joint development. An estimated 20 per cent of Soviet GNP was traded between republics, and Russia was still supplying oil at R70 a tonne ($2), while the world price was $70. The republics were also aware that without agreement on how to repay the USSR's $68 bn debt new credits would not be forthcoming. The disintegration of the USSR, and the precarious political position of the new republican leaders within their own countries, meant that no effect agreement could be reached on these issues. The creation of the Commonwealth of Independent States (CIS) in December 1991 merely created a political shell which left these crucial economic issues unresolved.

The Decision to Launch Shock Therapy

In late 1991 Boris Yeltsin presided over a political and economic system which was in ruins. Drastic measures were clearly required, but there were no blueprints or models explaining how to build capitalism out of the ruins of centrally planned economy. The only model available – and one which was urged on Yeltsin by Western advisors such as Jeffrey Sachs of Harvard – was the shock therapy introduced by Poland in January 1990, involving policies of liberalisation, stabilisation and privatisation. On 2 January 1992 the Gaidar government launched its version of shock therapy – liberalisation of domestic prices and foreign trade, combined with a tough fiscal and monetary policy. These policies were subsequently encapsulated in a memorandum submitted to the IMF in February 1992, as a result of which the IMF released $3 bn in financial support.

It may be useful to summarise the problems which Russia faced in January 1992, to convey the enormity of the challenge facing the new government.

1. Long-term structural problems

- chronic economic inefficiency;
- intensive use of material and energy resources;
- lack of incentives for improvements in productivity and technical progress;

- lack of clearly-defined property rights;
- a bloated military industrial sector;
- onerous subsidies paid by Russia to the other republics in the USSR and to client states further afield;
- separation from prevailing world markets. Much of Soviet industry was 'negative valued added' (i.e. at current world prices their inputs were worth more than their outputs).

2. Medium-term problems

- inability to create policy consensus among political elites within Russia;
- growing splits with leaders of republics outside Russia;
- mounting incapacity of governmental bureaucracies to perform normal functions.

3. Short-run breakdown factors

- collapse of supply system;
- absence of usable currency and financial system;
- rising budget deficit;
- rising foreign debt;
- the collapse of Comecon.

This is only a partial list of the problems Russia faced at the end of 1991 – but one can immediately see that it would be unrealistic to expect *any* single economic programme to deal successfully with such an array of challenges.

On the positive side, Yeltsin perceived that he had one major advantage in late 1991. The August coup had discredited Yeltsin's major political adversary – the party–state apparatus – and gave him the opportunity to shut it down overnight. His political popularity was unchallenged, and he had virtually a free hand (within Russia, at least) to impose whatever economic programme he wanted. How long this window of political opportunity would remain open was difficult to predict. The radical economic reformers who Yeltsin brought into his government adopted a 'kamikaze' mentality. They expected to be in power for only a few months, and wanted to move quickly to dismantle the remnants of central planning and set the economy irreversibly on a course towards the market.

Yeltsin decided that he had sufficient political authority to dispense with fresh parliamentary elections. Later developments proved this to be an erroneous decision, since by spring 1992 the Russian parliament parted company with Yeltsin and managed to block many of his economic reforms. It proved fairly easy to implement 'negative' policies – to abolish the CPSU's Central Committee apparatus, to disband the central ministries, to lift restrictions and controls. But it proved far more difficult to implement 'positive' policies, which involved the government actually doing something – such as raising taxes or privatising industry. For this, the cooperation of other political actors was required – and their compliance could be bought only at a price.

Price Liberalisation

Around 85 per cent of domestic prices were freed in January 1992. Producers responded by cutting output and raising prices, causing an inflationary surge of 400–500 per cent. On the positive side, this meant that price rather than rationing became the dominant mode of allocation in the economy. On the negative side, living standards were cut by 40 per cent and people's ruble savings were wiped out overnight.

Unfortunately, freeing prices before breaking up the monopolies which dominated Soviet industry proved to be a recipe for hyperinflation. Under pressure from their workers, managers continued pushing up prices, in order to generate cash to pay higher wages. The absence of working capital in the economy meant managers also solicited massive credits from the Central Bank, at highly negative rates of interest.

The economic turmoil which resulted from these measures eroded the government's political support, forcing them to back off from liberalising energy prices in April. There were fears that farmers (who had sold their harvest at 1991 prices) would be unable to buy gas and fertiliser for the 1992 season. Thus oil and gas prices continued to be held at 20–30 per cent of world levels, choking off investment in the energy sector and causing these price distortions to ripple through the economy.

Fiscal and Monetary Stabilisation

Central to the government's strategy of creating a price-driven economy was the establishment of a stable currency which would serve as a reliable means of exchange. In order to stabilise the ruble, the government would have to balance its budget and bring money emissions under control. Despite some success in the first two months of the year they proved unable to achieve either of these goals, due to strong political pressure from the industrial and agrarian lobbies. Firms continued to make deliveries to each other without payment, expecting the Central Bank to cover the wage bill or face massive social unrest.

The battle over inter-enterprise credit and the money supply was effectively lost in July 1992 when Gaidar ceded control over the Central Bank to the Russian parliament, with Viktor Gerashchenko, former head of the Soviet State Bank, being appointed as bank chairman. Gerashchenko proceeded to triple the money supply over the next quarter, reigniting the inflationary spiral. By the end of 1992 inter-enterprise debt stood at R4 trillion out of a GDP of R15 trillion, and the government deficit was R3.5 trillion.

The Finance Ministry made intermittent efforts to rein in credit emissions over the next 18 months, but a succession of political crises saw Yeltsin repeatedly retreating from tough stabilisation measures in order to shore up his political support. This pattern held true from the confrontations with the Congress in April and December 1992 (the latter of which saw the departure of Gaidar from the government) to the run-up to the referendum in April 1993 and the parliamentary elections in December 1993. Thus inflation continued to race forward, rising from 13 per cent per month in 1992 to 20 per cent per month in 1993. By January 1993 retail prices had risen 1780 per cent over December 1991 and 4340 per cent over December 1990.

Currency Convertibility

Achieving full convertibility for the ruble was a top priority for the Russian economic reformers. Western advisors believed that a convertible ruble could play the role of nominal anchor for the

TABLE 6.3 *Russian prices and wages, 1991–3*

	Consumer price index (1990 = 100)	Bank ruble $ exchange rate	Nominal wage (rubles)	Real wage (1990 = 100)	Nominal wage ($)
Apr. 1991	151	30	400	80	13
Jan. 1992	484	180	1,438	51	8
Jul. 1992	2,746	136	5,452	61	40
Jan. 1993	7,673	442	15,890	59	36
Jul. 1993	24,290	1,025	55,995	65	55

Source: G. Ofer and B. Bosworth, 'Deeper integration of formerly planned econo-mies', Brookings Institution (January 1994).

stabilisation policy, in the absence of reliable indicators of fiscal and monetary rectitude. A convertible ruble would introduce world market prices to the Russian economy, undermining the monopolistic pricing by Russian producers.

The government moved quickly to allow businesses and private citizens to freely exchange rubles for dollars, and a sort of con-vertibility was achieved. Exchange booths sprang up on every street corner, and an inter-bank ruble–dollar exchange was opened in Moscow. In order to protect Russian commercial bankers, new regulations were introduced in 1993, severely limiting the operations of foreign banks.

Unfortunately, the utility of the ruble as a currency was under-mined by the runaway inflation caused by the budget deficit and reckless credit creation. The value of the ruble plummeted from R180 per dollar in January 1992 to R400 in December. It eventually stabilised at around R$1200 per dollar in July 1993. In January 1992 the ruble fell to a level some 30 times below its real purchasing power parity. Subsequently, domestic prices rose faster than the rate at which the ruble fell against the dollar, which meant the ruble appreciated to 30–50 per cent of its purchasing power parity by December 1993. After the December 1993 elections, however, its value against the dollar plummeted once more.

Thus chronic political instability drove the ruble down to a highly undervalued level, undermining its possible role as a nominal anchor of the government's stabilisation programme. The obstinate pursuit of ruble convertibility proved to be one of the most illusory aspects of the government's economic programme, and wreaked havoc with Russian foreign trade. (Manufacturers and oil producers could not afford to purchase urgently-needed equipment, for example.)

Economic Performance and Living Standards

By October 1993 Russian industrial production was down 43.8 per cent on 1990 and 15.8 per cent on October 1992. Curiously, this massive fall in output took place without generating mass unemployment. Throughout 1993 unemployment stayed at about 1 million – less than 2 per cent of the 71 million labour force. Managers still saw themselves as responsible for the social protection of their workers – and the reforms provided few effective penalties (or incentives) to force them to shed excess labour.

After the initial drop in living standards at the beginning of 1992, real wages mostly managed to keep pace with inflation throughout 1992 and 1993, although differentials increased as some sectors (such as mining) did much better than others (such as textiles). The average wage rose from R15,000 ($35) in January 1993 to R100,000 ($75) in December. However, many workers faced delays of 2–3 months in payment of wages – by which time they had lost half their value. Pensioners and workers in state organisations (such as education and health care) did worst of all, with some 35 per cent of the population living below the poverty level (R54,000, or $40, as of December 1993).

However, considering the degree of economic and social turmoil, Yeltsin has in fact encountered surprisingly little organised social opposition to his reforms – less than in Poland, for example. Strong testimony to social acquiescence in the reform programme was provided by the April 1993 referendum, in which a surprising 53 per cent of voters voiced their support for Yeltsin's economic reforms. It was resistance from the industrial managers, from the parliament and from within the governmental apparatus itself which blocked the economic reforms, and not opposition from society at large.

Foreign Trade Liberalisation

Despite Yeltsin's initial declaration of his intention to liberalise foreign trade, the only concrete step that was taken was the lifting of import controls in January 1992. Exports remained subject to strict (albeit laxly enforced) controls: licensing requirements for strategic materials; quotas allocated by decree rather than through auction; and confiscatory rules for the conversion of dollar earnings into rubles. The structure of export controls is rather similar to the old pre-1991 system, the main difference being that many more firms (8000) are now directly engaged in foreign trade. The collapse in the value of the ruble obliged the government to subsidise the costs of necessary imports. Thus from mid-1992 import tariffs and quotas were haphazardly re-imposed.

Corruption is rife, with many of the exports and imports being channelled through private trading organisations with close ties to leading government officials. It became extremely lucrative to buy commodities like oil and metals on the domestic market and sell them on international markets. This was possible because the ruble sank to a highly undervalued level (in purchasing power parity terms). Unprocessed or semi-processed fuel and minerals account for 70 per cent of total exports. Unfortunately, the dumping of large quantities of aluminium, copper and fertiliser on world markets caused their prices to fall by 50 per cent. This, together with a slump in oil prices, meant a sharp deterioration in Russia's terms of trade.

In 1992 Russian exports fell 12 per cent to $45 bn and imports dropped 20 per cent to $35 bn. In the first 11 months of 1993 the corresponding figures were $36 bn and $16 bn. Thus Russia was able to post a $10 bn surplus in 1992 and a $20 bn surplus in 1993. An additional $5 bn may have been illegally exported each year, with the proceeds sitting in offshore bank accounts. Despite this trade surplus, Russia only paid $3.5 bn on the outstanding foreign debts of $81 bn in 1993! Russia's biggest trading partners in 1992 were Germany ($7.5 bn exports and $9.3 bn imports) and Italy ($5.2 bn exports and $3.5 bn imports).

Contrary to the reformers' hopes, foreign trade liberalisation did not trigger a boom in the exports of Russian manufactures. On the contrary, their share in exports fell from 38 per cent in 1988 to 13 per cent in 1992. Russia's political and economic elites are uncomfortable with the idea of Russia becoming a mere source of raw materials for the global economy (what they call 'Kuwaitisation'). They believe that there are markets for Russia's sophisticated aerospace and armaments industries, and complain that political pressure from the US is preventing Russia from gaining access to these markets. The fact is that many of Russia's traditional customers (Iraq, Syria, Libya, Yugoslavia) are bankrupt or politically discredited, while Russian weaponry is increasingly outdated compared to the latest foreign offerings. Soviet arms exports, in consequence, fell from a peak of $22.6 nm in 1987 to $6.78 bn in 1991, $1.3 bn in 1993 and perhaps $2 bn in 1993.

Some of Yeltsin's Western advisors promised a massive pro-gramme of Western aid would be forthcoming if Russia embraced market reform. In the end, despite some grandiose but vague promises at G7 meetings in April 1992 and 1993, the aid failed to materialise. In 1990–1 some $70 bn worth of aid flowed into the USSR, but only some $2–4 bn was forthcoming in 1992 and 1993.

The Rise and Fall of the Ruble Zone

The Russian government was so preoccupied with its domestic reform programme that it neglected the question of trade links with the other ex-Soviet states. The non-Russian republics tried to insulate themselves from the impact of Russia's shock therapy (for example, by continuing to subsidise food prices), but these efforts eventually led to even worse inflation and economic dis-location than in Russia.

At first, old trade patterns continued to operate under force of inertia. In the USSR 20 per cent of GNP used to be traded across the borders of the union republics. Firms carried on shipping goods to each other across state boundaries, although deliveries fell 34 per cent in 1992 as it became more difficult to clear payments through the banks. Trade mostly took the form of bilateral deals signed by individual firms or regional governments at Russian domestic prices. This meant that prices were inflating, while energy was still being sold at 20–30 per cent of world market levels. This meant that in 1992 Russia gave an implicit subsidy to the other states of some R1500 billion ($7 bn), equal to about 10 per cent of its GDP and 25 per cent of the recipient countries' GDP. Some 63 per cent of Russia's exports went to the CIS in 1992, from which she took 41 per cent of her imports. The other states were heavily dependent on Russian energy imports, and had little to offer in return.

This growing trade imbalance was covered by credits issued by the Russian Central Bank (RCB). In June 1992 the RCB began keeping separate accounts for each state (effectively ending the non-cash ruble zone) and began issuing 'technical credits' to the other national banks. In October 1992 Armenia, Belarus, Kazakhstan, Uzbekistan and Kyrgyzstan signed an agreement to create a common currency zone managed by the Russian Central Bank. Ukraine did not sign, and continued to print its temporary currency (coupons) at an accelerating rate. The IMF decided it was unrealistic to expect the Russian ruble to stabilise, and they began encouraging the other countries to leave the ruble zone. In June 1992 Estonia introduced its own currency, followed by Latvia (July 1992) and Kyrgyzstan (May 1993).

In 1993 energy prices were increased to about 50 per cent of the world market price for CIS partners and to world market levels for the Balts. In theory trade prices were supposed to be cleared every quarter, but in practice the deficits continued to mount. Russian fuel deliveries to Ukraine and Kazakhstan fell to around 60 per cent of their 1992 levels. By July 1993 the cumulative credits from Russia amounted to R2,300 bn ($3 bn). In 1993 the RCB began issuing new 1993 notes inside Russia, and on 24 July announced the withdrawal of all pre-1993 rubles from circulation. This effectively killed off the ruble zone. Henceforth, Russia would only issue new rubles to countries which were prepared to accept RCB control over their bank emissions. By the end of 1992 only Tajikistan and Belarus had agreed to these terms. Even countries what were enthusiastic advocates of the ruble zone, such as Kazakhstan and Uzbekistan, were forced to introduce their own national currencies in November. By late 1993 the inter-state payments system had almost totally broken down, and inflation in countries such as Ukraine and Georgia had topped 100 per cent per month. The newly-independent countries are in such desperate economic straits that some sort of reimposition of Russian hegemony is looking increasingly likely.

The Privatisation Programme

Laws allowing for the privatisation of housing, shops and factories were introduced in July 1991, but were not seriously implemented because of the confusion caused by the coup and the collapse of the USSR (for a fuller discussion, see Chapter 7). The new Gaidar government concentrated its efforts on shock therapy and structural reform took a back seat. By mid-1992, as the stabilisation programme faltered, Gaidar switched attention to privatisation as a way to regain the reform momentum. Anatolii Chubais, the energetic head of the new State Committee for Administrative of State Property (GKI), argued that privatising industry through a Czech-style voucher scheme would build a popular constituency for change and outflank the opposition to reform. In June 1992 Yeltsin persuaded the parliament to pass an ambitious privatisation programme, which obliged all firms to convert themselves into joint stock companies (JSCs) with openly traded shares.

Fierce political disputes arose between federal and regional authorities for control over the corporatisation of industry. Many of the ethnic republics inside Russia (such as Tatarstan) refused to implement the federal programme, and in Moscow itself privatisation ground to a halt because of a dispute between the council and GKI over the valuation of real estate. The lucrative oil and gas industry has been largely excluded from the privatisation process, since the government is locked in conflict with the regional councils and the oil corporations for control over the profits. Gaidar lost a crucial battle in May 1992 when Yeltsin fired the reformist Minister of Fuel Energy, Vladimir Lopuhkin. Lopuhkin was replaced by Viktor Chernomyrdin, the former head of the Soviet gas industry, and in December 1992 Chernomyrdin went on to replace Gaidar as prime minister.

Under pressure from the parliament, Chubais' programme was modified to give some privileges to worker ownership. Each firm's workers would vote on which type of privatisation their firm would adopt:

1. the workers are given 25 per cent of the shares (non-voting), and can buy 10 per cent of voting shares at 30 per cent discount;

2. the workers buy 51 per cent of voting shares (with no discount); or
3. the workers can buy 20 per cent of voting shares at the end of one year of profitable operation.

By the end of 1993 about 40 per cent of firms had been privatised. Three-quarters opted for the 'second variant', that is the worker buyout, in which effective control usually remains with the current managers. In some respects, therefore, the programme represents the continuation of the '*nomenklatura* privatisation' which began under *perestroika*. There have been only a handful of cases in which new outside owners have bought firms for cash in auctions. (One example is Philip Morris's purchase of 49 per cent of the Krasnodar Tobacco Factory for $60 mn.)

In November 1992 GKI started distributing vouchers to citizens, which they could use to bid for company shares. The vouchers have a face value of R10,000 ($20 in 1992 prices). More than 90 per cent of citizens picked up their vouchers, whose cash value fell to R4000 ($4) before recovering to R25,000 ($20). The first voucher auction took place in a blaze of international publicity at the Bolshevik biscuit factory in Moscow in December 1992. However, there was little incentive for firms to sell shares for vouchers (which would not bring any new capital into the firm). Most firms only sold 29 per cent of their shares for vouchers – the legal minimum.

The government encouraged the formation of investment funds to encourage the concentration of shareholdings. The investment funds, which have been dogged by scandal, control about 20 per cent of vouchers, but have not managed to establish a controlling interest in a significant number of firms. Most of the funds buying up vouchers are seeking a quick profit through speculative resale (e.g. to plant managers).

The most successful field for privatisation has been the small-scale retail sector, the administration of which was entirely delegated to municipal authorities under a December 1991 decree. By August 1993 some 70,000 shops, cafes and service outlets had been privatised by auction or direct sale, raising R450 bn. This represents perhaps 30 per cent of the total number of outlets and 60 per cent of all shops (two-thirds of these shops have been purchased by their current workers). Model projects for small privatisation were set up by the International Finance Corporation (an arm of the World Bank) in Nizhnii Novgorod and Volgograd, beginning in March 1992. In addition, 6 million apartments have been privatised (17 per cent of the total) – mostly by being given free of charge to the sitting tenants.

Leaving aside the privatisation of small shops, in only a very few cases has privatisation achieved its avowed goal of putting *new* owners in control of enterprises. The process is better described as 'commercialisation' than 'privatisation', since what it involves is the conversion of state-owned and centrally-planned enterprises into profit-seeking, legally independent companies, owned and controlled by their former managers and workers. Nevertheless, steps towards the legal definition of property rights – even if they are enjoyed by the managers and workers – should be a positive step towards a market economy.

What of the political goals of the privatisation programme? It has enjoyed partial public support (see Table 7.1) – no small achievement in a land of massive public alienation from political institutions. However, a June 1993 poll showed that while 69 per cent approved of the idea of small private firms, only 27 per cent favoured large private firms, and only 13 per cent approved large firms owned by foreigners.

Conclusion

The economic transformation of Russia is proving to be a slow and painful process – more slow, and more painful, than anybody predicted. The old structures of the centrally planned economy have been destroyed, but the translation process is not following anyone's blueprint for reform. Rather, it is a product of complex political and economy struggles, with an unknown outcome.

The future economy will almost certainly be one in which market forces play a major role. However, factories and farms will probably remain under the control of the local economic and political elites inherited from the old regime. And although they will no longer be subject to a central plan, the regions and republics will interact through an unstable mixture of political dealing and market trading.

7

Privatisation: The Politics of Capital and Labour

SIMON CLARKE

To understand the significance of privatisation in Russia it is important to look behind the ideological stereotypes which dominate political debate and to locate the privatisation process in its economic, social and political context. This chapter will attempt to place Russian privatisation in this wider context, building on the discussion of economic reform more generally that has been presented in Chapter 6.

The economic significance of privatisation in Russia is its role in the transformation of collective state property into capitalist private property, as the basis for the transition to a capitalist market economy. However, this process is not as straightforward as it is often presented, but involves three quite distinct stages. The first stage is the transformation of the form of property from undifferentiated state property to differentiated forms of property, which nevertheless remain formally in state ownership. This stage in Russia was largely achieved by the end of 1991. The second stage is the transfer of ownership of this property to individual or corporate private owners, which in Russia began on a large scale in 1993. The third stage is the transformation of this privatised property into productive capital, which in Russia has hardly begun.

The social significance of privatisation in Russia is its role in the process of class formation. The transformation of collective state property into capitalist private property is supposed to create a property-owning meritocracy, in which the privatisation process leads to the formation of a strong middle class based on the wide distribution of property and the recruitment of professional and managerial strata on the basis of their ability. However, a redistribution of property without any fundamental changes in social organisation risks leading not to a transformation in the class structure, but to an intensification of existing social antagonisms and the emergence of class polarisation.

The political significance of privatisation in Russia is its role in the reconstitution of state power. The state has not stood above the disintegration of the Soviet system – on the contrary the central feature of that disintegration has been the disintegration of the state and the dissipation of its powers. This has meant that the state has not been able to play a determining role in the privatisation process, but has been largely confined to giving juridical recognition to changes that have already taken place. However, although the state has to accommodate itself politically to the existence of social forces it does not control, the state can still play an important role in influencing the balance of forces in play and so in conditioning the future pattern of social relations and social conflicts in Russia.

The study of the privatisation process therefore has a broader significance for understanding the political development of post-Soviet society, since privatisation provides a means by which the state can attract to itself a constellation of interests and social and political forces on the basis of which it can reconstitute its own power. This reconsolidation of the political and economic elite, and its reconciliation with the exercise of centralised state power, has been played out in the give and take between the reformist politicians who command the state apparatus and the 'industrial *nomenklatura*', the state-appointed directors of large enterprises who still control the commanding heights of the economy. In the short term this bargaining revolved around the issues of taxation, state credit and subsidies, in which the government tempered its free market principles with a shower of money. In the longer term it has revolved around the issue of privatisation, in which the political elite has eventually been forced to concede the ownership claims of the industrial *nomenklatura*, nominally on behalf of the 'labour collectives', in return for a growing political allegiance which strengthens not just one political faction, but the state itself.

This is not the place to recount the political struggles of the Yeltsin years (see Chapters 2 and 3). Suffice it to say that behind the political theatre of the conflict between President and parliament the government effectively served the interests of the industrial *nomenklatura*, while denying the latter a forum in which to constitute itself as an independent political force. By late 1993 an implicit alliance had been sealed between the executive apparatus and the (depoliticised) industrial *nomenklatura* on the basis of which it became possible to construct the strong state that both sides sought, in order to reimpose 'order' and 'discipline' on society. If the period between 1991 and 1993 was dominated by factional conflicts within the ruling stratum, the consolidation of the elite makes it likely that the next years will see the emergence of conflicts which have an increasingly overt class character.

Privatizatsiya or *Prikhvatizatsiya*?

'Privatisation' is usually identified simply as the transfer of ownership of particular assets from state to private hands. However, even in the capitalist world such a transfer of ownership is only a small part of the process of privatisation. Before ownership can be transferred the assets in question have to be constituted as private property, that is to say the rights which are to be transferred have to be demarcated and delimited juridically. For various reasons state enterprises in the capitalist world have already tended to take on the juridical form of private property, as in the public corporation, in which case privatisation may involve simply the sale of state-owned shares. However, in the case of public utilities and services the definition of the respective rights and claims of users, providers and prospective owners can be much more complex, and the object of considerable conflict.

The definition and demarcation of property rights is not a sufficient condition for privatisation in the West. Even when the assets in question already have the form of private property they still have to be 'prepared' for privatisation, since they are sold not simply as private property for the personal use and enjoyment of their new owners but as income-generating assets – as *capitalist* private property. Privatisation in the West is often associated with debt write-offs, injections of investment funds and tax holidays to ensure the profitability of the assets involved, but even this is not sufficient if the underlying conditions for long-term profitability have not been established. The British coal mining industry, for example, has been going through a process of state-sponsored restructuring to establish its competitiveness in the face of world competition for almost 50 years, although by the time it is ready for privatisation there may be nothing left to privatise. The Russian coal-mining industry, by contrast, was given 2 months to carry through the complete process of 'privatisation'. This alone should lead us to doubt that privatisation East and West are comparable processes.

For all the rhetoric that surrounds the redeeming power of privatisation, in practice in the West it is taken for granted that privatisation is the culmination of a process of state-sponsored restructuring, with profitability a precondition of privatisation, not its result. In Russia, on the other hand, there is little connection between privatisation and profitability or the transition to capitalism. Privatisation in Russia is not about the transformation of the social relations of production, but is about the juridical constitution of private property and recognition of *de facto* ownership rights.

The process of privatisation in Russia has not played the leading role in the transformation process attributed to it by liberal economists, but has tailed behind the real changes through which *de facto* ownership rights have been asserted. At the heart of the process of privatisation lies the attempt of those who have established such *de facto* rights to secure juridical protection for those rights. Privatisation is not about selling state property, since the state has long since lost control over its property, nor is it about the transformation of the social relations of production, since such a transformation has barely begun. At its crudest it is about the legalisation of theft, the process of *prikhvatizatsiya* – 'grabbing'. If there are analogies with the transition to capitalist in the West they are with what Marx called the 'primitive accumulation' of capital in the 18th century. At best Russian privatisation is the equivalent of the 'bloody legislation', clearances and enclosures in Britain at this time, which may arguably have paved the way for the capitalist transformation that followed. At worst it is the equivalent of the colonial plunder which financed the lavish consumption of a parasitic ruling class, and left the plains of Bengal littered with the bleached bones of a generation of peasants and artisans.

The Disintegration of the Soviet System and the Destatisation of Property

State ownership in the Soviet bloc was not defined on the basis of capitalist property forms but was a qualitatively different form of property, corresponding to a different social form of production. According to the Soviet legal doctrine of the 'unitary fund' all social property was owned exclusively by the state (apart from consumer and agricultural cooperatives). As such, state property was absolute and undifferentiated, expressing the principle of the centralisation of authority within the administrative–command system of production. Although the state delegated rights of possession, use and disposition to particular bodies, including ministries, enterprises, municipal authorities, trade unions of the Communist Party, user-rights did not imply any rights of proprietorship. This meant, for example, that the state could transfer assets between different institutions at will, without any question of compensation arising. It meant that the 'profits' of an enterprise did not belong to that enterprise but were at the disposal of the state, which could redistributed them at will. Privatisation in Russia therefore involves not simply a transfer of ownership, but a transformation of the form of property: before any change of ownership can take place, the assets in question have to be transformed into private property.

The basis of the process of privatisation in Russia has been the 'destatisation' of property, which has expressed the disintegration of the monolithic administrative–command system to leave independent enterprises, associations and concerns, cooperatives, leasehold and shareholding companies and individual entrepreneurs, all appropriating and using, buying and selling state assets over which the central state apparatus had lost control, but to which no single individual or corporate entity had established clear ownership rights. The disintegration of the old system made a redefinition of property rights essential. This is why the essential issue in contention has not been the fact of privatisation but its form. The form of privatisation defines the rights and obligations attached to ownership, and so plays an important role in structuring the conflicts around the future economic and social development of postcommunist Russia.

The process of destatisation was initiated by the legislation of private economic activity under the 1986 Law on Individual Labour Activity, the 1988 Law on Cooperatives and the 1989 Law on Small Enterprises. In practice the vast majority of private economic activity which developed under these laws had to make use of state productive assets and secure supplies through state distribution channels for want of any alternative. The emerging private sector was therefore closely integrated into the dominant state of the economy, using public assets for private gain. Most of this private economic activity was of dubious legality and much of it was simply illegal, with no clear dividing line between the violation of obstructive laws and straightforward criminal activity. It is arguable that the diversion of state assets was socially beneficial, to the extent that the private gains derived from the more productive employment of those assets, but much private economic activity amounted to little more than theft and extortion, private fortunes deriving not from productive activity but from the exploitation of the growing gap between state and market prices, particularly in industrial raw materials and urban commercial property.

The liberalisation of the laws governing private economic activity enabled a few individuals to accumulate substantial fortunes, but it did not provide the basis for the emergence of a new capitalist sector of independent small and medium enterprises which could displace the state monoliths. The significance of the liberalisation was much more in its impact on the state sector, since it provided a juridical framework within which state enterprises could begin to evade the straightjacket of ministerial control. Thus about 85 per cent of all cooperatives were not private enterprises at all, but operated under the wing of the state enterprises which had established them and which were their main suppliers and customers. The development of private enterprise therefore accelerated the disintegration of the administrative–command system, without providing an alternative to it. The basis of privatisation is not the new forms of capitalist property, but the transformation of state ownership.

The transformation of state ownership was an inevitable consequence of the attempt to replace 'administrative' by 'economic' methods of regulation which lay at the centre of Gorbachev's reform programme. This programme involved the decentralisation of decision-making within the administrative–command system, with the replacement of gross output by financial indicators and an increased reliance on the market regulation of contractual relationships between enterprises. This implied the general application of the principles of self-financing, the juridical autonomy of the enterprise as an accounting unit, and its constitution as a juridical subject able to enter into commercial and financial contracts. This in turn implied the transformation of the unitary form of state property into the differentiated form of private property. However, the programme of *perestroika* was based on a fundamental contradiction: although *perestroika* was based on democratisation and the decentralisation of responsibility, these were seen only as the means to strengthen centralised control which would be asserted by economic and ideological rather than administrative means. This contradiction ran through both policy and legislation between 1987 and 1991, until it finally broke the whole system as local bodies, including state enterprises, increasingly asserted their independence of central control.

The process of destatisation of the state enterprise was initiated by the 1987 Law on the State Enterprise (Association), which defined the enterprise as an independent unit although still subject to central controls. Although the ministries constantly thwarted the provisions of the law, this led to growing demands for the destatisation and formal privatisation of property as the only means of securing the juridical independence of the enterprise, while the reform itself defined the basis on which ministerial power was rapidly eroded. As market prices diverged increasingly from state prices it became more and more profitable for enterprises to produce for the market and to cut back on their state orders, even if they had to buy supplies at market prices. The result was that contractual deliveries began to make headway at the expense of state orders, and a growing proportion of transactions took place at market prices rather than state prices, rapidly eroding the administrative–command system.

The 1987 law not only gave the enterprise the rights of possession, use and administration of its assets, but also the right to transfer its assets, and this provided a loophole through which enterprises could escape from central control prices, wages and financial transactions by transferring activities to subsidiary enterprises which were not subject to ministerial regulation or control. Typically, a state enterprise or association would assign the productive assets of a particular factory, shop or department to a cooperative or leasehold enterprise, would sell the subsidiary the raw materials it required, and sometimes purchase some of the product so that the enterprise could meet its obligatory plan deliveries, while the subsidiary would sell the rest on the open market. Similarly, commercial subsidiaries provided a channel through which the enterprise could, often illegally, sell its products, and even its machinery and raw materials, at free market prices, while financial subsidiaries provided a way of laundering bank credit.

The cooperative, leasehold and small enterprise sectors all provided more differentiated forms of property through which state enterprises could shelter activities from central control. The final step in the 'destatisation' of state enterprises was the freeing of the enterprises themselves through their conversion to the form of joint-stock and limited companies, which was provided for by the 1990 Law on Property, implemented by a decree of June 1990.

Meanwhile, the disintegration of the administrative–command system progressively loosened the grip of the ministries over state enterprises. Interbranch State Associations (MGOs), Concerns and State Associations were authorised by an amendment to the Law on the State Enterprise in August 1989. Unlike the ministerial system, these forms of association are built from the bottom up, the powers and property of the association being delegated from its component enterprises, which enter or leave the association voluntarily. The formation of associations proceeded relatively slowly at first, but as privatisation loomed on the horizon, and ministries were faced with break-up in the wake of the disintegration of the Soviet Union, ministries rapidly transformed themselves into concerns and associations, which were in effect giant holding companies for the branches they had formerly supervised. By the middle of 1991 it was estimated that over half the ministries had privatised themselves in this way and most of the rest did so in the wake of the August coup, although some were brought back under central control with the formation of republican ministries. On the other hand, the formation of concerns and associations transferred juridical rights to the component enterprises, and the final disintegration of the administrative–command system gave increasing substance to these rights as the association was no longer able to guarantee supplies to its component enterprises. It would therefore be wrong to see the conversion of ministries into associations as no more than a change of name, since it also marked a real shift in the balance of power from the ministry to the enterprises.

The 'destatisation' of property in Russia was more or less completed with the disintegration of the system in the second half of 1991, so that social property had taken on a 'private' form. However the precise juridical status of property claims and the valuation and ownership of assets were still at best ill-defined.

From Destatisation to Privatisation

The process of destatisation prepared the way for privatisation by defining juridical forms within which state property could be assigned to the differentiated forms of private property. It was inevitable that once state property came to assume the juridical form of private property the question of ownership would arise, and destatisation would give way to privatisation. By late 1990 the momentum towards privatisation was unstoppable, if only because the destatisation of property meant nothing until the ownership of that property was defined. Just who was to own this property was another matter.

The All-Union Law on Destatisation and Privatisation, which was approved in July 1991, allowed the conversion of state enterprises to leased, collective, cooperative, joint-stock or private ownership. However, the Law was not so much about the transfer of state assets to private ownership as about the transformation of state property into other forms of corporate property, and particularly to the form of the joint-stock company. At the same time the various republics passed their own privatisation laws, which conflicted with the all-union law. However, the various laws and decrees on privatisation expressed no more than a vague commitment to privatisation in an indefinite future.

Through 1991 the commitment of both Russian and Soviet governments to privatisation remained primarily rhetorical, as a means of appealing for political support. The Soviet government still sought to reconcile privatisation with centralised control by leaving the majority of shares in state hands for the foreseeable future. The Russian government's plans had a more populist thrust, with the promise of a wider distribution of share ownership. However, there was no privatisation programme, there were no clear procedures by which enterprises which wanted to privatise could actually do so, no bodies with appropriately defined duties, and none of the forms and documents necessary to carry the process through. The result was that private ownership made very little headway in the productive sphere. At the beginning of January 1992 in the Russian Federation there were 21,945 state-owned industrial enterprises, of which 3042 were leased, and only 992 non-state industrial enterprises, of which 272 were collectively owned, 162 were joint-stock companies, and 70 in private ownership. State enterprises still accounted for 96 per cent of industrial production. In terms of their turnover the collectively-owned enterprises were relatively small, and the private ones minute, while the joint-stock companies were relatively large, accounting together for 1.5 per cent of industrial production. The bulk of the shares in the joint-stock companies, however, were still owned by the state or by other state enterprises (see *Ekonomika i zhizn'*, no. 14, April 1992).

While the contending forces in the state apparatus saw privatisation primarily as a means of transforming and reconstituting state power, enterprise directors had quite different ambitions. Enterprise directors had established their independence as the system disintegrated around them, and saw privatisation as the means of securing juridical recognition for this independence. They were not going to sit quietly by and see themselves placed under the control of new owners. However they did not press their claims in their own name, but in the name of the people, in the form of the 'labour collective' of the enterprise.

First Steps in Privatisation: Russia's Managerial Revolution

During 1990 and 1991 the increasing divergence between state and market prices created almost unlimited opportunities for private enterprises to profit by buying at state prices and selling in the market, while making the central regulation of prices and financial transactions increasingly burdensome for managers of state enterprises. In this period the appeal of privatisation to enterprise directors was not so much the change in the form of ownership, since directors had already acquired *de facto* control of their enterprises, as the opportunity to escape from the straightjacket of state control. Enterprise directors saw privatisation as the means of securing the relative prosperity which, at that stage, was the almost universal concomitant of economic independence. Despite formidable bureaucratic and legal barriers some enterprise directors were able to exploit the provisions of the law to assert their independence, resting on the support of their workforce to press their claims against those of external economic and political structures to carry through the first stage of Russia's 'managerial revolution'.

The pioneers of privatisation were those enterprises that had already established their independence on the basis of their transformation into cooperatives or, more often, leasehold enterprises. The Law on Leasehold had included the right of the labour collective to buy out the enterprise on a two-thirds majority vote, although it did not establish a procedure through which this could be done. As the Law on Cooperatives became increasingly restrictive many cooperatives also transformed themselves into joint-stock companies or small enterprises, usually of a closed type with share ownership restricted to employees of the enterprise.

Whether privatisation went via the cooperative or the leasehold form the pattern was the same. Typically shares would be sold to employees at a discounted price, subsidised from the profits of the enterprise, with the enterprise offering cheap credit to finance share purchases. Share allocations would generally take account of a workers' grade and earnings, length of service and, sometimes, disciplinary record. Pensioners of the enterprise and workers on military service or maternity leave were also usually included in the share allocation. A residual package of shares was usually held back, to be sold at a later date either internally or to raise external finance, with voting rights meanwhile in the hands of management.

This form of privatisation appealed to both workers and managers. Workers were attracted by the offer of high dividend payouts, the end of centralised control over wages and the implied promise of job security attached to share ownership. Privatisation provided the managers with juridical guarantees of the independence of the enterprise from state control. The closed type of joint-stock company ensured that control of the enterprise could not pass to outsiders. The relatively equal distribution of shares among the labour force enabled the management to continue to use the well-established mechanisms through which they controlled worker representation, and made it unlikely that they would face any concerted internal challenge.

Although this first wave of privatisation embraced relatively few enterprises, mostly of small and medium size, it was a direct expression of interests of enterprise directors, and so set the pattern to which the industrial *nomenklatura* as a whole aspired, and to which the privatisation process eventually conformed.

Privatisation and the Struggle for Power

Through 1991 Yeltsin ruthlessly exploited divisions within the 'conservative-reformist' camp and encouraged the forces of decentralisation to further his own political advance. The coup and counter-coup of August 1991 not only swept away the conservative-reformists, but also marked the disintegration of the authority of all centralised state structures and so the unviability of any conservative reform programme based on such structures.

Yeltsin seized power in the autumn of 1991, but the means by which he did so had fatally weakened the political, juridical, economic and administrative mechanisms through which he could exercise that power. In this sense the character of Yeltsin's political revolution determined that he had no choice but to follow a liberal economic strategy which would be based on the attempt to retain some control over the disintegrating economy through the use of fiscal and monetary instruments. It equally determined that the struggle for power over the following two years would have little to do with the apparently implacable opposition between the 'liberals' and 'conservatives' whose histrionics dominated the political stage.

The struggle for power was represented rhetorically as a struggle between liberal democrats, supported by the international financial institutions, who sought to subject enterprises to the discipline of the market through restrictive fiscal and monetary policies, and the conservative industrial *nomenklatura*, who wanted to consolidate their power by stabilising the economic and financial prospects of their enterprises on the basis of subsidies and privileges. The day-to-day struggle centred on the struggle for control of the central bank and the budgetary process in which the executive sought to limit monetary emission and the growth of credit, while parliament responded to regional and sectoral demands for budgetary support. However, this struggle was not so much an expression of fundamental differences of political principle as an expression of a real contradiction between the long-term need for a fundamental restructuring of the economy and the short-term need to maintain incomes and employment and avoid economic collapse, a contradiction which appeared within the industrial *nomenklatura* itself as a contradiction between its collective interest in constituting itself as a class in control of a viable economy, and the interests of individual directors in securing the best conditions for their own enterprises. The outcome of this struggle was necessarily a compromise, however arbitrary and irrational the form of such a compromise might be. The political advantage of such an apparently chaotic means of determining economic policy was that both parliament and President could tacitly endorse the compromise, while denying responsibility for its outcome.

The issue of privatisation was in many respects a crucial battleground between the liberal democrats, who had command of the state apparatus, and the industrial *nomenklatura*, who controlled the industrial enterprises which dominated the economy. However it was also the battleground in which it first became clear that neither side could prevail over the other, and that the interests of each were best served by the reconsolidation of the political and economic elites into a unified ruling stratum. Indeed, to some extent the issue was decided even before the conflict began, by the decision to give priority to the liberalisation of prices over privatisation and demonopolisation, a decision that was sealed by Yeltsin's appointment of Gaidar as deputy prime minister and economic strategist at the end of October 1991.

The liberal democrats were nominally committed to privatisation as the means of forcing a rapid transition to capitalism on state enterprises. However there was a fundamental division within the liberal camp, which was essentially between the neo-liberal economists whose priority was the economic transformation of Russia, and the 'democrats' who controlled the state apparatus and those ambitions were primarily to secure the fiscal, monetary and political stabilisation of their power.

The neo-liberal economists insisted that to be effective privatisation should be as rapid as possible, but most importantly that privatisation should be closely linked to a policy of demonopolisation, without which it would simply be the means of handing power to the industrial *nomenklatura*. The form of privatisation was of much less concern to the neo-liberals. Provided that enterprises are subject to the pressure of competition, in their view, it does not much matter who is the owner of the enterprise. If those who initially acquire the enterprise do not manage to make it profitable, it will soon pass into the hands of those who can. Thus the neo-liberals were not opposed to a '*nomenklatura* privatisation' that transferred ownership to the labour collective, controlled by the enterprise director. As Gavriil Popov argued, 'it is necessary first . . . to give privileges to the labour collectives. They will be, so to speak, "pre-owners". They will enter the market. Competition will show who is able to conduct business . . . It is not difficult to predict that quite a few of these "pre-owners" will end up having their enterprises go to the auction block' (*Izvestiya*, 20 May 1992). Within this strategy the bargain between the state and the industrial *nomenklatura* which held the reins of economic power was one in which the industrial *nomenklatura* would become the effective owners of their enterprises, but would be subjected to the coercive force of competition which would impose a transition to capitalism.

The 'democrats' were much more concerned with the political than with the economic consequences of privatisation, seeking through the privatisation process to consolidate their political base and to strengthen the financial position of the state. The principal problem faced by the 'democrats' was the need to neutralise the industrial *nomenklatura* politically. Despite their extravagant rhetoric, they were in no position to confront the industrial *nomenklatura* head-on. Thus the strategy which gradually emerged during 1992 and 1993 was a pragmatic one, in which the government sought to strengthen the state by constructing a popular political base in opposition to the self-proclaimed political representatives of the agrarian and industrial lobbies, while in practice its policies increasingly reflected the economic interests of the industrial *nomenklatura*.

Gaidar, a politically ambitious liberal economist, was the ideal man to bridge the gap between liberals and democrats, borrowing the liberal rhetoric to cloak what was in practice a pragmatic strategy of accommodation and compromise with the 'conservative' forces of the industrial *nomenklatura*. Gaidar defended his reversal of the liberal priorities, by pressing price liberalisation over demonopolisation and rapid privatisation, as being unavoidable in the face of rampant inflation, a soaring budget deficit and a credit explosion. But this reversal nevertheless also corresponded to the economic interests of the industrial *nomenklatura*. The immediate result of price liberalisation was to cut the ground from under the feet of the commercial and financial capitalists, who had been able to exploit their freedom from restraint to make large profits. State enterprises could now consolidate their monopoly powers, establish commercial relations directly without having to go through intermediaries, and sell directly for market prices.

Privatisation and the Labour Collective

The political battle over privatisation was marked by a progressive weakening of the government's initial principles as it accommodated itself to the demands of the industrial *nomenklatura* and to popular pressure. Initially the government envisaged privatisation as involving the sale of assets both to raise revenue and to create a new class of owners, while it was implacably opposed to giving assets away for nothing and to handing control to the existing management in the name of the 'labour collective'. In the event the failure to find buyers, the need to secure popular support, and the need to come to terms with the power of the industrial *nomenklatura* led the government progressively to reverse its position during 1992.

The final privatisation programme issued in July 1992 marked an almost total capitulation to the demands of the industrial *nomenklatura*. Enterprises were offered three routes to privatisation, with the choice being a matter for a meeting of the labour collective. The first option allocated 25 per cent of the shares to the workers free in the form of non-voting stock, with a right to buy a further 10 per cent with a 30 per cent rebate (and the senior management would have an option on a further 5 per cent). The remaining shares would remain in the hands of the Federal or regional State Privatisation Committees, to be sold by auction at a subsequent date. The second option allowed the workers to purchase a controlling interest in the enterprise directly, instead of having to bid at auction, on a decision of at least two-thirds of the labour collective, with individual share ownership bid for in a closed subscription, and the remaining shares to be sold at auction. The third option, primarily for small enterprises in trade and services, allowed a minimum of one-third of the workers to form a partnership to buy the enterprise outright through auction with a 30 per cent rebate; or, if the enterprise is sold at auction, the workers receive up to 30 per cent of the proceeds. Additional variants provided for leasing with a subsequent right to buy, primarily designed for the privatisation of bankrupt enterprises.

Various measures ensured that workers would have the money needed to buy the shares allocated to them. First, enterprises were permitted to use their funds to establish personal privatisation accounts for the benefit of their workers, which could be augmented by additions from current profits, and would also receive 10 per cent of the revenue raised from the privatisation itself. Second, commercial banks and local councils were permitted to extend credit for the purpose of privatisation. Third, shares did not initially have to be paid for in full. Fourth, the voucher scheme would provide 10,000 roubles for every man, woman and child to participate in the privatisation exercise. Overall the government expected 20 per cent of the money subscribed to come from private funds, 15 per cent from foreigners, and 65 per cent from enterprise funds, on top of that made available in the form of vouchers. Fifth, the privatisation scheme grossly under-valued the assets of the enterprises for the purpose of defining the nominal value of their shares. The net result was that the personal privatisation accounts paid for out of enterprise funds, supplemented by the workers' privatisation vouchers, would cover the cost of purchase of the labour collective's shareholding in the vast majority of enterprises, sometimes leaving funds for workers to buy additional shares through open bidding. Effectively the workers were being offered the controlling interest in the enterprise for next to nothing. The remaining 49 per cent of shares would then be the object of competitive bidding with the remainder of the 'funny money', since the main participants would be the investment funds set up with privatisation vouchers, and enterprise privatisation funds.

The privatisation programme was finally issued on 9 July 1992, just before the summer holidays, with the requirement that all medium and large enterprises subject to privatisation should have transformed themselves into joint-stock companies, draw up privatisation plans, discussed them with the labour collective, submitted them to a meeting of the labour collective for its approval, and got them to the appropriate privatisation committee for endorsement by 1 September (later extended to 1 October, and 1 January 1993 for the largest enterprises). Despite the fact that almost no documentation was available, and in many cases the relevant privatisation committee did not even exist, the industrial *nomenklatura* seized the opportunity presented to it with alacrity.

The principal decision which had to be made was which of the privatisation options to adopt. The decision was nominally a matter for the labour collective, but in practice enterprises established their own privatisation commissions which drew up proposals, and then conducted intensive propaganda throughout the enterprise to drum up support, primarily in the attempt to persuade workers to take up their allocation of shares so that they would not fall into outside hands.

In general the second option was more attractive both to management and to the workers. Although the first option provided a free allocation of shares, additional shares had to be bought at auction-related prices, while under the second option a full 51 per cent of the shares were available at a purely nominal price. Moreover the second option ensured that the controlling interest remained within the enterprise, so long as the workers bought the shares allocated to them. Although the bulk of the shares would be held by the workers, the management was very experienced at handling the 'representation' of workers' interests to ensure that its own nominees were elected to the shareholders' council, while worker share ownership provided a useful prop to the ideology of 'social partnership' through which the industrial *nomenklatura*

sought to maintain the stability of the enterprise and to consolidate its political base.

The second variant not only assured management of control of
the activity of the enterprise and the allocation of its resources,
but also enabled it to control the sale of the remaining 49 per cent
of shares, which the managers could buy themselves directly or
through 'pocket companies' or could sell to outside interests to
raise funds or to secure strategic alliances. Under the first option,
by contrast, the controlling interest remained in the hands of the
relevant State Property Committee, which could in principle
assert its rights and control the disposal of additional shares.
The first option was accordingly favoured by the privatisation
committees, and by those liberal democrats and worker activists
who still hoped to break the power of the industrial *nomenklatura*.

The principal conflicts raised by the privatisation process were
those between component parts of large enterprises and associations. The privatisation legislation did not define the unit of
privatisation, which meant that the component units of large
enterprises or associations were free to apply to privatise independently. A profitable shop or factory had a very strong incentive to
privatise in this way, while the parent had an equally strong
incentive to keep profitable units under its own control. The
situation was made more complicated because of the overlapping
jurisdictions of federal, regional and municipal privatisation committees. Thus a large enterprise might fall under the jurisdiction
of the state or regional privatisation committee, but a smaller
factory or shop might fall under the jurisdiction of the regional or
municipal committee. Each could then submit independent privatisation plans to different committees, each of which could then
receive endorsement. Despite the nominal commitment of the
government to de-monopolisation, in all but one of the cases of
such conflict with which I am familiar the issue was resolved in
favour of the larger unit.

The drawing up of privatisation plans was a process which did
not usually involve the workers, and which did not give rise to
significant conflict between workers and management within the
enterprise. Workers had very little understanding of what privatisation involved, little faith that the purchase of shares would
improve their economic position, and little opportunity to develop

or express their own opinions. Management proposals were routinely endorsed through the traditional channels of 'representation', and workers were induced to subscribe for shares by various means, the most common being the promise of future dividend payouts and the implied threat that in the event of redundancy those without shares would be the first to go.

Once privatisation plans had been approved, the process of privatisation itself could begin with the formation of the shareholding company, the distribution of shares and the election of the council of shareholders. It was only at this stage, which got under way in industrial enterprises from the second quarter of 1993, that privatisation began to have any real impact on workers. At the time of writing it is too early to be able to generalise about the impact of privatisation on social relations in the enterprise, although our own case studies do provide a basis on which to identify some clear tendencies that are already defining new patterns of conflict within the enterprise (see Clarke *et al.*, 1994). These tendencies are most clearly identifiable in those enterprises that were pioneers of privatisation, in which management had had time to establish its dominant position and to exploit the security it has acquired in its capacity as effective owner of the enterprise.

The main significance of privatisation for the existing management is that it provides a basis on which the directors can secure their control of the enterprise on a juridical foundation. With the collapse of the Soviet system the enterprise directors became the *de facto* owners of their enterprise, but they had no guarantees of the security of their position. A strong opposition faction within the enterprise administration, sometimes with external commercial or political backing, could easily mobilise worker dissatisfaction to overthrow the existing senior management. The risk of such a development was the main reason why enterprise directors pursued a strategy of 'authoritarian paternalism', expressed in the rhetoric of 'social partnership', guaranteeing to protect the labour collective in return for its passive support for management's ownership claims. The cries of 'social partnership' reached a crescendo during the privatisation campaign as the directorate enlisted popular support for its demand for privatisation to the labour collective. However, once the shares are issued and the shareholders' council elected, the directorate's hand is freed from dependence on the labour collective as a whole, and a change of strategy is in order.

Privatisation also changes the relationship between the large state industrial enterprise and the new commercial and financial structures that oil the wheels of the market economy, and through which state resources are diverted into private hands. The majority of commercial and financial enterprises were established in close relationship with state enterprises, but this relationship was typically sealed by informal personal relationships in which managers of the state enterprise, their relatives or their close associates were partners in formally independent companies. The disadvantage of such arrangements was that the relationship between state and private enterprise at best sailed very close to the law, and more often was simply illegal. The privatisation of the state enterprise then makes it possible to bring these illegal and semi-legal activities within a secure legal framework, by incorporating the commercial and financial enterprises as partners or subsidiaries of the privatised state enterprise. In this way, paradoxically, privatisation provides a way of consolidating the dominance of the state enterprise directorate over the capitalist financial and commercial sector. Typically the privatised share-holding company is conceived as a kind of investment trust, established on the basis of its majority shareholding in the priva-tised state industrial enterprise, but also embracing a number of other commercial and financial subsidiaries. The shareholding company remains distinct from the enterprise or enterprises that it owns, with its own management, constitution and decision-making bodies. The outcome is a symbiotic relationship between the (former) state industrial enterprise and capitalist commercial and financial activities in which the two parts remain distinct, but their relationship ambiguous.

Privatisation and the Emergence of Class Conflict

Once management has incorporated and privatised the enterprise it is not very long before it begins to assert its ownership rights, and to subordinate the activity of the enterprise to its own inter-ests. Typically the first step is to undertake a restructuring of the management of the enterprise, removing or downgrading those branches of management which had been central to the administrative control of the enterprise, and expanding the commercial and financial branches of management which play the leading role in the adjustment to changing market conditions. Alongside this restructuring of the management hierarchy there is a substantial widening of pay differentials in favour of management as a whole, and within management in favour of senior managers. Finally, the process of concentration of share ownership gets under way almost immediately, as management offers to buy workers' shares for cash.

Privatisation also seems to be very closely linked to the introduction of large-scale redundancies. Although most large enterprises have been threatening redundancies for some time, and many have reduced their labour force substantially, these reductions have largely been through natural wastage. It is only following privatisation that enterprises introduce programmes of compulsory redundancy, focusing on older workers (those working beyond pension age), auxiliary administrative and manual workers (especially women), and workers with a poor disciplinary record. On the whole there has so far been very little resistance to redundancy, despite the fact that it violates traditional social guarantees, with management seeking support for its programme for those who remain by rationalising it on the grounds of the need to pay higher wages in order to preserve the 'backbone' of the labour collective intact.

Despite the promise of the regenerative powers of private ownership, privatisation provides very little incentive to invest in new production facilities, or even to the significant reorganisation of existing production. In the face of the disintegration of the Soviet system enterprise directors have shown themselves to be extremely resourceful in exploiting short-term opportunities, using the skills which had been necessary to meet the plan in the face of the shortages and chaos which masqueraded as a planned economy. Enterprises have proved extraordinarily adept at finding new markets and new sources of supply, and at using existing equipment, labour and raw materials to develop new lines of production in response to fluctuating demand. However, in conditions of extreme economic instability large-scale productive investment, except on the basis of state subsidies for production for state orders, is unprofitable, while the more modest restructuring of production to raise productivity risks provoking dangerous conflict with the labour force, and between senior and line management. It is far more profitable to invest in the exploitation of commercial and financial opportunities.

Although the workers were effectively excluded from active participation in the privatisation programme and had little understanding of its technicalities, it did not take them long to learn that 'privatisation to the labour collective' was not for their benefit but for that of the enterprise directorate. Soviet workers had been told for seventy years that productive labour was the basis of all wealth and the only true path to human self-realisation. They had been told that the enterprise had been created by their labour as the basis for their collective economic and social welfare. The 'managerial revolution' which grew out of the process of *perestroika* had been wrapped in the same rhetoric as enterprise directors asserted their independence from Moscow and the ministries in the name of the labour collective, holding out the promise of the realisation of what had been an ideological fiction, to use the resources of the enterprise for the benefit of its labour collective, and to gain control of profits in order to maintain wages, employment and social and welfare provision. In this sense the reality of privatisation violated the most fundamental values and beliefs of the Russian working class as the directorate sought to assert its rights of control, no longer as representative of the collective labourer, but on the basis of property rights bestowed by the state (see Table 7.1).

The conflict between the contradictory claims of labour and property is not an abstract conflict, and it is certainly not expressed in the direct collision of class forces, nor even in overt political conflict. It is a conflict that centres on the concrete rights and responsibilities of management and that is expressed in the first instance in small-scale conflicts within the enterprise, and in growing dissatisfaction within the workforce. The widening of pay differentials, which to the Western economist is a perfectly rational reform in a society in which managers were often paid less than manual workers, provokes immediate hostility on the part of workers who see management as an inflated bureaucratic apparatus whose incompetence condemns the workers to unsafe and unhealthy working conditions, with inadequate equipment and supplies, for wages which are being steadily eroded by infla-

TABLE 7.1   *Privatisation: the public response*

(A)   'Were you able to take part in the process of privatisation that is taking place in our country?' (percentages)

Yes		**62.8**
Of which:	exchanged vouchers for shares	29.8
	purchased housing	24.7
	purchased allotments	19.4
	purchased shares in own enterprise	11.6
	purchased shares of other enterprises	2.5
No		**35.2**
Of which:	not got round to it yet	7.2
	don't believe in privatisations	4.6
	have no voucher	2.3
	insufficiently informed	2.3
	nothing worthwhile privatised	1.2
	other reasons	6.4
	hard to say	8.5

Source: Adapted from *Mir mnenii i mneniya o mire*, 1993, no. 92.

(B)   'Who, in your view, will obtain the ownership of most enterprises as a result of privatisation?' (percentages)

	January 1993	*July 1993*
The population as a whole	15	11
A narrow group of people	64	74
Hard to say	11	15

Source: Adapted from *Ekonomicheskie i sotsial'nye peremeny: monitoring obshchestvennogo mneniya*, 1993, no. 5, p. 23.

(C)   'Will you personally gain or lose as a result of the privatisation of state property?' (percentages)

Likely to gain	17
Neither gain nor lose	37
Likely to lose	28
Hard to say	18

Source: As Table 7.1(B).

tion. Workers see reductions in the labour force as a means of intensifying labour and strengthening management control by increasing the workers' insecurity. The exercise of managerial authority is stripped of its former legitimation on the basis of the wellbeing of the enterprise, and is increasingly seen as a means by which managers line their own pockets at the expense of the workers.

Worker dissatisfaction does not appear in the first instance in the form of overt conflict because the workers have no independent organisation through which to articulate their grievances, the trade union being no more than a branch of the enterprise administration. Dissatisfaction appears more directly in the form of an increasing instrumentalism, a growing sense of 'them and us', and a sullen resistance to the exercise of managerial authority on the shop floor. The brunt of this resistance is born by line managers, who find themselves squeezed between the demands of the enterprise administration and the reluctance of the workers to meet those demands.

The privatisation programme has transferred property rights, and enabled the enterprise directors to claim authority as representatives of the 'owners' of the enterprise. But all the indications are that while workers are willing to see good managers well rewarded, they do not recognise the legitimacy of privileges and financial rewards based on ownership claims alone. In all the enterprises that we have studied levels of social tension were rising rapidly through 1993, and managers were constrained in their ability to enforce their ownership rights by their fear of provoking uncontrollable conflict.

It is one thing to pass a law on property; it is another thing to define a particular set of assets as the private property of a particular juridical subject, and something else again for that subject to be able effectively to assert that property right against other claimants. The process of privatisation involves a complex interaction between juridical claims to ownership and the effective assertion of control in which private ownership is only fully established when the two coincide. In the face of passive resistance on the part of the workers, sometimes backed by their line managers, many enterprise directors looked increasingly to a strong state to endorse their property rights and to reassert managerial control, whoever might head that state and whatever its political complexion might be. In my view this is the ultimate basis of the success of Yeltsin's coup of September and October 1993, consolidated in the constitution adopted in December; whether this will secure the long-term future of directors and their prerogatives is much more uncertain.

8

The Politics of Social Issues

MARY BUCKLEY

Disagreements over social policy, in early postcommunist Russia, were closely linked to divisions over broader issues. Paramount among these were the consequences of economic reform for the gap between rich and poor and for increases in crime. Rapidly increasing prices, disorientation, insecurity and fear were among the results of chaotic transitions to market economies in newly independent states which lacked smoothly functioning systems of legality and in which corruption found new opportunities to flourish. For many citizens, especially for the growing ranks of the Communist Party in its several forms, laudable values of the past such as equality, social justice, morality, security and order were being betrayed. A feeling of betrayal was heightened by the historical context of political disintegration in which social policy was being made.

The larger setting of loss of empire, diminished status on the world stage, ethnic hostility and an ongoing process of fragmentation within the Russian Federation fuelled political volatility and economic uncertainty which, in turn, exacerbated the inherited inability to formulate coordinate social policies within the Commonwealth of Independent States. Ethnic conflicts also intensified certain social problems, such as swelling numbers of refugees. But budget deficits meant that resources to deal with many problems were lacking or insufficient. The quality of health-care and social services took on a downward spiral at a time when diseases such as diphtheria and cholera were spreading in

Russia and Ukraine. In an economic context of unemployment, inflation and wiped-out savings, some citizens turned more readily to prostitution and crime to make a living.

The aims of this chapter are threefold: first, to comment on the legacy of the Soviet state without which current predicaments and reactions to them cannot be understood; second, to outline key features of changing social structure and healthcare which have prompted competing political reactions; and third, to consider deterioration in the selected issues of crime, drugs and prostitution.

The Legacy of the Soviet State

Soviet ideology held that ownership of property by the socialist state in the name of the working class ensured 'socially just public aims', through the 'planned development of the economy'. Ideologists contended that scientific planning had 'a socially purposeful orientation' because it was linked to the principle of 'from each according to their abilities to each according to their work'. Under communism, this principle would become 'from each according to their abilities to each according to their needs'. Above all, socialism offered its citizens what capitalism, by its very exploitative nature, could not. Genuine social justice was among the many benefits.

The promotion of social justice was officially described as a process which established the political, social and economic equality of social groups. 'Deliberate policies' aimed to 'promote the levelling of social conditions' irrespective of family status or level of pay. The right to work, rising real incomes and extensive welfare rights, including the constitutional right to housing, were cited as evidence of the system's 'democratic nature' (Mchledov, 1987, p. 26).

Gorbachev modified these ideas. While he remained officially committed to socialist social justice, he emphasised that it did not mean levelling. In his book, *Perestroika*, Gorbachev propagated the notion that socialism had nothing to do with equalising. The latter was a deformity resulting from the Brezhnev 'years of stagnation' which encouraged the development of attitudes of dependence. Genuine social justice required initiative and social responsibility. The social scientist Tatyana Zaslavskaya developed these ideas further, arguing that because different groups made different contributions to socio-economic development, there should be a 'differentiated approach to social policy' ensuring a 'differentiated growth of the well-being of population groups'. Those who contributed more should receive a higher standard of living.

Whereas official ideology stressed socialist social justice after the 27th Party Congress in 1986, the rhetoric of 'social protection' began to replace it after the 28th Party Congress of 1990. This was prompted by the increasing unpopularity of the word 'socialist' and also by deep fears of the hardships that a market economy would inflict. Citizens badly needed reassurance that they would be protected in a society of inevitably growing inequalities.

The Yeltsin government inherited this discourse of social protection and retained it. In addition, Yeltsin talked of the importance of the 'social factor'. In a speech to the Presidium of the Council of Ministers in May 1993, he stressed that the economy had to have a 'greater social orientation'. Yeltsin observed that stepped-up reforms 'cannot endlessly increase the burden of social costs'. But simultaneously he agonised that resources were limited. Herein lay the dilemma. Sufficient social protection cost money which he did not have. Yeltsin wanted a 'realistic' anti-inflationary policy which was only possible 'if we are sufficiently tough'. His solution was a 'balance of interests' of participants in economic life. Interests, however, did not 'balance' in practice. Instead, they conflicted.

One of Yeltsin's major problems was how to provide a necessary social safety net to cushion the painful results of rapid reform when the International Monetary Fund (IMF) and budgetary pressures required strict restraint. Whilst most deputies in the Russian parliament, with the support of pensioners and many workers, were keen to increase pensions and the minimum wage, Yeltsin's government wished to keep more closely to the expectations of the IMF, especially during 1993. Yeltsin became exasperated after 22 July when Parliament passed the 1993 budget which increased expenditure and the deficit. Spending was set at 44.7 trillion rubles, revenues at 2.3 trillion and the deficit at 22.4 trillion. During August there was deadlock over all major items of revenue and expenditure. Ruslan Khasbulatov charged that the policies of Yeltsin's government were 'destroying the country'.

Disagreements between parliament and government over the pace of reform and over aspects of social policy led Yeltsin to conclude that parliament was seriously jeopardising his reform programme. In response, Yeltsin's critics charged that 'wild capitalism' had brought unacceptable social divisions and hardship for the majority. A brash minority was flaunting its wealth, driving around in foreign cars and eating in expensive restaurants, whilst others were wondering how they could feed their families. The new constitution of December 1993 described Russia as a 'social state' which protected the work and the health of the people; there was to be a 'guaranteed minimum wage', 'state support for the family, motherhood, fatherhood, childhood, invalids and the elderly', and free medical care, depending upon the budget, insurance contributions and other revenues. Sceptics, particularly communists and some nationalists, viewed these commitments to social protection as empty in the current socio-economic context. Even after leading reformers including Ella Pamfilova, Minister of Social Security, had left the government in January 1994 due to its commitment to slower reform, many communists and patriots were still far from satisfied. Their discontent was fuelled in the same month by a 16 per cent increase in consumer prices.

A Changing Social Structure

Economic reforms had indeed resulted in accelerating social differentiation. In early 1993, *Izvestiya* reported that at the end of 1992 the income level of the richest 10 per cent of the population was 8.7 times higher than that of the poorest 10 per cent. Moreover, the richest 20 per cent enjoyed 41 per cent of all cash incomes. At the end of 1992, according to one economist, 11 per cent of Russia's population, more than 16 million, fell under the poverty line. But as many as 50 per cent of the people had incomes below subsistence level. A massive 86 per cent of those surveyed in 1992 declared that increases in incomes lagged behind price increases and that, on average, 70 per cent of earnings was spent on food.

In August 1993, Prime Minister Viktor Chernomyrdin declared that three-quarters of the population had incomes below subsistence level. Estimates, however, varied. Roskomstat, the state statistical committee, had suggested in July that subsistence required 16,000 rubles for that month and that one-third of the population fell below this. All poverty and subsistence 'lines' are artificial constructs, but the general message was clear: many people were buying basics only, and more sparingly than before. In response to these arguments, the IMF claimed that real wages at the beginning of 1993 were similar to those of 1987. The perceptions of many Russians, however, did not match this conclusion.

Pensioners, in particular, found it hard to make ends meet and generally relied upon the help of relatives in order to subsist. Predictably, pressure to raise pensions was immense. A 90 per cent increase was introduced in a new law of pensions, effective from February 1993. As a consequence, pensions reached 4275 rubles a month. But as Otto Latsis, writing in *Izvestiya*, pointed out, these larger pensions were effectively already eaten up by price increases in January and February 1993. Even with more money, pensioners would end up able to buy less than before since prices would continue to rise. The state, however, could not actually afford to double pensions due to the budget deficit. Moreover, due to the demographic structure of the population, the number of pensioners was nearly half the number of workers. Thus pressure on state resources was high, contributing to an overload of demands. Latsis also commented that it was odd that the minimum pension was now twice the minimum wage for workers of 2250 rubles a month.

In response to this predicament, the Supreme Soviet in July 1993 increased the minimum wage to 7740 rubles a month. The justification was that the previous minimum wage was three times lower than the subsistence minimum and goods and services had, in fact, doubled since April. The government, however, criticised the new law as inflationary, noting that the budget could not cope with increased wage costs. Parliament also set the minimum pension at 14,620 rubles a month, effective in August, following the advice of its Commission on Social Policy. Pensioners were relieved, but still considered the amount meagre; the government again asked how the bill could be met. Elected deputies felt conflicting pressures from constituents and Yeltsin's government, insisting that these increases were consistent with the law on indexation. Yuri Yarov, deputy prime minister, suggested that the indexation of pensions should stop and instead compensation payments of fixed amounts should be paid. Breaking this pattern, on the eve of the December elections, Yeltsin doubled pensions and the minimum wage. By then, however, voters were not prepared to be seduced by a last-minute electoral ploy.

Although society was becoming much more stratified, the extent of the gap between rich and poor varied according to geographic location. Researchers began talk about 'rich' and 'poor' regions, citing evidence on widening gaps in average per capita income. At the end of 1992, the average per capita income in 'rich' areas was 4.9 times higher than in 'poor' ones. The former included Moscow, Magadan, Murmansk, Sakhalin, Tyumen and the Sakha and Komi republics and the latter spanned the republics of Chechia, Ingushetia, Dagestan, North Ossetia and the Moscow and Penza provinces. The relevant explanatory variables were several. 30 per cent more pensioners lived in poor areas and the proportion of those employed was one-third less. The unevenness in the decline of production across regions contributed to the diversity. Regions rich in oil and minerals enjoyed obvious advantages.

Unemployment patterns are affected by the fate of industry in different regions. Although the general trend is that unemployment is increasing, job availability varies across the vast landmass. One source in early 1993 estimated that the total number of unemployed in Russia exceeded job vacancies by three to one, but in the textile town of Ivanovo the ratio was 36 to one. Moreover, official statistics were unreliable. *Rabotnitsa* (Working Woman) reported that workers in Ivanovo were given extended holidays in 1992 with no pay. This made them ineligible to register as officially unemployed. Such 'hidden unemployment' meant that official figures generally understated the problem. Hidden unemployment had arisen in this case because the textile industry could no longer rely on supplies of cheap cotton. Central Asian leaders were keen to sell cotton on world markets for hard currency. Agreements to trade oil for cotton were also poorly implemented. Deliveries of raw materials for the textile industry were months behind and in smaller amounts than requested. The result was 250,000 textile workers with no work to do on their obsolete equipment. A knock-on effect was the closure of pre-school creches.

Roskomstat reported that for the first half of 1993 there were 700,000 registered unemployed in Russia and over 1 million registered jobseekers. Estimates in late 1992 had projected much higher figures. In August 1993, Deputy Prime Minister Yarov put Russia's official unemployment at 1 per cent and hidden unemployment at 4–5 per cent. Patterns in other CIS states were similar. Belarus, for example, saw 1.2 per cent unemployment in the first half of 1993. However, projections for the near future reach 12–13 per cent.

In Russia, 66 per cent of the registered unemployed receive benefits, but most consider them inadequate. A well thought out system has yet to be developed. Low-paid workers, however, feel similarly aggrieved, angered by growing wage differentials. In 1993, gas workers could earn eight times the wages of many factory workers and ten times those of farm workers. Moreover, most workers lacked the industrial muscle of power workers. But this could also be shortlived. In March 1993, miners again threatened strike action if the government did not meet demands for increased wages. In July, news of redundancies in some mines redefined political battles. And in September, announcement of an end to state subsidies for coal meant that the threat of closure hung over some pits.

In this general context of price increases outstripping wages in most sectors, more citizens thought about working abroad. By the end of 1992, over 100,000 had left Russia for employment elsewhere. Research by the Ministry of Labour showed that 1.5 million were prepared to do so and that a further 5 million were considering this course of action.

Growing complexities in the social fabric and in polity are also influenced by the gender divide. Interviewed in the newspaper *Nezavisimaya gazeta* in 1993, Alevtina Fedulova, Chair of the Russian Union of Women, pointed out that more than 75 per cent of the unemployed were women between 35 and 40. Since women deputies made up only 5 per cent of the Russian parliament, Fedulova argued that women had little influence on policymaking despite the fact that a woman (up to this point) headed the Ministry of Social Protection. In sum, women's economic prospects and political representation had significantly worsened.

In the Soviet state, despite proclamations of equality, aggregate statistics showed that women earned less than men. There was also an inverse relationship between women and power. This picture, Fedulova regretted, had not improved in postcommunist Russia, where women's average pay was still one-third lower than men's. The same applied to women's pensions. And women were three times more likely than men to lose their jobs. In the past, a job had been guaranteed, although promotion prospects, as in the West, were weakened by discriminatory practices and also by patriarchal attitudes towards women.

With greater freedom of speech, sexual stereotypes have been under attack since 1989 by small women's groups, some female journalists and a handful of politicians. In March 1993, Yeltsin signed a decree calling for the 'liquidation of all forms of discrimination' in relations with women, consistent with United Nations criteria. To many, this came as a surprise since throughout 1992 women's groups were especially worried that draft legislation on the family would undermine women's legal rights, enshrining in law their second-class status. A draft law was circulating which proceeded from the assumption that the family unit was the main unit of society, itself an entity with rights and obligations. The document stated that the family, not individuals in it, owned a flat or land. Individual incomes automatically became part of the family budget. The decision to reproduce was not the woman's since the embryo was given rights. Critics pointed out that this anti-democratic draft facilitated discrimination against women and, in fact, violated the existing Russian Constitution and international human rights documents. Finally, the European Court of Human Rights ruled this to be the case.

The ideas in the draft law, however, enjoy a positive resonance in sections of the Russian population. Those who believed in the traditional and patriarchal elements of Russian culture would be happy to see women stay at home, reproduce when it suited the husband, and fulfil a traditional 'servicing' role. Advocacy of the patriarchal family, especially among patriots, has become louder as images of 'emancipated woman' created by the repressive socialist state have been discredited. The extent to which Yeltsin's new decree against discrimination will be taken seriously is likely to be low. Radical changes in social attitudes are a necessary prerequisite.

To further such changes, Fedulova insisted in 1992 that women must help themselves. She told this author in an interview in

Moscow that she was active in establishing courses for women to train to enter the business world. Informal women's organisations who were critical of the Russian Union of Women for growing out of the old communist *nomenklatura* were also putting on courses to instruct women in how to become entrepreneurs. The minority of women who are successful in business, however, cannot make a significant dent in the aggregate statistics which chart women's deteriorating economic position.

Whilst many citizens have been keen to enter the business world, be they black market racketeers, former *nomenklatura* bosses, members of family businesses, circles of friends or individuals, many also hesitate. By the end of 1993, a large number of people still believed that life had been more predictable and satisfactory under Brezhnev. Whilst many of the same people, especially the young, also supported *glasnost*, the freedom to go to pop concerts and the lifting of restrictions on foreign travel, they still lamented that basic job security had gone, that luxuries were unaffordable except by a minority of successful entrepreneurs, and that the system of healthcare was not only deteriorating but would soon require costly insurance policies. The elderly especially lamented that the comforting social props of state socialism that brought 'social justice' were being eroded.

Healthcare

Soviet healthcare had developed from a most rudimentary starting point. It became Soviet tradition for statistical yearbooks to pride themselves on increasing numbers of doctors and hospital beds. True to this spirit, 'strengthening the health of the Soviet people' and 'increasing life expectancy' were the main goals for healthcare adopted under Gorbachev. But alongside commitment to improve state services, a new emphasis on entrepreneurship meant that private medicine was encouraged. Charity, too, became acceptable again, resulting in a mushrooming of local groups devoted to philanthropy.

Following political disintegration and fragmentation, services worsened and the health of post-Soviet peoples deteriorated: official statistics, with all their limitations pointed to a deepening crisis. Investigative reporting continued to expose the many problems of healthcare that had begun to be revealed by *glasnost*; the picture constructed by the media at the same time became much bleaker. According to *Nezavisimaya gazeta*, for instance, 42 per cent of hospitals in Russia and 30 per cent of outpatients' clinics lacked a hot-water supply. 12 per cent of the former and 7 per cent of the latter had no water at all. 18 per cent of hospitals and 15 per cent of clinics had no sewage system. Similarly horrific, 70 per cent of these institutions violated sanitary and hygienic standards (see Tables 8.1 and 8.2).

These conditions prevail in a medical system which has to cope with an increasing incidence of disease. In 1992, there were over 2717 cases of diphtheria in Russia, 127 of whom died. By August 1993, there were 4000 further reported cases. The epidemic also spread to Ukraine. There were refusals to be vaccinated due to fears of unsterile needles which could give AIDS. Enthusiasm for the announcement of a special vaccination plan in Russia was therefore muted. Currently, only 43 per cent of babies in Moscow are inoculated against diphtheria before the age of one. Official reports suggest that only 59 per cent of children in Russia have been vaccinated against whooping cough, 69 per cent against diphtheria and 71 per cent against poliomyelitis. Other diseases on the increase include cholera, malaria, dysentery and encephalitis.

Environmental factors contribute to the spread of disease. It is estimated that 50 per cent of the drinking water falls below required standards. Apparently every year, there are 75,000 breaks in water mains which lead to secondary contaminations. Industry contributes to chemical contamination and there are high levels of bacterial and viral contamination in Russia's major rivers, such as the Volga, Don and Ob. Russia's air, too, is highly polluted. *Nezavisimaya gazeta* claims that just 15 per cent of those in urban areas breathe air which meets international health standards. And particular parts of the CIS suffer the consequences of radioactivity dating back to accidents in 1949. These include the southern Urals and the Techa river basin. The accident at Chernobyl in 1986 affected Ukraine, Belarus and Russia. The reactor in 1993 still emitted some radiation and its foundations and protective sarcophagus were feared unstable.

On top of these factors, poor working conditions and falling standards of nutrition due to high food prices mean that the

TABLE 8.1 Illness rates, medical provision and mortality in the Soviet Republics, 1989–91

	Tuberculosis (first diagnosis per 1000 popn)	Cancer (first diagnosis per 1000 popn)	Hospital beds (per 10,000 popn)	Doctors (per 10,000 popn)	Infant mortality (deaths per 1000 live births)	Maternal mortality (deaths per 100,000 births)
All USSR	36.9	265.9	130.9	42.3	22.3	43.8
RSFSR	34.2	274.5	134.7	44.3	17.8	49.0
Ukraine	31.9	281.5	135.2	44.2	13.6	32.7
Belarus	29.8	267.5	123.3	40.7	11.7	24.8
Uzbekistan	46.1	169.2	123.0	35.5	35.8	42.8
Kazakhstan	65.8	289.9	136.4	40.3	27.1	53.1
Georgia	28.9	140.9	110.7	59.2	15.9	54.9
Azerbaijan	36.2	224.9	99.4	38.9	25.0	28.6
Lithuania	30.9	268.8	124.4	46.1	14.3	28.7
Moldova	39.6	223.5	130.8	39.2	19.1	34.1
Latvia	27.4	270.9	148.1	49.6	15.6	56.5
Kyrgyzstan	53.3	219.0	122.0	37.3	29.6	42.6
Tajikistan	44.4	163.1	107.2	25.5	40.0	38.9
Armenia	17.6	223.1	89.4	42.8	17.1	34.6
Turkmenistan	63.6	203.0	114.2	36.2	46.6	55.2
Estonia	20.6	313.0	121.0	45.7	13.1	41.2

Source: Compiled from Okhrana zdorov'ya v SSSR (Moscow: Finansy i statistika, 1990) and other official publications.

TABLE 8.2   *Health indicators in the Russian Federation, 1990–June 1993*

	1990	1991	1992	First half of 1993
Birthrate (births per 1,000)	13.4	12.1	10.8	9.6
Salmonellosis (cases per 100,000)	70.4	74.2	80.1	82.0
Diphtheria (cases per 100,000)	0.8	1.3	3.1	4.6
Whooping cough (cases per 100,000)	16.9	20.8	25.0	29.0
Measles (cases per 100,000)	12.4	13.8	15.2	30.0
Cancer (first diagnoses per 100,000)	264.5	266.0	267.6	269.2
Tuberculosis (first diagnoses per 100,000)	34.2	34.0	37.7	45.3
Syphilis (first diagnoses per 100,000)	4.5	5.0	8.9	21.5
Hospital beds (per 10,000)	137.5	134.7	127.7	121.3
Doctors (per 10,000)	46.9	44.3	42.0	40.0
Invalids from childhood (per 10,000 children up to age 16)	43.1	61.6	62.0	62.0
Infant mortality (per 1,000 live births)	17.4	17.8	18.0	18.8
Maternal mortality (per 100,000 births)	47.4	52.4	50.8	52.0
Mortality of males aged 20–44 (deaths per 1,000 in group)	7.6	8.0	8.8	10.9
Crude death rate (deaths per 1,000)	11.2	11.4	12.1	14.4
Life expectancy (years at birth)	69.2	69.0	68.6	67.2

Source: As Table 9.1

probability of being healthy is falling. Average life expectancy in Russia is currently 74.3 years for women but a low 63.8 for men. And in areas like the dried-up Aral Sea, life expectancy has fallen to 55. Here 77 per cent of babies are born ill. Throughout Russia, infant mortality remains relatively high.

Newspaper reports in *Izvestiya* in 1993 pointed out that infant mortality had increased from 16.8 deaths per 1000 children under the age of one in 1991 to 17.1 per 1000 in 1992. Scanning statistics across the years from 1975 shows this to be a small fluctuation and a figure lower than most years in the preceding 20. But Russian infant mortality rates are likely to show a jump in future years to over 25 deaths per 1000 births. This is because Russia is about to calculate new rates according to the criteria of the World Health Organisation (WHO). Traditional Russian regulations date back to 1939 when the People's Commissariat of Health specified that a baby was considered to be alive only if it could breathe on its own. Babies that could not were deemed stillborn and no attempt was made to save them. And babies weighing under 1 kilogram were classified as a late miscarriage or a foetus, not a baby. WHO criteria, by contrast, stipulate four signs of life: breathing; heartbeat; pulsation of the umbilical cord; muscular contractions.

A decree signed by Yeltsin 'On sustaining the lives of infants', effective from January 1993, requires that doctors in Russia devote more care to saving the lives of babies weighing more than 500 grams. This requires doctors to revive what previously they labelled as stillborn. The decree has been controversial among doctors for the medical effort it will require and for the possible ill-health of the surviving child. Implementation of the decree, moreover, will require more special equipment for the intensive care of premature babies, which is already insufficient in most maternity homes. Critics of the decree have pointed out that the cost will be huge and that more specialists are required. *Moskovskie novosti* commented that Russia's medical profession was just not ready for this. The medical paper *Meditsinskaya gazeta* warned that proper care had to be taken of premature babies since future births were more likely to be early ones. This was due to malnutrition among women, irregular diet, stress, ecological factors, the psychological and emotional state of society and the high abortion rate. In the CIS, for many women abortion continues to be the unhealthy substitute for contraception. An estimated 20 per cent of Russian women use contraceptives. In 1991, there were twice as many abortions as live births in state hospitals.

These numerous health problems occur in a system whose government is attempting to encourage medical insurance. For decades, citizens have expected state medical care, been prepared to bribe within that system or, when necessary, resort to private care for payment. The idea of personal insurance, however, goes against the ideological grain of a welfare state. Moreover, the confusion surrounding the process of insurance and privatisation has led to further disorientation. Most of Russia's regions in 1993 were unwilling to adopt a system of medical insurance. Indeed, the law on medical insurance has proved highly controversial. Supporters expect it to improve standards and inject some dignity into dealings with patients. Critics fear that it will mean good healthcare for a minority. Like the USA and Britain, Russia is grappling with the dilemma of how to deliver a more efficient system. Unlike them, it lacks modern equipment, drugs and sufficient standards of hygiene; it suffers from increasing levels of disease, a lack of money and no political consensus on how best to proceed.

Crime

It was not until 1989 that journalists were able to report freshly released crime statistics to the Soviet people. Thereafter quarterly and yearly updates were given. Every new bulletin revealed escalating increases in registered crimes and crime rates among minors. Given the unreliability of crime statistics worldwide, precise interpretations were hazardous. Nonetheless, it was clear that reported crime was increasing and that the people experienced heightened fear and anxiety about mugging, theft and rape.

These statistics and fears continued to grow in the CIS. In recognition that crime was soaring, Alexander Rutskoi, then vice-president, was put in charge of preparations for a national conference on combatting crime which took place in February 1993. Here it was reported that in 1992, 2.76 million crimes had been committed in various parts of the Federation. Assaults and robberies were up over 60 per cent and premeditated murder increased by 40 per cent. In July 1992, 17 per cent of citizens were entirely in favour of owning firearms for self-defence and 31 per cent were in favour with some reservations.

Crime fell into different categories. Mugging on the street or in lifts for cash, especially hard currency, targeted foreign visitors. More systematically organised crime run by racketeers demanded protection money from entrepreneurs setting up kiosks, market stalls or shops. One documentary on Russian television argued that every street in Moscow had been sewn up by organised crime. Once its tentacles were deeply rooted in developing business they were hard to curb by law enforcement agencies, especially if these, too, were corrupt and well-practised in receiving bribes. In 1992, over 4000 organised criminal groups were identified in Russia, one-quarter of these with connections outside the Federation.

Other categories of crime include the making of counterfeit money, illegal petroleum sales, the resale of illegal videos, non-payment of taxes and blackmarket services in car repair, housing construction and arms sales.

In 1993 journalists paid special attention to corruption within state agencies. Data collected by the Ministry of Security suggested that thousands of state bureaucrats were corrupt. The 'new ways' that Gorbachev had called for had in many senses not developed; and the vehement attacks that Yeltsin had made against corruption among the *nomenklatura* under Soviet socialism were still relevant to his own apparatus. Some journalists argued that new laws were needed to control bureaucrats. But in a situation in which laws were generally ineffective anyway because rarely implemented, law alone is unlikely to be a remedy.

Cynicism also surrounds the Interdepartmental Commission on Combating Crime and Corruption. In October 1992, Yeltsin created this commission by presidential decree. Initially few people knew of its existence since no statute was signed for several months. When one appeared, it stated that the commission was permanent and intended to help the Security Council draft decisions on crime prevention in society and in governmental structures. It is also supposed to coordinate the duties of the Ministry of Internal Affairs, the Ministry of Security, the Ministry of Defence, Foreign Intelligence and other relevant structures. *Izvestiya* wondered what 'coordination' really meant in a context of a proliferation of new government agencies.

A new criminal code has incorporated some legal changes. The number of offences punishable by fines rather than imprisonment will increase. Imprisonment for mercenary and violent crimes will rise from 15 to 25 years. The number of crimes punishable by the death penalty has been reduced from 28 to 6. And criminal charges can be brought against those 14 years and over. How effectively to police societies undergoing rapid change when resources are stretched and crime is rising is the central question of law and order facing Russia and the other post-Soviet states.

Drugs

Apart from articles in specialist medical journals of the 1920s, recognition of a drugs problem in the USSR was not forthcoming until the late 1980s. Like unemployment, prostitution and suicide, official Soviet ideology declared that drug addiction was characteristic of capitalism's moral decay.

Thanks to *glasnost* and to the investigative reporting of journalists Illesh and Shestinsky, drug addiction was finally exposed in *Izvestiya* in 1987 as 'an evil that experts acknowledge is growing around the world'. These journalists informed readers that the authorities drew a distinction between 'classical drug abuse' and 'vulgar drug abuse'. The former referred to plant substances, such as marijuana; the latter included 'new, home-made narcotic substances, . . . produced by processing preparations of various kinds . . . similar to those that are produced industrially for medical purposes'. The distinction was similar to Western categories of 'soft' and 'hard' drugs.

The statistics released during Gorbachev's leadership pale in comparison with subsequent ones. Despite the unreliability of official estimates, it is hard not to conclude that an alarming increase in drug addiction is accompanying the transition to market economics. According to the newspaper *Megapolis Express*, the Ministry of Internal Affairs estimated that in January 1992 turnover in drug trafficking totalled 6 billion rubles. By November 1992, the figure had reached 100 billion. Allegedly, a professional dealer could make 200,000 to 300,000 rubles a day.

Journalists pointed out that his money could only be pumped into the process of privatisation, thereby greasing the mechanisms of corruption and organised crime.

Statistics released by the Ministry of Internal Affairs suggested that there are 1.5 million drug addicts in Russia and 5.5 million in the CIS. The head of one drug rehabilitation hospital in Moscow, however, considers these figures to be a serious understatement. When his department offered anonymous treatment for payment, it was inundated with clients who were not on official registers. He regretted that money was not available to create the necessary infrastructure for psychotherapeutic care. *Megapolis Express* considered in December 1992 that the average daily dose cost an addict about 3000 rubles. Inevitably crime increased from attempts to obtain the necessary money. In 1992, there were 1800 such reported crimes.

Given the interregional nature of organised drugs crime, *Izvestiya* stressed in 1993 the importance of CIS states coordinating their activities in this sphere. Already in October 1992, top police officers and internal affairs ministers from the former Soviet republics, excluding Lithuania and Latvia, agreed to work together.

Prostitution

During the Gorbachev years, sensational stories were printed in *Literaturnaya gazeta*, *Komsomolskaya pravda*, *Nedelya* and *Sovetskaya Rossiya* with explicit moral messages. Young women who 'worked' hotels in tourist spots in Sochi, soliciting foreigners, were an insult to society. Madames who lured women to work in brothels, taking advantage of their lack of residence permits and their poverty, were corrupt. Pimps who demanded protection money, and who beat up prostitutes if they did not get it, were violent parasites. Early articles focused on moral degradation, deception, crime, violence and venereal disease.

More systematic analyses followed. A study of prostitutes in Georgia found that women saw discrepancies between the lives they dreamed of and everyday reality. Images of elegant and successful women in the media underlined the mediocrity of their lives. Some women found prostitution attractive as a form of supplementary income.

In 1992 and 1993, journalism highlighted child prostitution and the spread of child pornography. According to *Komsomolskaya pravda* there were more than 1000 girls under 18 working as prostitutes in Moscow. Allegedly, the 13 to 15 age-group preferred to work near hotels, whilst those aged 12 and younger frequented Red Square and casinos. 7–8-year-olds waited at home for clients. Girls aged 12 to 15 cost more than adults – about $100 to $150 an hour. In some cases, parents sold their daughters into prostitution for 30,000 rubles. Adult prostitutes reacted violently to the appearance of younger prostitutes by beating them up or shaving their heads.

During the late 1980s, debate had raged about whether to criminalise prostitution. Prostitutes could then be issued a warning and be fined up to 100 rubles for the first offence. The debate continued in Yeltsin's Russia where, in early 1993, prostitutes could be fined up to 900 rubles, but not criminally prosecuted. An article in the legal code on the corruption of minors is applicable to under-age prostitutes. But this is extremely hard to enforce. In order to prove that a pimp has exploited a young girl, her clients have to testify.

A special temporary unit, however, had been set up to combat brothelkeeping. Within two months, its 10 police officers had closed eight establishments. They were easy to find by looking at classified advertisements in newspapers. Criminal charges had been brought against the owners of firms such as 'Emmanuelle' and 'Anastasia'. Women working for them could bring in from 8000 to 15,000 rubles an hour, themselves receiving 30 per cent of the takings. Yevgenii Kozlov, head of the special unit, commented that charges can be brought against owners under Article 226 of the Russian Criminal Code which deals with brothelkeeping. The offence is punishable by up to 5 years' deprivation of freedom with or without internal exile. But clients and prostitutes are required to be witnesses.

So long as unemployment and low wages are suffered by women, prostitution will remain a lucrative source of income, especially while inflation outstrips wages. As the dollar continues to penetrate the economy, prostitution for hard currency lures young girls. It is distressing that in response to questionnaires, schoolgirls note that prostitution is high on their list of preferred professions.

Conclusion

Russian sociologists have become preoccupied with what they call the 'socio-psychological situation'. This refers to psychological states in a rapidly changing social context and is linked to questions of how much unhappiness, discontent and despair a population can endure before mass action ensues. Survey research in 1993, before the crisis of September and October, showed that 75 per cent of Muscovites were unhappy with their lives and that 44 per cent found it hard to cope with new price increases. Especially demoralising was the importance of obtaining dollars in a society in which most citizens were paid in rubles. As many as 44 per cent of Muscovites claimed never to have possessed dollars, nor even seen them, while 29 per cent had seen but not possessed them and 27 per cent had acquired them. Greatest optimism about the future was found among the young.

When in September 1993, Yeltsin unconstitutionally dissolved parliament, the majority of citizens showed disinterest. They were more concerned about queueing for as many plastic tokens for the metro as possible since prices were rumoured to be increasing from 10 rubles to 30. The newspaper cartoon 'Not another revolution' summed up weariness with political battles. Whilst over 70 per cent of Muscovites finally approved of Yeltsin's 'firm hand' and hoped that crime would fall as a result, they remained uncertain about their own socio-economic futures. And support for Yeltsin was far less enthusiastic in many regions.

The election results of December 1993 confirmed that a majority of voters opposed economic shock therapy and its consequences. But the failure of nearly half of the electorate to turn out to vote indicated that the low level of interest in politics evident during the two constitutional crises of 1993 persisted. Many citizens had come to believe that politicians would not alleviate their daily plight and so voting was not worth the effort.

During the election campaign, the leaders of all 13 political blocs and parties commented upon social policy and social issues, keenly aware that voters were troubled by poverty, inflation, unemployment, crime and a moral vacuum. What different leaders emphasised about social issues, however, predictably varied. Zyuganov of the Communist Party of the Russian Federation stressed labour, justice, 'civic peace' and prosperity for everyone rather than for the few. A potential ally, the Agrarian Party, focused on regulating the land and how to combat 'speculation'. Vladimir Zhirinovsky's Liberal-Democratic Party emphasised the need to combat crime, re-establish Russia's greatness and reunite separate Slav countries. And for over two years Zhirinovsky had crudely been championing vodka, sausage, and the right of men to decide whether their wives should work and how many children they should produce. His fairy-tale economic promises and national chauvinism won over many destitute Russians keen for improved lives and for a great Russia no longer dependent on humanitarian aid from foreigners.

The divided democrats delivered varied social messages. Amid the slick professionals of Russia's Choice who argued for 'a normal market', a softer Pamfilova spoke of the need 'to care about the suffering of ordinary people'. Voters remained unconvinced that Russia's Choice would do so. The Russian Movement for Democratic Reforms gave proportionally far more television coverage to social problems. Sobchak talked of extensive housing repairs, guarantees of a minimum standard of living and protection for invalids. Shakhrai of Russian Unity and Concord stressed the need for 'a humanitarian way' through agreement, family and spirituality. The Yavlinsky–Boldyrev–Lukin bloc stressed the importance of listening to the people and of developing a state which 'no longer deceived'. Travkin's Democratic Party of Russia declared its main social policy to be the tackling of poverty and deteriorating services, particularly for children and the elderly. Women of Russia gave priority to a social programme with guarantees for the unemployed. Fedulova emphasised the need to defend light industry, education and medicine, while Lakhova delivered the loud message that 'no-one except us looks at female unemployment'. Zhirinovsky's sexist leer after the elections at the possibility of cooperating with Women of Russia was met with an appropriate rebuff.

The centrist Civic Union declared a commitment to stability, justice and development, warning of the danger of hidden unemployment becoming a future explosion of real unemployment. Of the smaller parties, the ecological group Cedar advocated 'clean' products, good healthcare insurance and legal mechanisms for the rights of individuals. The Future of Russia–New Names bloc concentrated on the importance of incentives for the young in production and on social problems in the countryside. Finally, Dignity and Charity attempted to appeal to everyone by addressing the poor, women, the young, the old, teachers, invalids, the blind and war veterans. It also advocated the regulation of television advertisements such as women in bikinis promoting Western chocolate bars in order to protect moral standards.

Above all, the election campaign illustrated the politicisation of social issues and highlighted competing public discourses about how best to tackle pressing social problems. But the fate of social policies remains complex, linked as they are to a range of factors: government economic policy, budgetary constraints, IMF requirements, executive–legislative relations, the readiness of citizens not to rebel in adversity, reformers' fears of Zhirinovsky's popularity, and the outcome of future presidential elections.

The relationship between society and state in Russia has always been a close one, but with different implications in different historical periods. In this context of free elections, the nature of that relationship may crucially determine future directions of economic and social policy. In the sharply divided society that is Russia in the 1990s, stable outcomes depend not only upon the nature of the policies favoured by the next president but also upon the readiness of the losers to accept that they have lost without recrimination. Thus a great deal also hangs upon whether the political culture can be successfully redefined to allow a greater space for toleration, compromise and coalition among parties and social groups that at present are irreconcilably divided.

9

The Politics of Foreign Policy

ALEX PRAVDA

One of the reasons why the West seeks to promote democratisation in Russia is the widely-held belief that democracies tend to have peaceful relations with the outside world. At its strongest this argument contends that democracies do not go to war with one another. If political elites become used to reaching compromises at home, they apply them in their external dealings. Governments relying on popular legitimacy and electoral support may find it more difficult to use violence abroad. More plausible than the contention that democracies are inherently peaceful is the general line of reasoning that associates them simply with more transparent, flexible and pragmatic foreign policies. The fact that the West hopes democratisation will make Russia a more 'normal' foreign policy actor, one more acceptable to the international community, is appreciated by most Russian officials. Andrei Kozyrev, the Russian Foreign Minister, has defined his goal as being 'to create a normal state with a normal policy and a normal diplomacy'. He defines 'normality' in terms of democracy and laments that achieving this 'has turned out to be the most difficult task, apparently because we have become used to living in abnormal conditions'. Those conditions have made the achievement of normality (democracy) an elusive goal in a politics of foreign policy, as in all spheres of Russian public life.

How the politics of foreign policy has fared in the difficult

208

conditions over the last two years sheds an interesting light on the nature of those conditions and on the triple legacy of the Soviet, *perestroika* and early post-Soviet eras. Much of the foreign policy process still bears the heavy imprint of the old Soviet system: executive domination, Byzantine decision-making, and over-lapping jurisdictions and rivalries between government agencies. To these features the *perestroika* period added public controversy over foreign policy and the use of criticism of international issues for domestic power purposes. In 1992–3, the organisational dis-location that grew under Gorbachev deepened. A top-heavy pre-sidential apparatus presided over a fragmented foreign policy institutional structure which generated a confusion of policies. At the same time, the Yeltsin period has seen the airing of public dif-ferences over foreign policy questions become more pronounced, more loudly expressed and used more disruptively in the struggle between president and parliament. The tussles over domestic issues became increasingly entangled with those over international ones.

It is a truism that foreign policy is to a large extent the product of domestic concerns and political battles. Under Gorbachev foreign policy was placed more explicitly than ever at the service of domestic strategies. Yet, in the years since Gorbachev, the overlap between domestic and foreign has increased further. The end of the USSR transferred a large sector of what had been domestic issues into the international sphere. Overnight Russia's relations with the other union republics became a matter, formally at least, of foreign policy. This sudden encroachment of foreign on domestic policy created a large penumbra of 'inter-mestic' policy. Relations with the other members of the former Soviet Union, the 'near abroad', have made links between domestic politics and foreign policy closer and more intense than ever before. These links have emerged clearly in the public politics of foreign and security policy, but have also been evident in the more hidden processes of executive policy formulation and decision-making. The first part of this chapter focuses on public political debates and controversies surrounding external policy issues; the second examines the ways in which executive agencies shape foreign policy; and the conclusion briefly assesses the outlook for the politics of policy towards the 'far' and 'near abroad'.

Public Politics

One would not expect foreign policy issues to figure very prominently in people's minds at a time when the Russian population has experienced such turmoil in everyday life. Predictably, economic changes and accompanying deterioration in living conditions preoccupy most Russians. Inflation stands out clearly as the greatest cause of concern, with the collapse of industrial production a considerably less alarming second. External disruptions follow surprisingly hard on the heels of domestic material ones. Foreign policy problems, especially those involving the 'near abroad', have figured quite prominently in public concerns. In late 1992, for instance, the breakup of the USSR and, more saliently, the conflicts in Moldova, North Caucasus and Central Asia, worried Russians almost as much as falls in industrial production. This was particularly the case among the younger and better educated as well as among those who supported Yeltsin and his government. Among those more critical of Yeltsin, 'far abroad' issues seemed to be a particular cause of concern. If only one in every four Russians in late 1992 expressed regret at the loss of Great Power status, a substantial majority wanted to see Russia's high international standing restored.

Such public concern is perhaps not surprising, coming as it does in the aftermath of a triple national humiliation – the loss of the global contest with capitalism, the end of the outer empire in Eastern Europe and the breakup of the inner empire of the USSR. It is this last development that has particularly alarmed the political elite and the population at large. It has created a climate in which all foreign policy issues have become highly politicised and vigorously contested.

Foreign policy questions have figured prominently in general political debate. The salience of international issues for political groups and parties reflects the instrumental as well as substantive importance of these problems. There is no doubt that most of the Russian political elite feel strongly about foreign policy questions especially where the CIS and the defence of Russian minorities 'abroad' is concerned. For the reform democrats openness to the West is central to their overall strategy for Russia as a modernising European state. For the nationalist opposition the need for Russian independence and assertiveness are emotional issues fundamental to their basic philosophy and political identity. At the same time the nationalists and others opposed to domestic economic and political reform have often used foreign policy issues as cudgels with which to hit out at Yeltsin and his ministers. The government may receive more popular support for its international achievements than for its economic performance. Nonetheless, opposition groups have often found it easier to put forward persuasive alternatives on external policy than on the economic front. The frequent instrumental use of foreign policy issues is hardly surprising in the climate of Russian politics. Its confrontational nature and the sheer confusion of political debate, with its extensive overlaps between domestic and external policies, all make criticism highly transferable across issue areas.

Whatever the contribution of belief and utility in shaping political groups' and parties' attachment to foreign policy issues, there is an overall consistency between their alignments on domestic and international matters. Those supporting radical marketisation and democratic reform also advocate a Western-oriented foreign policy. By the same token those who caution against too rapid a pace of economic and political reform warn against too great a dependence on the West. The correlation between the domestic and foreign policy stances is most apparent where opinions are most polarised, at the extremes of the political spectrum. Many policy issues are distorted by being viewed through the prism of political confrontation. The need to oppose the other side has often played a more important role in determining policy stances than the substance of the policies themselves. At the centre views are somewhat more differentiated and the connections between attitudes towards external and internal issues often less clear. Much depends on the shifts in the general political climate. What is important is that these shifts embrace both domestic *and* international policy. The period from autumn 1992 to spring 1993, which saw hesitation about radical economic reform and a general strengthening of the opposition, also witnessed the emergence of doubts about unquestioning cooperation with the West. The movement towards slower economic reform since late 1993 has been accompanied by a more assertive stance in the 'far' and especially in the 'near abroad'.

These parallel movements along internal and external policy tracks are similar in broad outline rather than specific detail. This reflects in part the level and quality of foreign policy discourse among Russian political groups and parties. Poorly organised and ill-equipped to deal even with domestic policy issues, most political parties have displayed little expertise in foreign affairs. Party pronouncements on international issues tend to remain at the level of fundamental declarations of principle. Foreign policy proposals amount to statements reiterating those principles in somewhat greater detail and reacting against official policy rather than putting forward specific policy alternatives.

The poverty of foreign policy programmes and the fragmented and volatile nature of party organisation make it difficult to categorise in any very precise fashion. Whatever divisions one draws, they often correspond more to the views of individual party leaders than the parties as a whole. Nevertheless, it is possible to group politicians and their parties into three clusters distinguished by their stances on foreign policy issues: liberal internationalists, patriots, and pragmatic nationalists. These labels reflect basic orientations as well as attitudes towards foreign policy and highlight the distinctions between committed pro-Western reformers, those who feel emotionally attached to Russia as a cause as well as a state, and those whose stance reflects a pragmatic calculation of Russian interests.

These different political perspectives on foreign policy are sometimes divided into two major groups: Westernisers or Atlanticists on the one hand and Eurasians on the other, echoing the 19th-century controversy between Westernisers and Slavophiles. However, to describe the politicians and parties engaged in the current foreign policy debate in such a dichotomised fashion is to oversimplify a far more complex clustering of opinion. While it is clearly true that liberal internationalists identify most closely, and patriots identify least, with the Westernising perspective, pragmatic nationalists favour elements of Westernism. Even patriots are not wholly opposed to some aspects of Western association for Russia. Eurasianism differs considerably in meaning and is distributed unevenly between the groups. Eurasianism in the sense of supporting a certain degree of isolation from and defiance of Europe and the West is associated with the patriots. Insofar as it denotes a wariness of integration with the West and a preference to ensure that Russian priorities reflect its two-continent geostrategic position, Eurasianism is espoused by pragmatic nationalists. And even liberal internationalists acknowledge that Russia is a very peculiar kind of European country and, in an effort to make a virtue of that peculiarity, talk of its bridging and mediating role between Europe and Asia. The approaches taken by all three groups thus contain elements of Eurasianism. Emotional Eurasianism predominates among patriots, while pragmatic nationalists subscribe to a more sober version. The overall weight of Eurasianism in the orientation of all three groups has increased over time. It figured least prominently across the board in the first half of 1992, became central to the pragmatic nationalists in the latter half of that year and emerged as an element even in the liberal internationalists' platform in the course of 1993.

The Great Debate

The debate on foreign policy has been intense and far-reaching, covering both specifics and fundamentals. The intensity of the debate reflects the poverty of serious public discussion of foreign policy even under Gorbachev. Not until 1990–1 was there any wide-ranging public debate on Soviet foreign policy and then it was absorbed largely with negative criticism of Gorbachev and Shevardnadze, rather than with the advancement of alternatives. This negative tradition persisted into the Yeltsin period. A second and more obvious 'historical' reason for the intensity and depth of debate is the simple fact that the physical reconfiguration of Russia – now reduced to its 17th-century dimensions – forced a rethinking of fundamentals.

Liberal Internationalists

This label applies to groups, parties and individual politicians who support priority being given to collaboration and even integration with the West and the international community. Liberal internationalist views have been closely linked with those supporting democratic political and marketising economic reforms in Russia. Views of this kind were initially identified with movements such as Democratic Russia and, more recently, the electoral and parliamentary bloc 'Russia's Choice'. The fullest and most articulate

exposition of liberal internationalism has come from Andrei
Kozyrev, the Foreign Minister. He has taken a somewhat idealist
view of the international system, reflecting his past association
with those in the old Soviet Foreign Ministry who promoted the
shift in the late 1980s towards greater collaboration with international organisations, especially the UN. Kozyrev has claimed,
however, to take a pragmatic rather than idealist view of Russia's
international role. Anxious in the early months of 1992 to distance
Russia's new foreign policy from that of Gorbachev, he went out
of his way to criticise the moralising qualities of New Thinking
and to stress his own sober, practical approach. He justified
cooperation with the USA and the international community on
pragmatic grounds. Kozyrev and his fellow liberal internationalists have repeatedly stressed the economic necessity of a
collaborative policy towards the G7 states, and have also highlighted the security advantages of a cooperative strategy towards
the West.

Both pragmatic arguments justifying their Westernism rest on
certain assumptions and tenets. Liberal internationalists in fact
share many of the beliefs of the Gorbachevian New Thinkers
from whom they have tried to distance themselves. They take an
idealist view of international relations, seeing economic and political collaboration and the observance of international norms as
the most effective way of advancing national interests. A corollary
of this idealism is that they play down the existence of any
national 'enemies'. They depict Western states as potential, and in
many cases, notably that of the USA, actual partners. Underlying
and reinforcing such contentions is the belief that the West
provides the best model for Russian economic and political
modernisation. This belief rests in turn on their identification of
Russia as an essentially European state and civilisation. It follows
that Russia's foreign policy interests lie with giving preference to
economic and strategic alignment with the West, indeed to efforts
to integrate into its structures – hence the goal of gaining
membership of GATT and the G7. According to the electoral
programme of Russia's Choice in late 1993, careful assessment of
national security strategy led to the conclusion that Russia's
interests lay with those of the developed democratic countries.
Only in alliance with them could Russia hope to maintain stability and progress.

The other side of this Westernising coin is the relative down-grading of relations with the less developed world. Liberal internationalists of course deny that they in any way neglect Southern relations and many have talked of Russia as a bridge between Europe and Asia. Such denials were a way of responding to charges of excessive Westernism and a way of attracting support from the large majority of the political establishment – three-quarters according to an early 1993 survey – which thought Russia should provide a link between East and West, without alienating the almost equally large proportion of elite opinion which approves of Russian integration into the Western international system.

Liberal internationalists have also sought to adjust to wide-spread elite and mass preferences where the 'near' abroad is concerned. In the early months of 1992 Kozyrev underscored the importance and viability of creating effective multilateral CIS relations. By 1993 continued commitment to multilateralism, to creating a common security and economic space within the CIS, was accompanied by a growing stress on bilateral agreements and, more importantly, on the need to safeguard Russian minority rights. Adjustments on the 'far' and 'near' abroad notwithstanding, liberal internationalists have continued to advocate a foreign policy that gives high priority to cooperation and identification with the West and to the observance of international norms.

Patriots

Standing in 'irreconcilable opposition' to Yeltsin, this cluster of movements and parties couched most of its statements about foreign policy in highly negative terms. Both the communist and non-communist components of this 'Red–Brown' grouping launched violent attacks on Kozyrev and what they dubbed his betrayal of Russian national interests. One of the most virulent critics of Kozyrev's foreign policy, Sergei Baburin, leader of the National Union in the Russian Supreme Soviet (later elected as a deputy to the State Duma), depicted the political struggle in Russia as one between the patriots and the party of betrayal. Further out still on the extreme patriotic wing, Vladimir Zhirinovsky called Kozyrev a CIA agent and the secretary of the

American Ambassador in Moscow. Communist and non-communist patriots alike agreed in 1993 that the government's foreign policy had produced only failures by following a naively pro-Western line. In the eyes of the patriots the West continued to pose a threat to Russian interests. This did not take the form of a direct military threat even in the view of the most extreme groups. Rather, the West in general and the USA in particular as pursuing aims inimical to Russian interests. A few patriots claimed that the West sought the further disintegration of Russia itself; most contended that the West wished to take advantage of the economic and political weakness of Russia to exploit its raw material wealth. According to the electoral programme of the Communist Party of Russia in late 1993 Yeltsin and his government were out to turn the country into a 'raw material colony of international capital'. Patriots generally rejected the need for Western aid, insisting that independence was the only way out of Russia's deep economic crisis. On this question of self-reliance in the economic sphere as in many others, patriots' views find widespread support among the military elite.

Self-reliance and independence were also patriots' watchwords of Russian policy in major regional conflicts, where Russia, they considered, should have supported traditional allies rather than siding with the USA and other Western states. In the Middle East, patriots objected to Moscow's endorsement of sanctions against Libya and Iraq. Some went so far as to express support for Baghdad as a traditional Russian ally which had fallen victim to US aggression. Russian policy in the former Yugoslavia was repeatedly criticised as kowtowing to Western interests and betraying traditional allies such as Serbia. Calls were frequently made for solidarity with Serbia and some of the patriotic organisations, including the Liberal-Democratic Party of Russia and the Russian National Assembly, sent volunteers to fight in the former Yugoslavia. While not going as far as to object to cooperation with the UN, the patriots insisted on placing Russian interests, conceived in traditional terms, above all other considerations. Similarly, while there was no outright rejection of arms control and disarmament, parity was placed before partnership as an essential ingredient of any agreements with the USA.

Running through the patriots' arguments was a determination to assert Russian dignity as a Great Power or what some described as a great world power, though few tried to advocate global influence along old Soviet lines. What all patriots agreed on was that Russia had to pursue its interests as a Eurasian rather than a Western-oriented power. They rehearsed some of the old Slavophile theses about the unique qualities of Russian civilisation and its incompatibility with Western notions of liberalism and democracy. If the negative meaning of the patriots' emotional Eurasianism was clear as an objection to the Westernisation of Yeltsin's and Kozyrev's foreign policy, its positive attributes were ambiguous. Many of the patriots favoured alliances with the countries of the South and Far East, especially with India and China. At the same time they saw the South as a source of threat, issuing in particular from militant Islam. These two views were reconciled by those who argued that links with the South were vital to defend Russia against these dangers. Only extremists, such as Zhirinovsky, put forward outlandish ideas about the need to foster war in the South in order to use conflict to pressure Afghanistan, Turkey and Iran.

Most of the patriots were far closer to Zhirinovsky in their views on Russia's interests and policies within the former Soviet Union. The majority regretted the passing of the old Soviet Union and sought its effective reconstitution by all means available, including the use of economic and military pressure. They saw the need for the Russian state to build up a strong military force to bring recalcitrant former republics into line and, most importantly, to defend the rights of Russians living beyond the borders of the Russian Federation. The issue of protecting the 25–27 million Russians living in the rest of the former Soviet Union lie at the heart of the patriots' arguments, both in terms of their emotional appeal and their resonance among the Russian political elite and population. Condemning some of the policies discriminating against Russian minorities as apartheid, communist leaders, such as Zyuganov, went on to recommend forceful action in the Baltic to ensure that Russian rights were observed. Going well beyond the protection rights, patriots also supported Russian separatist movements, whether in Kazakhstan, Dnestr or the Crimea. Those like Zhirinovsky have condemned the new states of the former Soviet Union as illegal and see the main task of Russian foreign policy as one of restoring the Russian state within the borders of the old Soviet Union, if not beyond them.

Pragmatic Nationalists

Movements and parties within this cluster were associated with what may loosely be called the political centre. In 1992–3 the centre included individual parties, such as Renewal and the Democratic Party of Russia, various social democratic parties, and umbrella blocs such as the Civic Union and, more recently, the Yavlinsky–Boldyrev–Lukin electoral alliance. Through these years the centre and pragmatic nationalism have thus embraced a wide spectrum of views, ranging from representatives of older, conservative managerial groups to younger entrepreneurs. The range of politicians was equally wide from fairly traditionalist figures, such as Volsky, to reformers including Sergei Stankevich and Vladimir Lukin. For the most part these leaders took a moderate position on foreign policy, combining elements from both the liberal internationalist and patriotic camps. They supported political democratisation and economic marketisation though at a pace adapted to avoiding political confrontation and social instability. Likewise, on the international front, they endorsed Western links while taking a more Eurasianist position on the need for more assertive policies in the 'far' and especially the 'near' abroad. Unlike the other two clusters, the centre group avoided doctrinaire positions, preferring to adjust pragmatically to the changing political climate abroad and, particularly, within Russia.

The pragmatic nationalists produced by far the most detailed and coherent foreign policy criticisms and proposals. Given the vague and muddled nature of most foreign policy pronouncements, such primacy in elaborating foreign policy programmes was relatively easy to achieve. To a greater extent than the other groups the centre drew on the expertise of academic specialists as well as on that of academics-turned-politicians, including Vladimir Lukin and Yevgenii Ambartsumov. Both took a hard-nosed realist view of international relations and decried the idealism of the liberal internationalists, notably of Kozyrev. They certainly saw the developed Western states as important partners, but wanted partnership to be based on mutual benefit, on a balance of interests, rather than on terms that favoured the West. Avoiding much of the patriots' emotional rhetoric about Western exploitation, the pragmatic nationalists talked critically about the inadequacies of Western aid and ineffectiveness of the Russian government's 'begging bowl' approach. They warned against the dangers of 'Kuwaitisation', against allowing Russia to become simply an exporter of raw materials. To ensure the balanced foreign economic policy they advocated diversification. This involved carrying out relationships with new partners, including newly industrialised countries (NICs), while building on old relations with some of the former CMEA countries. Among the trading relations highlighted by the pragmatic nationalists were those with China and the Gulf States, areas which provided good markets for Russia's military exports. Here, as on other external policy issues, the centre adopted an approach which the Yavlinsky–Boldyrev–Lukin programme described as one of 'reasonable egoism'.

These 'reasonable egoists' took a pragmatic rather than emotional view of Russia's status as a Eurasian Great Power. Russian national interests required a policy that fostered good relations with the advanced industrial states while building ties with the South. In this way Russia could avoid the dangers of becoming an outpost of the developed world, guarding the North against the South. Russia had to steer a pragmatic, balanced, and independent course, whether in the Middle East or in former Yugoslavia. Centrists rejected the emotional appeals for open support of Iraq or Serbia while criticising the excessive passivity of Kozyrev's policies in these regions.

A similar approach was applied to Russian relations in the 'near' abroad on which politicians, such as Stankevich, were particularly vocal. Many pragmatic nationalists regretted the passing of the Soviet Union, though they did not advocate its resurrection. Rather, they wanted to put Russia first and pointed to the importance of ensuring that the CIS served Russian economic and security interests. This meant creating a common economic market and a defence union and stabilising relations through bilateral as well as multilateral agreements without dictating to the other states. While they stressed the need for a voluntary union, they effectively made the case for continued Russian primacy. Ambartsumov was the first to raise the idea of a Russian 'Monroe Doctrine', seeking to establish the CIS and indeed the former Soviet Union as an area in which Moscow would exercise predominant influence. Such influence had to be brought to bear first and foremost to protect the rights of Russians living in the new states in order to prevent discrimination and to minimise large-scale emigration to the Russian Federation. Pragmatic nationalists sought, quite successfully, to champion assertive policies to defend Russian minorities without endorsing the openly militaristic near-imperialism of the patriots. Even on issues relating to the 'near' abroad, where emotions clearly ran high, they managed to maintain a sober Russia First approach.

The Role of Parliament

The great debate on Russian identity, interests and international role was conducted in the media, on the hustings and, most fully and vigorously in parliament. Parliament, the Congress of People's Deputies and especially the Russian Supreme Soviet played a central role in the public politics of foreign policy in 1992–3. Whatever the differences in the composition and constitutional position of the parliament elected in December 1993, the broad political make-up and likely differences with President and government over foreign policy are sufficiently similar to those of the Supreme Soviet to produce some of the old patterns.

The general political circumstances in which the Russian Supreme Soviet operated in 1992–3 made it difficult to achieve the kind of parliamentary scrutiny of government foreign policy practised in the Western democracies which served as its notional model. Lack of experience in conducting parliamentary proceedings contributed to the confusion and inefficiency of much of the work relating to foreign policy (and to other spheres). Attendance at committee and plenary sessions was often poor, the standard of debate low and its results unimpressive. Lack of expertise was particularly marked where 'far' abroad policy was concerned. More importantly, the tenor and nature of parliamentary debate and action on foreign policy issues (as on others) often reflected power political rather than policy considerations. While this is plainly a common feature of any system of parliamentary politics, it was taken to extremes in the Russian Supreme Soviet. What began as a flexing of new institutional muscles to establish relations between legislature and executive increasingly became a bitter political power confrontation which polarised views on foreign policy, as in other questions.

As the Supreme Soviet leadership came increasingly to see itself as an alternative government, so original notions of parliamentary scrutiny were vitiated by attempts to undermine and replace official policy. In these circumstances, parliamentary debate on the substance of foreign policy was rare, and political sparring over weaknesses of government actions frequent. Government liberal internationalists and opposition patriots alike tended to play up their differences over policy; pragmatic nationalists, in contrast, sought to concentrate on policy substance and find compromise solutions. Such compromise proposals typically had more effect on government policy than opposition criticism and gradually helped steer the official course in a more pragmatic nationalist direction. The unreservedly pro-Western policies of the first half of 1992 became qualified, from mid-1992 to early 1993, by growing assertiveness which subsequently developed into a more independent if still cooperative policy. These shifts in foreign policy gear were determined within the executive (see below) yet were in part responses to the general changes in the political balance of forces which parliament both reflected and shaped.

Constitutionally the Russian Parliament had important if limited rights bearing on external policy. It had a say in the overall direction of foreign policy, the right to approve certain personnel appointments, to sanction the despatch of armed forces abroad, and the power to ratify or reject international treaties. To help parliament to fulfil these responsibilities, as well as general scrutiny of government performance, the Russian Supreme Soviet had three committees dealing in one way or another with external policy: the Committee on Defence and Security Questions; the Committee on Inter-Republican Relations and Regional Policy and Cooperation; and the Committee on International Affairs and Foreign Economic Relations. Of the three, the International Affairs Committee was by far the most prominent, active and influential. In terms of organised political groupings, the Committee's membership gravitated towards the centre of the parliamentary spectrum. Both of the Committee's chairmen set themselves up as leading detractors of Kozyrev's foreign policy, much to the irritation of the Foreign Ministry. Ambartsumov and other committee members were active in conducting their own shadow diplomacy. Parliamentary delegations to the former Yugoslavia in August 1992 and April 1993 came out with pro-Serbian statements which consciously departed from the official Moscow line.

The Foreign Ministry saw such behaviour as typical of the openly adversarial attitudes adopted by the International Affairs Committee and the Supreme Soviet in general. The Committee, for its part, considered the Ministry uncooperative. Problems were increased by the fact that both sides had little notion of how to shape and manage the relationship. The early sessions of the Committee were often confused and tense, with patriots grilling Ministry officials unaccustomed and unresponsive to such pressures. Committee members complained that the Ministry withheld vital information and failed to consult them adequately on policy developments. In the hearings on the Kurils, as during those relating to nuclear weapons agreements, patriot members capitalised on the general feeling that Foreign Ministry sleight-of-hand would get agreements past the Committee which were detrimental to Russian interests. If many of the Committee debates and some of its resolutions (as those on Ukraine in mid-1992) were highly critical of the Foreign Ministry, most of the final recommendations were reasonable and balanced. As chairman, Ambartsumov was in large part responsible for steering Committee decisions in a pragmatic nationalist direction.

Ambartsumov was less successful in his efforts to temper the foreign policy actions of the full Russian Supreme Soviet. The tone of much parliamentary debate was set by the Supreme Soviet leadership under Khasbulatov which used foreign policy issues to attack Kozyrev and thereby get at the government and President. The Foreign Minister and his deputies regularly came under assault for betraying Russian interests and, in Kozyrev's case, for being too closely involved in domestic politics. The politicisation of these struggles was highlighted when Kozyrev made a dramatic speech, at the December 1992 Conference on Security and Cooperation in Europe (CSCE) meeting in Stockholm, warning of the dangers of the patriots gaining power and bringing Cold War elements back into Russian foreign policy. The higher the political tensions between opposition and government, the harsher the parliamentary criticism of foreign policy became. The summer of 1993, for instance, saw a barrage of parliamentary resolutions designed to obstruct the progress of the government's foreign policy on a range of important issues from Ukraine to arms exports.

In much of the discussion of foreign policy issues the scoring of political points was accompanied by the airing of substantive concerns. Pragmatic nationalist as well as patriot deputies proved very sensitive about the excessive willingness of the government to make concessions to Western states in security arrangements. The 'Open Skies' agreement was among those criticised as asymmetrical and therefore not ratified. Neither was the accord on the transfer and destruction of nuclear materials, the provisions of which were thought to give Americans excessive rights on Russian soil. Deputies' misgivings about the START 2 accord with the US obstructed the ratification of this key treaty.

Passive compliance with US policies in major areas of regional conflict was lambasted by patriots and questioned by pragmatic nationalist deputies. Particular anxiety was voices about the high cost (estimated at $15–16bn) of the sanctions against Libya, Iraq and Serbia. Inadequate support for Russia's traditional ally Serbia was one of the refrains of the numerous parliamentary debates on the former Yugoslavia. Resolutions in December 1992 and February 1993 called on the government to instruct the Foreign Ministry to secure a relaxation of sanctions against Serbia, to seek their extension to the other warring parties and to take all steps, including the use of the veto in the Security Council, to prevent outside military intervention. The thrust of the criticism levelled against the government over Yugoslavia, as over purported readiness to make territorial concessions to Japan, was that the Foreign Ministry was far too willing to subordinate Russian national interests to the priority of increasing its international reputation for cooperation.

The need to put Russia first was also the underlying theme of deputies' critical discussion of policy in the 'near' abroad. Most members of the Supreme Soviet showed relatively little enthusiasm for the CIS. Many of those at the patriot end of the spectrum, and even some in the centre, wanted Moscow to take a strong line with the new states. As one Foreign Ministry official observed, many deputies equated a strong policy with a policy of strength. The patriots took every opportunity to champion the cause of Russian minorities. In the case of the Russian movement in the Dnestr region of Moldova, radical nationalists almost managed to get through a resolution supporting separatism. Similarly, Khasbulatov tried, albeit without success, to get the Supreme Soviet to endorse his policy of encouraging South Ossetia to become part of the Russian Federation. The Parliament's attitude towards Russian military involvement in CIS conflicts depended on particular circumstances. The Supreme Soviet reportedly rejected the proposal of the Ministry of Defence to deploy two peace-keeping divisions in Georgia, although it approved participation in peace-keeping activities in Tajikistan.

By far the most frequent, prolonged and heated debates on 'near' abroad policy concerned relations with Ukraine. In early 1992 the Supreme Soviet and the 6th Congress of People's Deputies pressed hard on the issue of the Crimea. In May 1992 Parliament annulled the 1954 transfer of the Crimea to the Ukraine and deputies repeatedly objected to what they saw as unwarranted Russian concessions on the Black Sea Fleet. In July 1993 the Supreme Soviet rejected an agreement negotiated by Yeltsin and Kravchuk to divide the Fleet, and drove home the point by declaring Russian sovereignty over Sevastopol.

Parliamentary treatment of Ukraine points up the complex nature of the Russian Supreme Soviet's responses to government policy in the 'near' abroad. On the one hand, parliament, as in July 1993, sought to undermine government efforts to reach negotiated settlements. On this and other occasions parliamentary action inflamed the situation, evoking Ukrainian ripostes. To some extent, therefore, the sharp political conflicts characteristic of parliamentary–government relations in the 'far' abroad area were repeated in the 'near' abroad. On the other hand, Supreme Soviet and government positions on CIS matters often seemed to be closer than on other foreign policy issues. Rather than venting their anger on the Foreign Ministry, as tended to be the case on 'far' abroad policy, deputies attacked the leaderships of the ex-Union republics. On some occasions – annulment of the 1954 transfer of the Crimea was a case in point – the Supreme Soviet took steps which the government broadly welcomed. Here as elsewhere, parliament could afford to adopt public positions which tactical considerations made difficult as far as the government was concerned.

It was precisely where the gap between the government and

parliament strategies was small that Supreme Soviet actions had most impact on policy by affecting the climate of thinking within the political establishment. The December 1992 resolution on policy towards the former Yugoslavia was not carried out by the government, yet Moscow did subsequently adopt a tougher tone and abstained in a vote to tighten sanctions against Belgrade. The strong objections voiced by deputies in summer 1992 to Yeltsin making any territorial concessions to Japan played some part in the decision to postpone his visit to Tokyo. By highlighting the objections to concessions on the Kurils, parliamentary debate may have even increased public hostility to the idea (nearly three out of four Russians opposed making any concessions). However, insofar as parliamentary objections affected the postponement of Yeltsin's visits to Tokyo in late 1992 and the spring of 1993, this was due in large part to deputies' views reflecting the overall balance of political forces in Moscow and reinforcing doubts already present within the executive. On issues where few such doubts existed, even the non-ratification of agreements had little effect. Such was the domination of the executive over the actual running of foreign policy that several agreements, such as that on the transfer of nuclear materials, were put into operation without receiving parliamentary ratification.

Executive Dominance

As vigorously as parliament discussed foreign affairs and contested the government line its impact was more often on policy climate and tactical adjustment rather than on substance. The shaping of that substance remained overwhelmingly in executive hands. Executive dominance of the foreign policy sphere was one legacy of the Soviet period which Yeltsin did not seriously seek to alter. The concern of the presidential machine to keep all foreign policy reins in its hands tended to foster institutional uncertainty about policy jurisdictions and thus to increase confusion and dislocation in policy-making. Uncertainty about policy roles further weakened coordination and control over implementation. Mixed and even conflicting policy signals from Moscow allowed for, and sometimes encouraged, local actors to use their own initiative and follow their own policy agenda. This only added to the difficulties of coping with multiple and frequently simultaneous crisis developments.

The goal of leaving a strong presidential imprint on foreign policy-making was clear from the start. In late 1991 Yeltsin put himself in overall charge of what was then an embryonic Russian Foreign Ministry. From early 1992 to the autumn, Presidential control over the Ministry was exercised on Yeltsin's behalf by Gennadii Burbulis. The political protection Burbulis provided proved sufficient, by and large, to sustain the Foreign Ministry line on key areas, such as Yugoslavia. This was due not so much to any deep-seated liberal internationalism on Yeltsin's part or to the personal persuasiveness of Kozyrev. The Foreign Minister reportedly had no regular access to the President, in contrast to the privilege of weekly meetings enjoyed among others by the head of the Intelligence Service. It is likely that Yeltsin's endorsement of the Foreign Ministry's line was due largely to the influence of Burbulis, a proponent of liberal internationalism and a close political associate of the President.

The decline in the political fortunes of Burbulis in the last quarter of 1992, which saw defensive concessions by Yeltsin in the face of growing patriot and centrist opposition, weakened the Ministry's political standing and its pro-Western policy. Yeltsin himself criticised the performance of the Ministry and gave increasing weight in late 1992 and early 1993 to the more conservative views of Yuri Skokov, the chairman of the Security Council, a key executive body (established in mid-1992) whose members inclined towards a more assertive policy in the 'far' and especially the 'near' abroad. In December 1992 Yeltsin formally reversed his previous support for the institutional primacy of the Foreign Ministry in the external policy area by assigning overall coordination in this sphere to a new Foreign Policy Commission operating under the Security Council (*ex officio* members included the Foreign Minister and the Minister of Defence).

Political considerations play a dominant part in Yeltsin's shift in position, but there were also other reasons for his doubts about the capacity of the Foreign Ministry to oversee the formulation and implementation of policy, particularly in the 'near' abroad. The Ministry suffered from the failure of ministers, from Shevardnadze to Kozyrev, thoroughly to overhaul its structure and staff. While Kozyrev did more than any of his predecessors to reorganise and to promote younger officials, the continued presence of older, conservative-minded personnel helped to maintain rivalries between and within departments and to make the Ministry less attractive to new entrants. Recruiting bright new diplomats was made particularly difficult by the low pay the Ministry could offer. This was one of the main reasons for its loss of around a tenth of its 3000 plus staff in 1992, including many of the most talented and enterprising. In autumn 1992 Yeltsin berated the Ministry for its inefficiency and compared its information gathering and analysis unfavourably with that of the Intelligence Service.

The under-resourcing that lay behind some of the Ministry's recruitment problems created difficulties for it in coping with the most important foreign policy sector: the 'near' abroad. The Ministry made a very slow start in expanding its operations to relations with the other members of the CIS. Despite calls for a new and separate ministry for CIS relations, Yeltsin gave the Foreign Ministry full authority over the 'near' abroad. (A separate Ministry for Cooperation with the Member States of the CIS was established only in January 1994.) The Ministry's CIS Department grew apace and was soon claiming to be carrying over half of the Ministry's workload without anything like matching resources. Greater organisational capacity, however, failed to give the Ministry anything like a dominant say in CIS policy. This remained largely within the control of the presidential apparatus which seemed to regard the Ministry as an executor rather than the main source of strategy for the 'near' abroad. At the same time, the President and his team paid increasing attention to the views and policy preferences of the Ministry of Defence and the military establishment.

The Military

As the military came to play a crucial role in the political struggle in the course of 1993, so they gained a growing say in decisions affecting foreign as well as security policy. What has also given military preferences policy weight has been the presence of Russian armed forces in many of conflict areas that dominate Moscow's decisions on the 'near' abroad. The institutional strength and access of the military to the foreign policy and decision-making process has grown steadily from mid- to late 1992. While initially not a full member of the Security Council, the Minister of Defence was included in the composition of the Council's Foreign Policy Commission (he became a member of the Council itself in late 1993–early 1994). The Secretaries of the Security Council (Skokov, Shaposhnikov and Lobov) have all been associated closely with the military and the military industrial sector. More important to military influence than such institutional representation has been informal access to Yeltsin and his closest advisers. This is a matter determined more by political expediency and loyalty than by policy criteria. The events of October 1993 clearly gave the military far greater access and political capital.

At the level of basic security and foreign policy thinking military influence expanded significantly during the course of 1993. The military leadership were asked to develop the political as well as the military dimensions of military doctrine. The final version of the Russian Military Doctrine (published in November 1993) reflected Ministry of Defence rather than civilian preferences. It defined threats in such a way as to steer external policy towards the forceful assertion of Russian interests, especially in the 'near' abroad.

The general political climate from mid-1992 has certainly favoured a more forceful defence of Russians and Russian territory. Where the military have seen diplomatic moves threatening such preferences they have openly sought to influence policy. The General Staff's public stand in mid-1992 against territorial concessions to Japan, and the probable military–industrial impetus behind moves for rapprochement with Iraq in early 1993, were cases in point. As far as disarmament agreements were concerned, the military, while less than enthusiastic about the provisions of these accords, did not apparently place any serious obstacles in their path, allowing the Foreign Ministry to make a successful case for diplomatic priorities.

Military priorities have made themselves far more clearly felt in policy towards the 'near' abroad. Disputes about the nature of security relations between the CIS states resulted in the adoption of the Russian Defence Ministry's preference for a Moscow-centred structure and the end of the CIS joint command (dissolved in June 1993). Russian military leaders, notably Pavel Grachev, played a central role in negotiating troop withdrawal agreements with the Baltic states. It was the Ministry of Defence, rather than that of Foreign Affairs, which seems to have exercised tactical control over this aspect of Baltic policy, using the threat of halting withdrawals to extract concessions. A similarly tough line has been taken by the Defence Ministry wherever conflicts raised issues of Russian border security. The military proved successful in persuading a far from unwilling Yeltsin to adopt a general policy of treating the borders of the CIS as extensions of the Russian frontier. This became the guiding principle of intervention in Tajikistan, where the military felt that they needed to secure the border only against Afghanistan but also against interference from Iran. Similar concerns about extended border security affected the Russian Defence Ministry's policy towards Georgia, which they helped to tie into close military association with Moscow.

The ascendance of military priorities in the 'near' abroad should be viewed as the product of local as well as central military interests and actions. The Defence Ministry has been susceptible to the radical stance of some local commanders (such as General Lebed, head of the 14th Army in the Dnestr region, who has remained defiantly independently of official Russian government policy), both because of its own sympathies and those of the wider officer corps. The very presence of Russian troops in the 'near' abroad, often in difficult conditions of conflict, have given the Defence Ministry ample reason to support assertive security objectives. In some cases, however – Abkhazia being a notable instance – the military in Moscow have found themselves responding to rather than directing the initiatives of local commanders.

The high-stake interest of the military plus their physical resources throughout the former Soviet Union gave them clear advantages over the Foreign Ministry in influencing policy in the 'near' abroad, especially in conflict zones. However, the apparent prevalence of military priorities should not be interpreted as necessarily denoting the defeat of political and diplomatic ones. In many instances of 'near' abroad policy, the military have expressed, albeit more forcefully, preferences favoured by the political leadership, if not always by the Foreign Ministry.

As far as issues relating to the 'far' abroad were concerned, diplomatic priorities have often found favour with the political leadership. This seems to have been the case in the vexed issue of exports of rocket engines to India in 1993. The military–industrial lobby pressed for the agreement with India to go ahead, while the Foreign Ministry highlighted the importance of US objections to the deal. In the event, Yeltsin decided on balance in favour of the USA. Clearly, there was much more to the equation than the relative policy weight of the Defence and Foreign Ministries – maintaining good relations with the USA was probably the decisive factor. This case illustrates the importance of the overall political context in shaping institutional influence over policy.

Disarray and Coordination

The case of engine exports to India also highlighted the inconsistency and lack of coordination frequently found in Russian foreign policy. The leader of the Russian delegation in the talks with the USA was dismissed for opposing the Foreign Ministry line. Immediately after agreement was reached with the Americans Foreign Ministry officials, without any further consultation, presented the Indians with an effective abrogation of the contract. Examples of uncoordinated activities abound in Russian policy towards the 'near' abroad. In Tajikistan several Russian policies ran for a time in tandem in 1993. Similar differences between the Foreign and Defence Ministries were evident in Russian policy in the Georgian–Abkhazian conflict. Local and central military authorities generally took the Abkhaz side while the Foreign Ministry and government officially supported Georgia.

Inconsistency and dislocation in Russian foreign policy can be explained in various ways. Conditions within the presidential administration seem hardly to have been conducive to regularise policy and decision-making. The presidential apparatus has been overblown, lines of authority uncertain and personnel constantly in flux. Appointments to key positions within the machine have depended more on loyalty than competence. Elaborate advisory arrangements have long existed, yet advisors have found it extremely difficult to gain access to Yeltsin and have remained reliant on aides who reportedly have frequently proposed ideas off-the-cuff. A further problem has been Yeltsin's impulsive approach to decision-making, which has led him sometimes to take up such ideas without consulting the appropriate minister. Examples of impulsive presidential decision include the announcement of the recognition of Macedonia in August 1992 and, a year later, the statement that Russia had no real objection to Polish membership of NATO. In both cases the Foreign Ministry had to clarify Yeltsin's declarations and put policy back on course. These occasions left Kozyrev in the embarrassing position of what the French Ambassador to St Petersburg in the reign of Nicholas II described as 'a Minister of Foreign Affairs *à la Russe*, which is to say that he [does] not have charge of the foreign policy but only of the diplomacy of Russia, with the mission of adapting the latter to the former'.

Impulsiveness, improvisation and dislocation within the presidential apparatus was compounded in 1992–3 by the departmental and institutional rivalries we have already noted. Some of the measures taken to counter these, such as the creation of problem-based commissions and inter-departmental delegations for relations with the other CIS states, tended to compound difficulties of communication and coordination. To overcome these problems Yeltsin established the Foreign Policy Commission in December 1992 to operate under the Security Council. Chaired by the Council Secretary, this Commission included the heads of the eight ministries and agencies most closely associated with security and foreign affairs. The Commission was supposed to coordinate the work of all these agencies, examine their policy proposals and produce draft decision for the President. The original Commission experienced severe operational problems and was reportedly replaced in late 1993 by a somewhat smaller body. While the appointment in January 1994 of a National Security Advisor marked a further step towards more effective inter-agency coordination, Moscow still had a long way to go to achieving the establishment of an equivalent of the US National Security Council, long an objective of Soviet and Russian policy makers. One serious obstacle along the path towards this goal has been the tendency of the presidential staff to guard Yeltsin's and thus their own policy prerogatives.

Trends

Continuing problems of coordination notwithstanding, Russian foreign policy looked set in early 1994 to develop in a more rather than less coherent and stable fashion. 1993 saw signs of a foreign policy consensus begin to emerge in official policy documents and statements. The Foreign Policy Concept, approved in spring 1993, was transformed in its passage through the Security Council into a tougher document than the Foreign Ministry's original draft. It struck a note of qualified rather than enthusiastic Westernism, stressing the need for Russia to pursue its interests assertively in the 'far' and especially the 'near' abroad. The document pointed up Moscow's responsibility for the defence of all Russians and for stability within the former Soviet Union. Assertion of Russia's role as regional gendarme was expressed more explicitly in the military doctrine, published in November 1993. Among the threats defined in the document were interference with Russian military installations in the whole of the former Soviet Union, and the expansion of blocs and alliances.

Official statements in late 1993 and early 1994 confirmed the general adoption of this more assertive line of policy. Kozyrev's diplomatically couched appeals to the West to take into account Russian sensitivities when reviewing security arrangements in Europe came steadily closer in tone to Grachev's categorical objections to the eastward expansion of NATO. A certain rapprochement with the military line was also evident in the Foreign Ministry's stance on peace-keeping within the CIS. While continuing to favour international collaboration in peacekeeping, Kozyrev made increasingly clear that Russia would fulfil her special responsibilities in the region regardless of international endorsement. Such shifts of tone and policy were symptomatic of a degree greater agreement of alignment between the positions of these two key ministries.

The emerging policy consensus marked the ascendance of pragmatic nationalism. Liberal internationalist elements remained quite strong in 'far' abroad policy, but even here the Foreign Ministry adjusted to the pragmatic nationalist priorities favoured by growing majorities within the military and political establishment. In 'near' abroad policy a tough pragmatic nationalism prevailed, as was evident in the assertion of Moscow's rights to maintain military bases throughout the former Soviet Union.

The results of the 1993 elections and the subsequent cabinet reshuffles looked likely to reinforce these trends towards a pragmatic nationalist consensus in foreign policy. The new State Duma showed early signs of reiterating some of the old Supreme Soviet criticism of the Foreign Ministry. However, the old differences between parliament and government on foreign policy (as on other issues) are likely to be tempered by the sensitivity of all politicians with regard to future presidential elections and public preferences. Those Russians who supported the Communists, Agrarians and Liberal Democrats were particularly concerned not just about economic hardship and social inequality, but also about the loss of Russia's Great Power prestige. Greater 'normality' in the shape of democratic responsiveness as well as considerations of *Realpolitik* may therefore tend to induce the powerful executive to continue to steer foreign policy in a tough and pragmatic nationalist direction.

PART THREE

Post-Soviet Nations and States

10

Nationality and Ethnicity in Russia and the Post-Soviet Republics

ZVI GITELMAN

The Soviet Union inherited a multinational state from the Russian Empire. That empire had gained a reputation as 'the prisonhouse of nations', and the Bolsheviks exploited the grievances of non-Russians in rallying support for their cause. Leaders of the Soviet state claimed to have the solution to the 'national question': all peoples would be equal and then they would come to realise that class, not ethnicity or religion, was the important dividing line in society. In line with Marx's teachings, the Bolsheviks expected ethnic consciousness to recede and nations to disappear, just as the state would.

In practice, the Soviet regime elevated some nationalities to positions they had never enjoyed before the revolution, even creating written languages and state structures for them, while repressing and persecuting other peoples, both culturally and politically. By the 1950s, it appeared to some that the USSR was a state that successfully managed a multiethnic society. But toward the end of the Soviet period, ethnic tensions and even violence arose to the surface and played a role in the disintegration of the Soviet Union. In the 1990s, ethnic conflicts are highly visible in many of the successor states. There are ethnic wars in Georgia, Azerbaijan and Armenia, and ethnic tensions in the Baltic states,

237

parts of Russia, Ukraine, Moldova, and some areas in Central
Asia. A new issue, the fate of the 25 million Russians living
outside the Russian Federation, has become an international one,
conditioning the relations between Russia and some of the successor states and drawing the attention of some Western countries
and world bodies. On the other hand, economic and military exi-
gencies have forced Georgia and Azerbaijan to swallow national
pride and join the Commonwealth of Independent States (CIS)
which they had earlier refused to do. Moldova came close to
doing the same. Many in the former Soviet republics see the CIS
as Russian-dominated and the rise of nationalistic political parties
in Russia stir fears that some will try to re-establish a Russian-
dominated empire.

The Disintegration of the USSR

Writing just as World War II ended, the distinguished historian,
E.H. Carr, asserted that 'In Europe some of the small units of the
past may continue for a few generations longer to eke out a
precarious, independent existence . . . But their military and
economic insecurity has been demonstrated beyond recall. They
can survive only as an anomaly and an anachronism in a world
which has moved on to other forms of organization'. He reasoned
that 'just as the movement for religious toleration followed the
devastating religious wars of the 16th and 17th centuries, so the
movement for national toleration will spring . . . from the
destructive 20th century wars of nationalism' (Carr, 1945, pp. 37,
66). More than forty years later, the USSR, a state which claimed
to have solved the 'national problem' and to have created a new
type of harmonious multiethnic society, began to disintegrate,
largely because of the emergence of militant nationalisms and
demands for independent existence, no matter how politically and
economically 'precarious' that existence might be.

By late 1991, power had drained away from the centre of what
had been considered one of the most powerful states in the world.
The Soviet republics first declared sovereignty, meaning that their
laws took precedence over federal laws. Following the failed coup
attempt in August, all republics declared independence and the
Soviet Union ceased to exist as a state. It was replaced, in

December 1991, by a Commonwealth of Independent States, which had originated as a federation of Russia, Belorussia, and Ukraine, Slavic states which had agreed to form a new state with its headquarters in the Belorussian capital of Minsk. Several Central Asian republics, put out by the formation of a purely European entity, made their feelings known and the Slavic federation was hastily expanded to include five Central Asian republics, Armenia, Moldova and Azerbaijan. The former Soviet republics in the Baltic, Estonia, Latvia and Lithuania, remained resolutely outside the Commonwealth, as (initially) did Georgia, itself rent by ethnic and political strife. The state that had once been feared as the propagator of world revolution and later as a nuclear superpower disintegrated into a loose association of regions beset by economic crisis, political instability and civil strife.

How did this highly integrated state, which maintained a facade of ethnic peace, fall apart so rapidly? What explains the resurgence of nationalism so long after both Soviet and Western observers had concluded that acculturation and assimilation had advanced so far in the USSR that the Russians had succeeded in denationalising, politically and even culturally, large numbers of peoples?

The general collapse of the economic and political systems in the USSR enabled national disintegration as well, though the latter was also a cause, not just a result, of that collapse. Not only did the three Baltic republics leave the federation, and others followed in the chaos of late 1991, but within the remaining entities, peoples demanded autonomy or even independence from the titular nationality. Thus, Abkhazians and Ossetians protested against Georgian rule, and in November 1991 Chechen-Ingushetia declared a republic independent of the Russian republic, renamed Chechnya and separate from the Ingush Republic, which remained inside Russia. Politicians and publics alike are learning to deal separately with many entities which formerly could be dealt with through Moscow, and cartographers have returned to their drawing boards.

One person who had to learn much about national feelings is Mikhail Gorbachev. In the late 1980s he became painfully aware that the country over which he presided was a multinational one and that many people were acutely conscious and proud of their nationality, to use the Soviet term, or ethnicity, a roughly equivalent term more often used in the West. The 'nationalities problem' emerged as one of the greatest challenges to Gorbachev's own position and to the political viability of the Soviet Union.

In 1926, when the first Soviet census was taken, there were 178 officially recognised nationalities. By 1979 their number had declined to 101, but the 1989 census enumerated 128 nationalities. The number of nationalities at a given time was a function both of their own shifting demographics as well as of government decisions about how to classify peoples. In 1979 there were 23 ethnic groups with populations over 1 million. 15 of them had Soviet republics named for them, and they were the majority of the population in all but one of those republics. As has been discussed in earlier chapters, the Union of Soviet Socialist Republics was a federal state. In addition to the 15 republics, reduced to 12 in 1991 when Estonia, Latvia, and Lithuania gained independence, the USSR comprised 20 'autonomous republics', smaller units within four of the larger republics (16 of the 20 'autonomous republics' were in the largest former republic, the Russian Soviet Federated Socialist Republic or RSFSR). Their official languages were those of the majority indigenous nationality. Smaller nationalities had autonomous national regions (*oblasti*). There were eight of these regions. The smallest nationality unit was the national district (*okrug*), of which there were 10. The numbers of these units, including the republics, fluctuated over the years, reflecting changes in borders and in Soviet nationality policy. In the post-Soviet period, these borders have been disputed, with several group arguing that the Soviet division of lands had been either arbitrary or politically motivated, designed to dilute the potential power of several ethnic groups. Such issues have arisen between Russia and several entities in the Caucasus, between Tajikistan and Uzbekistan, Armenia and Azerbaijan and several other new states.

Russians constituted barely half of the Soviet population (50.8 per cent in 1989), and their proportion had been slowly declining. The rate of natural increase among Central Asians (except for Kazakhs) was between 33 and 46 per cent in 1979–89, while the rate for Russians was only 5.6 per cent, and rates for the other major Slavic peoples, Ukrainians and Belorussians, were about the same. Some Russians were apprehensive about the prospect of their becoming a statistical minority in the country. It was projected that by the year 2000 at least 20 per cent of the population would be of Muslim background, and the USSR already had the fifth largest population in the world. Today, Russians constitute 83 per cent of the population of the Russian Federation, and a substantial number of the others are native speakers of Russian. Nevertheless, some Russian nationalists argue that it is better to be an imperial power, dominating other peoples, than to have a more 'purely' Russian state, because the 'historical destiny' of Russia is to control a huge land mass and its inhabitants.

The ethnic heterogeneity of the USSR naturally brought with it cultural diversity. There were significant numbers of people whose traditions, if not their current practices, were Russian Orthodox, Uniate, Protestant, Catholic, Muslim, Jewish, and Buddhist, among others. Georgians and Armenians have ancient and independent Christian churches. There were five alphabets in use – Cyrillic, Latin, Hebrew, Georgian and Armenian. About 130 languages were officially recognised by the state. They ranged across a wide variety of linguistic groups, and some were unique to the USSR. Some of the nationalities had been historic enemies, others historic allies, and still others had had little contact with each other. The lifestyles of the Soviet peoples range from nomadic peoples of the far north-east of the country, related and similar to North American Eskimos, to the Turkic peoples of Central Asia, to the Northern European types found in Karelia, and many others. Perhaps it is almost inevitable that in such a diverse country ethnic issues should play a major role in politics, as nationalities vie for recognition, resources, and representation. Until the late 1980s, Soviet politicians and scholars claimed that nationality conflicts had diminished to the point that the 'nationalities questions' had been definitively solved, and the ethnic diversity of the country was yielding to a unity which would approach and eventually reach homogeneity. Like other dogmas long proclaimed as scientific truth, this one was called into question both by policies of *glasnost* and by dramatic events which seemed to contradict official beliefs. In fact, the nationality question emerged in the late 1980s as one of the most sensitive and troublesome. It played a major role in the disintegration of the Soviet state and is also shaping the character of the political systems within its former component parts. The nationalities tested the viability of the system and it was found wanting.

The Ethnic Map of the Former USSR

There are several families and groups of nations and nationalities which inhabited the former USSR (see Table 10.1). The three large Slavic nations were located in the European, western part of the country, though members of all three migrated eastwards and southwards over the centuries. The Russian Republic, by far the largest in the former Union, stretched from Europe across Siberia and out to the Pacific Ocean, just across the water from Japan. Over 82 per cent of the 145 million Russians (1989 figure) lived in what was the RSFSR. Ukraine is about one and a half times as large as neighbouring Poland, the largest country in Eastern Europe, and with its more than 50 million people, it is comparable to some of the largest countries of Western Europe. Ukraine is an important centre of both industry and agriculture. About 85 per cent of the 44 million Ukrainians live in the Ukrainian republic, the western part of which was annexed from Poland in 1939. Aside from Ukrainians, Russians and Jews constitute significant proportions of the urban population of Ukraine. Belorussia, now Belarus, is considerably smaller than Ukraine, with a population of just over 10 million. Historically, Belorussian national consciousness and literature were not as developed as their Ukrainian counterparts. Western Belorussia, which used to have a mixed population of Russians, Poles, Belorussians, Jews and others, was also annexed from Poland in 1939.

The three Baltic republics, Latvia, Lithuania and Estonia, now independent, also were 'latecomers' to the Soviet Union, assigned to it in secret protocols of the Nazi–Soviet treaty of 23 August 1939. Red Army troops moved into these countries and insured that the 'elections' held shortly thereafter would show the great majority of the local populations asking to join the USSR. Exactly 50 years later, on 23 August 1989, two million people in the three republics joined hands in a human chain symbolising their protest at being forced to join the USSR, an act that would have been unthinkable 20, 10, or even five years before. Estonia has less than 2 million inhabitants, ethnic Estonians constituting 65 per cent of the total. The Estonian language is related to Finnish. This, together with Estonia's location and Protestant heritage, made that republic more attuned to Western culture than perhaps any other.

TABLE 10.1   *The major Soviet nationalities, 1989*

	Census popn. (1989, m)	% of total	Linguistic group	Traditional religion
The Slavs				
Russians	145.1	50.8	East Slavic	Russian Orthodox
Ukrainians	44.1	15.5	East Slavic	Russian Orthodox
Belorussians	10.0	3.5	East Slavic	Russian Orthodox
The Balts				
Latvians	1.5	0.5	Baltic	Protestant
Lithuanians	3.1	1.1	Baltic	Roman Catholic
Estonians	1.0	0.4	Finno-Ugrian	Protestant
The Caucasians				
Georgians	4.0	1.4	Kartvelian	Georgian Orthodox
Armenians	4.6	1.6	Indo-European	Armenian Orthodox
Azerbaijanis	6.8	2.4	Turkic	Muslim (Shi'a)
The Central Asians				
Uzbeks	16.7	5.8	Turkic	Muslim (Sunni)
Kazakhs	8.1	2.9	Turkic	Muslim (Sunni)
Tajiks	4.2	1.5	Iranian	Muslim (Sunni)
Turkmenians	2.7	1.0	Turkic	Muslim (Sunni)
Kirgiz	2.5	0.9	Turkic	Muslim (Sunni)
Other				
Moldavians	3.4	1.2	Romance	Romanian Orthodox

Source: Based on *Vestnik statistiki*, 1990, no. 10, pp. 69–71.

Latvia also has a Protestant heritage and a language that is unrelated to any other language of the former USSR. About 54 per cent of the republic's population of some 2.6 million are ethnic Latvians. Here, too, a militant movement to wrest autonomy or even independence from the USSR surfaced in the 1980s and culminated in independence in 1991.

Unlike the other two Baltic states, Lithuania has a Catholic background and was historically associated with Poland, though the two nations fought over possession of the present capital of Lithuania, Vilnius. The result was that the city was in Poland, where it was called Wilno, between the two world wars. A higher proportion of the population than in the other two Baltic states – about four-fifths – belongs to the indigenous nationality, and the rate of population growth is higher. Religion plays a greater role in Lithuania and buttresses national sentiment. Until the Holocaust, Lithuania was one of the most important Jewish cultural centres. Like the Latvians and Estonians, Lithuanians organised a national movement, called *Sajudis*, in 1988. It led the fight to gain autonomy from Moscow and managed to elect three-quarters of the delegates from Lithuania to the USSR Congress of People's Deputies which began to meet in May 1989. The Lithuanian Communist Party was the first to declare itself independent of the national party in December 1989, and Lithuania, along with the other Baltic republics, formally recognised political parties other than the Communists before this was done elsewhere in the USSR.

Now that the Baltic states are independent, Russians and others who are not of the titular nationality feel discriminated against. Indeed, the republics have passed legislation on citizenship which asserts residence and language requirements for those who wish to be citizens of the new republics. The aim is obviously to disenfranchise those who came to the Baltic after Soviet annexation and/or those who refuse to learn the languages of the titular nationalities.

The Caucasus mountains are inhabited by a great variety of nationalities with different religious and cultural traditions. The major nationalities, each of whom has a republic, are Armenians, Azerbaijanis and Georgians. The Armenian and Georgian languages are old and unique, as are their Christian churches. Azerbaijanis are Muslim and related to peoples in Iran and Turkey. The Armenian republic serves as a magnet for the large Armenian diaspora. Of all the republics, Armenia has the highest percentage of its population (90) made up of the titular nationality. It is ethnically the most homogeneous republic, although nearly 2 million Armenians live outside Armenia, where 2.8 million reside. Georgia has a larger population, over 5 million, and nearly 70 per cent of the population is Georgian. This republic had the reputation of being economically more independent and enterprising than other Soviet regions. Armenians and Georgians, who have not always enjoyed the friendliest relations, were among the most educated nationalities and hence well represented in the Soviet intelligentsia, and in the economic and, at times, the political elites. Nearly 6 million of the 7 million inhabitants of Azerbaijan are Azeris. In 1988–9 Armenians living in the Nagorno-Karabakh region of Azerbaijan protested against what they viewed as cultural deprivation and Azeri discrimination against them. Armenians in the home republic supported them, violence broke out, the two republic legislatures passed opposing resolutions about the proper jurisdiction under which Nagorno-Karabakh should fall, and a major ethnic, constitutional and political crisis ensued. The central leadership temporised by placing Nagorno-Karabakh under the direct jurisdiction of the federal government in Moscow, thus avoiding a decision as to which republic had the stronger claim to the region. The issue has not been settled, and has led to an Azeri–Armenian war in which, it is estimated, some 13000 have been killed and several hundred thousand made homeless. The Russians at first tried to mediate the dispute but more recently they have been charged with supporting one side over the other.

There are five republics in Central Asia: Uzbekistan, Turkmenistan, Kirgizia (now Kyrgyzstan), Tajikstan, and Kazakhstan. The titular nationalities are all Muslim in background, and all the peoples but the Tajiks, who are of Persian stock, are Turkic. Some were nomads until forcibly settled by the Soviets. Nearly all were illiterate at the time of the revolution. Their alphabets and literacy were given to these peoples by the Soviet authorities, partly out of a desire to socialise them politically through written media. Like the Caucasus, these areas had come under Russian rule before the revolution as a result of tsarist imperialism and wars that Russia had fought with her neighbours. All these peoples have high fertility rates: for example, in recent years, when fertility among Slavs was 13 per 1000, among Tajiks and Uzbeks it was 45 per 1000. Despite migration to their republics by Europeans, the proportion of indigenous nationalities in the population grew because of this high birth rate. In the post-Soviet period, the tendency has been accelerated by the out-migration of Slavs and other Europeans. One estimate is that 4 to 5 per cent of the Russians had migrated to Russia from Central Asia by mid-1993. Turkey, Iran and Saudi Arabia are now engaged in an economic, religious and political competition to gain the sympathies, and perhaps even loyalties, of the Central Asian peoples and the largely Shi'ite Muslim population of Azerbaijan.

There is a diversity of other territorial groups. The Moldavians, living in the southern part of the European USSR, are very closely related to the neighbouring Romanians though, in order to justify their annexation of the area from Romania in 1940, the Soviets insisted that the Moldavians are a distinct nationality. To widen the differences, the Soviets changed the Moldavian alphabet from Latin (Romanian and Moldavian are Romance languages) to Cyrillic, a decision reversed in 1989. The Moldavians have renamed their now independent republic 'Moldova'. Slavs in the former Moldavian SSR formed a breakaway 'Dnestr Moldavian Republic' on 10 per cent of Moldova's territory. It is claimed that of Dnestr's population of 742,000 (1993), 40 per cent are Moldavian, 26 per cent Ukrainian and 24 per cent Russian. Moldavian, Russian and Ukrainian are the three official state languages. The Dnestr republic seems to be supported by Russia, which uses the presence of the 14th Russian Army to extend its influence and curb Moldovan expansion.

The Buryats and Kalmyks are Mongolian by language and culture and Buddhist and Shamanist by religion. Yakuts and Chukchi are Siberian peoples, while the Turkic-speaking Tatars are Muslims by tradition.

Finally, non-territorial nationalities of the former USSR include Germans, Jews, and Poles, as well as smaller groups of Magyars (Hungarians), Greeks, Bulgars, Kurds and others. The 2 million Germans, some of whose ancestors came at the invitation of Catherine the Great to improve Russian agriculture, used to have an autonomous republic in the Volga River region but were deprived of it and forcibly exiled at the beginning of World War II when Joseph Stalin presumed they would collaborate with the Nazis. Germans were settled mostly in Kazakhstan and other parts of Central Asia, as well as in the Baltic. In the 1970s and 1980s thousands of Germans emigrated, almost all to the Federal Republic of Germany. In the late 1980s and early 1990s there was a huge upsurge in German emigration, with over 450,000 leaving in 1987–91. Only in 1989 did articles begin to appear in the Soviet press which exonerated the Germans of the false accusations Stalin had made and which spoke sympathetically of their cultural and political demands. With the fall of the USSR, the Federal Republic of Germany stepped up its pressure on Russia to restore a German political entity within its borders. Germans in the former USSR are currently debating whether to continue to

emigrate or to try and rebuild German cultural and political institutions in one or more of the successor states.

The 1.4 million Jews counted in the 1989 census were the most
urbanised and educated nationality, but whereas they were once
overrepresented in the government, party and military, since the
1940s they were systematically excluded from the higher echelons
of those hierarchies as well as from other positions where political
loyalty or ideological considerations were important. Jews are the
only nationality of any significant size who did not have a single
school of their own until 1989 when two schools were opened in
the Baltic. Since the late 1960s over 600,000 have emigrated,
mainly to Israel and the USA. In 1990, a record 184,300 Soviet
Jews immigrated to Israel, and another 210,000 did so in 1991–3,
with 85,000 going to the USA.

The Poles live mostly in Belarus, Ukraine and Lithuania. Their
linguistic assimilation is almost as complete as that of the Jews:
only 14 per cent of the Jews and 29 per cent of the Poles listed their
national language as their native one in the 1979 census. Some
movement of Soviet Poles to Poland was observed in 1990–1.

Soviet Nationalities Policy: Ideology and History

Marx and Engels provided little guidance to their followers on
how to deal with ethnic issues. The ideological forefathers of the
Soviet state assumed that the fundamental cleavage in modern
society was class, not ethnicity. They assumed that nations were
an artificial construct of the capitalist epoch and that national
sentiments were exploited by the bourgeoisie to pit one segment
of the proletariat against another, thereby diverting workers from
venting their spleen against the exploiting capitalists. It followed
that in the classless society to be established after the socialist
revolution nations would disappear as they no longer served any
useful social and economic purpose. This theory did not prevent
Marx and Engels from taking sides in the national disputes of
their day, nor even exhibiting personal prejudices in regard to
races and nationalities.

Lenin began thinking about nationalities issues from an
orthodox Marxist point of view. He severely criticised the Jewish
Labour Bund in the Russian Empire which had borrowed the

concept of 'national–cultural autonomy' from Marxists in another multi-national empire, the Austro–Hungarian. This provided for the right of nationalities to administer their own cultural institutions and make independent decisions in the cultural sphere even after the advent of socialism. Lenin rejected even more decisively the Bund's proposal that the Russian Social-Democratic Labour Party, from which the Bolsheviks emerged, allow the formation of national groupings within it which would deal with the cultural affairs of the respective nationalities. The Bolshevik leader felt that such concessions to the nationalities would divert attention from the overall objective, the overthrow of tsarism.

In the years before the revolution Lenin came to appreciate how sensitive and important the nationalities issue was in the tsarist empire. He realised that ethnic issues were among the grievances many people felt against the tsarist system, and was flexible enough to modify his earlier positions in order to make tactical use of these grievances. Thus, he conceded that geographically compact and distinct national groups might be granted territorial autonomy within a socialist structure. After the revolution he agreed to the establishment of a Commissariat of Nationalities, headed by Joseph Stalin, himself a Georgian, and even to the creation of nationality sections within the Bolshevik Party. Once the Bolsheviks reconciled themselves to the temporary existence of a state – ultimately, it was supposed to 'wither away' – they agreed to organise it along federal lines in order to meet the demands of the nationalities. In the course of the revolution and the civil war, several areas that had been wholly or partly in the Russian empire – Poland, Finland, the Baltic states – managed to break away from the Russian-dominated state. Others which attempted to do so – Ukraine, Georgia, Armenia, for example – were forcibly reincorporated into the USSR, successor state to the Russian empire.

In the 1920s Soviet leaders declared that Russian chauvinism was the main problem in nationality relations and that the non-Russians, having been discriminated against for so long, should be assisted in developing their cultures. This would not contradict the ultimate Marxist–Leninist goal of the disappearance and amalgamation of nations, because if one thought 'dialectically' one would appreciate that oppressed nationalities needed to have their cultures flourish first in order to realise that this was not the main purpose of their existence. Once having maximised their cultural freedom the nationalities could then move on to mutual assimilation. The concrete application of this paradoxical idea came in the policy of *korenizatsiya*, 'nativisation' or indigenisation. That meant that members of the non-Russian nationalities were encouraged to take government and party posts; schools in their languages were set up and vigorously promoted; courts, trade unions, and even party cells were encouraged to operate in local languages; and the press, theatre, research institutes and other cultural organisations operating in the local languages were supported by the state. It was during this period of the 'flowering of the nationalities' that the peoples of Central Asia, many of whom were organised in tribes and clans, were given national status, state structures, and written languages. This was the heyday of ethnic pluralism and cultural development.

When Stalin began his drive to modernise and industrialise the country as quickly as possible, he tried to shift all energies toward that goal. By the early 1930s the goal of promoting national cultures yielded to the overarching aim of rapid industrial development at any cost. What had been laudable efforts to develop national cultures just a few years before now became 'petit bourgeois nationalist deviations'. Cultural and political leaders of the nationalities were arrested and often killed. Cultural institutions were purged, closed down, or allowed to disappear by attrition. Parents became fearful of sending their children to national schools and many hesitated even to speak in their native languages. Stalin declared that the cultures of the USSR were to be 'national in form, socialist in content'. That meant that ideological uniformity was to be imposed on all cultures, and only the linguistic and other forms of culture were to be preserved. Indeed, all of Soviet culture became subject to a deadly uniformity and conformity. At the same time, there were many who genuinely believed that the epoch of flourishing national cultures had passed and that it was time to move on to a more 'internationalist' mode. Marriages among peoples of different nationalities became more common. As people streamed from the countryside to the city, driven both by the horrors of collectivisation and the lure of modernity, they began to lose their traditional ways of life, native languages, distinctive dress, foods, and styles of life. Russian was the common language of the cities, housing and food became more uniform, and many began to abandon their former cultures.

Already in the 1930s, but certainly in the next decade, Stalin stressed the historical and contemporary virtuosity of the Russian people and made it clear that they were to be regarded as the 'elder brother' of all other peoples. During World War II the Russian Orthodox church, severely persecuted in the two preceding decades, was revived. Historic Russian heroes were lauded, and the message was sent that the war was being fought to defend historic Russia as much as it was to safeguard the Soviet system. Simultaneously, several peoples, among them the Germans, Crimean Tatars, Chechen and Ingush, were deported *en masse* on the grounds that they had intended to collaborate with the German invaders or had actually done so. Collective punishment was meted out for what were often individual crimes.

In his victory toast in the Kremlin in 1945 Stalin singled out the *Russian* people for especial praise, and in the following years Russians were given credit for all kinds of inventions and achievements that properly belonged to people of other nations. This was part of a militant anti-Western and 'anti-cosmopolitan' campaign which sought to isolate the Soviet population from the world outside and which singled out the Jews, especially, as aliens and potential or actual traitors. The 'flowering of the nationalities' seemed long forgotten.

In his 'secret speech' to the 20th Party Congress in 1956, Nikita Khrushchev criticised Stalin for many crimes, including some – but not all – that had been perpetrated against the nationalities. Though Khrushchev curtailed some of the Stalin's excesses in regard to the nationalities and opened up the elite to Ukrainians and some others, he was not especially sympathetic to ethnic claims, having been Stalin's party secretary in Ukraine at the height of the purges. Khrushchev launched a vigorous campaign against religions, which indirectly impinged on several nationalities associated strongly with certain faiths. In 1958 he initiated an educational reform which eliminated the required study of the native language in the non-Russian regions. His plan to divide the country into economic regions, known as *sovnarkhozy*, threatened to diminish the importance of the national republics.

Under Khrushchev's successor, Brezhnev, dissident nationality movements, among others, began to be more visible. Crimean

Tatars demanded to return to their ancestral homeland in the USSR while Jews and Germans demanded to return to theirs outside it. Lithuanian Catholics pressed for religious and cultural concessions, as did Ukrainians. Brezhnev doggedly asserted, however, that the nationalities question had been solved definitively and that the protestors were deviants and criminals who should be punished accordingly – and many were. During the period of detente in the 1970s, however, in order to improve relations with Germany and the United States, relatively large numbers of Germans and Jews, and later Armenians, were permitted to emigrate. However, many were denied permission to leave the country and were imprisoned or harassed for their efforts to do so. In the 1970s also the concept of a 'Soviet people' was developed and widely promoted. According to one Soviet scholar, Academician P.N. Fedoseev, this was not a nation or an ethnic entity but 'a new historical form of social and international unity of people of different nations' which eliminated antagonistic relations between classes and nations and was based on 'the flowering and drawing together of nations'. It remained unclear whether this 'Soviet nation' was ultimately to replace the peoples of the Soviet Union, though this was presumably the intention.

The official doctrine explaining the present and future of the nationalities was for a long time encapsulated in two terms, *sblizhenie* and *sliyanie*. The former means the 'drawing together', or rapprochement, of peoples, while the latter means their fusion into each other, or amalgamation. The two were presumed to exist in a sequential and causal relationship. That is, over time *sblizhenie* would lead to *sliyanie*, because as nations mingle with each other they would lose their specific characteristics and assimilate into one another. The prospect of fusion and loss of identity frightened those who cherished their particular cultures, but they were reassured that *sliyanie* was a rather distant prospect. Both components of the formula came under empirical scrutiny and serious questioning in the 1980s. The emergence of militant nationalisms rendered them irrelevant.

Regarding *sblizhenie*, in the late 1980s Soviet commentators began to admit that nationalism and ethnic prejudices and tensions existed in Soviet society. These evils were usually dismissed as 'survivals of the past' but, as one high official of an autonomous republic put it, the great majority of Soviet citizens today were born after the revolution, so how can the fiction of 'survivals' be maintained? It was suggested that nationalism existed because peoples' consciousness changed more slowly than the reality in which they lived and because some peoples entered the USSR relatively recently and had not been fully resocialised. Moreover, religion survived, reinforcing national exclusivity, and 'bourgeois elements' outside the country tried to fan ethnic tensions. Furthermore, 'subjective' factors had to be taken into account: insensitive bureaucrats insulted people on an ethnic basis or tried to hasten assimilation 'artificially'.

Soviet ethnographers discovered in the 1970s and 1980s that national consciousness was not fading, as the theory had predicted, but was growing. Indeed, Gorbachev told the All-Union Party Conference in 1988 that 'The development of our multinational state is, naturally [sic], accompanied by growth in national consciousness. This is a positive phenomenon . . .' (*Pravda*, 28 June 1988). As for *sliyanie*, the 1986 Party Programme said that the 'complete unity of nations' would take place 'in the remote historical future'. In a speech to scientists and 'cultural figures', Gorbachev stated, 'Of course, we cannot permit even the smallest people to vanish or the language of the smallest people to be lost, nor can we permit nihilism with respect to the culture, traditions and history of both large and small peoples' (*Pravda*, 8 January 1989). In theory, at least, this was a far cry from Lenin and Stalin's assimilationism. The judgement that national consciousness had not faded, and had even grown among some peoples, was borne out by events in the USSR.

Soviet Nationality Policy

The Soviet Union brought dramatically higher standards of living to many of the peoples of the Caucasus and Central Asia. Industry and modern agriculture were brought to these areas by the Soviet government, along with higher standards of health and education. Still, at the end of the Soviet period it was revealed by the Minister of Health that nearly half the hospitals in Turkmenistan had no running water. Infant mortality is shockingly high in parts of Central Asia, and the USSR as a whole ranked thirty-second in the world, behind Barbados and Mauritius, in this respect. For many nationalities there were trade-offs between higher standards of living and improved economies, on one hand, and the loss of some or even much of their traditional cultures and religion, on the other. Jews are perhaps an extreme example of this trade-off: the revolution liberated them from the Pale of Settlement, allowing them to live where they chose, and opened educational and vocational opportunities to them that had been denied to them by the tsars. At the same time their religious institutions were almost completely destroyed, they were denied the opportunity to study or use Hebrew, and later they were discriminated against in education, employment and culture. Ukrainians are an example of a nationality whose very existence was denied by the tsars but who received republic status from the Soviets, though they were denied independence. Great economic progress was made in Ukraine, and Ukrainian cultural institutions flourished. However, there was steady pressure for Russification within Ukraine, and few opportunities in their native culture for Ukrainians living elsewhere. Like most multinational countries, the USSR tried to balance the perceived needs of centre and periphery, though ever since the 1930s the centre's interests took precedence. In 1991, the combined centrifugal forces of the peripheries destroyed the centre.

How did the central authorities previously control this heterogeneous and potentially fractious population? This was accomplished with a mix of normative and coercive incentives and through structural devices. First, the spread of Marxist–Leninist ideology throughout the country imbued the ideologically committed or conforming with the conviction that 'all-Union' interests and those of the party took precedence over the 'narrow, parochial' interests of this or that nationality. They were also taught to believe that nationalism was an evil and that 'internationalist' attitudes and actions were the only ones admissible under socialism. Nations were, in any case, transient. Thus, political elites of the nationalities were generally chosen for their 'internationalist' outlooks in addition to any other attributes they might have possessed. As the power of ideology faded rapidly, and with the devolution of power away from the centre, some republic leaders in the late 1980s became more responsive to their constituencies than to the central authorities.

Second, the Communist Party, in great disarray and seriously weakened by the failed coup of 1991 and then suppressed, was organised as a hierarchical, disciplined organisation in which orders flowed from the top down and had to be obeyed. This was the device which effectively weakened Soviet federalism and made inoperative the constitutional right of the republics to secede. The logic of this device has the following: since the nation was represented by its leading class, and since the leading class of all Soviet nations was the proletariat, and since, furthermore, the party was the only authentic representative of that class, ultimately it was the party which decided whether a particular nation would secede or not. Because the party was centralised and hierarchical, no republic-level party organisation could unilaterally recommend secession. By 1990, the new Union Treaty, to be discussed later, implicitly rejected this doctrine and conceded the right of republics to secede with no reference to the party.

A third control mechanism was the cooptation of native elites. Promising people were recruited into the party and imbued with an 'internationalist' world view. Those who aspired to higher education had to have, in almost all cases, an excellent command of Russian, the language of most higher educational institutions. The peoples of the USSR were given the impression that, at least on the republic and lower levels, they were being ruled by people of the indigenous ethnic groups. Of the 44 republic party first secretaries in 1954–76, over 86 per cent were non-Russians. In 1990–1 the first secretaries of all republics were members of the titular nationality of that republic. As we shall see, political mobility of non-Russians seemed to stop at the republic level, but perhaps most of the non-Russians did not aspire to run the country as a whole and were more concerned with running the affairs of their respective regions. During the 18 years of the Brezhnev period, later labelled in the Soviet media the 'era of stagnation', republic leaders, particularly in Central Asia, were given considerable latitude in running republican affairs, apparently in return for their acquiescence to national policy as formulated by the Slavic leadership in Moscow. This resulted in the creation of fiefdoms wherein the local leaders' power was enormous. That power was used, according to the Soviet press, to discriminate against national minorities, mainly Russians, in the republics. It also resulted in enormous corruption and nepotism, with several of the republics looking like the personal possessions of local bosses.

On the other hand, traditionally the second party secretary in the republics was not of the indigenous nationality and was usually dispatched from the central apparatus in Moscow. He was assumed by many to be the 'eyes and ears' of the centre. About two-thirds of the second secretaries from the mid-1950s up to 1976 were Russians or other Slavs. While the second secretary probably did not run things in the republic, he may at least have exercised some influence over his superior.

The centre was also able to exercise great economic leverage on the republics. Investment and trade decisions were, like most economic decisions in the country, highly centralised. It was Moscow which decided, though not always unilaterally, what was to be built where, and how much was to be invested around the country. There is considerable debate about whether the centre equalised the distribution of wealth through its policies, or whether some regions, and hence peoples, were favoured over others. Gorbachev's reforms promised that the republics would have greater say in economic decisions, but that was not enough to assuage feelings of exploitation nor to stem the tide of autonomism.

A sixth instrument of central control was coercion as exercised by the militia (police), KGB, and armed forces. The KGB played a major role in the repression of nationality dissent in the 1970s and early 1980s. The police were used to break up ethnic and other demonstrations. In especially serious instances the armed forces were called in. When large-scale violence broke out between Armenians and Azerbaijanis or between Uzbeks and Meskhetis, several thousand troops of the regular army intervened. On quite a few occasions the threat of army intervention was used to head off nationality demonstrations. In the post-Soviet period, Russia has claimed it would not allow Russian or CIS troops to be used in the non-Russian republics. During serious fighting between Georgian political factions, Soviet troops stationed in the republic made no attempt to intervene. By 1993, however, it was widely believed that the Russian military was helping Abkhazian forces fighting the Georgians, and this successfully pressured the Georgians to join the CIS. Russian troops are active in the Dnestr area and they have guarded the border between Tajikstan and Afghanistan on the grounds that an invasion of Tajikstan could lead to foreign troops entering

Russia. Russia has also used her dwindling military presence in the Baltic as a counterweight to what Russians see as Baltic discrimination against their co-ethnics residing in those republics.

Finally, there were policies whose obvious aim was to hasten *sblizhenie*, or more concretely, to nudge the nationalities in the direction of Russianisation. The Russian language was clearly the favoured one. Though official doctrine spoke of the 'mutual enrichment of languages', in practice the other languages took much of their scientific, technological and political vocabulary from Russian, while the latter borrowed little from them. As pointed out, the educational system was heavily slanted toward Russian. The armed forces operated exclusively in Russian and they were supposed to have a role in the teaching of Russian to those of other nationalities. As a greater and greater proportion of recruits came from Central Asia, and since large numbers of rural Central Asians have only a rudimentary command of Russian, the army's role in teaching Russian was increasing.

Perhaps the dominance of Russian was the only practical arrangement in such a multilingual country, but non-Russians complained that the media and publications were disproportionately weighted toward Russian. Publication data seem to bear them out. About 41 per cent of the Soviet people considered their native language to be one other than Russian, but in 1983 only 23 per cent of the titles and 16 per cent of the total runs of books and brochures were in non-Russian languages. Still, among most nationalities there was little erosion of native-language loyalty. That is, the proportions of people declaring the language of their people to be their 'mother tongue' (*rodnoi yazyk*) changed very little over the decades, though this is not true of the non-territorial nationalities. Over 90 per cent of most nationalities considered the language of their people to be their native or mother tongues. At the same time, there was an impressive growth in the Russian-language facility of all peoples, though a leading Soviet ethnographer complained that in some republics the older generation is more conversant with Russian than the younger. There is some debate over the extent to which bilingualism was achieved, or was even desirable, but on the whole Soviet citizens of all nationalities were able to communicate with each other through Russian. No doubt, Russian will remain for at least a generation the language of communication among the peoples of the successor states.

Russian's influence was exercised even in what might be called alphabet policy. When written languages were invented for the Central Asians, the first script used was Arabic. For fear of the spread of pan-Arabism and other reasons, this was changed to a Latin script, but by 1940 all of these languages had gone over to a Cyrillic script, the script of the Russian language. As mentioned, even Moldavian was switched to Cyrillic after the incorporation of that republic. Today, the trend is in the opposite direction.

Russianisation was also promoted by migration of Slavs to non-Slavic areas. Not only the Russians, but Ukrainians and Belorussians also, tended not to learn the local languages and used Russian as the common language of Europeans as well as with indigenous nationalities. This is now costing them, as the Baltic states have made knowledge of the indigenous languages a prerequisite for citizenship, and the other states are favouring the indigenous languages in education and employment. In the Soviet period Central Asians tended to stick to their own republics, even eschewing movement from the countryside to the city. Thus, many remained basically monolingual, since the countryside had few Slavs. Baltic peoples complained about the migration of Slavs to their republics as a result of industrialisation. Factories brought Slavic workers and managers, thereby diluting both the ethnic and linguistic character of the countries. For this reason the national fronts in the Baltic in the late 1980s demanded that the republics be given the right to limit migration into the republics. Now they demand that the indigenous languages be learned by all non-native speakers and that all official business be transacted in the indigenous languages.

Compared to many other multinational countries, irrespective of political system, the Soviet Union was quite tranquil until the late 1980s. Certainly, when one thinks of Yugoslavia, Lebanon, Iraq, Nigeria, or even Canada and Belgium, the Soviet record in granting opportunities to nationalities and maintaining peace among them looks quite good. It might fairly be asked, however, whether this was due more to actual and implied coercion or repression than to genuine harmony and cooperation. When in 1991 the reins were loosened, Soviet nationality policy was severely tested, and the results indicate that the policy, if it ever was as successful as it appeared, had ceased to be effective.

Ethnopolitics in the Post-Soviet Period

With the breakup of the Soviet Union, states are free to follow
their own ethnopolitical courses. Thus far, some have moved
toward becoming ethnic states, where the criterion for full membership is membership in one, favoured ethnic group, while others
are tending toward civic statehood, where membership is determined by residence and political allegiance rather than by ethnicity. Georgia, Estonia, Latvia, Moldova, the self-declared Dnestr
Republic and perhaps some Central Asian states are becoming
ethnic states, whereas so far Russia, Belarus, Ukraine, Kazakhstan, and Lithuania look more like civic states. Thus, in Georgia
the Abkhazians and Ossetians feel that they are being ruled by
foreigners, while the Georgians see the desire for independence by
those nationalities as betrayal of Georgia. In Estonia and Latvia
the Russian-speaking population, which has to pass tests in order
to acquire citizenship, sees itself as the object of discrimination,
whereas the Balts argue that the Russian speakers were invaders
who have no claim to citizenship. In the civic states no distinctions are made *de jure* among the peoples resident there.

The major manifestations of ethnopolitical issues are ethnic
'hot' wars and ethnic 'cold' wars, and the consequences of each.
The 'hot' wars began in February 1988 when the ancient historical dispute between Christian Armenians and Muslim Azerbaijanis, who had territorial claims on each other, flared into violence
in the Nagorno-Karabakh enclave of Azerbaijan. The claims of
the local, overwhelmingly Armenian population that they were
being discriminated against and denied cultural facilities were
supported in the Armenian republic. Thousands were killed in
Armenian–Azerbaijani clashes over the next years, as we have
seen, and several hundred thousand people became refugees from
the conflict.

In April 1989 Abkhazians living in an autonomous republic of
Georgia demanded a republic of their own and Georgians, in
turn, demanded independence from the USSR in a series of mass
demonstrations and hunger strikes. Troops called in to restore
order killed 20 Georgians and the events became a subject of
heated discussion in the Congress of People's Deputies. Later,
Abkhazian–Georgian clashes, Georgian–Ossetian skirmishes,
combat in the North Caucasus, and attacks by Uzbeks on Mes-

khetis, a Turkic minority who had been exiled by Stalin from Georgia to Central Asia, added to the casualties of inter-ethnic disputes. By the end of 1993, about 10,000 people had died in such wars.

Having spent his entire career in his native and mostly Russian Stavropol province, in the south of the RSFSR, and in Moscow, Gorbachev had no direct experience in nationalities issues. And in his first year or so in office he paid little attention to them. But *glasnost* allowed people to express national sentiments and grievances and to criticise the cliches and shibboleths that had marked Soviet rhetoric about ethnic issues. *Perestroika* showed them the possibilities of institutional and policy change. The two together led to the explosion of national sentiment and demands that we have described. On one hand, Gorbachev acknowledged that there was a much higher consciousness among the Soviet peoples than his predecessors were willing to admit and that not all was well in relations among nationalities. He tolerated actions and rhetoric in the Baltic that none of his predecessors would have countenanced. On the other hand, his personnel policies indicated a stronger inclination to promote Russian and Slavic dominance than that show by any of his four predecessors. Nearly all government ministers were replaced by Gorbachev. Yet, only two of them were not Slavs. It is as if Gorbachev had been telling the non-Slavs that while they could continue to wield some power in their republics, they would not have any share in running the country as a whole.

In his search for a new formula to guide nationalities policy and a new programme to implement it, Gorbachev proposed a new 'Union Treaty' which would restructure the USSR, now to mean the 'Union of Soviet *Sovereign* Republics'. It was presented to the Congress of People's Deputies in December 1990, was revised in March and June 1991, and was due to be signed on 20 August by 10 republics. The treaty defined each republic as a sovereign state and gave the republics the right to appoint one house of the legislature which could veto new laws. Republics would have a vote in the cabinet and block amendments to the Union Treaty. Republics were given ownership of their lands, water and other natural resources. They would collect taxes and give a share to the centre, reversing traditional arrangements. The nuclear power and arms industries, rail, sea and air transport would be controlled by the centre, as would fuel and energy policy. Foreign policy and the military would also be controlled by the centre.

One aim of those who mounted the attempted coup on 19 August 1991 was to block the signing of this treaty on the following day, on the grounds that it would destroy the Soviet Union by giving too much power to the republics. Ironically, the coup's failure led to great losses of central power and to declarations of independence by the republics.

In late 1991 the reconstitution of at least part of the former USSR, albeit on a different basis, began to evolve slowly. Russia, Belorussia, Armenia and the five Central Asian republics signed an agreement to create a free market economic community, and the Commonwealth of Independent States emerged.

How long this 'Commonwealth' will last and how its component parts will relate to each other are not clear (see Chapter 11). From the outset the former Soviet republics have had to grapple with such questions as uniform or separate currencies; coordination of price reforms among them so that prices in one region would not be radically different from those in another; general economic coordination in such areas as trade and supply; control of armed forces; and nuclear weapons. Russia and Ukraine have disputed the 'ownership' of the Soviet Black Sea Fleet and whether and to what extent Ukraine would give up its nuclear weapons. Four republics with strategic nuclear forces – Russia, Belarus, Ukraine and Kazakhstan – came under international pressure to give up some of their leverage and agree to place control of strategic nuclear weapons under centralised, which is to say Russian, command. But the volatility of national and political relations made the possession of even tactical nuclear weapons a cause of widespread unease well beyond the borders of the CIS.

The 'cold wars' among the republics went beyond this issue and centred on citizenship, language rights, and schools. These are matters of contention in Estonia, Latvia, Moldova, parts of the Russian Federation and, less visibly, Lithuania and Central Asia. In Ukraine, for example, the Crimea, transferred from Russia to Ukraine by Khrushchev, is the scene of a three-way struggle for power, involving Ukraine, which wants to regain it, Russia, which wants to keep it, and Crimean Tatars, who want to make it independent. There are tensions between West Ukraine, the centre of radical Ukrainian nationalism where Ukrainian is widely spoken, and East Ukraine, with its large Russian and acculturated, Russian-speaking Ukrainian population. As the economic situation deteriorates rapidly in Ukraine, extremist and demagogic appeals to antisemitism and anti-Russian sentiments are heard increasingly. In the Transcarpathian area of Ukraine, Hungarians demand cultural autonomy. In Moldova, in addition to the Slavs who declared independence, the Gagauz, an Orthodox Christian, Turkic-speaking minority, declared autonomy, against the wishes of the republican government.

These wars and tensions have created several million refugees, mainly Armenians, Azerbaijanis and Russians. The Armenian refugees are mostly people who lived in Azerbaijan, the Azerbaijanis have fled Armenian-occupied territory and have crowded near the Iranian border, and the Russians – 3 million of them – have fled actual or expected discrimination and persecution in the Baltic, Central Asia and the Caucasus. It is estimated that of 388,000 Slavs living in Tajikstan before the outbreak of civil war, 300,000 have fled that Central Asian republic. Thus, while they may have gained independence, the former Soviet republics took on responsibility for an awesome array of social and economic problems and have been forced to confront ethnic issues that had been swept under the rug by the Soviets and had been repressed by the kind of power the successor states do not have. Moreover, whereas in the Soviet period these problems were contained within one state, today they spill across new international borders and become issues of inter-state relations. There is tension between Uzbekistan and Tajikstan over the identity and cultural rights of Tajiks living in Uzbekistan. Russia feels obliged to defend the rights of the 25 million Russians outside the Russian Federation. Armenia felt compelled to support the demands of Armenians in Nagorno-Karabakh, part of Azerbaijan. As these and other similar issues are dealt with in other parts of this book, we shall turn our attention to ethnopolitics within the Russian Federation.

Ethnopolitics in the Russian Federation

Although Russians are more than four-fifths of the population of the Russian Federation, or 'Russia', that country has not avoided ethnic problems. The ethnic issues most prominent on the Russian political agenda include acting as protector of Russians in other states; the refugees from those states; autonomist tendencies within the Russian Federation; and the structure of the federation itself. We have already touched on the first two issues and now take up the latter two.

Gorbachev's new 'Union Treaty' having been aborted in 1991, a Federation Treaty for Russia alone was signed in March 1992. This was really three treaties, with republics, regions (*oblasti* and *kraya*), and autonomous regions (*oblasti* and *okrugi*). Republics within the Russian Federation obtained the right to conduct foreign policy and foreign trade. Land and natural resources were to belong to the republics, though federal law would govern ownership and use. The republics are not really ethnic strongholds since apparently the titular (eponymous) nationality constitutes less than 40 per cent of the populations of the republics. Barely half, on average, of the titular nationalities live in 'their' republics. The regions, not based on nominal ethnic groupings as the republics are, were angered because 'their' land and resources would be controlled by the republics of which they were formally a part. So some of them simply declared themselves republics. Moreover, Tatarstan held a referendum which resulted in a declaration of sovereignty in March 1992, but a rejection of a separate defence policy. The Caucasian territory of Chechnya was already acting independently of Moscow, and was instrumental in forming a Confederation of Mountain Peoples of the Caucasus, including 16 ethnic groups, in 1991. Some people from the North Caucasus fought with the Abkhazians against the Georgians, and the latter held the Russians responsible for allowing this. In July 1993, the Ural Mountains province of Sverdlovsk declared itself a Urals Republic, not sovereign and not claiming the right to secede from the Federation, but establishing its own organs of government. Federation President Boris Yeltsin angrily abolished the republic in November.

Obviously, part of the problem was that the regions of the Federation are of two types: ethnically based and territorially based. In April 1993, Yeltsin released a draft of his proposed constitution which provided for 21 republics, based on nominal ethnicity, 50 provinces, 6 territories, 10 autonomous regions, two 'federal cities' (Moscow and St Petersburg) and one autonomous province. The constitution approved by voters in December affirmed this structure. A majority of the republics protested that the constitution did not recognise their status as sovereign states and focussed on individual rights to the neglect of the 'rights of peoples'. Republics wanted to retain all rights except those which they explicitly ceded to the federal centre. They pressed for the right to establish their own foreign policies and a Council of the Heads of the Republics, which some saw as a counterweight to both the federal presidency and the legislature. The proposed Council was regarded by many as a 'boyars' duma' or assembly of the medieval nobility, a body of regional leaders who could check presidential power. Yet, the speaker of the parliament, Ruslan Khasbulatov, backed the territories and provinces against the republics, as the regions felt the republics were getting too much power and demanded to have as many rights as the republics. In turn, Yeltsin seemed to be wooing the republics. However, after he ordered the attack on parliament on 3–4 October 1993, in the course of which Khasbulatov was arrested, Yeltsin greatly reduced the powers of the regions by peremptorily disbanding local soviets and ordering new elections for smaller regional assemblies. Heads of regional administration were now to be appointed or dismissed exclusively by the President. Yeltsin also defined the republics by omitting any mention of republican sovereignty from the constitution passed in the December 1993 referendum.

The new constitution makes Russian the official state language but in the republics the language of the dominant nationality may also be used as a state language. Foreign policy, defence and taxation are the province of the federal government. A Council of the Federation (as we have noted in Chapter 1) is one of the two houses of the legislature. Each component of the Federation elects two deputies to the Council. The two houses jointly draft legislation, adopt the budget, and may amend the constitution. The Council confirms internal border changes, may vote no confidence in a government or one of its ministers, and 'decides the question of removing the President of the Russian Federation from Office'. How the new institutional arrangements work out remains to be seen, especially since the struggle between an increasingly authoritarian Yeltsin and a more nationalistic and anti-reformist legislature will be as difficult as that between the parliament and president before October 1993.

As the peoples of the former Soviet Union search for new formulas and programmes to deal with their nationalities, they can find little inspiration in other East European countries. Yugoslavia has dissolved in a violent and tragic manner. It serves as a warning to all peoples of the dangers inhering in intolerant nationalism. Czecho-Slovakia broke apart, though in a more benign manner. Bulgaria and Romania have dealt with their national minorities through combinations of emigration (in the Bulgarian case, actually deportation) and repression. Clearly, the nationalities question is complex and differentiated and is not solved simply by the abolition of the old centre. Some Jews, Germans and others might prefer emigration, but others of those nationalities would like to have greater cultural opportunities and experience less discrimination in the CIS. Other nationalities are not at all interested in emigration. Some stress cultural issues, others economic or political concerns, and some have a broad agenda of changes they would like to see. The 4 million Ukrainians in Russia, for instance, have established 40 cultural societies. Some have expressed the wish to obtain Ukrainian citizenship. They point out that there is not a single Ukrainian school in Russia, whereas there are 5000 Russian schools in Ukraine. Jews, Koreans, Germans, Greeks, Mordvins, Poles and several other non-territorial minorities in Russia have developed local, regional, and in some cases national organisations. They spoke of forming a Minorities Bloc for the parliamentary election but were unable to organise one in the limited period that was available. The Russian government has supported the formation of these national organisations, though not financially.

On the other hand, extremist forms of Russian nationalism have also surfaced. For example, an organisation calling itself *Pamyat*, or Memory, has urged that Russians be given more control of the country, and has adopted explicitly anti-semitic platforms. They view the current system as conceding too much to non-Russians. Much more significant is the Liberal-Democratic Party led by Vladimir Zhirinovsky, which won 24 per cent of the vote in the party-list elections to the new parliament. The party stands for the dominance of the Russian people and the restoration to Russia of the borders of the Soviet Union. All of the 'near abroad', the states formerly part of the USSR, are understandably nervous about the emergence of a Russian imperialist force in the new Russian government.

Conclusion

The ethnopolitical agenda of Russia must include maintaining the territorial integrity of the CIS without permitting nationalist forces to push Russia into 'adventures' in the former Soviet republics; balancing the needs of the republics within the Russian Federation with those of the federal centre; guaranteeing the rights of the non-Russians; and intervening effectively on behalf of Russians outside the Federation. If Russia continues to use her military and economic power to nudge republics back into the CIS or form a stronger union, she may succeed in restoring some of the lost assets, territory, and glory of the USSR. On the other hand, she will be saddled with the responsibility of helping keep the peace and propping up failed economies in the republics. At present, it would seem that Russia's own political, social and economic challenges are of sufficient magnitude to focus her efforts on the Federation alone. But it is precisely these difficulties that prepare the ground for an extremist Russian nationalism which feeds on the frustration born of the failure to turn around the economy and polity, the humiliation of the loss of empire and of superpower status, and the fears aroused by an uncertain future.

11

Politics Outside Russia

DARRELL SLIDER

The breakup of the Soviet Union created a new set of nations on Russia's periphery – the 14 other former Soviet republics, which had suddenly become independent republics. The term used most commonly in Russia to describe these nations is the 'near abroad'. Many Russians had difficulty adjusting to the idea that these nations were truly independent, and there was considerable support among Russians for policies that would re-establish some of the patterns of relations that had characterised the Soviet and tsarist empires. Among the proponents of such policies were the former vice-president, Alexander Rutskoi, and Vladimir Zhirinovsky, leader of the Liberal-Democratic Party, which received the most votes in party-list voting in the December 1993 parliamentary elections.

Russia, as the creator and centre of previous empires, had served as the cultural, administrative, and economic core. The Russian language and Russian-language newspapers and television were widely used in non-Russian republics. The central leadership and administrative bodies of the Communist Party of the Soviet Union and the Soviet government were dominated by ethnic Russians. Both the party and government bureaucracies, located in the Russian capital, were highly centralised, and they exercised close supervision over the activities of party officials, local administrators, and enterprises in the non-Russian republics. Defence and security issues were also decided in Moscow.

Many of the ties between Russia and former Soviet republics, forged through the decades, were difficult or impossible to change in short order, despite the wishes of the more impatient nationalists in the republics. The most widespread second language in the republics was Russian, and for many residents (even non-Russians) it was their first language. Most of the population continued to watch television programming from Moscow. Transportation and communication links with the outside world often continued to pass through Russia. Russia remained an important source of raw material and fuel, while the larger factories in the non-Russian republics were almost all dependent on enterprises in Russia that provided equipment and spare parts, and that were the main purchasers for their output. The breakdown of traditional supply relations after the collapse of communism led to a near economic disaster in several republics, and industrial output plummeted in all of them. Russia also had considerable military forces stationed at former Soviet bases in the republics, and controlled strategic nuclear weaponry deployed in Belarus, Ukraine and Kazakhstan.

The question of borders and their 'transparency' was one of the most vexing to the Russian government. Russia was slow to set up border installations that corresponded to its new international boundaries with the Baltic states, Belarus, Ukraine, Kazakhstan, Georgia, and Azerbaijan (Russia shared no boundaries with the now independent states of Moldova, Armenia, Kyrgyzstan, Uzbekistan, Turkmenistan and Tajikistan). The result was that Russia depended on the willingness of its new neighbours to accept the continued presence of Russian border troops and customs officials on their territories. It was not surprising that one of the most nationalistic of the former republics, Estonia, was the first republic – in July 1992 – to require visas and the first to set up its own customs points for citizens of Russia entering the country. The other Baltic states soon followed this example. It was only in October 1993 that Russia opened the first international customs post on its new borders, between Ivangorod and the Estonian city of Narva.

A powerful emotional issue for Russia was the problem of Russians who, because of the breakup of the Soviet Union, were now located outside its borders. Over 25 million ethnic Russians were living in the 'near abroad', according to the 1989 Soviet census. Particular problems arose in places where Russians and

TABLE 11.1   *The Commonwealth of Independent States, 1994*

Name of state	Population			Chief executive
	m *(1990)*	*%* *titular*	*%* *Russian*	
Armenia	3.3	93.3	1.6	Levon Ter-Petroysan
Azerbaijan	7.1	82.7	5.6	Gaidar Aliev
Belarus (Belorussia)	10.3	77.9	13.2	Mechislav Grib
Georgia	5.4	70.1	6.3	Eduard Shevardnadze
Kazakhstan	16.7	39.7	37.8	Nursultan Nazarbaev
Kyrgyzstan (Kirgizia)	4.3	54.2	21.5	Askar Akaev
Moldova (Moldavia)	4.4	64.5	9.4	Mircea Snegur
Russian Federation	148.0	81.5	81.5	Boris Yeltsin
Tajikistan	5.3	62.3	7.6	Ali Rakhmanov
Turkmenia	3.6	72.0	9.5	Saparmurad Niyazov
Ukraine	51.8	72.7	22.1	Leonid Kravchuk
Uzbekistan	20.3	71.4	8.4	Islam Karimov

Source: Nationality and population data are as reported in the 1989 census returns published in *Vestnik statistiki*, 1990, nos 10–12, and 1991, nos 1 and 4–6.

'Russian-speakers' (meaning Ukrainians and other non-Russians whose primary language of communication is Russian) formed a local majority. Politically restive concentrations of Russians confronted republic authorities in Estonia (in Narva and the northeast; overall they made up 30 per cent of the republic's population), Moldova (in the Trans-Dniester region), and Ukraine (in the Crimea and, in particular, the port city of Sevastapol). Russians in these regions sought at a minimum greater rights; the most extreme demands were for independence or incorporation into Russia. Russians also made up a large share, about 38 per cent, of the total population of Kazakhstan, and 34 per cent in Latvia. In Ukraine and Kyrgyzstan, about 22 per cent of the population was Russian. Elsewhere the share of Russians ranged from less than 2 per cent in Armenia, to 13 per cent in Moldova and Belarus, and 19 per cent in Turkmenistan. Russians tended to make up a disproportionate share of the skilled industrial labour force as well as of positions in management and science (see Harris, 1993, for an overview).

The newly independent states faced problems similar to those faced by Russia itself after the end of Soviet rule: the creation of new political and administration institutions and a new constitutional framework to govern their interrelations, facilitating the development of political parties, ethnic minorities and problems of regional or local autonomy, and rebuilding and redesigning their economies. At the time of independence, all of the republics were governed by parliaments and leaders who had been chosen for the most part in 1990. The rapidly changing political context in the republics made preterm elections (the term in office was to have been 5 years) an issue in almost every republic, as groups that felt underrepresented sought a greater share of political power. The simultaneous strengthening of presidential and executive power in most republics meant that gaining a substantial share of seats in new parliamentary elections would not necessarily result in a corresponding increase in their political power.

The former Soviet republics responded to these challenges differently, and in several cases they were embroiled in political and ethnic violence that threatened their existence as sovereign states. In some republics there were disputes between presidents or government leaders and parliaments that rivalled in intensity the conflict between Yeltsin and the Russian parliament in 1993. Elsewhere, the communist power structure remained essentially intact, and there was outward calm. Economic reforms were pursued quickly and radically by some of the former republics and hardly begun by others. These variations influenced relationships with Russia and other former Soviet republics, and they served to limit the extent of future mutual accommodation both in, or outside of, the context of the Commonwealth of Independent States.

The Baltic

The Baltic states of Latvia, Lithuania and Estonia were the most recent of the Soviet acquisitions, taken by the Red Army as it advanced against Hitler in the final stages of World War II. As such, the Baltic was somewhat less integrated into the Soviet system than those republics that had been brought under Soviet rule just after the 1917 revolution or in the 1920s. In their struggle for independence, the Baltic states benefited from at least a formal predisposition by the outside world to support their cause, since the incorporation of the Baltic states was not recognised as legal by many countries including the USA. All three had considerable numbers of their compatriots who had become emigres after the war, and they set up a network of organisations and unofficial 'consulates' that served to put political pressure on Western governments to keep alive the cause of Baltic independence. Once independence was achieved emigres became a ready source of expertise, advice, and capital – several even became candidates in presidential elections.

In all three republics, significant progress was made in the building of democratic and market institutions in the independence period. Politically, the Baltic states most rapidly of all the former republics developed effective party systems and legislatures. While there have been notable problems in dealing with local Russians and other ethnic minorities, the new politics of the Baltic republics did not suffer the level of violent conflict and political gridlock characteristic of other former Soviet republics. The parliaments elected in the last stage of communist rule were peacefully dissolved in Lithuania and Estonia in 1992 and in Latvia in 1993, and new parliaments were elected without public disorder in their place.

In Lithuania, the victory in October 1992 of the Democratic Labour Party (formerly the Lithuanian communists) brought back to power the former communist leader, Algirdas Brazauskas, who had helped steer Lithuania to independence in the *perestroika* period. Brazauskas had been pushed aside in 1990 elections by the victory of the nationalist front *Sajudis*. Its leader, Vitautas Landsbergis, adopted a more confrontational approach toward Moscow, under which Lithuania became the first republic to openly declare its independence in March 1990.

A strikingly different outcome resulted from the September 1992 elections in Estonia. The largest share of votes, 20 per cent, went to the Fatherland bloc, a coalition of right-wing, pro-market parties. Elections were held at the same time for the republic's first president. When no one received a majority, the decision was turned over to the parliament which chose Lennart Meri, who was associated with the Fatherland bloc. The leading vote-getter had been parliamentary speaker Arnold Ruutel, who had been in that post since 1983. A controversial law on citizenship kept most Russians from participating in the elections.

In Latvia, parliamentary elections in June 1993 gave the largest number of seats (though not a majority) to the centre-right group 'Latvia's Way'. This political bloc comprised a range of well-known figures, including Latvia's popular president, Anatolii Gorbunovs. The Latvian Popular Front, which had dominated the parliament in the 1990 elections, fractured, and what was left of the movement did not win even a single seat.

Moldova and the Caucasus

The region affected by the greatest political instability was the Caucasus, just north of Turkey and aligned along Russia's southern border between the Black and Caspian Seas. The region was awash in weapons that in Georgia and Azerbaijan were used both by separatist groups and internal political opponents of the regimes in power. Moldova (formerly Moldavia), on the Romanian border between Ukraine and Russia, was beset by similar problems. In all four republics, these armed conflicts – combined with the disruption of former economic relationships – resulted in a severe decline in the standard of living and under-mined economic reform.

In Georgia, the first democratically elected president in the republic, the former anti-Soviet dissident Zviad Gamsakhurdia, was overthrown by armed force at the beginning of 1992. The groups that ousted Gamsakhurdia invited Eduard Shevardnadze, former communist leader of Georgia and Gorbachev's foreign minister, to take over the government. He won popular election in October 1992 at the same time that a new parliament was elected. Georgia was beset, however, by a series of conflicts that tore the republic apart and reduced effective government control from the capital to less than half of the country. Gamsakhurdia's suppor-ters, mostly concentrated in Western Georgia, took effective control of part of the republic and fought for his return. Georgia also suffered from two serious ethnic conflicts. In late 1990, ethnic separatists fought to take the province of South Ossetia out of

Georgia. The cease-fire brokered by Russia did not bring the region under Georgian control, though both Gamsakhurdia and Shevardnadze continued to assert Georgia's claim to the region. In October 1993 separatists also took control of Abkhazia, the Black Sea region in the northwest of Georgia in which Georgians made up the largest ethnic group. (The Abkhaz were only about 1 per cent of the 1989 population of the region, and less than 2 per cent of Georgia's total population.) Abkhazia was vital to the Georgian economy, in part because rail links with Russia passed through the region. The war created tens of thousands of refugees, and Georgian leaders vowed to retake the region and re-establish their control over the whole republic.

In Azerbaijan, the chief factor destabilising political life was the war over the status of Nagorno-Karabakh, a predominantly Armenian enclave. The war went badly for Azeri forces, despite the fact that they had a much larger population and more resources. Military defeats had a direct impact on Azerbaijan's internal politics, resulting in the *de facto* overthrow of two elected presidents. By the end of 1993, about one-third of Azerbaijan's territory had been seized by Armenian forces and over 1 million Azeris had fled their homes. Aziz Mutalibov, the Communist Party leader at the time of independence, was elected in tainted elections in September 1991 and was forced to resign in March 1992. His subsequent attempt to return using military force was rebuffed. Abulfez Elchibey, a former dissident, was elected president in democratic elections in June 1992, but was forced out of office in June 1993 when a private army led by a young millionaire advanced on the capital. These events led to the return to power of Gaidar Aliev, a former communist leader in Azerbaijan and member of the CPSU Politburo in the pre-Gorbachev period. Aliev himself later won election to the post of president in October 1993 with over 90 per cent of the vote – Azerbaijan's third elected president in just over two years.

Armenia, of the three Caucasian republics, was the most politically stable in that its president, Levon Ter-Petrosyan, was elected in 1991 and remained in office at the end of 1993. He, like Gamsakhurdia and Elchibey, had been imprisoned under Soviet rule for his political activities. The parliament, elected in 1990, was dominated by Ter-Petrosyan's party, the Armenian Pan-national Movement, a group that had its origins in the chief nationalist opposition group, the Karabakh Committee. The dominant feature of Armenian politics was its economic crisis, since Armenia was virtually cut off from the outside world and energy supplies by an Azerbaijani blockade and the conflicts in Georgia.

Moldova was a Romanian-speaking republic, most of the territory of which had also been annexed to the Soviet Union after World War II from Romania. In the post-independence period, the republic was divided by disputes over whether Moldova should remain independent or seek reunification with Romania. The latter position was held by the nationalist Moldovan Popular Front. Significant problems developed in the work of the Moldovan parliament because of this and other issues. The impasse in parliament led to a decision to hold early elections for a new parliament in February 1994, in which the Agrarian Democratic Party (representing the old *nomenklatura*) did well; a referendum meanwhile overwhelmingly reasserted the principle of independence. In the Trans-Dniester region and among the Gagauz ethnic minority there were serious conflicts as non-Moldovan groups sought to break away from the republic. As in Georgia, Ukraine, and Estonia, leaders of the ethnic separatist movements appealed to, and collaborated with, Russian nationalists who fanned hopes of restoring the former Soviet borders. This latter group often included local Russian army commanders who were in a position to offer concrete assistance.

Ukraine and Belarus

Two of the largest former Soviet republics that, like Russia, are ethnically and linguistically Slavic are Belarus (formerly Belorussia) and Ukraine. The post-Soviet governments of Belarus and Ukraine were both dominated by people who had made their careers in the communist system and both were relatively conservative in their economic policies. Particularly in Ukraine, the 'new' leaders attempted to consolidate popular support by recasting themselves as nationalists. Leonid Kravchuk, the Ukrainian president, was once the ideology secretary of the Ukrainian Communist Party and thus was responsible for stamping out Ukrainian nationalism. Once independence was certain, Kravchuk became a vocal Ukrainian nationalist who used such appeals to win the presidency at the end of 1990. Stanislav Shushkevich, the chairman of the Belorussian parliament, had been a prominent physicist who was elected as a compromise candidate in a parliament that was dominated by communist-era functionaries. Shushkevich lacked his own political base, and this in part explained why Belarus remained one of the few post-Soviet republics that did not introduce the post of president (a new constitution, incorporating a presidency, was approved in March 1994; Shushkevich had meanwhile lost his position and real power appeared to rest with the former Communist apparatchik, Vyacheslav Kebich). The prime ministers in both Ukraine and Belarus resisted economic reforms, with the support of fairly stable parliamentary majorities; opposition parties, however, campaigned for new elections on the assumption that the 1990 elections had not fairly recorded their popular support. Early elections for parliament took place accordingly in Ukraine in March–April 1994 (former Communists and nationalists won the largest share of the 450 seats) and were also being planned in Belarus.

A major ethnic and territorial dispute surrounded Crimea, a region that had been transferred from Russia to Ukraine only in the 1950s. A majority of the population was Russian, and many objected to being subordinate to Ukraine. The region was also the base for the Black Sea fleet. Crimean officials, with only grudging acceptance from Kiev, held elections for a president and Supreme Soviet of the 'Crimean Republic' in January and March 1994, respectively. Demands to redraw the borders to reincorporate the Crimea into Russia or a declaration of independence appealed both to many Crimean Russians and Russian nationalists in Moscow. The issue was complicated by the rapid return of thousands of Crimean Tatars who had been forcibly deported from the region by Stalin.

Central Asia and Kazakhstan

Central Asia and Kazakhstan has been the most stable of the former Soviet regions, with the glaring exception of Tajikistan which suffered a bloody civil war. Very little changed in these republics in the period after the demise of the Soviet Union; in fact, they among the republics were the most reluctant to part with Soviet rule. They were also extremely reluctant to begin the process of privatisation, and even then retaining the major sectors of the economy under state control.

The first stirring of political reform in Central Asia was in the republics of Kyrgyzstan and Kazakhstan. Kyrgyzstan was the only one of the Central Asian republics not led by a former communist official. Askar Akayev had been head of the republic's Academy of Sciences, and he pursued a policy that was notably more reformist than leaders of other Central Asian states. Kazakhstan, the largest (in area) and richest of the republics outside Russia, was led even before independence by its former party first secretary Nursultan Nazarbaev. Little changed in the political life of the republic, but Nazarbaev aggressively sought to develop Kazakhstan's resources, attracting significant foreign investment for this purpose. New rounds of parliamentary elections took place in Kazakhstan in March 1994 to a professional 177-seat assembly (pro-government candidates did well but international observers pointed out that opposition candidates had been handicapped) and were scheduled for 1995 in Kyrgyzstan.

Uzbekistan and Turkmenistan developed a reputation as perhaps the most conservative of the former Soviet republics, particularly in their political structure. The ruling party was essentially the Communist Party under a new name, and both countries were led by former communist leaders. In Uzbekistan, President Islam Karimov used the familiar array of Soviet methods in an effort to stamp out the opposition party 'Erk'. The party newspaper was shut down. Opposition leaders were forced to flee the republic, and even rank-and-file party members have been dismissed from their jobs and harassed by the police. In one notorious incident, authorities sent secret police agents to kidnap a leading Uzbek dissident in Kyrgyzstan, where he had gone to attend a human rights conference (see Cavaunagh, 1992). Authorities in Turkmenistan, a republic with significant oil and natural gas reserves, also resisted change. Its president, Saparmurat Niyazov, created a personality cult around himself that rivalled those of the pre-Gorbachev Soviet Union. Just to give one example: Niyazov's face was printed on Turkmenistan's new currency issued in 1993. Only one political party was allowed, Niyazov's party, and all others were banned.

Tajikistan presented a significant exception to the relatively tranquil Central Asian scene. A powerful opposition arose when Islamic movements, the fledgling democratic movement, and regional groups that felt disadvantaged merged to oppose the republic's communist-era leadership. A civil war ensued that led to untold thousands of deaths and forced over 60,000 Tajiks to flee their homes. The opposition triumphed in September 1992. Russia and Uzbekistan saw their interests threatened by the relationship between the Tajik opposition and groups in Afghanistan, who moved freely across the border. Both were also frightened by the possibility of Islamic fundamentalism on their borders. In December 1992, with the help of direct military assistance from Uzbekistan, the old regime defeated (at least temporarily) the opposition. A former communist official, Imamali Rakhmonov, was made chairman of what remained of the parliament. In 1993 Russian forces began to actively defend Tajikistan's borders with Afghanistan, in a clear effort to influence the outcome of political struggles within Tajikistan and prevent the opposition from regrouping. The Tajik regime, for its part, made no efforts to conciliate the opposition or allow it a role in the republic's political life – thus setting the stage for future conflict.

The Commonwealth of Independent States

The final breakup of the Soviet Union was precipitated by the actions of the leaders of Ukraine, Belarus and Russia who met on their own – without inviting then Soviet president Mikhail Gorbachev – in December 1991. They decided to form a new relationship that effectively marked the end of the USSR. The new 'Commonwealth of Independent States' attracted the participation of Kazakhstan, all Central Asian republics, Armenia, Azerbaijan, and Moldova – though parliaments in the latter two were slow to ratify the agreement. Georgia was more steadfast in its refusal to join the Commonwealth. In October 1993, however, Shevardnadze requested that Georgia be added as a member, and it was formally admitted in December 1993. Georgia at the time was on the verge of collapse: rebels in Abkhazia had succeeded in defeating government forces and an attempt was under way by the former president, Zviad Gamsakhurdia, to return to power from his base in Western Georgia. Georgia was also in the throes of a severe economic crisis caused in part by its isolation from former trading partners.

Given the obvious political diversity of the former Soviet republics, the interrelations between and among them in the post-Soviet world was complex. The Baltic states consistently refused to join the CIS, though occasionally they would send observers when matters of concern to them were discussed. Latvia, Lithuania and Estonia rapidly shifted their orientation to Scandinavia and the West generally. Already by mid-1993, the value of exports from the Baltic to the West exceeded those to former Soviet republics. Economic integration among the Baltic states was advanced by the signing of a free trade agreement in September 1993 along with a declaration on cooperation in the area of defence and security. Radical, far-reaching reforms – monetary reform, price liberalisation, privatisation – were begun in the Baltic states often with direct reference to future trade partners. For example, when Estonia introduced its own national currency in June 1992, the *kroon*, it was pegged not to the ruble but to the German mark. In relations with Russia, they preferred a bilateral approach. For them the main issue involving Russia was the withdrawal of troops from their territories.

The organisers of the CIS were not setting out to create a new Soviet Union, and they wanted neither a federation nor a confederation. At first, the CIS was set up to provide a forum for what was termed a 'civilised divorce' between the former Soviet republics. The institutions and operation of the CIS were designed to assuage the newly attained sovereignty of its member-states. Its main administrative headquarters were located in Minsk, not Moscow, in order to be away from the Kremlin and the old seat of Soviet power, and it was not a CIS 'capital'. Negotiations or discussions by member-states took place on an equal footing with consensus as the decision rule.

A typical pattern of decision-making would be for initial discussions to take place at conferences of experts sent by each of the member states. These conferences or the CIS executive secretariat – formerly, the working group on preparing sessions – would draft documents or prepare alternatives. For many policy areas, the CIS framework provided for meetings at the ministerial level – for example, the councils of foreign ministers, energy ministers, or meetings of heads of state committees for environmental protection. In June 1993 a new Coordinating and Consultative Committee began monthly meetings; it included deputy prime ministers for economic matters and also prepared decisions for higher-level meetings. Sessions of these groups would further refine proposals for a session of the CIS Council of Heads of Government, made up of republic prime ministers, or the Council of Heads of State. This latter group, the highest body of the Commonwealth, was made up of the presidents of the member states (or chairmen of the Supreme Soviets of the republics that did not establish the institution of president, Belarus and Tajikistan).

A basic principle of the CIS was that its policies were binding only on that set of member states that agreed to sign the decision in question. This was designed to gain the maximum cooperation of now sovereign states who often zealously guarded their sovereignty; it was designed to facilitate the coordination of policy and avoid even the appearance of capitulating to Moscow on policy. Despite this process and the compromise decisions that resulted, policies that were agreed upon, particularly in the economic sphere, often were not carried out by the signatories (for an inside account of these negotiations see Shelor-Kovedyaev, 1993).

Of the eleven countries that were CIS members through most of 1992–3, Ukraine, Moldova, Azerbaijan, and Turkmenistan frequently refused to go along with policies that they saw as excessive moves toward integration or concessions to Russia. At the centre of support for stronger ties were generally found Russia, Belarus, Armenia, Kazakhstan, Kyrgyzstan, Tajikistan, and Uzbekistan. It was rare for any CIS decision to encompass more than six or eight of its members.

The slow progress on the CIS charter gave evidence of the diversity of opinions among member-states. This document outlined the general principles of the Commonwealth and set out its institutional framework. The charter was finally signed by republic leaders in January 1993, but only by seven of the ten members at that time – the leaders of Ukraine, Turkmenistan, and Moldova did not sign at that time, and Azerbaijan had temporarily withdrawn from the CIS (its parliament voted to affiliate again in September 1993).

Military Ties

Part of the Commonwealth structure was the CIS Joint Armed Forces, with headquarters in Moscow. Marshal Yevgenii Shaposhnikov, the Soviet air force chief who supported Yeltsin at the time of the August 1991 coup, was named commander-in-chief, and it was he who was entrusted with operational control over former Soviet nuclear weapons.

Initially, the joint CIS Joint Armed Forces were intended to be the successor of the Soviet military. Even before independence, however, several Soviet republics began creating their own armies, and they later sought and received a share of the equipment of the former Soviet military. This later proved to be a decisive blow to the creation of a joint military force, particularly when Russia decided to create its own army in April 1992. Republic officials were reluctant to place their newly created armed forces under the command of Russian officers. Within the CIS, a Council of Ministers of Defence was created to provide a mechanism for possible coordination that took into account the separate military structures of the newly independent states. Parallel to this, a Council of Commanders of Border Troops was created. In June 1993, the post of commander-in-chief of the CIS forces was abolished, and Shaposhnikov resigned, issuing a statement that 'today the CIS Joint Armed Forces do not exist, and their creation in the near future is problematic'. At the same time, Shaposhnikov turned over the nuclear 'button' to the Russian Minister of Defence, Pavel Grachev. It was clearly opposition from the Russian Ministry of Defence that prevented the development of a unified CIS force.

Republic leaders outside Russia soon discovered that it was difficult to create effective and disciplined military units in a short period of time. This was most obvious in Georgia, Azerbaijan, and Tajikistan where government military defeats at the hands of rebels threatened the very existence of these republics as sovereign states. Small, private armies arose in a number of regions in the absence of effective republic military structures. Such groups found it easy to obtain sophisticated weapons from the stockpiles of the former Soviet army. Threats from local armed groups in Azerbaijan led to the first forced withdrawal of Russian troops from a former Soviet republic.

Russia's formal military doctrine, released in November 1993, placed great significance on the role of Russia in intervening in local conflicts in bordering regions (a lengthy summary appeared in *Rossiiskie vesti*, 18 November 1993). This essentially ratified what had already been Russia's policy. The Russian military intervened unilaterally in several conflicts outside of Russian territory in 1992–3, though often it was unclear who adopted decisions that authorised a Russian military role. Sometimes the Russian military was far from being a stabilising presence. Russian forces secretly aided the Abkhaz rebels and even participated in some military operations, while official Russian policy proclaimed its support for the territorial integrity of Georgia and a cessation of hostilities. Earlier, in South Ossetia, another part of Georgia, Russian forces participated in a joint Russian–Ossetian–Georgian peacekeeping force – but this was after they had provided weapons and other support to South Ossetian rebels. In the Trans-Dniester region of Moldova, the Russian 14th army, which had long been stationed in that area, supported anti-government units among the local Russian population. In other situations, the Russian military played a role in peace-keeping efforts and sought to bring stability to regions beyond Russia's borders. The Russian military became involved in Georgia again in November 1993 at the request of Georgian leader Shevardnadze, to keep the main Black Sea port and railways open that had been blocked by forces loyal to former president Gamsakhurdia (who committed suicide, when his forces were defeated, at the end of 1993).

A treaty on collective security was worked out within the context of the CIS in May 1992, but only six members signed the agreement (Russia, Armenia, Kazakhstan, Kyrgyzstan, Tajikistan, Uzbekistan) and not all of them had ratified it by late 1993. Armenia, seeking guarantees against a possible attack from Azerbaijan in the context of the war in Nagorno-Karabakh, was especially interested in the pact and was the first to ratify it. The treaty provided for consultations in the event of a threat to any of the signatories in order to provide a collective response. Serious questions were raised about the willingness of signatures to adhere to the terms of the pact. Only with great difficulty was a small, *ad hoc* joint CIS force created in August 1993 to stabilise the situation in Tajikistan. The three countries that agreed to contribute to the joint operations were Russia, Kazakhstan, and Turkmenistan (which had a separate security agreement with Russia). Uzbekistan, according to many reports, already had its forces there and did not officially join in the operation.

Economic Ties

The economic decline that followed the end of the Soviet Union, experienced in all of the republics, was in part due to the disruption of traditional trade patterns. Liberalisation of prices, loose monetary policies, and the decline in production led to high rates of inflation that often affected real incomes dramatically. Incomes in 1993, adjusted for inflation, fell most rapidly in Armenia, Kyrgyzstan, Moldova, Tajikistan, Azerbaijan, and Georgia. In Tajikistan and Armenia, the average wage was below the amount calculated as the minimum needed to survive. Turkmenistan and Uzbekistan successfully preserved their earlier standard of living, though in Uzbekistan this was substantially lower than in the rest of the former Soviet Union. In all republics, the share of consumer expenditures going for food increased while expenditures on services and non-food items decreased (see *Rossiiskie vesti*, 11 November 1993).

A natural consequence of the differing political situations in the republics was the differing rate of economic reform from republic to republic. The Baltic states moved ahead rapidly and, among CIS members, Russia was in the forefront in the pace and scope of the changes introduced. Nevertheless, even in Russia much of the economy remained in state control and socialist policies such as subsidies and credits to state-owned enterprises continued unabated, a practice that led to the first trade disputes between the former Soviet republics as they began to exchange charges of 'price-gouging', 'protectionism' and 'dumping' that are familiar among other of the world's trading partners.

Russia, as the main supplier of fuel and raw materials to the former republics, played a key role in the economic life of all former republics, though as noted above this was less true in the Baltics. Disputes over fuel prices were a recurring theme as Russia began to increase the price of oil and natural gas deliveries to approximate the world market price. The former republics, accustomed to cheap energy supplies, were placed in an extremely difficult position. Combined with the economic downturn in the republics, increased energy expenses led many republics, with Ukraine in the forefront, to run up huge debts to Russia. By agreeing to allow republics to incur such debts, Russia was essentially subsidising their economies.

The financial policies of Russia's Central Bank, which often acted independently of and contrary to Russian government policy, provided massive financial support in the form of cash and credits to many republics from mid-1992 until mid-1993. The chief beneficiaries of this largesse were the two most conservative of Russia's neighbours: Turkmenistan and Uzbekistan. One Russian analyst has calculated that over this period, the amount of financial assistance they received equalled over half of their gross domestic product. The republics of Kazakhstan and Tajikistan were also major recipients (see *Izvestiya*, 16 September 1993).

The need to set up a new framework for economic relations among CIS members was generally acknowledged. At a Council of Heads of State meeting in May 1993, republic leaders agreed to take steps to form a Commonwealth Economic Union, designed to create a common market by establishing a free trade zone and a customs union, and also to coordinate legislation and policies on prices, taxes, investment, ownership, and in other spheres. Turkmenistan was alone in refusing to sign the preliminary accord, but Ukraine gave signs that it would not participate as a fully-fledged member. Ukrainian President Kravchuk objected to the term 'union', since it evoked memories of the USSR and offended national sensitivities – he preferred the term 'association'. Later he described the new union as creating 'supragovernmental centralised structures' that were unacceptable to Ukraine. A draft agreement was prepared, initially by the Russian State Committee for Cooperation with the CIS States, and it drew on the principles of European Economic Community.

An issue of special relevance to the future economic relationships among the former Soviet republics was monetary policy – the problem of how to agree upon a currency or other accounting unit for trade and other economic interactions. At first, in the aftermath of the breakup of the Soviet Union, all republics continued to use the Soviet currency, the ruble, as their currencies. The preservation of the 'ruble zone' became a policy prescription favoured not only by Russians who wanted to preserve past economic relationships but also the International Monetary Fund (IMF). Since rubles, as paper currency, were issued only in Russia by the Central Bank, this left the republics vulnerable to Russia's monetary and credit policies. As we have seen, the Russian Central Bank provided CIS member-states with large sums of 'free' money, thus contributing to the rapid inflation of the ruble. Nevertheless, many enterprises faced severe financial straits because of non-payment by their partners. Under these conditions trade between enterprises in different republics often took place through primitive barter arrangements. Inadequacies in the banking system meant that even when enterprises had money, they could not easily transfer it to accounts in other republics. There were frequent reports of trucks and airplanes filled with rubles being sent from one enterprise to another to pay for orders.

Shortages of rubles in many republics forced organisations and enterprises to delay paying their employees for months at a time. Already in 1992 this forced leaders in some republics to seek control over their monetary systems, and many began to introduce monetary substitutes (such as 'coupons') or their own national currencies.

In this context, an agreement by Russia, Belarus, Armenia, Kazakhstan, Uzbekistan, and Tajikistan in September 1993 centred on the creation of what was called a 'ruble zone of a new type'. Initially it appeared that an agreement had been reached that would have maintained the ruble zone and strengthened the monetary interdependence of the former republics. Russia, however, later added to the conditions necessary for countries continuing to use the ruble. A commonly advanced proposal to create a new CIS international bank that would control credit policy and ruble emissions was dashed when it became clear that Russia would insist on having a decisive voice in running the new institution. In effect, the Russian government began to insist that the former republics create their own currencies which would be allowed to fluctuate in value against the ruble. The effective end of the ruble zone came in November and December 1993, as republics that had continued to rely on the ruble quickly began to introduce their own national currencies; only Belarus and Tajikistan committed themselves to closer financial integration with Russia and re-established the ruble as their currency.

Conclusion

The creation of the newly independent states on Russia's periphery was unexpected, not only to the outside world, but to many of the states that became independent. While the Baltic states and a few other republics had been actively seeking to secede from the Soviet Union, most had been working to create a 'new' Soviet confederation. Once independence became a reality, however, internal political dynamics encouraged many leaders – even, or perhaps especially, former communists – to establish nationalist credentials. In attempting to advance their national interests, republic leaders were often unwilling to make even limited concessions on the sovereign right of their republics to make their own decisions. Naturally, this limited the potential integrating and coordinating role of the Commonwealth of Independent States. The experience of the CIS in the areas of defence and the economy illustrated the difficulty in arriving at a consensus even on issues that all of the successor states agreed were threatening their security and economic viability.

The attitude of Russia's own nationalists toward the 'near abroad' complicated the situation still further. Their activities and populist rhetoric were an unambiguous attack on the independent existence of the former Soviet republics. Extremists such as Vladimir Zhirinovsky advocated not simply an end to the policy of aiding the former republics, but the active use of Russian economic power to 'bring them to their knees'. This, combined with appeals to Russian minorities living in the newly sovereign states, stimulated republican leaders to reassert their independence and avoid concessions that could give Russia additional leverage. The Commonwealth of Independent States, it appeared, would survive; but by itself it offered no solution to these and the other difficulties that confronted the post-Soviet republics in the 1990s.

PART FOUR

Conceptualising the Politics of Post-Soviet Russia

12

Russia, Communism, Democracy

RICHARD SAKWA

The dissolution of communist power and the disintegration of the
Soviet Union represent one of the most important periods in
Russian history, a turning point at least as important as 1917.
The choices facing the country raise once again in the starkest
possible form the eternal question: what is Russia? Is the country
doomed forever to repeat cycles of reaction and reform, with
periods of authoritarianism marked only by spasms of somehow
always doomed modernisation? Or is a democratic, open, and
liberal Russia at last on the agenda and a realistic (or desirable)
prospect? Can the apparently universal principles of modernity
and modern civilisation be applied without destroying the distinctive character of Russia and its people?

The Russian Tradition

European Russia today occupies a territory roughly similar to
that of Muscovy at the time of Ivan the Terrible in the 16th
century. Some 400 years of the 'gathering of the lands' collapsed
in a mere blink of historical time. While the Soviet Union might
have lost the Cold War, Russia, it appeared, had to pay the price
and, in a geopolitical sense, was the greatest loser. Everything had
to be remade, but few nations in a time of peace have faced such

unpropitious circumstances in which to reconstitute their political and social institutions.

For most of the modern era Russia has been looking for a suitable political form to institutionalise its diversity and to defend its identity while searching for effective ways to interact with the rest of the world. The debate over the nature of the transition today is simultaneously a debate over Russia's past. Does the country's apparent lack of democratic traditions under both the Tsarist and communist regimes forever doom it to an authoritarian system, or will Russia this time be able to join 'the high road of world civilisation', as it is often put in Russia? More prosaically, will Russia be able to achieve a liberal democracy based on civil society and a market economy?

The role of political traditions in assessing the prospects for democracy is clearly a pivotal issue, yet there is no consensus over Russia's past. While the notion of the 'rebirth of history' is central in the East European transitions (for example, Glenny, 1990), in Russia the question is usually posed not as a return to the past but of 'overcoming the past', to use the phrase common in Germany after the war and once again following unification in 1990. Does Russia possess what is now called 'a usable past', traditions that can sustain and legitimise the attempt to build a democratic order?

Political traditions are more malleable and open-ended than the partisans of the political culture approach of an earlier generation suggested. There is always a choice of traditions from which to choose and very often they are 'invented' to sustain the ambitions of elites who hope thereby to gain legitimacy for their rule. The mass production of traditions in the post-Soviet area is now reaching an intensity and scale comparable only to that in Europe and Africa in the four decades before the Great War (see Hobsbawm and Ranger, 1984). The generation of the purported symbols and traditions of nationhood, called 'cultural artefacts of a particular kind' by Benedict Anderson (1983, p. 13), has now reached epidemic proportions. What is the nature of Russia's present *national* rebirth, and what relationship does it have to forms of *state* organisation? What constitutes the *community* in the first place, and will it be based on civic or ethnic principles (Jowitt, 1992)?

The Russian tradition is marked by a series of peculiarities, some of which continued into the Soviet period in new forms, and others which were sharply truncated in 1917 and are now being revived. While the 'peculiarities of German history' have been analysed in terms of the distinctive development of German society and capitalism (Blackbourn and Eley, 1984), discussion of Russia's path focuses far more on the over-development of the Russian state at the expense of society. From the struggle against the Mongol occupation (1240–1480) to the defeat of the Swedes and the Turks, the question of Russian statehood (*gosudarstvennost*) has been central. In political terms we can identify a four-fold dynamic to state development in Russia: the state as a geopolitical entity expanding to neighbouring territories; the internal organisation of the state (the state as administration); the relationship between state and society, in which societal development was subordinated to the pursuit of the geopolitical interests of the state; and the state as an element in the system of international relations.

The history of Russia is often written as the 'thousand-year process of unifying the Russian state, a process unexampled in perseverance and heroism' (Pozdnyakov, 1993, p. 5). For many Western visitors, however, this took on a rather less glorious aspect. In the 1830s the Marquis de Custine (1991) noted that 'In Russia, the government rules everything and vitalizes nothing' (p. 225), and added for good measure that 'Russia alone, coming late to civilization, has been deprived, by the impatience of its rulers, of a profound ferment and the benefits of a slow and natural cultivation' (p. 228). Tibor Szamuely (1988, p. 8) stresses this too: 'Most incomprehensible and alien of all, pervading and colouring every Western description of Russia, was the awesome sway of an omnipotent State exercising unlimited control over the persons, the property and the very thoughts of its subjects'. He went on to propose a variant on the 'frontier thesis', arguing that the absence of natural borders and a relentless cycle of invasions and repulsions, of occupation and colonisation, had shaped the omnipotent Russian state.

The thesis of the tsarist state's omnipotence has been challenged, especially by those influenced by Russian patriotic thought. Already in the mid-17th century the scholar Yuri Krizhanich observed in his *Politika* (Politics), a remarkable work analysing Russian statecraft at the time, that 'Autocracy is the best form of government', but he insisted that this should be tempered by 'reasonable, appropriate and just privileges' for society (Letiche and Dmytryshyn, 1985, p. 206). Contrary to the attempts by the communists (and by many Western writers) to paint a uniformly dark picture of prerevolutionary Russian politics, numerous commentators have argued that society did enjoy certain 'privileges' under tsarism.

The historian Sergei Pushkarev, for instance, insisted that 'The widespread belief that the Russian people have always lived in slavery, are used to it and are incapable of ordering their lives on the basis of freedom and independence is contrary to the historical facts' (1988, p. xv). He noted that the tsarist regime was very different from the communist totalitarianism that came later, and rather than the Soviet system being a continuation of tsarism he sought to demonstrate the elements of democracy and freedom that illuminated Russian history and which proved, in his view, that there were various alternatives for the free development of the country. Contemporary Russian patriots insist that a huge gulf separates the tsarist from the Soviet regime, namely the opposed moral and social contexts of the two systems and the very different nature of leadership politics, with religious and other moral constraints on the tsars. Despite its subordination to the state under Peter the Great, the Russian Orthodox Church continued to act as the conscience of the nation, although they admit that the tsarist political slogan of the 19th century, 'Autocracy, Orthodoxy and Nation', heralded an exclusiveness that ultimately subverted the regime itself. Many others have added their voices to this debate, with Alexander Sozhenitsyn (1991) stressing the democratic role of the *zemstvos*, the system of local government established by Alexander II in the 1860s as part of his 'great reforms'. These reforms also saw the establishment of trial by jury and many other achievements that were swept away by the Bolsheviks after coming to power in October 1917.

The debate over the relative mix of tyranny and the social and religious restraints on that tyranny in prerevolutionary Russia continues with new strength since the fall of communism, with various evaluations of the role of the peasant land commune (*mir*), of the reforms of Peter the Great and Alexander II, the role of the Orthodox Church and the *Zemskii Sobor* (Council of the Land), and the limits to structural despotism inherent in a Christianised polity. The question, however, can be examined from a rather different angle, and instead of focusing on the relative strength of the state *vis-à-vis* society, it might be useful to examine the nature of Russian statehood itself.

One of the central features of Russian development is that the invasive state is marked, paradoxically, by the extraordinary underdevelopment of modern forms of institutionalisation of state power. Peter Tkachev was convinced that the Russian state lacked roots in Russian society, and hence concluded that revolutionary change could be effected relatively easily by a coup at the top, a thought Lenin later appeared to prove by the relative ease with which the Bolsheviks came to power. The absence of a developed civil society, in other words, denied the Russian state a firm foundation and gave it a superficial and almost military occupational character. Like the Soviet regime that followed, tsarist politics became a struggle to achieve stability once order, defined as a polity grounded in and responsive to the realities of society, had been undermined by social and political changes.

The success of the early modern tsars in unifying the various principalities around Muscovy meant that by the 16th century Russia had become one of the most cohesive and strongest European nation states. The 'gathering of the lands' across ever wider distances, however, dissipated the 'national' element and the tsarist system increasingly operated on a supranational basis. Imperial Russia from Peter the Great's time was no longer a nation state but subsumed numerous ethnic identities in a system focused on the person of the monarch. In this respect, as in others, Russia appeared to evolve in a direction opposite to that of the Western European nation-states. Russia became a supranational state whose defining characteristic was the absence of ethnocentrism. There were attempts to combine imperial expansion with nation-building, especially from the 1880s when Russianisation took more overt forms of Russification, but the overall underdevelopment of ethnicised national consciousness only reinforced the stress on Russian state consciousness.

This was all very well, but the Poles, Finns and increasingly the Ukrainians too, sought their own independent statehood in which national and political borders would coincide. National consciousness could not be separated from state consciousness either in the tsarist or the Soviet periods. The late 19th century had seen a resurgence in national consciousness in the Russian empire, which in the 20th took the form of the creation of nation states. The collapse of the autocracy in 1917 saw the emergence of numerous independent states, but by the time of the creation of the USSR in December 1922 most were back in the imperial fold.

Another of the 'peculiarities' in Russian development is its messianism, reflected in notions of the 'Russian idea'. The term is used to express 'the conviction that Russia had been entrusted with the divine mission of resuscitating the world by sharing with it the revelation that had been granted to her alone' (Szamuely, 1988, p. 92). The monk Philotheus in 1510 penned his famous address to the tsar arguing that 'two Romes have fallen, but the third stands', suggesting that Moscow should take up where Rome and Constantinople had left off, a view that later took the form of the conviction that the Russian nation was a 'God-bearing people' (*narod bogonosets*). The theme of the individual's duties to the state, the idea that collectivism, known as *sobornost* or communality, is of a higher moral order than crass individualism, and the view of the Russian as other-worldly and idealist rather than grossly materialistic like the Westerner, all contribute to the Russian idea.

The belief that a country is fated to tread a distinct path is not unique to Russia (in the USA taking the form of 'manifest destiny'), but the messianic belief in the transcendental virtues of Russian exceptionalism is particularly strong. Almost every significant Russian writer has had something to say on the question of 'the Russian idea', and the whole notion is central to the debate over Russia's path of postcommunist development and the relevance of Western notions of liberal democracy to Russia. The Russian idea in one way or another suggests a unique path for Russia, and often reflected the philosopher Nikolai Berdyaev's view that Western capitalism and Soviet communism both represented blind alleys in the development of humanity (Berdyaev, 1946). Dostoevsky was not the only one who believed that from Russia would come the salvation of the world.

Russia and Communism

Now that the epoch begins to fade into the past, the sources and nature of communism in Russia are being examined anew. For some communism had been a distinctive expression of the Russian idea, whereas for others, almost certainly the majority, communism had subverted the very essence of what it means to be Russian. In the former camp, Alexander Yanov (1989, p. 157) argues that 'It wasn't communism that made Russia sick. In fact it was the other way round: Russia caught the left-wing extremist disease because it was sick'; and he adds for good measure that Russia is liable to catch the right-wing disease as well unless it changes its habits.

Berdyaev (1960), too, had stressed the national roots of Russian communism, noting in particular the role of an alienated intelligentsia and their messianic ambitions. However, he was part of the group who provided one of the most sophisticated analyses of the relationship between Russia and communism. Even when revolutionary socialism was no more than a spectre haunting Russia, a remarkable group of thinkers (who also included the philosopher Semen Frank, the economist and later theologian Sergei Bulgakov, and the political theorist Peter Struve) in the *Vekhi* (Landmarks) collection (1989/1967) warned of the ethical consequences of trying to implement a utopian project like communism. They draw on the Orthodox tradition and contributed to a remarkable flowering of religious and social philosophy.

Their critique of revolutionary socialism was continued in a sequel, *Iz glubiny* (From the Depths) (1918/1991). Even before the full effects of the Bolshevik revolution had become visible the authors unerringly identified the weaknesses of the ideology that had come to power. They sought to demonstrate the unviability of the communist project in its economic and ethnical aspects, and suggested an alternative based on a distinctive combination of humanistic Christian values and traditional civic virtues, a type of liberalism with a Russian face. The authors condemned the sectarian and narrow views adopted by Russian intellectuals. Rather than the Western Enlightenment tradition coming to Russia as a liberating experience, it was introduced in its 19th-century positivist, atheistic and materialistic guise, which in its Marxist–Leninist version combined to give the world 'scientific socialism'.

The *Vekhi* tradition was resumed in 1974 in a third remarkable volume entitled *Iz-pod glyb* (From Under The Rubble), which included articles by Solzhenitsyn, Igor Shafarevich and Mikhail Agursky (Solzhenitsyn, 1974). The contributors favoured the resumption of the intellectual traditions of Russian thought that had opposed the old revolutionary intelligentsia. Once again they stressed the need for a moral revolution and vigorously rejected the revolutionary socialist view that a world turned upside down would lead to universal happiness. This volume, like its predecessors, stressed Russia's unique path based on traditional spiritual values, but rejected the anti-capitalism typical of the Russian revolutionary intelligentsia. They condemned the politics of class warfare and thus, while stressing a distinctive Russian spiritual culture, welcomed the advent of liberal right.

The *Vekhi* tradition is both an expression of Russian exceptionalism, with its stress on spiritual and ethnical values, but at the same time reflected a historic turn by the Russian intelligentsia away from the utopianism of revolution towards the evolutionary development of society and incremental change, and thus represented an important step in the 'normalisation' of Russia. The *Vekhi* tradition is profoundly opposed to the authoritarian utopianism of communism, and these books and individual works by their contributors have been issued in numerous editions and have been at the centre of contemporary debates over paths of Russian development.

Rather than seeing communism as a natural outgrowth of Russian political traditions the thinkers mentioned above, and indeed most shades of Russian nationalist and patriotic thinking, see the source of communism in the West. In their view, Stalinism was not an exclusively Russian problem and 'cannot be fully understood unless it is treated as part of Western intellectual history' (Krasnov, 1991, p. 172). Whereas communism came to Eastern Europe from the Soviet Union, hence the 'return to Europe' and the renunciation of communism is reinforced by the rejection of Soviet imperialism, in Russia communism came from the West: thus the rejection of the former in many cases only serves to reinforce the traditional rejection of the latter.

The problem remains to understand the communist experience in Russia in the 20th century. While elements of communist political culture were congruent with Russian political traditions

(White, 1979), such as the stress on collectivism and messianism, Soviet rule as a whole represented a profound break with the earlier period. Russian statehood and culture was 'overlain' by the USSR, and Bolshevik rule was not simply 'tsarism in overalls'. Soviet rule took what it needed from the autocracy to support its distinctively modern dictatorship, and rejected the rest. So too, today, the postcommunist polity will no doubt borrow and stress traditions that enhance its historical legitimacy, and downplay the rest.

Although expounding an internationalist ideology, once in power the Bolsheviks were forced to recognise the strength of national feelings. Communism was a cosmopolitan and internationalist ideology, but it had come to power in one specific country and was forced to accommodate itself to the existing structure of international relations and to acknowledge the persistence of national identities. Rather than being resolved, the nationalities problem in the USSR was managed, and when that failed, suppressed. The elaborate ethno-federal system imposed by the regime, granting certain titular nationalities the trappings of statehood, gave formal expression to nationalism but deprived it of any real substance. Bolshevik policies sustained national identities, as in their insistence in Point 5 of the old Soviet passport for each citizens to register their nationality, and thus undermined their own goal of creating a new nationality, the Soviet people.

The Soviet regime, like the tsarist system earlier, was characterised by strong state power marked by the underdevelopment of autonomous institutions of the state, and by a relationship between regime and society that once again suggested military analogues. Marx had seen the solution of the class conflicts of modern society in the abolition of civil society; and Lenin had found that an effective way of achieving political integration in revolutionary society was simply to abolish politics. Lenin thus inaugurated the managerial rule of the Communist Party which lasted in Russia for more than seventy years. The Communist Party and personalised leadership, notably under Stalin, vied for dominance, but the state remained an administrative force rather than an autonomous political institution. When Gorbachev during *perestroika* attempted to separate the Communist Party from the state the result was the collapse of both.

It proved impossible to ground the Soviet regime in the national community, just as the tsarist regime had failed to root its rule in effective political institutions. As with the late tsarist regime, behind the facade of stability there was no order. The USSR represented a type of 16th republic, based on no nation and no history. While it would probably have been possible for the tsarist regime to have evolved from stability to order, the Soviet regime by definition sought to impose an order on Russian society from outside. As long as the regime tried to maintain its distinctive revolutionary socialist identity, the option of evolutionary adaptation to society and the community was closed.

Solzhenitsyn (1975) pointed out that the Soviet Union was an empire ruled not by a nation (a role usually considered to have been fulfilled by the Russians) but by a political party, the CPSU. There appeared to be no way out of the realm of ideology for the Soviet Union since there was no nation around which it could 'nationalise' the revolution. As part of the general attempt to revive the state under Gorbachev the trappings of national statehood came to life, in Russia and elsewhere, and the Soviet state found itself surplus to requirements. In the race for revival between the central institutions of the Soviet state and the republics, the latter won, though it is not too far-fetched to suggest that if Gorbachev had managed to modernise the Soviet state and democratise state–society relations speedily enough, then some form of genuine federalism might have been enough to keep a large part of the Soviet Union together.

Communism in the USSR was peculiarly rootless. The Chinese, as André Malraux told the American President, Richard Nixon, at the time of his visit in 1972, did not believe in ideology: 'they believed primarily in China' (Kissinger, 1979, p. 1052). Soviet communists could not make such a transference from Marxist–Leninist ideology to nationalism since the Soviet Union quite simply was not a nation, and when they began to shift the emphasis from ideological to nationalist (that is, Russian) motifs, the other republics objected. The Soviet regime failed to build an effective state, a viable nation or a recognised community. The artificial nature of the Soviet state perpetuated the artificiality of the ideology since there appeared to be no historical space in which it could evolve. Hence the sensation in the regime's last 25 years of going round in ever-decreasing circles.

Nationalism, Democracy and the West

The peculiarities of Russian history focus on such issues as strong but fractured statehood and supranationalism, on notions of Russian exceptionalism expressed through concepts like 'the Russian idea' and, as we shall see below, an ambivalent attitude to the West and democracy. It is not simply a question of identifying 'two Russias', one in a reformist mood and the other reactionary, but revealing the shifting features of a multi-layered tradition. While it is valid to argue that the communist regime represented the 'occupation' of Russia as much as it did any other country, it is equally true that the Soviet system reflected some of the traditional concerns of Russia as a great power. It is not always clear where the interests of the communist system ended and Russian imperial interests began. The red of communism and the white of Russia were often mixed, as during World War II. The reformulation of Russian national identity following communism has a rich store of competing traditions on which to draw.

Many of the questions that faced Russia at the beginning of the century remain unresolved today. These include the multiple challenges of state-building, national integration, regional and ethnic policies, economic reform and the creation of a national market, and finding a place for Russia in the world. A modern nation-state is struggling to be born out of a multinational empire. This involves the creation of the effective political institutions of statehood, and above all the establishment of constitutional law, the separation of powers between representative institutions and executive authorities, and a viable balance between the powers of the centre and the rights of the localities.

Democratisation is simultaneously about the 'recivilisation' of Russia, part of what Norbert Elias (1978) calls 'the civilising process'. In this respect it is no accident that the terms 'civil society' and 'civilisation' are often used interchangeably. The establishment of civil society, or 'civilised' forms of modern life, involves not only the creation of the economic bases of liberalism through private property regulated by the rule of law, but also the creation of a political system governed by a constitution and operating within the constraints of law. What we conventionally call 'democratisation', however, is more than changes in politics and the economy but entails a revolution taking place simultaneously in all spheres of life, society and manners.

The goal in postcommunist Russia is no longer stability but the generation of new political order (*Ordnungpolitik*), involving the simultaneous 'civilising' of the state by civil society and the 'politicising' of civil society through the formal organisation of competing interests in parties and movements. Only through the establishment of a symbiotic relationship between state and civil society can stability become transformed into order. Before a new order can be built, however, questions of ethnicity, nationality, democracy and the nature of postcommunist community in Russia and its relations with the world have to be resolved.

The tension between nationalism and the state continues into the post-Soviet epoch. Ethno-federalism remains a potent force for the disintegration of the Russian Federation. Russia is a multinational nation state, but at the same time it is increasingly becoming a multi-state, with areas, like Tatarstan and the Chechen Republic retaining only a tenuous unity with the rest of the Russian state as they develop the sinews of sovereign statehood. A multi-state is a precarious invention, and the future lies either in the establishment of a more ordered federation regulated by the rule of a single law and constitution, or the path of confederalisation and possibly disintegration.

Postcommunist Russian nationalism has been a broad church with many different and often opposed trends. Almost the entire Russian nationalist spectrum agree that Russia must find its own unique path of development, but the political consequences of this do not necessarily entail relying only on the authoritarian elements in the Russian tradition. The distinction between the nationalist and patriotic trends in Russian thought must be stressed. Solzhenitsyn's patriotism (1991) revived elements of the Slavophile critique of Western liberalism but sought to find a democratic way to institutionalise Russian exceptionalism. Right-wing nationalists, however, condemned the West in its entirety and retreated into isolationist policies. The basic division was between those who included the Soviet period as part of Russia's creative development, and those who considered the Soviet period as an almost unmitigated national disaster, destroying Russia's national heritage and repudiating its national traditions. The former group could more accurately be called National Bolsheviks, drawing on the ideology developed in the early 1920s by Nikolai Ustryalov asserting that in reconstituting the empire the Soviet regime was fulfilling Russian national tasks. Right-wing Russian nationalists and neo-communists insisted that the West was responsible for the disintegration of the USSR and now sought, through shock therapy and the like, to deindustrialise Russia and turn it into a Third World exporter of cheap raw materials.

Patriots (or the 'whites') found it extremely difficult to sustain a distinctive identity and were overshadowed at first by the radical nationalists. The alliance between the irreconcilables in the communist tradition, Stalinists and neo-communists, and right-wing Russian nationalists gave rise to what Yeltsin in December 1991 dubbed the 'red–brown' coalition (neo-fascists and neo-communists). The establishment of the Russian All-People's Union (*Rossiiskii obshchenarodnyi soyuz*, ROS) in December 1991, led by Sergei Baburin and Nikolai Pavlov, began as an attempt to combine democracy and patriotism, though the democracy was to be, as Baburin stressed, of a distinctively Russian sort that 'differs from that of Western Europe'. Under the impact of the disintegration the Soviet Union, however, ROS soon became one of the most implacable opponents of Yeltsin's domestic and foreign policies, and indeed the forerunner of the explicitly neo-imperial line in Russian politics that sought by fair means or foul to reconstitute the Soviet empire. This tendency was strong in the 'Russian Unity' bloc, dominated by former communists, in the old Russian legislature, and ultimately this was the force that Ruslan Khasbulatov and Alexander Rutskoi sought to use to defeat Yeltsin.

The formation of the National Salvation Front in October 1992 marked a step in the division between the Russian nationalist and patriotic movements, since several of the latter, like the Russian Christian Democratic Movement, refused to unite with neo-communist organisations. Moderate Russian nationalism gradually took on 'normal' political forms, and a number of 'liberal conservative' or 'moderate patriotic' groups emerged, some of whom drew on the ideas of the *Vekhi* thinkers. The establishment in early 1993 of Dmitrii Rogozin's Union for Russia's Renaissance (*Soyuz vozrozhdeniya Rossii*, SVR) marked an important stage in the evolution of a conservative patriotic, rather than nationalistic, opposition. The reconstituted Russian Communist Party, led by

Gennadii Zyuganov, also sought to combine nationalist and communist motifs within the framework of a new commitment to democracy, and enjoyed some success in the December 1993 elections.

In most of the other republics the democratic and national revolutions marched together in the struggle against the Soviet system, but in Russia the relationship between the two was much more ambivalent. Contrary to the views of nationalists and some patriots, the democrats insisted that the collapse of the Soviet empire represented not the ruin of Russia but the necessary condition for its political and national rebirth. The democrats were therefore associated, at least initially, with the destruction of the historical Russian state, while the liberals (largely but not entirely coterminous with the democrats) were seen as the squanderers of Russia's wealth and prestige at home and abroad.

However, under the pressure of centrifugal forces, which threatened Russian statehood in its entirety, a new synthesis of democratic and nationalist thinking emerged. An influential group of national democrats or statists (*gosudarstvenniki*) modified their democratic internationalism and universalism, so prominent following independence, to embrace a form of nationalism that stressed the need to defend Russia's state interests abroad and to build a strong state at home. National democrats increasingly took the view that the rights and status of the regions and the republics (the former 'autonomies') should be equalised, and balanced by a clearly defined division of powers between the centre and the localities.

The national democrats were sceptical about the viability of some of the Soviet successor states, arguing that deimperialisation had led to the abandonment of some of Russia's vital interests. They insisted that Russia should direct its policy far more actively towards what they called the 'near abroad', and in particular defend the rights of Russian compatriots there. This group in March 1992 sponsored the development of a Russian Monroe Doctrine, defining the whole area of the former Soviet Union as one vital to Russian national interests. In his speech to the United Nations in February 1993 Yeltsin proclaimed this view as the centrepiece of his foreign policy, and urged the international community to recognise Russia as the guarantor of security in the post-Soviet area.

One of the Decembrists, Pavel Pestel, stressed the third path between Western liberalism and Russian autocracy, and his advocacy of a type of nationalist authoritarianism devoted to modernisation from above commends him to many patriots and statists today. National democrats also draw on the Stolypin tradition of reform from above to force the market on Russia. Stolypin sought to build a strong country on the basis of a prosperous peasantry. Condemned during the Soviet period as the ultimate reactionary, Stolypin is now seen as a man who rose above the irreconcilable oppositionism of the revolutionary democrats to restore order following the 1905 revolution by putting Russian statehood on a firm foundation. However, while Stolypin understood the necessity for an economic and social basis to a modern Russia, he neglected the political aspect and contributed to the underdevelopment of the political (rather than administrative) institutions of the state.

Once again under Yeltsin the reformers launched a 'wager on the strong', and the combination of economic liberalism and an authoritarian state looked increasingly attractive. Following the defeat of his opponents in the old Russian legislature in October 1993, Yeltsin went on to implement some of the recommendations of the national democrats and liberal conservatives on strengthening the state, but now grounded in radical economic policies and democratic state-building. While there is some truth in the assertion that the radical democrats around Yeltsin tried to extirpate Bolshevism by Bolshevik means, in the main postcommunist Russia did not take the late tsarist, or indeed Chinese, path of authoritarian reform and instead gambled on democracy, with all of its attendant risks. Just as Hitler's authoritarianism marched through the gates of democracy in 1933, so too Vladimir Zhirinovsky exploited the dissatisfaction with the imperial and economic decline associated with the rule of Yeltsin's 'August regime' from 1991 to challenge the nascent democratic order in Russia.

The problem of democratisation in Russia is at the same time the question of Russia's relationship with the West. Opinion in postcommunist Russia is polarised between those who argue that Russia constitutes a separate and distinct civilisation of its own and those who insist that it represents no more than a variant of 'world civilisation', usually considered synonymous with the West.

The resistance to Western-style democratisation in Africa and Asia in the wake of decolonisation raises the question of the universality of liberal democratic values. Since Peter the Great's attempts to modernise Russia this resistance had focused on the contrast between idealised definitions of tradition and modernity: between how much better it was in the past or is in the West, with both sides agreeing that things are pretty bad in Russia at the time in question.

Before the revolution and again following communism Russian thinkers were divided over the degree to which the country was part of a single European experience, but 'all alike recognised that Russia had merely been in Europe, but not of it' (Szamuely, 1988, p. 10). The debate over Russia's distinctive identity peaked in the second half of the 19th century when Slavophiles and Westernisers presented starkly contrasting versions of Russia's future, and this ancient debate has once again been resurrected. Dmitrii Likhachev, the renowned expert on Russian culture, insists that Russia is part of the common cultural and spiritual development of the West, owing its religion and much of its culture to Orthodox Christianity and borrowing early concepts of statehood from the Scandinavians. He condemns nationalism as a pathology, reflecting a nation's weakness, but he considers himself a patriot in the belief that the 'ecology of culture' was formed in interaction with national traditions and, indeed, nature. He argues that an ethos of individualism has been developing since at least the 17th century to match the traditional collectivism of Russian society. On the question of change and continuity, Likhachev insists that 'simple imitation of the old does not necessarily follow tradition' and he condemns the 'mechanical imitation of that which has ceased to exist' (Likhachev, 1991, p. 80).

The establishment of sovereign republics on Russia's Western borders physically increased the distance between Russia and the heartlands of Europe and once again stimulated the geopolitical school of thinking, developed by Halford Mackinder in the early part of the century, in which Russia encompassed most of the 'geographical pivot of history', acting as the balanceholder in the World Island (Mackinder, 1962). This type of thinking was subsumed into the broader concept of Eurasianism, an idea very much in vogue in postcommunist Russia and which was taken up by the national democrats or statists. Russia's definition as a

European nation was once again questioned, and instead its unique geopolitical position as the 'balance holder' between Europe and Asia, neither of North nor South, was stressed. This view denies the need for Russian integration into Europe, part of which in terms of civilisation (they argue) Russia has never been (Ignatow, 1992). As far as the Eurasianists were concerned, Russia was a bridge between Western and Eastern civilisations.

Eurasianism is the moderate face of the Russian rejection of the West. Modern Eurasianists, drawing on the thinking of the National Bolsheviks of the early 1920s, questioned what they perceived as Yeltsin's and Kozyrev's uncritical pro-Westernism, and advocated a reorientation of policy towards the countries of the former Soviet Union. Stalinist xenophobia, in their view, had given way to a condition that Krizhanich had already diagnosed three centuries earlier: 'Xenomania (*chuzhbesie* in our language) is an obsessive love of foreign people and things. This deadly plague has infected our entire nation' (Letiche and Dmytryshyn, 1985, p. 128). Of all the Slavophiles Peter Chaadayev was the most pro-European, but his Westernising impulse was accompanied by a denigration of Russia. In his first *Philosophical Letter* he wrote 'We do not belong to any of the great families of humanity, to either the West or the East, and have no traditions of either. We exist outside time' (1991, pp. 320–39).

Eurasianism inspired policies of Russian exceptionalism, and was very strong among centrist organisations like the Civic Union as well as the more irreconcilable nationalists and patriots. Externally, Eurasianism served as a useful ideology to pursue an anti-Western critique and to advocate a reorientation of policy towards Asia; and domestically it suggested that a corporatist type of democracy was most appropriate for Russia. The debate over Eurasianism is essentially a debate over paths of development and the principles of political and economic reform. Times, however, have changed, and the concept of the West is no longer confined to Europe or America but now include Japan, South Korea and other newly-industrialised countries, none of whom have renounced their own civilisations to become part of the synthesis of global civilisation. The concept of Russia as a bridge is therefore meaningless, since links between Germany and Japan can quite happily bypass Russia. Eurasianism is a bridge leading nowhere (Zagorsky, 1993).

While 'the lie', as Solzhenitsyn termed communist ideology, might have been put to rest in 1991, there was no agreement over the organisation of the democratic reign of truth. There was broad acceptance that popular sovereignty should be the source of authority, but there was no consensus over how the new political order was to be institutionalised. While the principles of democracy might be universal, their application to each society is always specific. As in Africa, the political consequences of an ideology of exceptionalism are of crucial importance. If the forms of Western liberal democracy are rejected, how will the alternative be institutionalised? Does it have to be one-party authoritarianism, the only effective alternative that has been found so far, or can some novel combination of liberalism without democracy, or democracy without liberalism, or some other combination, be found? Is there a 'white' patriotic alternative, a form of Russian exceptionalism reflecting democracy with a Russian face, or is political modernity irremediably Western and all the talk of Russian exceptionalism no more than a smokescreen used to justify resistance to economic liberalisation and political democratisation?

Like communism, liberalism is also a universalistic, cosmopolitan and internationalist creed, though unlike the former it can coexist with most forms of nationalism. The very internationalism of liberalism leads to its rejection by various stripes of Russian nationalism in favour of a more organic view of the national community. The concept of *sobornost* or communality, drawn from the Orthodox tradition, has sometimes been suggested as an alternative to the anomie and amorphousness of Western forms of liberal democracy. In his article 'On Formal Democracy' the philosopher Ivan Ilin (1882–1954), much revered by today's patriots, distinguished between two types of polities: the mechanical, reflecting the instinctual individual and their private interests, measuring life numerically and formally; and the organic, arising out of the human spirit and leading to national unity and its general interests, seeking a qualitative source in spiritual roots (1992, p. 290). This distinction between organic and mechanical community, of course, reflects Ferdinand Tonnies' (1963) distinction between *Gemeinschaft* (community) and *bürgerliche Gesellschaft* (civil society), and places Russian exceptionalism firmly in the mainstream of sociological discussion on the tension between tradition and modernity. In politics and society *sobornost* and references to the collectivism of the old peasant commune suggests that Russia could maintain some sort of community as opposed to the alienation typical of Western 'bourgeois' civil society.

Democratic discourse is torn between the unabashed individualism of liberal democracy and the collectivism of commune democracy, and post-communist Russian *sobornost* is yet another way of trying to find a way of implementing the latter. Revolutionary socialism of the Marxist–Leninist type was the most ambitious attempt to implement elements of commune democracy in the 20th century, but the death of communism did not mean the end of the search for a way of institutionalising communitarianian forms of political life. Communism in Russia sought to create a new moral order, with disastrous results, but just as Marx threw out the baby of civil society with the bathwater of capitalist exploitation, so too postcommunist Russia is in danger of throwing out the baby of a compassionate society with the bathwater of bureaucratic state socialism. The questions raised by postcommunist Russian patriots on what makes a political and ethnical community are part of a broader attempt to develop the principles on which a postsocialist and postliberal social order can be built. However, in a society like Russia, where liberalism has traditionally been weak, an ideology of duty to the community must necessarily be balanced by secure and defensible individual rights.

Whereas Bolshevism began with an antagonistic view of society, riven by class divisions, the concept of *sobornost* implies an organic view of society and the nation as an extended community, in certain respects similar to Edmund Burke's classical conservatism in Britain. Solzhenitsyn (1991) and others (like Berdyaev) have advocated a type of corporatism that voices a critique of class-based party politics remarkably similar to that of a personalists in continental Europe, and indeed to the critiques of parliamentarianism by both left and right during the interwar crisis of democracy. How this can be reconciled with the pluralism and interest group politics of modern forms of representation is one of the main challenges facing advocates of a distinctively Russian form of democracy (Biryukov and Sergeev, 1993).

If ever there was a candidate to 'complete' the project of mod-

ernity, as Jürgen Habermas would put it, then Russia is it.
Marxism had represented an alternative path to achieve modernisation, but with its supreme disdain for the earth, land and
people, Bolshevism in Russia had revealed in the starkest form
possible the ambiguities in the modernisation project, and indeed
in the whole concept of modernity. Traditional Russian ambivalence about modernity, reflected for example in Likhachev's
'defense of Russian nature and Russian culture against "moder-
nization" ' (Krasnov, 1991, p. 81), is now reinforced by the rejection of communism. Moreover, a whole new agenda has
apparently been opened up by the prospect of a brave new postmodern age. Why should Russia endure the suffering associated
with the attempt to achieve modernity when the postmodern
agenda precisely returns to some of the features, such as community, extolled by Russian traditionalists? Yet another era of
Populist exceptionalism beckons.

Conclusion

One of the greatest state-building and nation-building endeavours
in history is taking place in Russia today. The dissolution of
communist power was a process with its own logic and
dynamism, whereas the disintegration of the geopolitical space
that came to be known as the USSR reflected a quite different
historical process. The coincidence of the two forced Russia to
deal with all four aspects of state-building simultaneously: the
shift from supranational imperial dynamics to the building of a
nation-state based on the civic principles of universal citizenship
and popular sovereignty; the administrative organisation of a
modern state marked by the separation of powers; placing state–
society relations on a new footing in which the 'privileges' of
society are guaranteed by law; and finding Russia a place in the
international community of nations.

The peculiarities of Russian history have bequeathed a rich
legacy of differing traditions over such issues as state structure
and nationality. While historical factors clearly have a role to
play in the current transition, there is always a choice of traditions, and the view of the future is coloured by the subjective
evaluation of the past. The past weighs particularly heavily on

Russian politics, and Russia has still to come to terms with its Tsarist and Soviet traditions, and elements to sustain the democratic experiment can be found although they come in a peculiarly Russian form. Decades of enforced isolation from Western political thought, for example, have only reinforced Russian philosophy's traditional penchant for thinking in transcendental terms, and the struggle against communism has imbued even the 'democratic' movement with the tendency to think in terms of absolute good and evil.

The basic elements of democracy, such as the establishment of legally defensible human and civic rights, the accountability of the government to a representative assembly, and an irreversible move from a one-party to a multi-party system, remain tenuous in Russia. Political power has not yet become rooted in social power, and hence the political process is marked by an extraordinary volatility. Politicians represent too often no one but themselves, and alliances are made and broken with startling rapidity. The question of 'governability' takes centre stage as social and political processes, like criminality and centrifugal regionalism, escape the ability of the centre to control them. Russia is not only a multinational nation, but increasingly also a multi-state. In these conditions the 'authoritarian temptation', one of Russia's traditions, may well come to the fore. The presidential system provides a focus of authority in a fragmented party system where the institutionalisation of democratic conflict resolution has proved remarkably difficult, but limits to executive power are fragile.

Democracy cannot simply be imposed on society but requires a degree of congruence with the evolving identity of that society. In other words, premodern traditions reworked in a modern guise, like nationalism itself, are crucial to the development of a new political order. Thus a moderate dose of nationalism (called patriotism in Russia), is an essential system-integrative element in the postcommunist transitions, but an excess is liable to be destructive. It is not enough to distinguish between civic and ethnic nationalism since ethnicised nationalism in a civic form is one of the essential ingredients in the state-building projects in countries as diverse as Estonia and Kyrgyzstan, not to mention Tatarstan and Ingushetia. The problem for Russia is to reconcile a multiplicity of identities, stretching both temporally back in time and spatially across a vast continent, within a viable political framework.

The concepts of modernisation, development and Westernisation in the Russian context have to be modified and no simple unilinear extrapolation of Western processes can hope to capture the manifold processes of social reconstitution now taking place. Russia presents a peculiar type of modernity and faces distinctive civilisational choices which incorporate elements of the Soviet past as well as (often mythologised) elements of prerevolutionary life. The postcommunist system in Russia remains in considerable flux, but it is clear that the emerging order is a unique combination of tradition and modernity which together are generating a new tradition.

13

Normalisation and Legitimation in Postcommunist Russia

LESLIE HOLMES

Since so many detailed aspects of Russia and post-Soviet politics are elaborated in other chapters of this book, the present one is intended to serve primarily as a basis for theoretical and comparative analysis. In it, some of the most significant developments will be considered from two contrasting perspectives. First, the issue of 'normal' politics, and the extent to which postcommunist politics are becoming 'normal', will be addressed. Following this, the difficult issue of legitimation crisis is considered in a Russian and more general context.

On 'Normal' Politics

There is no universal 'norm' of politics, from which it follows that any reference to 'normal' politics must be contextualised. Something that might be perceived as 'normal' in a Third World dictatorship could well be perceived as quite abnormal in a liberal democracy, for instance. Thus, whereas attempted coups for forced (even violent) shutdowns of elected parliaments might not be considered unusual in the former, they certainly would be in the latter. In this sense, the events in Moscow in August 1991 and

September–October 1993 could be used as evidence that post-communist Russian politics are anything but normal, by Western standards. But let us assume, for the sake of argument, that these two events – plus the disturbing electoral results of December 1993 – were merely (rather severe) teething problems of a new, postcommunist system that will soon settle down to a more reg-ularised – normal – form of politics, not so dissimilar from that typical in First World states. To do so would still be ethnocentric and restrictive. Partly in an endeavour to overcome this tendency, but also to broaden the base for understanding contemporary and future Russian politics, two principal conceptions of normal are employed in this chapter – although a third is suggested in the conclusion.

First, as already implied, there is an examination of what might be considered normal politics by a 'Westerner', particularly a West European, in the late 20th century. There are two justifi-cations for this conception. One is that most readers will them-selves be 'Westerners', for whom much of what will be described here as 'normal' will be the experienced norm. The other is that many East Europeans and Russians – far less so citizens of the former Central Asian republics of the USSR – describe them-selves as Europeans, and are overtly and consciously attempting to move towards a West European model of politics and eco-nomics.

It might be objected that references to 'the' West European model are unjustified. After all, one can find in Western Europe federal states (such as Germany and Switzerland) and unitary ones (like France and the UK); heads of state who are relatively powerful (as in France), others who are usually little more than figureheads (as in the UK, Italy and the Netherlands); a multi-plicity of electoral systems (such as first-past-the-post or propor-tional representation); and so forth. Whilst all the West European states are basically market-oriented, the degree of government planning and intervention in the economy has varied considerably from country to country, and in some cases even within one country over the past two or three decades.

In short, there are important differences between individual West European countries, and even *within* given countries over time (Belgium, for instance, became a federalised state only in mid-1993). Nevertheless, there are sufficient *fundamental* similarities between these various countries to warrant reference to a Western model; these are elaborated below.

The second conception of 'normal' is, if anything, even more problematic than the first. It is a notion of 'normalcy' that refers to the *precommunist* traditions of the postcommunist countries. Here, the focus is on perceptions of a 'return' to normal. One of the many problems of this conception is that it tends to conflict with the first. Thus, with the exception of Czecho-Slovakia, none of the communist states had an extended precommunist experience with liberal democracy and an advanced, industrial economy.

Although tensions exist between the two conceptions of 'normal' adopted here, it is still appropriate to employ both, for various reasons. One is that the very use of more than one conception emphasises the subjectivity of the term, the fact that there cannot be any single interpretation of it. Second, any attempt at a better understanding of postcommunist politics should, at the very least, consider individual countries both comparatively (*vis-à-vis* other countries) and longitudinally (in terms of their own history).

Postcommunist politics can now be examined in terms of the first definition of normalcy. In order to do so, it is necessary first to create a model of a 'normal' market-oriented liberal democracy that focuses on the *fundamentals* of Western systems rather than their more superficial differences.

Although the term 'separation of powers' is nowadays seen primarily as an American one, and is not often applied to West European systems, the notion of having some division of powers within the political system *is* a feature of all liberal democracies. For instance, it is a 'norm' of liberal democracies that there be a legitimate opposition within parliament. There are 'checks and balances', usually written down in constitutions, to ensure that no one branch of government – let alone any one politician or group of politicians – can dominate the system to such an extent that the system looks increasingly like a dictatorship or oligarchy. Some West European countries have a formalised judicial check on the constitutionality of the political system; the German Constitutional Court is probably the best-known example. Others – notably the UK – strive to keep the judiciary out of politics (the UK, atypically, does not have a written constitution anyway).

This very different approach still represents a notion of 'division of labour', however, with relatively autonomous branches of 'the system'.

Another manifestation of this division of labour in institutionalised politics is bicamerality of the legislatures. Thus most liberal democracies have an upper and a lower house of parliament, even though the basis for this division, and the relative powers of each house, vary from country to country.

The previous paragraphs hint at one of the key features of liberal democracy: pluralism, or the notion that power is not to be overconcentrated in any one set of hands. This is reflected in many other dimensions of 'normal' liberal democracy. For instance, liberal democracy implies a plurality of political parties. Although some liberal democratic countries are in practice two-party systems, whereas others are genuinely multiparty, the all-important point is that they are not one-party systems. Even where one party dominates the system over a prolonged period – as did the Liberal Democrats in Japan until 1993 – there must be regular and *relatively* frequent (usually every 3 to 5 years) opportunities for the citizenry to endorse or remove the ruling party through secret, competitive elections.

The acknowledgement of the superiority of pluralism in politics extends to both the economy and the socialisation process. In the economic sphere, there is a commitment to basic market principles, competition, and a plurality of both ownership and types of ownership. Regarding socialisation, most Western states accept that the state has a duty to provide cheap or free education (at least at the primary and secondary levels – there is less consensus about the tertiary level), but that parents should have the right to pay for private education for their children. Moreover, it is considered 'the norm' that there should be a plurality of electronic and printed media, reflecting a wide range of political and social viewpoints.

Liberal democracy does not usually specify 'correct' and 'incorrect' or acceptable and unacceptable belief systems. For instance, all religious beliefs are fully recognised by the state, unless they contravene general laws which are not specifically related to religion. Thus liberal democracies' tolerance of diverse value systems would not necessarily be expected to extend to polygamy or sex with children – largely on the grounds that to tolerate these would be to privilege male or adult rights over those of females and children respectively.

The last point leads to another important aspect of liberal democracy – its focus on the rights of both individuals and minority or underprivileged groups. For most analysts, a salient feature of the liberal democratic state is its acceptance of a duty to minimise the possibility of a tyranny of the majority. Not every Western state always performs this duty as well as it might, partly – and ironically – because the very pluralistic nature of liberal democracies means that politicians often believe it is more important to reflect the dominant wishes of their actual or potential electorates than to protect minorities. Nevertheless, few would openly reject the abstract notion that liberal democracy must seek to defend the interests of all groups – both large and small – and individuals.

Finally, liberal democracies are committed to the rule of law, broadly understood. Indeed, commentators such as Max Weber and Gianfranco Poggi have argued that 'legal-rationality' – the notion that the political system is depersonalised, and operates according to a set of rules that stand above, and are more powerful than, all political actors – is the key feature of the modern state (see for instance Poggi, 1978).

Many more variables could be included in an analysis of what might be meant by a 'normal' Western system. Unfortunately, space precludes a consideration of these. Therefore, the argument so far can be summarised by producing a minimal 'checklist' of components one would expect to see in a model of a normal Western or liberal democratic system:

1. a division of powers between the two or three main arms (legislative, executive, and possibly judicial) of the formal, ruling part of the political system, and a system of checks and balances;
2. political pluralism more generally – to include a plurality of political parties, and elections that are held regularly, reasonably frequently, and that are genuinely free and competitive;
3. a mixed economy, in which there is a basic commitment to market pricing, avoidance of monopoly (as part of a broader commitment to competition), a plurality of types of ownership, and limited government intervention;

4. a pluralistic approach to socialisation, especially in the areas of education and the media;
5. full acceptance of diverse belief systems, notably in terms of religion, within the limits of society's laws;
6. the ultimate supremacy of the individual, rather than of the state and/or collective;
7. the rule of law.

Shortly, recent developments in the postcommunist world and particularly Russia will be analysed in terms of this model. Before doing this, it is necessary to conclude the abstract part of the discussion by considering 'normalcy' in its second meaning – as a return to precommunist norms. Here, the focus is necessarily on Russia, since space does not permit even a cursory examination of the precommunist traditions of the nearly 30 postcommunist states (including 15 in the former Soviet Union) that existed by the mid-1990s. Although the focus is on Russia, the fact that the Russian Empire dates from the early 18th century, whilst evidence of – for instance – common Russian and Ukrainian history can be traced back for at least 1000 years, means that some of the points made about 'Russia' actually apply to several republics of the former USSR.

As analysts of Russian political culture (such as White, 1979) have pointed out, several features of it can be readily, and fairly uncontroversially (though see McAuley, 1984) identified. Perhaps the most useful starting point is the 19th-century government slogan of 'autocracy, orthodoxy and nationality'. Each of these concepts can be briefly elaborated.

Until its collapse in February 1917, the Romanov dynasty had ruled Russia for some 300 years (since 1613), although there were other dynasties before this. Thus the Grand Prince of Moscow first claimed to be the Grand Prince 'of all Russia' in the early middle ages, whilst Grand Prince Ivan IV (better known as Ivan the Terrible) had himself crowned first tsar (from the Latin 'Caesar') of Russia in 1547. The tsars wielded enormous power in Russia, although this was waning by the early 20th century. One of the reasons for this change was that the tsar so badly handled the unrest of the first years of this century that, in order to bring the subsequent turmoil in his country under control, he was compelled to make major political concessions in October 1905. In doing so, notably in permitting the establishment of a national elected parliament (the Duma), he seriously undermined his own legitimacy. Like most monarchs, the Russian tsar's authority rested largely on what Weber called the 'traditional' mode of legitimation, which is located above all in the 'divine right of monarchs' concept. Once the tsar had *de facto* acknowledged that he might have to share decision-making powers with a secular, popularly-mandated body, the mystique of his office began to fade. Perhaps ironically, Tsar Nicholas II only exacerbated the problem by shutting down the Duma whenever he thought it was seriously challenging his authority. This made him look increasingly like a petty tyrant, as distinct from a strong leader inspired and authorised by God.

By February 1917, then, the traditional image of Russia being led by a strong monarch had begun to tarnish. Whether or not most Russians *wanted* a strong leader, the fact is that they were being ruled by a *relatively* weak tsar, who had, albeit grudgingly, shared some of his powers with an elected assembly. Moreover, for a few months immediately preceding the Bolshevik (communist) seizure of power, there was *no* tsarist autocracy. Instead, there was a provisional government, based in Moscow, and a soviet (literally council), based in what is now St Petersburg, vying for power. This was the period of 'dual power' – or, as Trotsky so aptly described it, 'dual powerlessness'. This confusion of authority is often taken as one of the reasons for the collapse of the very short-lived democracy that succeeded the tsarist system.

In sum, the Russian Empire had a rather confused political system for approximately a dozen years before the Bolsheviks took power. Before then, there had been a tradition of highly centralised – if not always effective – autocratic government at least since the time of Peter the Great and, in Russia at least, since Ivan the Terrible.

In the pre-communist era, the Russian Orthodox Church played a significant role in the polity. One of its primary functions was to socialise citizens into accepting their position in society – a notion of hierarchy and 'natural' order. Although the revolutions of 1905 and 1917 (February and October) constitute clear evidence that such socialisation was far from totally successful by the early 20th century, the Russian masses were *relatively* obedient and quiescent for many centuries.

Finally, there was the tradition of official nationalism embodied in the state's emphasis on 'nationality'. Russia, as we have seen, became the Russian Empire under Peter the Great. As such, many Russians came to perceive of themselves as part of a larger and more diverse entity than even Russia itself. For instance, the area usually known during the Soviet era as the Central Asian republics came under Russian control in the 19th century, long before the communists came to power – whilst the Baltic states had been under Russian suzerainty since the 18th or 19th centuries (depending on the area). In a sense, then, there was a less dramatic break with tradition that might initially be assumed when the Soviet authorities encouraged Russians (and others) to think of themselves firstly as Soviet citizens and only secondly as members of a particular ethnic group. By the time of the collapse of communist power in the USSR, many Russians identified in only a limited way with Russia itself.

Once again space precludes a fuller analysis of precommunist Russian political traditions. Recent developments in Russia – and, to a much lesser extent, in other postcommunist countries – can now be examined in terms of the two models of 'normalcy' already outlined.

There is no question that *attempts* have been made in Russia, and several other postcommunist states, since the end of the 1980s to introduce both a clearer division of powers between the main arms of the formal parts of the political system, and the rule of law. Until September 1993 there was a clear distinction between the presidency and parliament in Russia, for instance, and a reasonably clear distinction between both of them and the Constitutional Court. The latter was seen by some as the most successful political development of 1991–2 and, under its chairman Valerii Zorkin, was not considered until about the middle of 1993 to have been clearly favouring either the presidency or the parliament. In this sense, both a system of checks and balances, and legal rationality, *were* beginning to emerge in Russia. But President Yeltsin, with some justification, believed that Zorkin and his Court were increasingly siding with parliament in the months following the April 1993 referendum – which is the major reason why, once Yeltsin had closed down the parliament, he also forced Zorkin's resignation from the Constitutional Court. By October 1993, there was very little in the way of a division of powers at the top of the Russian political system – largely because there was no real plurality of powers. The rule of law (as Sharlet demonstrates in Chapter 5) suffered in this process.

On the other hand, Yeltsin had not outlawed most political parties and groupings that had been emerging since 1988. Indeed, 13 political parties and blocs openly contested the December 1993 elections. As with so many other postcommunist states, one could argue that the number of parties was actually *abnormal*, in that there had not yet occurred a crystallisation into the small number of large parties that is the norm in most Western countries. Whilst such crystallisation is *beginning* to occur in both Russia and many other post-communist states (and is already well advanced in countries such as Bulgaria), it is quite understandable that a sudden legalisation of parties in all of these countries, following decades of *de facto* one-party systems, led to a mushrooming of organisations. Over time, many like-minded parties will merge, and others will simply disappear as some of the enthusiasm for newly-acquired political freedoms wanes and funds run out. In short, the recent emergence of so many parties is a healthy sign that Russia and other postcommunist states are on their way to 'normal' democracy – but it is unhealthy (notably in terms of efficient decision-making) to have a plethora of parties in parliaments and governments. Certainly, relatively stable party *systems*, as such, have still to emerge. Furthermore, Yeltsin was in late 1993 both privileging certain parties or blocs, and interfering with them (for instance, in strongly discouraging them from making negative comments about his draft Constitution), in a way that would be considered unacceptable in most Western systems. In terms of institutional and party politics, then, Russia – like the other postcommunist states – is still in transition, and has yet to arrive at 'normal' liberal democracy.

At present, the electoral process in Russia has not been fully regularised. The December 1993 elections were not approved by parliament – even though they were parliamentary ones. Just months before the election, it was still not clear which electoral law would be used. In these senses, one could still not talk of a 'normal' electoral process, despite genuine competition. Indeed, none of the postcommunist states could yet be held to have a really 'normal' electoral process. Electoral laws are often changed from one election to the next. For instance, Poland did not have a minimum threshold law at the time of the October 1991 elections, but did – at 5 per cent for individual parties and 8 per cent for coalition groups – by the time of the September 1993 elections. Moreover, the fact that at least two parliamentary elections have been held in each of the former communist states of Eastern Europe since 1989 reveals that the frequency is still higher than would be normal in established liberal democracies.

As of early 1994, it could not be said that Russia had proven itself totally committed to the kind of mixed economy typical of Western systems. Yeltsin had been openly arguing for such a system since at least 1990, and had for a time had a deputy or acting prime minister (Yegor Gaidar) who was firmly committed to radical privatisation. But many members both of the parliament that existed until September 1993, and of the one elected in December 1993, were hesitant about too rapid and too radical a push towards the market, while a small number even appeared to want to return to some form of centrally-planned economy. In addition, as part of his policy of compromising with parliament during 1992–3, Yeltsin demonstrated his preparedness to sacrifice his most radical market reformer (Gaidar) and replace him with a more moderate reformer as prime minister, Viktor Chernomyrdin.

The messy results of the December 1993 election, with a highly polarised parliament, mean that the confusion in economic policy is likely to continue – unless President Yeltsin again shuts down parliament, which is quite possible. In another – disturbing – scenario, Yeltsin would be replaced as president of the extreme nationalist Vladimir Zhirinovsky, or someone similar. If this were to happen, economic policy would *still* be confused. There are two main reasons. First, Zhirinovsky's own economic policy is not particularly clear; nationalism is at most an incomplete ideology, and does not *per se* provide a blueprint for economic management. Secondly, the new leader would have to acknowledge that Russia is part of the global economy, whether he likes it or not. There would thus be a tension between his professed abhorrence of 'the West' and his need both to trade with and seek aid from it. This tension would almost certainly result in continued confusion in Russian economic policy.

Russia has moved more rapidly towards normalcy in the area of socialisation. The media have been highly pluralistic by any criteria ever since the *glasnost* era of the late 1980s, and newspapers have been far more market-driven than they were throughout almost the entire communist era. This said, it would be most unusual for an established liberal democratic government to force major changes on a newspaper for political reasons, as did Yeltsin with *Pravda* in October 1993 – or to shut down some altogether (as he did with approximately 20 newspapers in October–November 1993). The educational system *has* become much more pluralistic and less controlled by government in recent years.

Russian citizens are now essentially free to pursue whatever religion they choose, as long as this does not involve transgression of the general laws of society.

Finally, individual rights are so far being treated with greater respect by the state than was the case during the communist era, for instance in terms of freedom of speech, association and travel. This said, a culture of individualism has not yet become a salient feature of the 'new' Russia.

Before drawing conclusions about Russian 'normalcy', recent developments in that country can be compared with pre-communist traditions.

Although a small group of monarchists has called for the return of the Romanov dynasty, the vast majority of Russians do not appear to favour a return to this traditional form of autocracy. This said, it is far from clear that Russia has given up its traditional penchant for strong and charismatic leadership. As in so many other postcommunist countries (such as Poland, Romania, Croatia, Azerbaijan – Hungary is a marked exception), there is a strong president, and – as suggested once again by the results of the December 1993 constitutional referendum – many citizens appear to favour this. Yeltsin gained considerable kudos in August 1991 when he stood atop a Russian tank in Moscow and defied those who had just attempted a *coup d'état*. The April 1993 referendum revealed that a clear majority (at least of voters) basically supported the President and his approach. The forcible closure of parliament in September 1993 followed what in some ways was reminiscent of the period of 'dual powerlessness' in 1917 (in that two bodies were vying for power, and it was unclear whose legislation was to be heeded). By this action, the use of violence against parliamentarians in October 1993, and the subsequent (short-term) declaration of a state of emergency, Yeltsin demonstrated once again that he was prepared to be a strong

Russian leader if, as he saw it, the situation required this. In doing so, he can be located in a long line of Russian leaders stretching back over the centuries. He believes that his mandate is above all from the Russian masses, and to some extent the West; this distinguishes him from most previous strong Russian leaders, who claimed legitimacy more in terms of the divine right of monarchs or Marxism–Leninism.

In one sense, there was a continuity – in terms of orthodoxy – between the precommunist and the communist eras that has now been broken. Although the Orthodox church itself always had a somewhat precarious existence during the communist era, the highly structured value system of the church was replaced by the highly structured value system of Marxism–Leninism. One dominant ideology was replaced by another. In contrast, there has been no clear-cut and agreed value system in society since the collapse of communist power and the USSR – as was amply demonstrated by the results of the December 1993 elections. Indeed, one of the major problems of contemporary Russia is precisely this ideological and moral confusion. Although the Orthodox Church has made something of a comeback in recent years, it is operating within a far more pluralistic context than was the case in the last century, for instance.

In some ways like Helmut Kohl in Germany, Boris Yeltsin is having to create a 'new' national identity among his subjects, based simultaneously on a new political unit and an old conception of what constitutes the nation. As indicated earlier, and further suggested by Zhirinovsky's success in December 1993, many Russians are finding it difficult to identify with a post-imperial Russia. The Soviet 'external empire' collapsed in 1989–90, whilst the 'internal empire', focussed on Moscow, collapsed in 1991 and has been only very partially resurrected in the form of the Commonwealth of Independent States.

One of the problems the Russian authorities face in attempting to create a 'new' Russian identity (official nationalism) is that such attempts can encourage unofficial nationalism among non-Russians. It can also exacerbate tensions between ethnic Russians and indigenous groups in the former republics of the USSR (in the early 1990s, approximately 25 million Russians were living in former Soviet republics other than Russia itself). Since ethnic and nationalist politics have already proven to be such a dangerous force in several of the successor states of the USSR (such as Azerbaijan, Armenia and Georgia), any policy that is likely to make the situation worse is obviously undesirable. On the other hand, the ideological void and economic problems alluded to earlier mean that state-sponsored (official) nationalism might be seen as a necessary 'glue' to hold Russian society together in a time of major change and great uncertainty. Certainly, the (quite inappropriately named) Liberal Democrats in the new Russian parliament will, given the chance, argue this. Unfortunately, their anti-semitic and chauvinistic form of nationalism carries with it precisely the kinds of dangers that have resulted in bloodshed in other parts of the former Soviet Union.

It has been argued that the term 'normal', when applied to Russia (and other postcommunist states), can have at least two quite different meanings. It should by now be clear that, in many ways, the two meanings of 'normal' used here are not merely different, but are to a considerable extent mutually exclusive. The first focuses on plurality, and an avoidance of any excessive concentration of power in the political, economic or ideological fields. The second, by contrast, implies just such a concentration. It follows from this that a move to 'normalcy' in one may very well imply a move away from 'the norm' in the other. Moreover, it should be borne in mind that the *choice* of one or other definition or 'normal' is itself normative. In an important sense, it is not up to outsiders to determine which version of normalcy Russians should opt for (if either). But Russians *themselves* are clearly divided on this issue. Of course, for the purpose of analysis, two relatively clear-cut *models* of normalcy have been produced here, and it has to be acknowledged that many individual Russians would probably like to see a Russian system that involves elements of both. For instance, there is no obvious reason why someone cannot advocate a system that is pluralistic, market-oriented, and nationalistic; many Westerners do this. This said, there does not appear to be much consensus on either one model or the other *or* on an eclectic mixture drawing on both of them. This lack of basic consensus on almost everything (other than, perhaps, that civil war should be avoided) is one of the biggest problems of contemporary Russia.

In a sense, the problem of consensus and common identity is more acute in Russia than in most other postcommunist countries. In nearly all of the latter (Albania and the former Yugoslavia being exceptions), the revolutions of 1989–91 were 'double rejective', in that they were simultaneously anticommunist *and* anti-Soviet (in the case of the external empire) or anti-Russian (in the case of several former republics of the USSR). Whereas the revolution in Russia involved the first component, it clearly could not involve the second. This is important, since it meant that, for all their differences, most citizens in most postcommunist states had something in common – their desire to be a truly sovereign people, free of Soviet or Russian domination. This 'gel' can be a negative phenomenon when it goes too far (when, for instance, it becomes racism directed against Russians or ethnic minorities within a given postcommunist country). Nevertheless, it has so far acted as some sort of common ground for most citizens in most communist states in a way that has not yet clearly crystallised within Russia. But what is in some ways a similar phenomenon *may* now be developing in Russia – in the form of a bonding, either in reaction to the anti-Russian feelings of others, or because of a sense of humiliation, as the West is seen to dictate terms to a once-proud and powerful Russia that is now on its knees. Thus, although the development of a Russian national identity may from *some* perspectives appear to be desirable (if it provides a common sense of purpose to Russians, that could overcome the current deep divisions and lack of direction), it could also – as indicated earlier – be very dangerous. Precisely because of its imperialistic past, a 'new' or 'resurrected' Russian identity could prove to be highly chauvinistic and expansionist. This could constitute a threat not only to other postcommunist and especially post-Soviet states, but also – given that Russia is still a nuclear power – to the rest of the world.

In sum, despite moves in the direction of both, Russia is not yet 'normal' by either of the definitions suggested in this chapter. If it were to move clearly towards the second model – as at least partially, and in different ways, advocated by people such as Alexander Solzhenitsyn and Vladimir Zhirinovsky – it would be turning back the clock of history. Moreover, and ironically, greater domestic stability on the basis of this model would almost certainly result in a further destabilising of the already fragile international order. In this important sense, and at the risk of appearing ethnocentric, it would be preferable if the Russian bear were to continue to stumble along the rocky path to the first model, as modernisation theorists always claimed would happen. Russia is currently trapped between at least two opposing models, with different sections of society pulling in different directions. In a real sense, we are witnessing yet another episode of the struggle between 'Westernisers' and 'Slavophiles' that can be traced back at least to the time of Peter the Great.

Legitimation Crises and Postcommunism

The question of legitimation crisis became a major one for social theorists in the 1970s. At that time, the focus was primarily on the capitalist world, with analyses such as O'Connor (1973, 1987) and Habermas (1976) tending to concentrate on the economic crises of Western states, and on the ways in which such crises could lead to rationality and legitimation crises. Apart from their concentration on the capitalist world, there were a number of problems with these early – and seminal – arguments, for instance in terms of being able to identify legitimation crises in 'the real world'.

Despite these limitations, a modified and refined version of legitimation crisis is useful for studying the collapse of communist systems (as in Holmes, 1993) and for considering from a more theoretical perspective some of the larger problems of the transitional, postcommunist systems. The analysis begins with a statement of three premises.

First, it is assumed that all political systems exercise power on the basis of a mixture of coercion (force) and legitimacy (here, in the simple sense of authority to govern), but that one or other of these is dominant at any given point in time. The process whereby governments seek legitimacy is what is meant here by legitimation.

Second, it is useful to distinguish between a 'regime' and a political 'system'. This distinction is a contested one in political science literature; for our purposes, a system can be defined as an amalgam of structures, processes, and conventions underpinned by an official ideology, whereas a regime is a particular team of politicians that is running a system at a given time. A regime, as the term is used here, is often named after a leader (say, the

Gorbachev regime), although it may – especially in a pluralist and competitive system – also be named after a particular ruling political party or coalition.

Third, an extreme legitimation crisis (this term is explained below) can only occur in a situation in which legitimation is the dominant mode of the exercise of power.

Having stated our three assumptions, a highly simplified and abbreviated version of legitimation crisis theory can be provided; it may apply to any system in which legitimation is more salient than coercion.

For most analysts, the starting point for what can develop into a legitimation crisis is economic crisis. In an endeavour to overcome such a crisis, governments often attempt to make significant changes to their policies – to such an extent that they begin to contradict the putative ideological underpinnings of the system. In the case of capitalist systems, for instance, many governments attempted in the 1930s to overcome the crisis that was the Depression by dramatically increasing the involvement of the state in the economy, to 'kick-start' the latter back into growth. President Roosevelt's 'New Deal', and the theories of Keynes, can be interpreted from this perspective. Communist governments also attempted to extricate themselves from the grave economic situation in which most of them found themselves during the 1980s by moving away from one of the key tenets of communist power, the centrally planned economy, and towards capitalist methods.

In both the above scenarios – the capitalist world of the 1930s and the communist world of the 1980s – the changes were significant enough to constitute what Habermas calls a 'rationality crisis'. This is a point at which the theoretical (ideological) underpinnings of a system are in *serious* conflict with current policies. This rationality crisis can then begin to undermine the legitimacy of both a regime and a system, at which point a legitimation crisis has begun to occur.

This last scenario is not a necessary one, however. If the move into rationality crisis results in marked economic improvement, the system's ideologists might be able to legitimise a (substantially) modified version of the original ideology to the masses. Certainly, such a crisis need not lead to collapse; if hardly anyone has a clear image of what kind of system could replace the existing one, or of how to move to such an alternative system, then the crisis may resolve itself without resulting in collapse. Thus, many 'capitalist' liberal democracies came to accept some form of state welfarism by the 1930s, even though the exact level has varied in the 20th century from country to country and decade to decade; whilst this has represented a major change in capitalist ideology, it has not resulted in system collapse. But if the economy does not improve and the state is unable to justify a radically altered ideology – and if there is a clear vision of an alternative system and of how to there is some vision of an alternative system and a belief that the existing system is vulnerable – then the legitimation crisis may well result in system collapse.

Let us now examine the concept of legitimation crisis more closely. The term 'crisis' is most frequently used in a medical context. Whilst it often refers to a life-or-death situation (*extreme* crisis), it is also used in less dramatic contexts, to refer to a critical point at which an illness may worsen or improve. It is argued here that legitimation crisis can also refer both to 'life-threatening' (system-threatening) situations, and serious but less dramatic ones. Before elaborating the four main forms it may assume, however, it is useful first to consider very briefly the different possible modes of legitimation.

Although there is as yet no widespread agreement on the number and classification of such modes, it is suggested here that 10 – seven domestic, and three external to a given system – can be identified. The domestic ones are old traditional (for instance 'divine right'); charismatic (often relating to the revolutionary role of a leader); goal-rational (or teleological – based on a claim to superior understanding of society's long-term goals and of how to achieve these); eudaemonic (focussing on performance, particularly in the consumer-related and social welfare spheres); official nationalist; new traditional (a regime acknowledges there are serious problems, but maintains that a return to the system's roots will solve them); and legal-rationality (briefly defined earlier). The external modes are formal recognition (as by foreign governments); foreign support (rulers retain faith in themselves because foreign institutions and/or specialists assure them they are pursuing appropriate strategies); and external role-model (rulers believe in their own legitimacy because they are emulating a foreign role-model in which they have faith).

It is acknowledged that several of these legitimation modes will coexist in a given society at a given time. However, it is further argued that the salience of different modes varies over time, and that one or two modes are usually predominant.

In light of the above, four types of legitimation crisis can be outlined. The first two are relatively minor, the third is moderately serious (a 'medium' form of legitimation crisis), whilst the fourth is an extreme – system-threatening – form that often results in system collapse.

In the first situation, regime becomes aware that its current balance of legitimation modes is markedly suboptimal – is not increasing legitimacy – but believes it can escape this minor legitimation crisis by shifting the balance of legitimation modes. For example, if a regime has been attempting to increase its legitimacy through better performance (eudaemonic legitimation), but finds that living standards are not rising (perhaps even falling) and that unemployment is increasing, then it might substantially reduce the emphasis on the economy and, instead, intensify its focus on official nationalism.

The second is abnormal or irregular regime change, in which a given leadership team loses faith in itself, but there are others with sufficient faith both in themselves and in the system to take power.

In the third scenario, a regime realises that its attempts at ruling primarily on the basis of legitimation are failing – or have already failed – and so reverts to coercion as the dominant form of exercising power. Inasmuch as the regime has acknowledged its failure to rule through legitimation, this is a fairly serious legitimation crisis. On the other hand, since the regime still has faith in its own right to rule, and is able to secure the compliance of the state's coercive agencies – notably the police and/or the military – in suppressing popular unrest, this is not yet an extreme legitimation crisis. A prime recent example from the communist world is the Tiananmen Square massacre of 1989 and its aftermath.

Finally, if the whole – or at least the key elements – of the elite loses faith in itself and the system it is supposed to maintain, an *extreme* legitimation crisis has occurred. One major reason for the development of such self-doubt is the growing awareness by the elite that a rationality crisis has occurred, and that it does not know how to overcome this. If, in their endeavours to overcome economic crisis, political elites adopt policies that are not merely at odds with past ideological tenets, but also appear to be emulative of the theories and practice of what had for long been portrayed as a system's principal ideological enemy, then an identity crisis arises. If, despite these *volte-faces*, the economy still does not appear to be improving sufficiently anyway, political elites can lose faith in themselves altogether; the system may collapse at this point.

Recent developments in Russian politics can now be analysed in terms of this theoretical framework. The collapse of communist power in 1991, for instance, can be interpreted in terms of the fourth (extreme) type of legitimation crisis. The reader will also recall the earlier argument that one of the salient features of Russia in the early 1990s is that it has no clear-cut ideology; whilst many would argue that 'anti-communism' is an ideology that is common to most Russians, even this is not clear. As recent elections in Bulgaria, Lithuania, Poland, Hungary – and to some extent Russia itself – have suggested, the more durable and acute the problems of early postcommunism appear to be, the greater the likelihood that many citizens will begin to seek a return to *some* aspects of what they associate with traditional communism – particularly its employment security and guaranteed subsidies on many basics.

It follows from this point about ideological confusion – which in turn implies no stable or clearcut 'system' – that the fourth type of legitimation crisis cannot *yet* emerge in the former Soviet Union. Moreover, if Russia were to continue in the direction of our first model of normalcy, there would be no *fundamental* contradiction between its values or policies and legal-rationality; unlike the situation in late communism, when Marxism–Leninism was unable to justify its dramatic turnaround on issues such as unemployment and inflation, postcommunism – with its putative commitment to market economics and pluralist democracy – is able to accommodate on a theoretical level most of the economic and social problems it is currently experiencing.

If, however, there were to be a major reversion to central planning and socialised ownership of the means of production, or the emergence of a clearly dictatorial system, this would contradiction the present vague – but not totally non-existent – ideological commitments of the Russian regime. As was demonstrated by many capitalist countries in the 1930s, such a dramatic shift would not *necessarily* result in collapse. But it would necessitate a revamping and clarification of the official ideology, and would succeed only if the change resulted in major economic improvement or there were high levels of coercion. In the case of future Russian politics in the short-to-medium term, such a move away from market economics and pluralist democracy would almost certainly be strongly criticised by much of the most influential section of the international community, which would have serious negative repercussions for Russia's ability to improve its economic performance. The implications of this have already been touched upon.

Does this argument suggest that early postcommunist Russia cannot fall into a legitimation crisis – if it continues along the path it was pursuing to mid-1993? Many have suggested that the events of late 1993 and the new constitution are clear evidence of a move away from democracy and towards dictatorship, but it is assumed here that the events of late 1993 were serious hiccoughs on the path to a freer, more pluralistic society. Whilst there currently appear to be few reasons for such an optimistic scenario, the fact that Russians have tolerated as much hardship as they have in recent years without (yet!) descending into civil war is enough to serve as a counter-argument to the more depressing, and in some ways more convincing, interpretations of recent events.

Assuming, then, no *fundamental* shift away from the current basically pluralist and market-oriented policies, it *is* still quite possible for Russia to fall into a legitimation crisis. Indeed, inasmuch as coercion was ultimately used to resolve the conflict between the president and the parliament in 1993, and that this was followed by a brief 'state of emergency', it can be persuasively argued that Russia has already had a (so far short-lived and relatively minor) version of the third type of legitimation crisis.

The chances of Russia having the first of two minor types of legitimation crisis are strong. At present, the continuing economic crisis in Russia means that the Yeltsin regime can hardly place much emphasis on eudaemonism. Given the aversion of so many leading Russian politicians to communism, coupled with their inability to agree on a plan for the future, teleologism also cannot be a predominant legitimation mode at present. Rather, the focus is primarily on charismatic and official nationalist legitimation, with Yeltsin himself also having faith in his own authority because of a blend of *some* aspects of legal-rationality (notably, his popular mandates in June 1991 and in the April 1993 referendum), and foreign support. As already argued, official nationalism becomes dangerous beyond a certain point. Past precedent would suggest that charismatic legitimation can be *relatively* durable, although this has usually been the case when, for instance, the means of socialisation have been far more centrally controlled than they have been in Russia in the early 1990s. Moreover, there is a limit to how well charismatic and legal-rational legitimation can coexist. Excessive emphasis on the former invariably casts doubt on the regime's commitment to the latter. At present, the excessive *personalisation* of Russian politics – the focus of one man (currently Boris Yeltsin, though this could change) – is clearly straining the credibility of claims to be moving towards legal-rational legitimation in Russia.

The probability of an abnormal/irregular regime change in the foreseeable future is greater because of 'natural' reasons – rumours abound concerning the state of Yeltsin's health – or coercion (in the form of a successful coup) than because of a type two minor legitimation crisis. The likelihood of the latter seems, as of 1994, to be remote, in that Yeltsin still *appears* to have considerable confidence in his own authority.

Earlier, the possibility of the fourth type of legitimation crisis was discussed, and it was argued that this is unlikely to occur in the near future on the basis of factors already identified. But another possible scenario is that Russia as a political unit, and centralised power, will become delegitimised. Without elaborating the complex debates about *who* legitimates the system or regime, suffice it to say that if the senior leaders believe in one kind of arrangement, but their staffs or large sections of the population lose faith in this and believe in both an alternative arrangement (such as regionalism – or even the establishment of the formal sovereignty of the present component parts of Russia) and the possibility of achieving this, then there could be fundamental system collapse. It is precisely in an endeavour to avoid this that the draft Russian constitution released by Yeltsin in November 1993, and approved by a referendum in December, placed greater emphasis than earlier versions on maintaining Russia as a unified and rather centralised whole.

Conclusions

In this chapter, a number of theoretical interpretations of the recent history and current politics of Russia have been explored. In the section on 'normalcy', two – contrasting – versions of 'normal' were analysed, on one level precisely to highlight the contradictory nature of post-Soviet Russia. In fact, there is at least a *third* version of normalcy – which is, in some ways, the most appropriate one of all, and which was briefly alluded to earlier. This is the traditional communist system. The vast majority of today's Russians have lived under communist rule for almost all their lives. What appears to be a growing minority of citizens now seem to believe – at least in their more pessimistic moments – that life may have been better in the Brezhnev era, before all the turmoil associated with Gorbachev and his successors. There was a certainty and a stability to that period, for all its negative features. If this third conception of normalcy is added to the two already elaborated, it becomes even clearer why there cannot be any widespread agreement on what 'normal' might mean in today's Russia. The country is still in revolutionary flux, as it was in 1917 or as France was in and after 1789. It is this uncertainty that makes it so difficult to forecast Russia's future, and that means that all 'models' of transition – especially predictive as distinct from comparative or descriptive ones – must be treated with caution.

Guide to Further Reading

All the chapters in this volume are based, to varying extents, on the contemporary Russian press and periodical literature. A substantial selection of these sources is available in translation in the *Current Digest of the Post-Soviet Press* (Columbus, Ohio, weekly) and in daily monitoring services such as the American-based *Foreign Broadcast Information Service* and the *BBC Summary of World Broadcasts*. Detailed commentaries on current developments are available in the *Research Report* issued by Radio Liberty in Munich; a separate series of *News Briefs* is also issued on a daily basis (and is available, like many of these services, on-line).

More extended scholarly commentaries are available in the journals that specialise in Soviet and post-Soviet affairs, among them *Europe–Asia Studies* (formerly *Soviet Studies*, eight issues annually), *Slavic Review* (quarterly), *Russian Review* (quarterly), *Post-Soviet Affairs* (formerly *Soviet Economy*, quarterly), the *Soviet and Post-Soviet Review* (formerly *Soviet Union*, quarterly), the *Journal of Communist Studies and Transition Politics* (formerly the *Journal of Communist Studies*, quarterly) and *Communist and Post-Communist Studies* (formerly *Studies in Comparative Communism*, quarterly). A helpful collection of statistics is available in Ryan (1993), which includes data on the population and public opinion as well as housing, crime and the environment.

Chapter 1   Introduction: From Communism to Democracy?

There are several detailed assessments of the Gorbachev leadership and of the post-communist years that have followed it (see for instance Sakwa, 1990; Parker, 1991; White, 1993; and Miller, 1993). An early biography of Gorbachev is available in Medvedev (1988); see also Schmidt-Hauer (1986), Doder and Branson (1990), and Ruge (1991). Gorbachev's speeches and writings are available in several editions, among them *Selected Speeches and Articles*, 2nd ed. (Moscow: Progress, 1987); *Socialism, Peace and Democracy* (London and Atlantic Highlands, NJ: Zwan, 1987); *Speeches and Writings*, 2 vols. (Oxford: Pergamon, 1986 and 1987); *Meaning of My Life: Perestroika* (Edinburgh: Aspect,

1990); and his best-selling *Perestroika* (Gorbachev, 1987). Boris Yeltsin has set out his early life in *Against the Grain* (Yeltsin, 1990); an interim biography is available in Morrison, 1991.

A broader view of Soviet and post-Soviet change is presented in Grey (1990), Hosking (1991), Hahn (1991a), Gibson, Duch and Tedin (1991), Finifter and Mickiewicz (1992) and Miller (1993), which explore public responses and the development of a 'civil society', in many cases through the use of survey evidence. The 'New Russian Barometer', conducted annually by the Centre for the Study of Public Policy at the University of Strathclyde, is reported in Boeva and Shironin (1992) and Rose *et al.* (1993). Among Russian-language sources of survey data, the most important are the All-Union Centre for the Study of Public Opinion's monthly *Ekonomicheskie i sotsial'nye peremeny: monitoring obshchestvennogo mneniya* and Vox Populi's *Mir mnenii i mneniya o mire.*

Chapter 2   Yeltsin and the Russian Presidency

A number of texts offer useful overviews of the evolving late Soviet and post-Soviet national leadership and political system. Among these, White (1993) and White, Gill and Slider (1993) offer especially detailed treatments. Huber and Kelley (1991) and Huskey (1992) provide a broad overview of institutional and elite issues for the Gorbachev period. Bremmer and Taras (1993) contains focussed chapters on the politics of each of the 15 successor states. The weekly background analyses of the RFE/RL *Research Reports* provide a wealth of timely information on institutional and political elite developments in the post-Soviet Russian Federation and other successor states. An insightful examination of Arkadii Volsky and other Russian centrists in this connection is available in Lohr (1993); on Yeltsin and his support since 1991, see White, McAllister and Kryshtanovskaya (1994).

For a comprehensive review of the Soviet-period political leadership see Hough and Fainsod (1979) and Hough (1980). Breslauer (1982) provides a thorough treatment of the policy dilemmas and authority-building efforts of the Khrushchev and Brezhnev regimes. A discussion of Soviet elite generational change and its consequences is found in Bialer (1980) and Breslauer (1984). Two collections of T.H. Rigby's work (1990a and 1990b) provide a comprehensive overview of one leading scholar's careful study of the Soviet system and elite. Edited volumes by Lane (1988) and Brown (1989) include a diversity of analyses by leading scholars on political elite and leadership issues. Willerton (1992) offers a comparative study of the Brezhnev and Gorbachev period elite mobility and regime formation norms. A series of articles that appeared in the journal *Soviet Economy* between 1989 and 1991 span a range of perspectives on Gorbachev's leadership style and effectiveness: see particularly Breslauer (1989 and 1990), Brown (1990), Hough (1991) and Reddaway (1990). Among studies of Soviet and post-Soviet subnational political and leadership are

Bahry (1987), Urban (1989), Brovkin (1990a), Gleason (1991), Willerton and Reisinger (1991), and Friedgut and Hahn (1994).

Chapter 3   Representative Power and the Russian State

Detailed discussion of electoral and representative politics are included in several more general studies of the late Soviet and post-Soviet periods, among them White (1993), White, Gill and Slider (1993) and Sakwa (1993). Studies that focus more particularly on the representative system include Urban (1990a), Huber and Kelley (1991), Kiernan (1993), Chiesa (1993) and Remington (1994). On the wider issue of parliamentary versus presidential forms, see for instance Lijphart (1992), Shugart and Carey (1992) and Mainwaring (1993).

Chapter 4   Parties and the Party System

For a general account of the CPSU's traditional role and structures see Hill and Frank (1987). Two standard histories of party development, from its origins to the 1960s, are Rigby (1968) and Schapiro (1970). The Party Programme and Rules, as adopted in 1986, are conveniently available in White (1989); for the Rules since their adoption up to 1986 see Gill (1988). For a selection of more research-oriented studies see for instance Potichnyj (1988) and Rigby (1990b), which expertly examines a number of the issues central to the CPSU, its role and performance. Contributions to the CPSU in its changing identity and role include Hill (1988), Hill (1991a and 1991b), White (1991b), Rees (1992), Millar (1992) and the relevant chapters of Miller (1993). A preliminary survey of the emerging multiparty system in Tolz (1990); Urban (1990b) records Russian views at the beginning of the decade; and a long chapter in Sakwa (1993) looks at the emerging system as of early 1993. For various surveys of the emerging Russian parties, see for instance Lentini (1992), Dallin (1993) and *Spravochnik* (1993); for 'Communists after communism' see White and McAllister (1994).

Chapter 5   Citizen and State under Gorbachev and Yeltsin

White (1993) and Sakwa (1993) provide close analyses of both the Gorbachev and Yeltsin reform programmes as contexts for citizen–state relations. For a study and the texts of the four Soviet constitutions, see Unger (1981); for the 1978 Russian Constitution, as revised, and the alternative drafts that were prepared in 1992–3, see *Konstitutsii* (1993). The text of the constitution that was approved at the referendum in December 1993 is available in *Izvestiya*, 28 December 1993. For an analysis of the evolution of Soviet constitutional reform from the 1977

USSR Constitution up to the end of the Soviet Union in 1991, see Sharlet (1992b). On human rights in the post-Stalin period up to *perestroika* see Reddaway (1972), Rubenstein (1985) and Alexeyeva (1987). On human rights under Gorbachev, see Sharlet (1992a) and Juviler and Gross (1993). The Soviet legal system is covered in Butler (1988), and the Russian system that succeeded it in Feldbrugge (1993); the *East European Constitutional Review* (Chicago, since 1992) is useful on more recent developments.

Hopkins has written on the post-Stalin media up to Gorbachev, including the official media (1970) and the *samizdat* or underground media (1983). Two comprehensive studies of *glasnost* are Laqueur (1989) and Nove (1989); for the late Soviet and postcommunist period see Benn (1992). Entin (1991), one of the authors of the Soviet law on the press, discusses the drafting process, while Remington (1991) provides a case study of the law's passage. Finally a well-edited selection of letters to the editor during the period from 1987 and 1990 can be found in Cerf and Albee (1990); see also Riordan and Bridger (1992).

Chapter 6   The Economy: The Rocky Road From Plan to Market

Given the rapid pace of developments in recent years, the best sources are journals such as *Europe–Asia Studies* (Glasgow), *Post-Soviet Affairs* (Berkeley), and the weekly *Research Report* issued by Radio Free Europe/Radio Liberty (Munich). Translations from Soviet and Russian journals and newspapers are available in the *Current Digest of the Soviet* (since 1992, *Post-Soviet*) *Press* and in the Foreign Broadcast Information Service series on Central Eurasia. For analyses of the development and deepening crisis of the Soviet-period economy see Hewett (1988), Nove (1992), Campbell (1992) and Rutland (1985 and 1993); on the post-communist period the best monographs are Aslund (1991) and Aslund and Layard (1993). An authoritative overview is the IMF study completed in late 1990 (IMF, 1991). Also useful is the collection of articles from the journal *Soviet Economy* (Hewett and Winston, 1991). On privatisation more particularly see Chapter 7 and Frydman *et al.* (1993); on foreign economic relations, Smith (1993).

Chapter 7   Privatisation: the Politics of Capital and Labour

For a survey of the post-1990 debates over privatisation see Flaherty (1992), Clarke (1992) and Clarke *et al.* (1993). Frydman *et al.* (1993) provide a recent and general account. On the early stages, see Hanson (1990), Johnson and Kroll (1991) and Filatotchev *et al.* (1992). There are several case studies of enterprises in the course of privatisation: see for instance Burawoy and Hendley (1992), Burawoy and Krotov (1992), Hendley (1992), and Clarke *et al.* (1994). The most sophisticated (and utopian) liberal theorist of privatisation is Naishul' (1990a, 1990b). Articles in *Moscow News* by Larisa Piyasheva (no. 5, 1992, pp. 8–9) and by Gavriil Popov (*Moskovskie novosti*, 21 February 1993) offer the most scathing liberal critiques of the Gaidar programme. On public opinion, see for instance Rose *et al.* (1993) and Duch (1993).

Chapter 8 The Politics of Social Issues

Soviet arguments about *perestroika*, social policy and 'socialist social justice' can be found in Gorbachev (1987), Klavdienko (1986), Mchedlov (1987) and Zaslavskaya (1988). Statements by Yeltsin, Khasbulatov, Chernomyrdin, Gaidar, Pamfilova and others can best be traced in Radio Free Europe/Radio Liberty *News Briefs* and in the *Current Digest of the Post-Soviet Press*.

Smith (1991, Chap. 11) offers an introductory account of the Soviet welfare state. A more detailed discussion is provided by George and Manning (1980). Employment policies and comparative wages are examined by McAuley (1979), Echols (1986), Lane (1987), Aslund (1991), Whitlock (1993) and Smith (1993). On housing, see Andrusz (1984) and Trehub (1992). On healthcare, see Ryan (1978 and 1991), Hyde (1974), Navarro (1977) and Davis and Feshbach (1980). An up-to-date discussion of disease in the states of the former Soviet Union and of infant and maternal mortality is provided by Davis (1993a). Comparisons with Eastern Europe are drawn in Davis (1993b). Helmstadter (1992) looks at medical insurance in Russia.

Feshbach (1991) links issues of population, health and environment; Feshbach and Friendly (1992) offer a more sensational account of 'ecocide'. Pryde (1991) gives an overview of environmental policy. Marnie and Slater (1993) look at the growing problem of refugees. On youth, see Wilson and Bachkatov (1988), Riordan (1989) and Pilkington (1992). On children's homes, refer to Waters (1992). For discussions of gender, see Buckley (1992), Einhorn (1993) and Posadskaya (1994). On crime, prostitution, drug abuse, alcoholism and other issues see Jones *et al.* (1991) and Joyce (1992). Galeotti (1993) looks at crime and policing; Waters (1990) considers prostitution; and Ann White (1993) discusses charity and self-help.

Chapter 9 The Politics of Foreign Policy

An accessible introductory text is Nogee and Donaldson (1990). The standard history is Ulam (1974) and its continuation (Ulam, 1983). More recent developments are covered in Hasegawa and Pravda (1990) and Laird and Hoffmann (1991); for the postcommunist period Crow (1994) and Malcolm (1994) are useful. On domestic aspects in the Soviet period, consult Bialer (1981) and Valenta and Potter (1984). For security issues, see MccGwire (1991) and more recently Blacker (1993). The changing Soviet theory of international relations, up to and including Gorbachev's 'new thinking', is considered in Light (1988) and Woodby (1989).

Chapter 10　Nationality and Ethnicity in Russia and the Post-Soviet Republics

There is a large general literature on the national question in the former USSR. See, for instance, Katz (1975); Carrère d'Encausse (1979); Connor (1984), a study that includes other communist-ruled systems; and Wixman (1984), an ethnographic handbook. Karklins (1986) uses interviews with Soviet Germans to provide a perspective 'from below'. A historical survey of the national question is provided by Nahaylo and Swoboda (1990). Analytic reconsiderations of the Soviet experience with nationalities can be found in two volumes edited by Alexander Motyl (1992a, 1992b). The role of ethnic issues in the collapse of the Soviet Union is explored in Gitelman (1992). For the early post-Soviet period, Bremmer and Taras (1993) is helpful.

Chapter 11　Politics Outside Russia

A comprehensive overview of the breakup of the Soviet Union and its implications is contained in White, Gill and Slider (1993). For a review of economic reform measures in some of the former republics, see Frydman *et al.* (1993). Current developments within the CIS, its member states and the Baltic states are analysed in the Radio Free Europe/Radio Liberty *Research Report*. A good source of translated primary source materials on these topics, as on others, is the *Current Digest of the Post-Soviet Press*. There are substantial studies of most of the individual post-Soviet republics, including at least two series: 'Studies of Nationalities in the [former] USSR', published by the Hoover Institution, and 'The Post-Soviet Republics', published by Westview. Several of the newly independent states are well served: see for instance Motyl (1993) on Ukraine, and Lieven (1993) on the 'Baltic revolution'.

Chapter 12　Russia, Communism, Democracy

Suggestions for further reading are contained at the appropriate point in the text of this chapter. For a representative selection of views see for instance Berdyaev (1960), *Iz glubiny* (1918/1991) and *Vekhi* (1909/1967, both available in translation), Jowitt (1992), Likhachev (1991), Solzhenitsyn (1991) and Yanov (1989).

Chapter 13   Normalisation and Legitimation in Postcommunist Russia

This chapter has been written on the assumption that most of the basic 'facts' (for instance, concerning the September–October 1993 events) are already known to the reader, or can be found elsewhere in this book. Two of the best, most up-to-date analyses of Soviet and Russian politics in the late communist and early postcommunist period are White, Gill and Slider (1993) and Sakwa (1993). For a detailed introduction to the successor states of the former Soviet Union see Bremmer and Taras (1993). A more comparative examination of postcommunism is available in Holmes (1994).

For legitimation crisis literature, see Habermas (1973 and 1976); the concept of crisis more particularly is elaborated in O'Connor (1973 and 1987). Of particular relevance on the issues of legitimacy and legitimation crisis in the former Soviet bloc are Rigby and Feher (1982), Lewis (1984) and Holmes (1993). For a full-length analysis of Russian political culture see White (1979); there are further discussions and of the cultural approach to politics in McAuley (1984) and Hahn (1991a). Standard introductions to Russian history include Florinsky (1969), Pipes (1974) and Riasanovsky (1993). Finally, an interesting analysis of what might be meant by 'democracy' (in the context of this chapter's discussion of 'normalcy') can be found in Held (1990). On Sovietology and postcommunism more generally, see for instance Solomon (1993) and Fleron and Hoffmann (1993).

Bibliography

This bibliography contains full details of items cited in the chapters or in the Guide to Further Reading section, together with a number of other items that students and specialists may be expected to find useful.

Aage, Hans (1991) 'Popular attitudes and *perestroika*', *Soviet Studies*, vol. 43, no. 1, pp. 3–26.

Afanas'ev, Yu. (ed.) (1988) *Inogo ne dano*. Moscow: Progress.

Aganbegyan, Abel (1988) *The Challenge: Economics of Perestroika*. London: Hutchinson.

Alexeyeva, Ludmilla (1987) *Soviet Dissent: Contemporary Movements for National, Religious and Human Rights*. Middletown, CT: Wesleyan University Press.

Anderson, Benedict (1983) *Imagined Communities: Reflections on the Origin and Spread of Nationalism*. London: Verso.

Andrusz, Gregory D. (1984) *Housing and Urban Development in the USSR*. London: Macmillan.

Anweiler, Oskar (1974) *The Soviets: The Russian Workers', Peasants', and Soldiers' Councils, 1905–1921*, trans. Ruth Hein. New York: Pantheon.

Arbatov, G.A. (1991) *Zatyanuvsheesya vyzdorovlenie*. Moscow: Mezhdunarodnye otnosheniya.

Armstrong, John A. (1973) *The European Administrative Elite*. Princeton NJ: Princeton University Press.

Aslund, Anders (1991) *Gorbachev's Struggle for Economic Reform*, 2nd ed. Ithaca NY: Cornell University Press.

Aslund, Anders and Layard, Richard (eds.) (1993) *Changing the Economic System in Russia*. London: Pinter.

Azrael, Jeremy R. (1966) *Managerial Power and Soviet Politics*. Cambridge MA: Harvard University Press.

Bahry, Donna (1987) *Outside Moscow: Power, Politics and Budgetary Policy in the Soviet Republics*. New York: Columbia University Press.

Bahry, Donna L. and Moses, Joel C. (eds.) (1990) *Political Implications of Economic Reform in Communist Systems*. New York: New York University Press.

Bahry, Donna L. and Silver, Brian D. (1990) 'Soviet citizen participation on the eve of democratization', *American Political Science Review*, vol. 84, no. 3 (September), pp. 821–48.

Balzer, Harley J. (ed.) (1991) *Five Years that Shook the World*. Boulder CO: Westview.

Barry, Donald D. (ed.) (1992) *Toward the Rule of Law in Russia: Political and Legal Reform in the Transition Period*. Armonk NY: Sharpe.

Benn, David Wedgwood (1989) *Persuasion and Soviet Politics*. Oxford: Blackwell.

Benn, David Wedgwood (1992) *From Glasnost to Freedom of Speech: Soviet Openness and International Relations*. London: Pinter.

Berdyaev, Nikolai (1946) *The Russian Idea*. London: Bles.

Berdyaev, Nikolai (1960) *The Origins of Russian Communism*. Ann Arbor: University of Michigan Press.

Berezkin, A.V. *et al.* (1990) *Vesna 89: Geografiya i anatomiya parlamentskikh vyborov*. Moscow: Progress.

Berman, Harold J. (ed.) (1972) *Soviet Criminal Law and Procedure: The RSFSR Codes*, 2nd ed. Cambridge MA: Harvard University Press.

Bialer, Seweryn (1980) *Stalin's Successors*. New York: Cambridge University Press.

Bialer, Seweryn (ed.) (1981) *The Domestic Context of Soviet Foreign Policy*. London: Croom Helm.

Bialer, Seweryn (ed.) (1989) *Politics, Society and Nationality inside Gorbachev's Russia*. Boulder CO: Westview.

Blackbourn, David and Eley, Geoff (1984) *The Pecularities of German History: Bourgeois Society and Politics in Nineteenth-Century Germany*. Oxford: Oxford University Press.

Blacker, Coit (1993) *Hostage to Revolution: Gorbachev and Soviet Security Policy, 1985–91*. New York: Council on Foreign Relations.

Boeva, Irina and Shironin, Viacheslav (1992) *Russians between State and Market*. Glasgow: University of Strathclyde Centre for the Study of Public Policy, SPP 205.

Bremmer, Ian and Taras, Ray (eds.) (1993) *Nations and Politics in the Soviet Successor States*. Cambridge: Cambridge University Press.

Breslauer, George (1982) *Khrushchev and Brezhnev as Leaders: Building Authority in Soviet Politics*. London: Allen & Unwin.

Breslauer, George (1984) 'Is there a generation gap in the Soviet political establishment? Demand articulation by RSFSR provincial party first secretaries', *Soviet Studies*, vol. 36, no. 1 (January), pp. 1–25.

Breslauer, George (1989) 'Evaluating Gorbachev as leader', *Soviet Economy*, vol. 5, no. 4, pp. 299–340.

Breslauer, George (1990) 'Gorbachev: diverse perspectives', *Soviet Economy*, vol. 7, no. 2, pp. 110–20.

Brovkin, Vladimir (1990a) 'First party secretaries: an endangered Soviet species?', *Problems of Communism*, vol. 39, no. 1 (January–February), pp. 15–27.

Brovkin, Vladimir (1990b) 'Revolution from below: informal political associations in Russia, 1988–1989', *Soviet Studies*, vol. 42, no. 2 (June), pp. 233–58.

Brown, A.H. (1974) *Soviet Politics and Political Science*. London: Macmillan.

Brown, Archie (1985) 'Gorbachev: new man in the Kremlin', *Problems of Communism*, vol. 34, no. 3 (May–June), pp. 1–23.

Brown, Archie (ed.) (1989) *Political Leadership in the Soviet Union*. London: Macmillan.

Brown, Archie (1990) 'Gorbachev's leadership: another view', *Soviet Economy*, vol. 6, no. 2, pp. 141–54.

Brown, Archie and Gray, Jack (eds.) (1977) *Political Culture and Political Change in Communist States*. New York: Holmes & Meier.

Brudny, Yitzhak M. (1993) 'The dynamics of "Democratic Russia", 1990–1993', *Post-Soviet Affairs*, vol. 9, no. 2, pp. 141–70.

Brzezinski, Zbigniew (1989/90) 'Post-communist nationalism', *Foreign Affairs*, vol. 68 (Winter), pp. 1–25.

Buckley, Mary (ed.) (1992) *Perestroika and Soviet Women*. Cambridge: Cambridge University Press.

Bunce, Valerie (1981) *Do New Leaders Make a Difference? Executive Succession and Public Policy under Capitalism and Socialism*, Princeton, NJ: Princeton University Press.

Bunce, Valerie and Echols, John M. (1980) 'Soviet politics in the Brezhnev era: "pluralism" or "corporatism"?' in Donald Kelley (ed.), *Soviet Politics in the Brezhnev Era*. New York: Praeger.

Burawoy, Michael and Hendley, Kathryn (1992) 'Between *perestroika* and privatization: divided strategies and political crisis in a Soviet enterprise', *Soviet Studies*, vol. 44, no. 3, pp. 371–402.

Burawoy, Michael and Krotov, Pavel (1992) 'The Soviet transition from socialism to capitalism: worker control and economic bargaining in the wood industry', *American Sociological Review*, vol. 57, February, pp. 16–38.

Butler, William E. (1988) *Soviet Law*. London: Butterworths.

Butler, William E. (ed.) (1991) *Perestroika and the Rule of Law: Anglo–American and Soviet Perspectives*. London: Tauris.

Butler, William E. (ed.) (1992) *Basic Legal Documents of the Russian Federation*. Dobbs Ferry: Oceana.

Campbell, Robert W. (1992) *The Failure of Soviet Economic Planning: System, Performance, Reform*. Bloomington IN: Indiana University Press.

Carr, E.H. (1945) *Nationalism and After*. London: Macmillan.

Carrère d'Encausse, Helene (1979) *An Empire in Decline*. New York: Newsweek.

Cavanaugh, Cassandra (1992) 'Crackdown on the opposition in Uzbekistan', Radio Free Europe/Radio Liberty *Research Report*, vol. 1, no. 31 (31 July), pp. 20–4.

Cerf, Christopher and Albee, Marina (eds.) (1990) *Small Fires: Letters from the Soviet People to Ogonyok Magazine, 1987–1990*. New York: Summit Books.

Chadaaev, P.Ya. (1991) *Polnoe sobranie sochinenii i izbrannye pis'ma*. Moscow: Nauka.

Chiesa, Giulietto, with Northrop, Douglas T. (1993) *Transition to Democracy: Political Change in the Soviet Union, 1987–1991*. Hanover and London: University Press of New England.

Clarke, Simon (1992) 'Privatisation and the development of capitalism in Russia', *New Left Review*, no. 196, pp. 3–27.

Clarke, Simon *et al.* (1994) 'The privatization of industrial enterprises in Russia: four case studies', *Europe–Asia Studies*, vol. 46, no. 2, pp. 179–214.

Cohen, Stephen F. (1985) *Rethinking the Soviet Experience*. New York: Oxford University Press.

Connor, Walker (1984) *The National Question in Marxist–Leninist Theory and Practice*. Princeton, NJ: Princeton University Press.

Corrin, Chris (ed.) (1992) *Superwomen and the Double Burden. Women's Experience of Change in Central Europe and the Former Soviet Union*. London: Scarlet Press.

Crow, Suzanne (1994) *The Making of Foreign Policy in Russia under Yeltsin*. Munich: RFE/RL Research Institute.

Crummey, Robert (ed.) (1989) *Reform in Russia and the USSR: Past and Prospects*. Urbana and Chicago: University of Illinois Press.

Custine, Marquis de (1991) *Letters from Russia*. Harmondsworth: Penguin.

Dahl, Robert A. (1971) *Polyarchy: Participation and Opposition*. New Haven CT: Yale University Press.

Dallin, Alexander (ed.) (1993) *Political Parties in Russia*. Berkeley: University of California Press.

Dallin, Alexander and Lapidus, Gail W. (eds.) (1991) *The Soviet System in Crisis: A Reader of Western and Soviet Views*. Boulder CO: Westview.

Davis, Christopher (1993a) 'Health care crisis: the former Soviet Union', *Radio Free Europe/Radio Liberty Research Report*, vol. 2, no. 40 (8 October), pp. 35–43.

Davis, Christopher (1993b) 'Health care crisis: Eastern Europe and the former USSR: an overview', *Radio Free Europe/Radio Liberty Research Report*, vol. 2, no. 40 (8 October), pp. 31–4.

Davis, Christopher and Feshbach, Murray (1980) *Rising Infant Mortality in the USSR in the 1980s*. Washington DC: Bureau of the Census.

Dawisha, Karen and Parrott, Bruce (1994) *Russia and the New States of Eurasia*. Cambridge: Cambridge University Press.

Denber, Rachel (ed.) (1991) *The Soviet Nationality Reader: The Crisis in Context*. Boulder CO: Westview.

Di Palma, Guiseppe (1990) *To Craft Democracies: An Essay on Democratic Transitions*. Berkeley: University of California Press.

Dibb, Paul (1988) *The Soviet Union: The Incomplete Superpower*, 2nd ed. London: Macmillan.

DiFranciesco, Wayne and Gitelman, Zvi (1985) 'Soviet political culture and "covert participation" in policy implementation', *American Political Science Review*, vol. 78, no. 3 (September), pp. 603–21.

Djilas, Milovan (1957) *The New Class. An Analysis of the Communist System*. London: Thames & Hudson.

Doder, Dusko and Branson, Louise (1990) *Gorbachev: Heretic in the Kremlin*. London: Futura.

Duch, Raymond M. (1993) 'Tolerating economic reform: popular support for transition to a free market in the former Soviet Union', *American Political Science Review*, vol. 87, no. 3 (September), pp. 590–609.

Dunlop, John B. (1993) *The Rise of Russia and the Fall of the Soviet Empire*. Princeton NJ: Princeton University Press.

Echols, John M. (1986) 'Does socialism mean greater equality? A comparison of East and West along several major dimensions', in Stephen White and Daniel N. Nelson (eds.), *Communist Politics: A Reader*. London: Macmillan.

Edmonds, Robin (1983) *Soviet Foreign Policy: The Brezhnev Years*. Oxford: Oxford University Press.

Einhorn, Barbara (1993) *Cinderella Goes To Market: Citizenship, Gender, and Women's Movements in East Central Europe*. London: Verso.

Elias, Norbert (1978) *The Civilising Process*. Oxford: Blackwell.

Entin, V.L. (1991) 'Law and glasnost', in Butler (ed.) (1991).

Farrell, R. Barry (ed.) (1970) *Political Leadership in Eastern Europe and the Soviet Union*. Chicago: Aldine.

Feher, Ferenc, Heller, Agnes and Markus, Gyorgy (1983) *Dictatorship over Needs*. Oxford: Blackwell.

Feldbrugge, F.J.M. (1993) *Russian Law: The End of the Soviet System and the Role of Law*. Dordrecht: Martinus Nijhoff.

Feldbrugge, F.J.M. (ed.) (1985) *Encyclopedia of Soviet Law*, 2nd ed. Dordrecht: Martinus Nijhoff.

Feshbach, Murray (1991) 'Social change in the USSR under Gorbachev: population, health and environmental issues', in Balzer (ed.) (1991).

Feshbach, Murray and Friendly, Alfred (1992) *Ecocide in the USSR: Health and Nature under Siege*. London: Aurum.

Filatotchev, Igor, Buck, Trevor and Wright, Mike (1992) 'Privatisaion and buy-outs in the USSR', *Soviet Studies*, vol. 44, no. 2, pp. 265–82.

Finifter, Ada W. and Mickiewicz, Ellen (1992) 'Redefining the political system of the USSR: mass support for political change', *American Political Science Review*, vol. 86, no. 4 (December), pp. 857–74.

Fischer, George (1968) *The Soviet System and Modern Society*. New York: Atherton House.

Flaherty, Patrick (1992) 'Privatisation and the Soviet economy', *Monthly Review*, vol. 43, no. 8, pp. 1–14.

Fleron, Frederick J. and Hoffmann, Erik P. (eds.) (1993) *Post-Communist Studies and Political Science. Methodology and Empirical Theory in Sovietology*. Boulder CO: Westview.

Florinsky, Michael (1969) *Russia: A Short History*. Toronto: Collier-Macmillan.

Friedgut, Theodore (1979) *Political Participation in the USSR*. Princeton NJ: Princeton University Press.

Friedgut, Theodore H. and Hahn, Jeffrey W. (eds.) (1994) *Local Power and Post-Soviet Politics*. Boulder CO: Westview.

Friedrich, Carl J. and Brzezinski, Zbigniew (1956) *Totalitarian Dictatorship and Autocracy*. Cambridge MA: Harvard University Press, 2nd ed. New York: Prager, 1961; revised ed. by Carl J. Friedrich, Cambridge MA: Harvard University Press, 1965.

Frydman, Roman *et al.* (1993) *The Privatization Process in Russia, Ukraine and the Baltic States*. Budapest: Central European University Press.

Fukuyama, Francis (1992) *The End of History and the Last Man*. New York: Free Press.

Galeotti, Mark (1993) '*Perestroika, perestrelka, pereborka*: policing Russia in a time of change', *Europe–Asia Studies*, vol. 45, no. 5, pp. 769–86.

Gambrell, James (1993) 'Moscow: Storm over the press', *New York Review of Books* (16 December), pp. 69–74.

George, Vic and Manning, Nick (1980) *Socialism, Social Welfare and the Soviet Union*. London: Routledge.

Getty, J. Arch (1985) *The Origins of the Great Purges. The Soviet Communist Party Reconsidered, 1933–1938*. New York: Cambridge University Press.

Getty, J. Arch and Manning, Roberta T. (eds.) (1993) *Stalinist Terror: New Perspectives*. Cambridge: Cambridge University Press.

Gibson, James L. (1993) 'Perceived political freedom in the USSR', *Journal of Politics*, vol. 55, no. 4 (November), pp. 936–75.

Gibson, James L., Duch, Raymond M. and Tedin, Kent L. (1991) 'Democratic values and the transformation of the Soviet Union', *Journal of Politics*, vol. 54, no. 2 (May), pp. 329–71.

Gill, Graeme (1987) 'The single party as an agent of development: lessons from the Soviet experience', *World Politics*, vol. 39, no. 4 (July), pp. 566–78.

Gill, Graeme (ed.) (1988) *The Rules of the Communist Party of the Soviet Union*. London: Macmillan.

Gitelman, Zvi (ed.) (1992) *The Politics of Nationality and the Erosion of the USSR*. London: Macmillan.

Gleason, Gregory (1991) 'Fealty and loyalty: informal authority structures in Soviet Asia', *Soviet Studies*, vol. 32, no. 4, pp. 613–28.

Glenny, Misha (1990) *The Rebirth of History: Eastern Europe in the Age of Democracy*. Harmondsworth: Penguin.

Goble, Paul A. (1991) 'Nationalism, movement groups, and party formation', in Sedaitis and Butterfield (eds.) (1991).

Goldman, Marshall I. (1991) *What Went Wrong with Perestroika?* New York and London: Norton.

Golubeva, V. (1980) 'The other side of the medal', in Women in Eastern Europe Group, *Women and Russia: First Feminist Samizdat*. London: Sheba.

Gooding, John (1990) 'Gorbachev and democracy', *Soviet Studies*, vol. 42, no. 2 (April), pp. 195–231.

Gorbachev, Mikhail (1987) *Perestroika: New Thinking for Our Country and the World*. London: Collins.

Grey, Robert D. *et al.* (1990) 'Soviet public opinion and the Gorbachev reforms', *Slavic Review*, vol. 49, no. 3 (Summer), pp. 261–71.

Grossman, Gregory (1977) 'The "second economy" of the USSR', *Problems of Communism*, vol. 26, no. 5 (September–October), pp. 25–40.

Habermas, Jürgen (1973) 'What does a legitimation crisis mean today? Legitimation problems in late capitalism', in William Connolly (ed.), *Legitimacy and the State*. Oxford: Blackwell.

Habermas, Jürgen (1976) *Legitimation Crisis*. London: Heinemann.

Hague, Rod and Harrop, Martin (1987) *Comparative Government and Politics*, 2nd ed. London: Macmillan.

Hahn, Jeffrey W. (1988a) 'An experiment in competition: the 1987 elections to the local Soviets', *Slavic Review*, vol. 47, no. 2 (Fall), pp. 434–47.

Hahn, Jeffrey W. (1988b) *Soviet Grassroots: Citizen Participation in Local Soviet Government*. Princeton NJ: Princeton University Press.

Hahn, Jeffrey W. (1989) 'Power to the Soviets?', *Problems of Communism*, vol. 38, no. 1 (January–February), pp. 34–46.

Hahn, Jeffrey W. (1991a) 'Continuity and change in Russian political culture', *British Journal of Political Science*, vol. 21, no. 4 (October), pp. 393–421.

Hahn, Jeffrey W. (1991b) 'Developments in Soviet local politics', in Alfred J. Rieber and Alvin Z. Rubinstein (eds.), *Perestroika at the Crossroads*. Armonk NY: Sharpe.

Hammer, Darrell P. (1986) *USSR: The Politics of Oligarchy*, 2nd ed. Boulder CO: Westview.

Hanson, Philip (1990) 'Property rights in the new phase of reforms', *Soviet Economy*, vol. 6, no. 2, pp. 95–124.

Harasymiw, Bohdan (1984) *Political Elite Recruitment in the Soviet Union*. London: Macmillan.

Harding, Neil (ed.) (1984) *The State in Socialist Society*. London: Macmillan.

Harris, Chauncy D. (1993) 'The new Russian geography: a statistical overview', *Post-Soviet Geography*, vol. 34, no. 1 (January), pp. 1–27.

Hasegawa, Tsuyoshi and Pravda, Alex (eds.) (1990) *Perestroika: Soviet Domestic and Foreign Policies*. London: Sage.

Hazard, John, *et al.* (eds.) (1984) *The Soviet Legal System: The Law in the 1980s*. Dobbs Ferry: Oceana.

Held, David (ed.) (1990) *Models of Democracy*. Cambridge: Polity.

Helmstadter, Sarah (1992) 'Medical insurance in Russia', Radio Free Europe/Radio Liberty *Research Report*, vol. 1, no. 31 (31 July), pp. 65–9.

Hendley, Kathryn (1992) 'Legal development and privatization in Russia: a case study', *Soviet Economy*, vol. 8, no. 2, pp. 130–57.

Hewett, Ed. A. (1988) *Reforming the Soviet Economy*. Washington DC: Brookings.

Hewett, Ed. A. and Winston, Victor (eds.) (1991) *Milestones in Glasnost and Perestroyka: The Economy*, 2 vols. Washington DC: Brookings.

Hill, Ronald J. (1988) 'Gorbachev and the CPSU', *Journal of Communist Studies*, vol. 4, no. 4 (December), pp. 18–34.

Hill, Ronald J. and Dellenbrant, Jan Ake (eds.) (1989) *Gorbachev and Perestroika*. Aldershot: Edward Elgar.

Hill, Ronald J. and Frank, Peter (1987) *The Soviet Communist Party*, 3rd ed. London: Allen & Unwin.

Hirszowicz, Maria (1980) *The Bureaucratic Leviathan*. Oxford: Martin Robertson.

Hobsbawm, Eric and Ranger, Terence (eds.) (1984) *The Invention of Tradition*. Cambridge: Cambridge University Press.

Holmes, Leslie (1993) *The End of Communist Power*. Cambridge: Polity.

Holmes, Leslie (1994) *Post-Communism*. Cambridge: Polity.

Hopkins, Mark (1970) *Mass Media in the Soviet Union*. New York: Pegasus.

Hopkins, Mark (1983) *Russia's Underground Press: The Chronicle of Current Events*. New York: Praeger.

Hosking, Geoffrey A. (1991) *The Awakening of the Soviet Union*, rev. ed. London: Mandarin.

Hosking, Geoffrey *et al.* (1992) *The Road to Post-Communism: Independent Political Movements in the Soviet Union 1985–1991*. London: Pinter.

Hough, Jerry F. (1971) 'The apparatchiki', in H.G. Skilling and Franklyn Griffiths (eds.), *Interest Groups in Soviet Politics*. Princeton, NJ: Princeton University Press.

Hough, Jerry F. (1980) *Soviet Leadership in Transition*. Washington DC: Brookings.

Hough, Jerry F. (1991) 'Understanding Gorbachev: the importance of politics', *Soviet Economy*, vol. 7, no. 2, pp. 166–84.

Hough, Jerry F. and Fainsod, Merle (1979) *How the Soviet Union is Governed*. Cambridge MA: Harvard University Press.

Huber, Robert T. and Kelley, Donald R. (eds.) (1991) *Perestroika-era Politics: The New Soviet Legislature and Gorbachev's Political Reforms*. Boulder CO: Westview.

Huskey, Eugene (ed.) (1992) *Executive Power and Soviet Politics. The Rise and Fall of the Soviet State*. Boulder CO: Westview.

Hyde, Gordon (1974) *The Soviet Health Service*. London: Lawrence & Wishart.

Ignatow, Assen (1992) *Der 'Eurasismus' und die Suche nach einer neuen russischen Kulturidentität. Die Neubelebung des 'Jewrasijstwo'-Mythos*. Cologne: Berichte des BIOst.

Il'in, Ivan (1992) *Nashi zadachi: Istoricheskaya sud'ba i budushchee Rossii*, vol. 1. Moscow: Rapog.

IMF (1991) *A Study of the Soviet Economy*, 3 vols. Paris: IMF and World Bank.

Iz glubiny: sbornik statei o russkoi revolyutsii (1918/1991). Moscow: Novosti; translated into English by W.F. Woerhlin (ed.), *Out of the*

Depths: A Collection of Articles on the Russian Revolution (1986), Irvine CA: Schlacks.

Johnson, Chalmers (ed.) (1970) *Change in Communist Systems*. Stanford CA: Stanford University Press.

Johnson, Simon and Kroll, Heidei (1991) 'Managerial strategies for spontaneous privatisation', *Soviet Economy*, vol. 7, no. 2, pp. 143–74.

Jones, Anthony, Connor, Walter D. and Powell, David E. (eds.) (1991) *Soviet Social Problems*. Boulder CO: Westview.

Jones, Ellen (1986) *Red Army and Society. A Sociology of the Soviet Military*, paperback ed. London: Allen & Unwin.

Jowitt, Kenneth (1983) 'Soviet neotraditionalism: the political corruption of a Leninist regime', *Soviet Studies*, vol. 35, no. 3 (July), pp. 275–97.

Jowitt, Kenneth (1990) 'Gorbachev: Bolshevik or Menshevik?', in White, Pravda and Gitelman (eds.) (1990).

Jowitt, Kenneth (1992) 'A world without Leninism', in K. Jowitt, *The New World Disorder: The Leninist Extinction*. Berkeley: University of California Press.

Joyce, Walter (ed.) (1992) *Social Change and Social Issues in the Former USSR*. London: Macmillan.

Joyce, Walter, *et al.* (eds.) (1989) *Gorbachev and Gorbachevism*. London: Cass.

Juviler, Peter and Gross, Bertram (eds.) (1993) *Human Rights for the 21st Century: a U.S.–Soviet Dialogue*. Armonk NY: Sharpe.

Kaplan, Cynthia S. (ed.) (1988) 'Local party organizations in the USSR', *Studies in Comparative Communism*, vol. 21, no. 1 (Spring), pp. 3–98.

Karklins, Rasma (1986) *Ethnic Relations in the USSR. The Perspective from Below*. Boston: Allen & Unwin.

Katz, Zev (ed.) (1975) *A Handbook of Major Soviet Nationalities*. New York: Free Press.

Keane, John (ed.) (1988) *Civil Society and the State*. London: Verso.

Kiernan, Brendan (1993) *The End of Soviet Politics: Elections, Legislatures and the Demise of the Communist Party*. Boulder CO: Westview.

Kissinger, Henry (1979) *The White House Years*. Boston: Little, Brown.

Klavdienko, V. (1986) *People's Wellbeing in Socialist Society*. Moscow: Progress.

Knight, Amy W. (1988) *The KGB. Police and Politics in the Soviet Union*. Boston: Unwin Hyman.

Konrad, George and Szelenyi, Ivan (1979) *The Intellectuals on the Road to Class Power*. New York and London: Harcourt Brace Janovich.

Konstitutsii (1993) *Konstitutsii Rossiiskoi Fedcratsii (al'ternativnye proekty)*, 2 vols. Moscow: RAU Press.

Kornai, Janos (1980) *Economics of Shortage*. Amsterdam: North-Holland.

Koslov, V.I. (1988) *The Peoples of the Soviet Union*. London: Hutchinson.

Krasnov, Vladislav (1991) *Russia beyond Communism: a chronicle of national rebirth*. Boulder CO: Westview.

Laird, Robbin F. (ed.) (1987) *Soviet Foreign Policy*. New York: Academy of Political Science.

Laird, Robbin F. and Hoffmann, Erik P. (eds.) (1987) *Soviet Foreign Policy in a Changing World*. New York: Aldine.

Laird, Robbin and Hoffmann, Erik P. (eds.) (1991) *Contemporary Issues in Soviet Foreign Policy*. New York: Aldine.

Lampert, Nicholas (1985) *Whistleblowing in the Soviet Union: Complaints and Abuses under State Socialism*. London: Macmillan.

Lane, David (1976) *The Socialist Industrial State. Towards a Political Sociology of State Socialism*. London: George Allen & Unwin.

Lane, David (1987) *Soviet Labour and the Ethic of Communism*. Brighton: Harvester.

Lane, David (ed.) (1988) *Elites and Political Power in the USSR*. Aldershot: Edward Elgar.

Lapidus, Gail W. (1989) 'State and society: towards the emergence of civil society in the Soviet Union', in Bialer (ed.) (1989).

Laqueur, Walter (1989) *The Long Road to Freedom: Russia and Glasnost'*. London: Unwin Hyman.

Lawyers' Committee for Human Rights (1993) *Human Rights and Legal Reform in the Russian Federation*. New York: Lawyers' Committee for Human Rights.

Letiche, John M. and Dmytryshyn, Basil (eds.) (1985) *Russian Statecraft: The Politics of Iurii Krizhanich*. Oxford: Blackwell.

Lentini, Peter (1992) *Political Parties and Movements in the Commonwealth of Independent States*. Manchester: Lorton House.

Lewin, Moshe (1988) *The Gorbachev Phenomenon*. Berkeley: University of California Press.

Lewis, Paul G. (ed.) (1984) *Eastern Europe: Political Crisis and Legitimation*. London: Croom Helm.

Lieven, Anatol (1993) *The Baltic Revolution: Estonia, Latvia, Lithuania and the Path to Independence*. New Haven and London: Yale University Press.

Light, Margot (1988) *The Soviet Theory of International Relations*. Brighton: Wheatsheaf.

Lijphart, Arend (ed.) (1992) *Parliamentary versus Presidential Government*. Oxford: Oxford University Press.

Likhachev, Dmitrii (1991) *Reflections on Russia*. Boulder CO: Westview.

Linz, Juan (1990) 'The perils of presidentialism', *Journal of Democracy*, vol. 1, no. 1 (Winter), pp. 51–69.

Lohr, E. (1993) 'Arkadii Volsky's political base', *Europe–Asia Studies*, vol. 45, no. 5, pp. 811–29.

Lowenhardt, John *et al.* (1992) *The Rise and Fall of the Soviet Politburo*. London: UCL Press.

Lynch, Allen (1989) *Gorbachev's Intellectual Outlook: Intellectual Origins and Political Consequences*. New York: Institute for East–West Security Studies.

Mackinder, Halford J. (1962) 'The geographical pivot of history', in H.J. Mackinder, *Democratic Ideals and Reality*. New York: Norton.

Mainwaring, Scott (1993) 'Presidentialism, multipartism, and democracy', *Comparative Political Studies*, vol. 26, no. 2 (July), pp. 198–228.

Mandel, David (1993) *Perestroika and the Soviet People*. Toronto: Black Rose.

McAuley, Alastair (1979) *Economic Welfare in the Soviet Union*. London: Allen & Unwin.

McAuley, Mary (1984) 'Political culture and communist politics: one step forward, two steps back', in Archie Brown (ed.), *Political Culture and Communist Studies*. London: Macmillan.

McAuley, Mary (1992) *Soviet Politics 1917–1991*. Oxford: Oxford University Press.

McCauley, Martin (ed.) (1987) *The Soviet Union under Gorbachev*. London: Macmillan.

MccGwire, Michael (1991) *Perestroika and Soviet National Security*. Washington DC: Brookings.

Malcolm, Neil (1994) 'The new Russian foreign policy', *The World Today*, vol. 50, no. 2 (February), pp. 28–32.

Marnie, Sheila and Slater, Wendy (1993) 'Russia's refugees', Radio Free Europe/Radio Liberty *Research Report*, vol. 2, no. 37 (17 September), pp. 46–53.

Mchledov, M.P. (1987) *Socialist Society: Its Social Justice*. Moscow: Progress.

Medvedev, Zhores (1988) *Gorbachev*, rev. ed. Oxford: Blackwell.

Meyer, Alfred G. (1965) *The Soviet Political System. An Interpretation*. New York: Random House.

Mickiewicz, Ellen (1988) *Split Signals. Television and Politics in the Soviet Union*. New York: Oxford University Press.

Millar, James P. (ed.) (1987) *Politics, Work, and Daily Life in the USSR. A Survey of Former Citizens*. New York: Cambridge University Press.

Millar, James R. (ed.) (1992) *Cracks in the Monolith. Party Power in the Brezhnev Era*. Boulder CO: Westview.

Miller, Arthur H. *et al.* (eds.) (1993) *Public Opinion and Regime Change. The New Politics of Post-Soviet Societies*. Boulder CO: Westview.

Miller, John (1993) *Mikhail Gorbachev and the End of Soviet Power*. London: Macmillan.

Miller, John H. *et al.* (eds.) (1987) *Gorbachev at the Helm: A New Era in Soviet Politics?* London: Croom Helm.

Morrison, John (1991) *Boris Yeltsin*. Baltimore MD: Penguin.

Moses, Joel C. (1989) 'Democratic reform in the Gorbachev era: dimensions of reform in the Soviet Union, 1986–1989', *Russian Review*, vol. 48, no. 3 (July), pp. 235–69.

Motyl, Alexander, J. (1987) *Will the Non-Russians Rebel?* Ithaca: Cornell University Press.

Motyl, Alexander J. (1993) *Dilemmas of Independence: Ukraine after Totalitarianism*. New York: Council on Foreign Relations.

Motyl, Alexander J. (ed.) (1992a) *Thinking Theoretically about Soviet Nationalities*. New York: Columbia University Press.

Motyl, Alexander J. (ed.) (1992b) *The Post-Soviet Nations*. New York: Columbia University Press.

Nahaylo, Bohdan and Swoboda, Victor (1990) *Soviet Disunion. A History of the Nationalities Problem in the USSR*. London: Hamish Hamilton.

Naishul', Vitalii (1990a) 'Problems of creating a market in the USSR', *Communist Economies*, vol. 2, no. 3, pp. 275–90.

Naishul', Vitalii (1990b) 'Can the Soviet economy stay left of the American?', *Communist Economies*, vol. 2, no. 4, pp. 481–97.

Navarro, Vincente (1977) *Social Security and Medicine in the USSR*. Lexington: Lexington Books.

Nelson, Daniel N. (1988) *Elite-Mass Relations in Communist Systems*. London: Macmillan.

Nelson, Lynn *et al.* (1992) 'Perspectives on entrepreneurship and privatisation in Russia: policy and public opinion', *Slavic Review*, vol. 51, no. 2 (Summer), pp. 271–86.

Neznansky, Fridrikh (1985) *The Prosecution of Economic Crimes in the USSR, 1954–1984*, ed. Robert Sharlet. Falls Church VA: Delphic Associates.

Nogee, Joseph L. and Donaldson, Robert H. (1990) *Soviet Foreign Policy since World War II*, 4th ed. Oxford and New York: Pergamon.

Nove, Alec (1989) *Glasnost' in Action*. Boston: Unwin Hyman.

Nove, Alec (1992) *An Economic History of the USSR 1917–1991*, 3rd ed. Harmondsworth: Penguin.

O'Connor, James (1973) *The Fiscal Crisis of the State*. New York: St Martin's.

O'Connor, James (1987) *The Meaning of Crisis*. Oxford: Blackwell.

O'Donnell, Guillermo *et al.* (eds.) (1986) *Transitions from Authoritarian Rule: Comparative Perspectives*. Baltimore MD: Johns Hopkins University Press.

Parker, John W. (1991) *The Kremlin in Transition*, 2 vols. London and Boston: Unwin Hyman.

Pilkington, Hilary (1992) 'Going out "in style": girls in youth cultural activity', in Buckley (ed.) (1992).

Pipes, Richard (1974) *Russia under the Old Regime*. New York: Scribner's.

Poggi, Gianfranco (1978) *The Development of the Modern State*. London: Hutchinson.

Posadskaya, Anastasia (ed.) (1994) *Women in Russia*. London: Verso.

Potichnyj, Peter J. (ed.) (1988) *The Soviet Union: Party and Society*. New York: Cambridge University Press.

Pozdnyakov, Elgiz (1993) 'Russia is a great power', *International Affairs* (Moscow), no. 1, pp. 3–13.

Pribylovskii, Vladimir (ed.) (1992) *A Dictionary of Political Parties and Organizations in Russia*. Moscow: Postfactum.

Pryde, Philip (1991) *Environmental Manaegment in the Soviet Union*. Cambridge: Cambridge University Press.

Pushkarev, Sergei (1988) *Self-Government and Freedom in Russia*. Boulder CO: Westview.

Pye, Lucian W. (1990) 'Political science and the crisis of authoritarianism', *American Political Science Review*, vol. 84, no. 1 (March), pp. 3–19.

Reddaway, Peter (1972) *Uncensored Russia: Protest and Dissent in the Soviet Union*. New York: American Heritage Press.

Reddaway, Peter (1990) 'The quality of Gorbachev's leadership', *Soviet Economy*, vol. 6, no. 2, pp. 125–40.

Rees, E.A. (ed.) (1992) *The Soviet Communist Party in Disarray*. London: Macmillan.

Remington, Thomas F. (1988) *The Truth of Authority. Ideology and Communication in the Soviet Union*. Pittsburgh: University of Pittsburgh Press.

Remington, Thomas F. (1991) 'Parliamentary government in the USSR', in Huber and Kelley (eds.) (1991).

Remington, Thomas F. (ed.) (1994) *Parliaments in Transition: New Legislative Politics in Eastern Europe and the Former USSR*. Boulder CO: Westview.

Riasanovsky, Nicholas (1993) *A History of Russia*, 5th ed. New York: Oxford University Press.

Rigby, T.H. (1968) *Communist Party Membership in the Soviet Union 1917–1967*. Princeton NJ: Princeton University Press.

Rigby, T.H. (1990a) *The Changing Soviet System*. Aldershot: Edward Elgar.

Rigby, T.H. (1990b) *Political Elites in the USSR*. Aldershot: Edward Elgar.

Rigby, T.H. and Feher, Ferenc (eds.) (1982) *Political Legitimation in Communist States*. London: Macmillan.

Rigby, T.H. and Harasymiw, Bogdan (eds.) (1983) *Leadership Selection and Patron–Client Relations in the USSR and Yugoslavia*. London: Allen & Unwin.

Riordan, James (ed.) (1989) *Soviet Youth Culture*. London: Macmillan.

Riordan, James and Bridger, Susan (eds.) (1992) *Dear Comrade Editor*. Bloomington IN: Indiana University Press.

Roeder, Philip G. (1993) *Red Sunset: The Failure of Soviet Politics*. Princeton NJ: Princeton University Press.

Rose, Richard *et al.* (1993) *How Russians are Coping: New Russian Barometer II*. Glasgow: University of Strathclyde Centre for the Study of Public Policy, SPP 216.

Rubenstein, Joshua (1985) *Soviet Dissidents: Their Struggle for Human Rights*. Boston: Beacon Press.

Ruge, Gerd (1991) *Gorbachev: A Biography*. London: Chatto.

Rutland, Peter (1985) *The Myth of the Plan*. London: Hutchinson.

Rutland, Peter (1993) *The Politics of Stagnation in the Soviet Union: the role of local party organs in economic management*. Cambridge: Cambridge University Press.

Ryan, Michael (1978) *The Organisation of Soviet Medical Care*. Oxford: Blackwell.

Ryan, Michael (1991) 'Policy and administration in the Soviet health service', *Social Policy and Administration*, vol. 25, no. 3 (September), pp. 327–37.

Ryan, Michael (comp.) (1993) *Social Trends in Contemporary Russia: A Statistical Source-Book*. London: Macmillan.

Saivetz, Carol R. and Jones, Anthony (eds.) (1994) *In Search of Pluralism: Soviet and Post-Soviet Politics*. Boulder CO: Westview.

Sakharov, A.D. (1974) *Sakharov Speaks*. New York: Knopf.

Sakwa, Richard (1989) *Soviet Politics: An Introduction*., London: Routledge.

Sakwa, Richard (1990) *Gorbachev and his Reforms 1985–1990*. Englewood Cliffs NJ: Prentice-Hall.

Sakwa, Richard (1993) *Russian Politics and Society*. London: Routledge.

Scanlan, James P. (1985) *Marxism in the USSR. A Critical Survey of Current Soviet Thought*. Ithaca: Cornell University Press.

Schapiro, Leonard B. (1970) *The Communist Party of the Soviet Union*, 2nd ed. London: Eyre & Spottiswoode.

Schmidt-Hauer, Christian (1986) *Gorbachev: The Road to Power*. London: Tauris.

Sedaitis, Judith and Butterfield, Jim (eds.) (1991) *Perestroika from Below: Social Movements in the Soviet Union*. Boulder CO: Westview.

Sergeyev, Victor and Biryukov, Nikolai (1993) *Russia's Road to Democracy: Parliament, Communism and Traditional Culture*. Aldershot: Edward Elgar.

Sharlet, Robert (1978) *The New Soviet Constitution of 1977: Analysis and Text*. Brunswick OH: King's Court.

Sharlet, Robert (1992a) 'The fate of individual rights in the age of *perestroika*', in Barry (ed.) (1992).

Sharlet, Robert (1992b) *Soviet Constitutional Crisis: From De-Stalinization to Disintegration*. Armonk NY: Sharpe.

Sharlet, Robert (1993) 'The Russian Constitutional Court: the first term', *Post-Soviet Affairs*, vol. 9, no. 1 (January–March), pp. 1–39.

Shelov-Kovedyaev, Fedor (1993) *Vyzov vremeni: politika novoi Rossii*. Moscow: Slovo.

Shevardnadze, Eduward (1991) *The Future Belongs to Freedom*. London: Sinclair-Stevenson.

Shlapentokh, Vladimir (1989) *Public and Private Lives of the Soviet People: Changing Values in Post-Stalin Russia*. New York: Oxford University Press.

Shugart, Matthew and Carey, John M. (1992) *Presidents and Assemblies: Constitutional Design and Electorical Dynamics*. Cambridge: Cambridge University Press.

Siegler, Robert W. (1982) *The Standing Commissions of the Supreme Soviet*. New York: Praeger.

Skilling, H.G. and Griffiths, Franklyn (eds.) (1971) *Interest Groups in Soviet Politics*. Princeton NJ: Princeton University Press.

Slavin, Boris and Davydov, Valentin (1991) 'Stanovlenie mnogopartiinosti', *Partiinaya zhizn'*, no. 18 (September), pp. 6–16.

Smith, Alan (1993) *Russia and the World Economy*. London: Routledge.

Smith, Gordon B. (1991) *Soviet Politics: Struggling with Change*, 2nd ed. London: Macmillan.

Smith, Graham (ed.) (1990) *The Nationalities Question in the Soviet Union*. London: Longman.

Smith, Hedrick (1990) *The New Russians*. London: Hutchinson.

Sobchak, Anatolii (1991) *Khozhdenie vo vlast'*. Moscow: Novosti.

Sobyanin, Alexander (1994) 'Political cleavages among the Russian deputies', in Remington (ed.) (1994).

Solomon, Susan G. (ed.) (1983) *Pluralism in the Soviet Union*. London: Macmillan.

Solomon, Susan G. (ed.) (1993) *Beyond Sovietology: Essays in Politics and History*. Boulder CO: Westview.

Solzhenitsyn, Alexander (ed.) (1974) *From Under The Rubble*. London: Fontana.

Solzhenitsyn, Alexander (1975) *Letter to the Soviet Leaders*. Boston: Harper & Row.

Solzhenitsyn, Alexander (1991) *Rebuilding Russia: Reflections and Tentative Proposals*. London: Harvill.

Spravochnik (1993) *Spravochnik: politicheskie partii, dvizheniya i bloki sovremennoi Rossii*, ed. R. Medvedev. Nizhnii Novgorod: Leta.

Steele, Jonathan (1985) *The Limits of Soviet Power*. Harmondsworth: Penguin.

Szamuely, Tibor (1988) *The Russian Tradition*. London: Fontana.

Szporluk, Roman (1990) 'The imperial legacy and the Soviet nationalities', in Lubomyr Hajda and Mark Beissinger (eds.), *The Nationalities Factor in Soviet Politics and Society*. Boulder CO: Westview.

Szporluk, Roman (1991) 'Dilemmas of Russian nationalism', in Denber (ed.) (1991).

Tatu, Michel (1988) 'The 19th Party Conference', *Problems of Communism*, vol. 38, nos. 3–4 (May–August), pp. 1–15.

Teague, Elizabeth (1990) 'Soviet workers find a voice', *Report on the USSR* (13 July), pp. 13–17.

Thompson, Terry L. (1989) *Ideology and Policy: The Political Uses of Doctrine in the Soviet Union*. Boulder CO: Westview.

Ticktin, Hillel (1991) *The Origins of the Crisis in the USSR*. Armonk NY: Sharpe.

Tolz, Vera (1990) *The USSR's Emerging Party System*. New York: Praeger.

Tonnies, Ferdinand (1963) *Community and Association*, trans. C.P. Loomis. New York: Harper & Row.

Trehub, Aaron (1992) 'Housing policy in the USSR/CIS', Radio Free Europe/Radio Liberty *Research Report*, vol. 1, no. 6 (7 February), pp. 30–42.

Trotsky, Leon (1937) *The Revolution Betrayed. What is the Soviet Union and Where is it Going?* London: Faber.

Tucker, Robert C. (1971) 'The image of dual Russia', in R.C. Tucker, *The Soviet Political Mind*, rev. ed. New York: Norton.

Tucker, Robert C. (1987a) 'Swollen state, spent society: Stalin's legacy to Brezhnev's Russia', in Tucker (1987b).

Tucker, Robert C. (1987b) *Political Culture and Leadership in Soviet Russia*. Brighton: Wheatsheaf.

Ulam, Adam (1974) *Expansion and Coexistence. Soviet Foreign Policy, 1917–1973*, 2nd ed. New York: Praeger.

Ulam, Adam (1983) *Dangerous Relations. The Soviet Union in World Politics, 1970–1982*. New York: Oxford University Press.

Unger, Aryeh L. (1981) *Constitutional Development in the USSR*. London: Methuen.

Urban, Michael E. (1985) 'Conceptualising political power in the USSR: patterns of binding and bonding', *Studies in Comparative Communism*, vol. 18, no. 4 (Winter), pp. 207–26.

Urban, Michael E. (1989) *An Algebra of Power: Elite Circulation in the Belorussian Republic 1966–1986*. Cambridge: Cambridge University Press.

Urban, Michael E. (1990a) *More Power to the Soviets*. Aldershot: Edward Elgar.

Urban, Michael (1990b) 'The Soviet multi-party system: a Moscow roundtable', *Russia and the World*, no. 18, pp. 1–7.

Valenta, Jiri and Potter, William C. (eds.) (1984) *Soviet Decision-Making for National Security*. London: Allen & Unwin.

Vanneman, Peter (1977) *The Supreme Soviet: Politics and the Legislative Process in the Soviet Political System*. Durham NC: Duke University Press.

Vekhi: sbornik statei o russkoi intelligentsii (1909, repr. 1967) Frankfurt: Posev.

Voslensky, Michael (1984) *Nomenklatura: The Soviet Ruling Class*. Garden City: Doubleday.

Walker, Rachel (1993) *Six Years that Shook the World*. Manchester: Manchester University Press.

Waters, Elizabeth (1990) 'Restructuring the "woman question": *perestroika* and prostitution', *Feminist Review*, no. 33, pp. 3–19.

Waters, Elizabeth (1992) 'Cuckoo mothers and apparatchiks: glasnost and Soviet children's homes', in Buckley (ed.) (1992).

White, Anne (1993) 'Charity, self-help and politics in Russia, 1985–91', *Europe–Asia Studies*, vol. 45, no. 5, pp. 787–810.

White, Stephen (1979) *Political Culture and Soviet Politics*. London: Macmillan.

White, Stephen (1989) *Soviet Communism: Programme and Rules*. London: Routledge.

White, Stephen (1990) ' "Democratisation" in the USSR', *Soviet Studies*, vol. 42, no. 1 (January), pp. 3–24.

White, Stephen (1991a) 'The Soviet elections of 1989: from acclamation to limited choice', *Coexistence*, vol. 28, no. 4 (December), pp. 513–39.

White, Stephen (1991b) 'Rethinking the CPSU', *Soviet Studies*, vol. 43, no. 3, pp. 405–28.

White, Stephen (1993) *After Gorbachev*, 4th ed. Cambridge and New York: Cambridge University Press.

White, Stephen and McAllister, Ian (1994) *Communists after Communism*. Glasgow: University of Strathclyde Centre for the Study of Public Policy, SPP 221.

White, Stephen and Pravda, Alex (eds.) (1988) *Ideology and Soviet Politics*. London: Macmillan.

White, Stephen, Gill, Graeme and Slider, Darrell (1993) *The Politics of Transition: Shaping a Post-Soviet Future*. Cambridge and New York: Cambridge Univesity Press.

White, Stephen, McAllister, Ian and Kryshtanovskaya, Olga (1994) 'El'tsin and his voters: popular support in the 1991 Russian presidential elections and after', *Europe–Asia Studies*, vol. 46, no. 2, pp. 285–303.

White, Stephen, Pravda, Alex and Gitelman, Zvi (eds.) (1992) *Developments in Soviet and Post-Soviet Politics*, 2nd ed. London: Macmillan and Durham NC: Duke University Press.

Whitlock, Erik (1993) 'The CIS economy', *Radio Free Europe/Radio Liberty Research Report*, vol. 2, no. 2 (1 January), pp. 46–9.

Willerton, John P. (1992) *Patronage and Politics in the USSR*. Cambridge: Cambridge University Press.

Willerton, John P. and Reisinger, William M. (1991) 'Troubleshooters, political machines, and Moscow's regional control', *Slavic Review*, vol. 50, no. 2 (Summer), pp. 347–58.

Willerton, John P., Jr. (1987) 'Patronage networks and coalition building in the Brezhnev era', *Soviet Studies*, vol. 39, no. 2 (April), pp. 175–204.

Wilson, Andrew and Bachkatov, Nina (1988) *Living with Glasnost. Youth and Society in a Changing Russia*. Harmondsworth: Penguin.

Wixman, Ronald (1984) *The Peoples of the USSR: An Ethnographic Handbook*. Armonk NY: Sharpe.

Woodby, Sylvia (1989) *Gorbachev and the Decline of Ideology in Soviet Foreign Policy*. Boulder CO: Westview.

Woodby, Sylvia and Evans, Alfred B. Jr. (eds.) (1990) *Restructuring Soviet Ideology: Gorbachev's New Thinking*. Boulder CO: Westview.

Yanov, Alexander (1989) 'In the grip of the adversarial paradigm', in Crummey (ed.) (1989).

Yeltsin, Boris (1990) *Against the Grain*. London: Cape.

Zagorsky, Andrei (1993) 'Russia and Europe', *International Affairs* (Moscow), no. 1, pp. 43–51.

Zaslavskaya, Tat'yana (1988) 'The human factor in the development of the economy and social justice', in Vladimir Gordon, trans., *Big Changes in the USSR*. Moscow: Progress.

Zaslavsky, Victor and Brym, Robert J. (1978) 'The functions of elections in the USSR', *Soviet Studies*, vol. 30, no. 3 (July), pp. 362–71.

Zhuravlev, V.V. *et al.* (1990) *Na poroge krizisa: narastanie zastoinykh yavlenii v partii i obshchestve*. Moscow: Politizdat.

Index

355